Pensions

and Corporate Restructuring

in American Industry

Pensions
and Corporate Restructuring
in American Industry

A CRISIS OF REGULATION

Gordon L. Clark

The Johns Hopkins University Press

Baltimore and London

The Johns Hopkins University Press
2715 North Charles Street
Baltimore, Maryland 21218-4319
The Johns Hopkins Press Ltd., London

Library of Congress Cataloging-in-Publication Data

Clark, Gordon L.
    Pensions and corporate restructuring in American industry : a crisis of
regulation / Gordon L. Clark.
        p.   cm.
    Includes bibliographical references and index.
    ISBN 0-8018-4523-8 (alk. paper)
    1. Consolidation and merger of corporations—United States.
2. Pension trusts—United States.   3. Pension trusts—Law and legislation—United States.   I. Title.
HD2746.55.U5C58   1993
331.25′2′0973—dc20   92-34553

A catalog record for this book is available from the British Library

[The Employee Retirement Income Security Act] represents a series of fundamental guarantees made to every American worker—guarantees which will secure for millions of Americans the expectation of a decent retirement income in combination with social security. These guarantees are nothing less than a pension "bill of rights" to which every worker—regardless of his occupation, salary or status—is entitled.

Sen. Jacob Javits, *Congressional Record*
120:29935 (1974)

[The motions of this case] in the context of the facts presented raise difficult and deeply perplexing issues concerning the reorganization of a corporate entity that includes the second largest steel company in the United States, the powers of a public corporation created by Congress to protect the pension benefits of more than 30 million American workers and their families, and the effect of congressionally sanctioned collective bargaining between the United Steelworkers of America and LTV. Underlying these issues is the fundamental question what processes and institutions are to be responsible for the casualties suffered by a basic American industry that has been battered by intensive and successful competition from abroad?

Judge Robert J. Sweet, *In re. Chateaugay Corp.*,
pp. 784–85 (1988)

FOR PETER BRUCE CLARK

Contents

List of Tables and Figures

TABLES

FIGURES

Preface

The restructuring of America's basic industries was a vital economic theme of the 1970s and 1980s, and its consequences promise to dominate the 1990s as the market for "corporate control" comes to terms with the events of the 1980s. Whether because of increased foreign competition, the accumulated inefficiencies of past business practices, or technological change, or a combination of all these factors, job loss and relocation of basic industry has been nothing short of spectacular. In all kinds of industries, including automobiles, steel, rubber, chemicals, and related industries, as well as in lesser known industries such as canning and packaging, and machine tools, corporate restructuring has become a fact of life for many workers and their communities. Corporations have discarded enormous amounts of capacity, have merged with other firms, have acquired new businesses, have sold many units and, in some instances, sought Chapter 11 bankruptcy status, all in a desperate struggle to become competitive in a rapidly evolving global economy.

This book is about the corporate restructuring process and the rights of workers to promised pension benefits. It is also, then, a book about the relationships between labor and management, union officials and corporate executives, and the mediation of those relationships by the federal courts involving government agencies, especially the Pension Benefit Guaranty Corporation (PBGC). As is demonstrated through a series of detailed case studies, pensions, corporate restructuring, and regulation are intimately connected, especially in those industries adversely affected by increased international and domestic competition and characterized by long histories of union representation.

As such, the book combines two of my essential research interests. One concerns the design and geographical consequences of corporate restructuring in U.S. industry. The other concerns the problematic nature of regulation in American society. In a sense, the book uses case studies of corporate restructuring as source material for explorations in the philosophy and practice of regulation in general, and judicial adjudication in particular. In another equally important sense, the book showcases case material on judicial adjudication in order to explore the hidden dimensions and complexities of corporate restructuring. By the interpenetration of the processes of restructuring with the institutions of regulation, I will analyze and conceptualize corporate behavior with respect to the law and public policy. Through a sequence of related chapters that analyze the dimensions of corporate restructuring with respect to pension obligations (Part 1), I work through the related issues of regulation and adjudication in the context of corporate restructuring (Part 2), and emphasize the ethical (or not so ethical) bases of corporate behavior (Part 3). In this manner, I aim to show how corporate restructuring has exposed the limits of regulation of the private pension system. Through this analysis, my aim is to demonstrate that a reinvigorated system of regulation is needed, one that reestablishes the connection between regulation and moral sentiments.

This project does not depend on complex econometric or statistical material; it is not an exercise in large-scale quantitative data analysis. It does, however, depend on detailed accounts of selected corporate restructuring practices in American industry. In this respect it relies on linking those practices to federal regulations, the federal courts, and the PBGC's policies and requirements, making an intensive (albeit focused) study of corporate practices and public policies. It is important to acknowledge from the outset that there are few relevant studies in the literature that can provide references points for analysis. While studies of private pension funds as sources of investment capital exist, as do economic studies of the patterns and determinants of pension benefit levels, there are very few studies of the private pension system, and even fewer studies of the status of pension obligations in the context of corporate restructuring. The Pension Research Council of the Wharton School at the University of Pennsylvania has made this issue an essential part of its programs; see in particular (and with respect to the issues raised in this book) Bodie and Merton (1992), Lewis and Cooperstein (1992), and Lockhart (1992).

To begin, secondary source data is presented on the significance and regulation of the private pension system. In doing so, the aim is to establish a brief benchmark from which to analyze the changing status of private pensions in American industry. Historical data on trends in coverage, benefit levels, and cost with respect to American industries, union, and nonunion representation are also presented. As well, data on the fiscal integrity of the PBGC are deployed to indicate how vital regulation is with respect to pension-oriented bankruptcies, pension terminations, and the status of the Employee Retirement Income Security Act (ERISA) with respect to Social Security. A historical account of the evolution of private pension benefits since 1945 is used to emphasize the past role of labor unions and the federal government in expanding the private pension system. Source material includes a historical narrative of the evolution of collective bargaining, and discussion of the original court decisions that legitimated expanded private pension coverage. This material is also related to the debates and arguments surrounding the passage of ERISA in 1974 to establish the PBGC's position on pension-oriented bankruptcies.

Cataloguing corporate pension-oriented restructuring strategies can be described by numbers (how many per year, how many workers are involved), and the consequences of those strategies for benefits such as pension terminations and bankruptcies. Other strategies can only be indicated and described through case studies, not literally counted. Three case studies are considered in detail in Part 2. *Gavalik v. Continental Can Co.* was a civil case consolidated with another related case brought against the same company. It was argued in federal courts and concerned the pension rights of displaced laid-off workers, members of the United Steelworkers of America employed by Continental Can Company. After about ten years of litigation, a federal appeals court found that the company had illegally denied a group of workers their eligibility for early retirement pensions. In doing so, the company violated Section 510 of ERISA. As part of the company's restructuring plan, it had relocated production and closed certain facilities so as to selectively and systematically lay off a particular set of workers just prior to their attainment of eligibility for early retirement pensions. Just recently, in a class action suit brought in a New Jersey federal district court on behalf of similarly affected Continental Can employees, the plaintiffs were awarded $415 million in damages. Recognizing that this case involves vital issues, such as the financing of restructuring as well as the implementation of the latest business strategies, the essential issues considered here are the interplay among the design of restructuring, the inherited pension obligations that went with the network of plants and employees, and the role of federal regulation in protecting the interests of affected workers.

The second case is that of *Wisconsin Steel Company v. International Harvester Corporation*, a suit involving the PBGC, International Harvester (now known as Navistar), and a group of affected employees who worked in the steel division of the company. This case has also gone through the federal courts with the PBGC arguing (in part) that the corporation deliberately and illegally sold its steel division to a sham corporation in order to wholly avoid, or at least limit, their pension liability if the plant closed. Other suits have followed, some charging fraud and others charging that the company deliberately misled workers about the consequences of agreeing to the sale of the steel division. On the issue of the sham corporation, the courts sided with the PBGC, suggesting that companies cannot use fictive shell companies to negate their pension obligations to employees and the federal government. This case is used to reflect on two questions that go to the heart of the restructuring process: first, how is restructuring to be financed, given the enormous potential liabilities involved in shutting down large amounts of capital plant? Second, what are corporations' rights with respect to selling off capital and equipment, given the public interest in protecting the integrity of the private pension system? There are no simple answers to these questions.

The third (and most involved) case concerns the status of the PBGC in federal bankruptcy proceedings *(PBGC v. LTV Corporation)*. At issue here is the relative status of one set of regulations compared to others, given compelling public interests that justify competing sets of responsibilities. The epigraph of this book (quoting Judge Robert Sweet) puts the problem most eloquently and most insistently, and is taken from the LTV case study. To bolster its competitive position in the U.S. steel industry, LTV Corporation bought and sold a number of smaller steel companies in the hope of creating a larger, more efficient network of plants. In doing so, however, it incurred billions of dollars of unfunded pension liabilities. With added competition and a downturn in the price for steel in the early 1980s, LTV terminated its pension plans, transferred its liabilities to the PBGC, and filed for protection from its creditors under Chapter 11 of the Bankruptcy Code. These actions have had severe, adverse consequences for the welfare of many thousands of workers, retirees, and their communities. At issue here are two most fundamental questions: first, what is the role and status of the PBGC in relation to U.S. corporations' economic imperatives? And second, what is the rationale for bankruptcy policy in general? In a country that has debated and rejected the need for an industrial policy, this case brings into the open the impossible job facing any court forced to rationalize the process of corporate restructuring.

Having considered the logic of corporate restructuring in the context of the emerging global economy as well as the evolution of pension regulation in the United States, I then consider in more detail the problematic status of regulation with respect to the process of corporate restructuring (Part 3). Generally, the issue considered in this part of the book is the most general of all issues: the relationship between economic imperatives and social obligations. In this book, I do not propose a simple recipe or formula for ordering that relationship as if it could be so easy to provide a technical solution. To do so would be both naive and misleading with respect to an issue that is at the center of any modern society. Moreover, such a move would ignore the deliberate attempts of Congress and the executive branch to shift resolution of this issue away from democratic and administrative forums to the courts. Why and how this has been the case in areas such as industrial policy is one way of understanding the complexity of the issue. In another way, though, I also consider the ethical value attributed to regulation with respect to economic imperatives. Here I argue that there is something profoundly disturbing about corporate executives' attitudes and behavior (as evidenced in the case studies). For many executives, regulation has lost its moral force, being now understood by managers and business consultants alike as just another cost of doing business. This attitude stands in contrast to the attitudes of unions and their members who look to the courts and the legal rules they would apply to specific cases as the embodiment of social right and wrong. Understanding the relationship between economic imperatives and social obligations in this manner allows us to go beyond simple recipes to the very philosophy of regulation.

This, I would argue, is one of the strengths of the book—linking corporate restructuring to the regulatory system and then understanding those tensions in the context of competing ethical theories of the "good" society. The only problem with this argument, however, is that it is an argument to reinvigorate the regulation of corporate restructuring in a manner that is both *comprehensive* (with respect to the overlapping interests of ERISA, bankruptcy law, and labor law) and *empowered* by significant penalties to protect American institutions. The book concludes by suggesting that the crisis of regulation of the private pension system with respect to corporate restructuring is a crisis of regulation in general. Perhaps we know this already: the deregulation of American industry during the late 1970s and 1980s has taught us a lot about the limits of market solutions. Still, I suggest that the roots of this current crisis of regulation are more likely to be found in Congress's dependence upon the courts than the particular circumstances of any one industry.

This book begins with the premise that regulation of restructuring is indeed a necessary task of government. In part, the agenda of the book is to document why this is true through the compilation of case study evidence about the practice of corporate restructuring in relation to private pension obligations. A related part of the agenda is to show how the regulation of restructuring occurs in reality, separate from but nevertheless based upon statutes such as ERISA and the federal Bankruptcy Code. Here I aim to make two contributions to the debate over industry policy. First, by focusing upon the costs of corporate rationalization I demonstrate how pension liabilities may become such an important variable in the restructuring process. While the federal government and those adversely affected by decisions to avoid pension liability appreciate this issue to some extent, there has been until recently little recognition of the significance of pension liabilities in the restructuring process. Second, by focusing upon the actions and motivations of corporate executives, I believe we are able to better understand how those actions are related to regulation and why regulation is so contested in court. It is not simply an issue of gaining justice, as if the court system is simply a forum for assigning legal responsibility for certain obligations. It is clear that the courts have become *both* the only available mechanism for rationalizing competing statutory claims (by fashioning crude solutions to what an industrial policy ought to have as part of its overall agenda for rationalizing economic imperatives with social obligations) and a means of punishing transgressions of trust and cooperation. Without an adequate industrial policy, the regulatory process is an increasingly dangerous place for citizens *and* corporations.

This conclusion ought to encourage policymakers to rethink the design and implementation of policy conceived to rationalize economic imperatives and social obligations. Even so, I should also acknowledge that this project has caught the restructuring process *in action*, not at the end of a long sequence of actions and events. That is, all the evidence suggests that restructuring will continue as a vital economic theme through the 1990s. Not only are the mergers and acquisitions of the 1980s going through a process of rationalization, the consequences of deregulation in the late 1970s and early 1980s in industries as diverse as airlines and savings and loans will raise fundamental doubts about the logic of regulation/deregulation. The purpose of the book is to reopen this debate, not to close off further analysis with a premature solution that in the end will not make a substantial difference to how we conceptualize regulation as a social practice.

Acknowledgments

This project began life at Carnegie Mellon University where I was a professor in the Center for Labor Studies and the Heinz School of Public Policy and Management. Without doubt, Carnegie Mellon literally made the book possible. Its special mix of academic talent and experience in labor-management relations provided a unique view of the intersection among unions, corporations, and government policy. In this regard, I would first like to acknowledge my personal debt to Ben Fischer, who more than any one else educated me about the intricacies of labor relations as a social practice. Acknowledging his influence is one thing. Anyone who knows him, though, will quickly realize that my ideas on the ethics of labor relations are quite unlike his, even antithetical to his version of pragmatism. Nevertheless, I cannot think of a more fitting testimonial to his importance in my thinking.

With respect to Pittsburgh, I must also thank Bennett Harrison and Richard Florida (colleagues at Carnegie Mellon), Karin Feldman, Carl Frankel, Eddy Ghearing, Rudi Milasich, Bill Payne, Jim Smith and Paul Whitehead (all of the United Steelworkers of America), who in their different ways helped me understand corporate restructuring as a problem of public regulation and social obligation. Somewhat removed from Pittsburgh, I would also like to acknowledge the related encouragement (past and present) provided by Meric Gertler. Elizabeth Warren of the University of Pennsylvania and Judge Robert Sweet helped me understand the value of my work in the context of bankruptcy theory and policy. I also benefited from the comments of Robert Beauregard and Julie Graham, and the editorial work of Therese Boyd at the Johns Hopkins University Press. But again with respect to Pittsburgh, no set of acknowledgments would be complete without thanking Brian Berry and Dick Cyert for the opportunity to work in such an extraordinary, stimulating environment.

Completing the book project has been more challenging than its initiation—a reality that all writers should appreciate. Making the connections among corporate restructuring, public policy, and the ethical obligations of corporate executives has demanded a broader conceptualization of economic and geographical theory than is typical in the mainstream literature. In this respect, Neil Wrigley, Nick Blomley, and Nigel Thrift provided at the right times support for the project, being an enthusiastic albeit critical audience for material that is somewhat at odds with the emerging new orthodoxy in regulation theory. At Monash University, I was lucky to join in a continuing conversation between Peter Marden and John McKay about regulation in theory and practice, seeing through their eyes how my perspective on regulation reflects work started more than a decade ago with Michael Dear on state theory. But what gives the project its distinctiveness is its ethical content. Here, my association with Michael Smith and the philosophy department at Monash gave me a special insight into ethical theory. From this association, it was a very short step indeed to Philip Pettit and John Braithwaite at the Australian National University. Philip has been especially valuable as an enthusiastic supporter, sharing his ideas on moral theory and the bases for a reconceptualized philosophy of public policy.

For research assistance, I was pleased to have the help of Kathy Barsom, Wayne Caldow, Karen Dreher, Rod Francis, Mary Huller, Tonia Stokes, and Tim Barta. As is true for all those who have helped me prepare this book, none of the above should be held responsible for the arguments and opinions expressed in the book. I am sure I have neglected as much good advice as I have tried to use. Most important, however, I would like to acknowledge the insight and understanding of the process of corporate restructuring and unionism given to me over the past few years by my wife, Shirley. Her own career and experience in the health care industry and the American labor movement gave me what most academics lack: a sense of the remarkable commitment involved when people stake their personal ideals on the performance of an institution. We are jointly responsible for the dedication of this book.

As this book is based upon a series of related papers, I should also acknowledge the permission of a number of publishers for use of that material in the book. In particular, John Ashby of Pion Ltd. permitted use of "Location, Management Strategy and Workers Pensions" and "Restructuring, Workers' Pensions and the Law," published in *Environment and Planning A* 22 (1990): 17–37, 149–68; and "Problematic Status of Corporate Regulation in the United States: Towards a New Moral Order," *Environment and Planning A* 24 (1992): 534–55. Cambridge University Press and the Regional Studies Association allowed the use of "Piercing the Corporate Veil: The Closure of Wisconsin Steel in South Chicago" and "Regulating the Restructuring of the U.S. Steel Industry: Chapter 11 of the Bankruptcy Code and Pension Obligations" published in *Regional Studies* 24 (1990): 405–20, and 25 (1991): 135–53. The Institute of British Geographers allowed use of "Unethical Secrets, Lies and Legal Retaliation in the Context of Corporate Restructuring in the United States" published in *Transactions* n.s., 14 (1990): 403–20. And finally, Clark University permitted use of "Limits of Statutory Responses to Corporate Restructuring Illustrated with Reference to Plant Closing Legislation" published in *Economic Geography* 68 (1991): 22–41.

Finally, I would like to thank Bruce and Dorothy Spratling for their dedication; proofreading is a difficult and exacting task. Once again they did an excellent job.

Abbreviations

AFL-CIO	American Federation of Labor-Congress of Industrial Organizations
BCG	Boston Consulting Group
CEO	Chief executive officer
DOL	U.S. Department of Labor
ERISA	Employee Retirement Income Security Act
GAO	U.S. General Accounting Office
GATT	General Agreement on Tariffs and Trade
IBM	International Business Machines
ICC	Interstate Commerce Commission
IHC	International Harvester Corporation (Navistar)
IMF	International Monetary Fund
IRS	U.S. Internal Revenue Service
LBO(s)	Leveraged buyout(s)
MITI	Japanese Ministry of International Trade and Industry
NICs	Newly industrialized countries
NIRA	U.S. National Industry Recovery Act
NLRA	U.S. National Labor Relations Act
NLRB	U.S. National Labor Relations Board
NRA	National Recovery Agency
OSHA	U.S. Occupational Health and Safety Administration
PBGC	U.S. Pension Benefit Guaranty Corporation
SLTE	Suitable long-term employment
SSA	U.S. Social Security Administration
UAW	United Auto Workers
USWA	United Steelworkers of America
WSC	Wisconsin Steel Company

PART 1

Background

1

ERISA and the Crisis
of Regulation

The alarm bells sound in corporate America when profits decline, when market share starts falling, when better and cheaper products are offered in corporations' marketplaces, and when competitors start shifting production sites around the country and throughout the world searching for lower costs of production and higher rates of labor productivity. For some corporations, the strategic response has been to mimic new competitors, a strategy fraught with many dangers, not least of which is the probability of always being behind the leading edge of innovation. Another response has been to shift resources from exposed product lines to other more sheltered products and industries—a strategy that may work in the short run but will not in the long run unless corporate executives are understood as portfolio managers instead of as product innovators. Yet another strategy has been to alter the very form of the modern corporation through mergers and acquisitions, which is one way to ensure a flow of new products through the company. The development of a "market for corporate control" has certainly added to the debt structure of many companies, while not necessarily improving their economic performance.[1]

These strategies had significant implications for the design and structure of corporations' production systems through the 1970s and (especially) the 1980s, as well as drastic implications for the continuity and use of existing plant and equipment. Plant closings, the reallocation and relocation of production within corporations' network of plants, and the outsourcing of components and parts are common indicators of these strategies in action. Of course, the past decade was not the first time economic forces have burst the fabric of established industries, their social relations of production, and the well-being of communities dependent upon those industries. B. Bluestone and B. Harrison's book (1982) on the deindustrialization of the U.S. economy documented a process underway during much of the post–World War II era. Furthermore, any review of the federal policies related to regulating the process of economic restructuring would show that Congress has initiated policies in response to dramatic economic changes wrought on communities around America. Witness the passage of ERISA in 1974 in response to well-documented instances of plant closings and corporate bankruptcy.

As this book is about the process of corporate restructuring, it depends upon a set of case studies to illustrate both the economic logic and regulatory structure that together determine the design of the restructuring process. It is also a book about the relative significance of economic imperatives in the light of corporations' social obligations, especially their statutory obligations to respect and protect the pension entitlements of their employees. The intersection of economic imperatives and social obligations is a problematic junction between arguments of private necessity (the imperatives of the market) and public aspirations about the proper boundaries of economic interests and social expectations. While there are many reasons to expect well-defined and policed boundaries between economic imperatives and social obligations, in fact the evidence presented here suggests that such boundaries are neither well defined nor well policed. The book documents a crisis of regulation amplified and exaggerated by the current economic crisis but nevertheless inherent in the American political economy. ERISA has not provided adequate protection from economic imperatives because there is no general regulatory framework through which competing statutory claims can be resolved and rationalized; the United States lacks a coherent industrial policy.

Logic of ERISA

The Employee Retirement Income Security Act (ERISA) was passed by Congress in August 1974 and signed into law by Pres. Gerald Ford on Labor Day, September 2, 1974. The conference report on the Pension Reform Act, as it was then known, passed both the House and the Senate with huge margins of support. In the House of Representatives only two members of Congress voted against the measure, and in the Senate no vote was cast against the bill (though fifteen senators abstained). In both, political support for the bill was demonstrably bipartisan and enthusiastic. Reading the *Congressional Record* (120 [1974]), it is obvious that passage of ERISA was a great victory for leading Democrats and Republicans, many of whom had worked for more than three years to bring the bill to the floor of Congress. Indeed, in Sen. Jacob Javits's case, the leading Republican supporter of the measure, he rightfully claimed that he had worked for pension reform for more than ten years. Most generally, the bill was conceived to be the first comprehensive piece of federal legislation designed to regulate the U.S. private pension system. Supporters of the bill believed it was essential to protect and enhance the pension rights of workers; as Rep. Joseph Gaydos (D-Pa.) intimated, the act was passed to ensure that employers' promises of retirement income were more than an "illusion" (p. 29207).

For many supporters of the bill, its significance was to be measured against the achievements of the New Deal. John Brademas (D-Ind.) noted that "this is one of the most important laws ever passed by Congress to protect the rights of American working men and women" (p. 29206). Representative Melvin Price (D-Ill.) suggested that it was "one of the most monumental pieces of labor legislation passed by any Congress" (p. 29209). Likewise in the Senate, supporters proclaimed its significance now and for the future. As noted in the epigraph to this book, Senator Javits (R-N.Y.) likened the bill to a set of "fundamental guarantees." He also claimed that "the pension reform bill is the greatest development in the life of the American worker" (p. 29933). Similarly, as Sen. Richard Schweiker (R-Pa.) suggested, although in a more restrained manner, "the bill will ultimately be considered to be one of the most significant pieces of social legislation to pass the Congress" (p. 29961). There can be very few pieces of social and labor legislation (including the related New Deal legislation) that began life with such high expectations and support. To understand why the bill was greeted with such enthusiasm is to simply remember the times. Notwithstanding the documented need and apparent hardship experienced by workers denied their pension benefits, passage of the bill came at a time of political crisis, immediately after the resignation of Pres. Richard Nixon and the Watergate scandal. Republican congressional representatives had a strong electoral interest in appearing on the side of Congress, just as the new president had an interest in supporting legislation that had received strong congressional support. Elections were looming, and even Democrats were concerned to project an image of a strong and independent Congress.

It would be misleading, however, to leave an impression that ERISA was a piece of legislation made possible by the political exigencies of the moment. In fact, its logic was quite unlike past labor-oriented legislation in a number of vital ways. Most generally, Senator Javits captured the essential logic of the act: it was conceived to guarantee workers' pension rights rather than to set uniform benefit levels or requirements. Put slightly differently, the act was designed to ensure that employers' unilateral or contractually negotiated promises of retirement income were honored and legally protected. The act did not require employers to offer pension plans as part of their employment benefits or to offer a certain level of benefits. What the act did was provide workers with federal legal rights to promised benefits while ensuring that the vesting, as well as the funding and management of private pension plans, met federally mandated minimum standards of operation. Thus, the rhetoric of supporters of the bill who suggested, as Gaydos did for example, that it was "the most important piece of labor-related legislation since the establishment of the federal minimum wage" (p. 29207), was not as accurate as one might initially suppose. In fact, the bill was more like civil rights legislation than it was a piece of New Deal legislation concerned with mandating the substantive welfare of American workers.

The distinction made here between the rights logic of ERISA and the welfare logic of comparable New Deal legislation is a distinction that matches other commentators' notions of the distinctiveness of 1960s and 1970s social legislation (see Sunstein 1990). In making this distinction, I do not mean to belittle the achievement of Congress in passing ERISA, nor do I wish to imply that the vesting, funding, and fiduciary standards set out in the act were of small consequence. There can be no doubt that these minimum standards were of vital significance in ensuring that private pension plans are administered fairly and equitably. These standards provided the Internal Revenue Service (IRS) and the secretary of the Department of Labor (DOL) with strong levers for monitoring and regulating the private pension plan system that, previous to the passage of the bill, was essentially unregulated.

For Rep. Daniel Rostenkowski (D-Ill.), the basic purpose of the act was to strengthen the rights of existing pension plan participants and beneficiaries. Like many other members of Congress, he was most concerned with ensuring that plant closings and pension plan terminations did not result in workers losing their promised benefits. As evidence for the significance of these problems, advocates of the bill often cited a 1972 study by the DOL which showed that in nearly half of all pension plan terminations workers lost benefits. To give this study greater emotional force, advocates for the bill often invoked instances of this occurring in different regions of the country, the most notable being the bankruptcy and closure of the Studebaker company in South Bend, Indiana, in 1964. Like so many other cited examples, the closure of Studebaker resulted in many workers losing all promised benefits. Those who did receive some benefits were provided hardly enough to live on. Suicide and extreme deprivation were cited as the inevitable consequences of lost retirement benefits (as was the case in the closure of Rheingold Beer Company in New York). In other cases, workers lost promised benefits while company executives were voted large pensions just before plants closed. And in other cases, pension plans made arbitrary and discriminatory decisions regarding benefits and

eligibility (a case cited from the United Mine Workers' welfare and retirement plan). In part, these instances are issues of equity and fair treatment. They are also the kinds of circumstances and events consistent with
the logic of corporate restructuring during the 1970s and 1980s.

Notwithstanding the political rhetoric, the cited cases of hardship, and
the strengths of the act with respect to the federal regulation of vesting
and fiduciary standards, the bill was less than perfect—a "delicate compromise," on many fronts, according to Rostenkowski (p. 29210). The bill
had to satisfy organized labor, especially the United Auto Workers (UAW)
and the United Steelworkers of America (USWA), but could not alienate
business. It was a compromise between Democrats and Republicans, between the House and the Senate, between standing committees in both
parts of Congress, and between leading Democrats. It was even a compromise between the need for a technically sophisticated bill (which defined, for example, the actuarial standards necessary for effective regulation) and the interests of Congress in fashioning an intelligible document
of public policy. Even at the time, many members of Congress (including
its most forceful advocates) noted deficiencies in the bill and promised that
Congress would carefully monitor its implementation and return, if necessary, to make amendments and corrections. What began life as a complex
and large bill has become through subsequent amendments and additions
a massively complicated and extraordinarily wide-ranging act.

But in many ways, the initial compromises necessary to ensure passage
remain at the heart of the act. In strengthening workers' pension rights,
care was taken to ensure that plans were not regulated "out of existence"
by virtue of their particularities just as it was recognized that the nation
had an interest in encouraging the expansion of existing plans and the
creation of new plans. Just thirty years before debate over passage of the
act, only 4.1 million workers were covered by pension plans. By 1972,
nearly 30 million were covered by plans (about one-half of the workforce),
and in 1987 about 66 percent of the workforce were covered by a pension
plan (Short and Nelson 1991). The argument repeated many times in debate
over passage of the act was that it could not and should not impose an
undue financial burden on employers. The added costs attributed to the
nature and requirements of meeting minimum vesting and fiduciary standards were rationalized as necessary, but acceptable. To guarantee workers' pension benefits, a new agency (the Pension Benefit Guaranty Corporation [PBGC]) was established, modeled on the federal deposit
insurance agencies of the banking and the savings and loan industries.
Pooling the risk of default and termination between companies, separating
companies from the actual control of pension funds, and requiring the

present funding of expected liabilities were thought to be effective ways of limiting a company's liability while also limiting the federal government's liability. But, again, to ensure companies were not overburdened financially, provision was made for short-term waivers in funding liabilities and amendments to plan benefits—a compromise that has come back to haunt the private pension system (Bodie 1992).

As we shall see throughout the book, Congress's ambition to both protect workers' pension rights and minimize individual corporations' financial responsibility for those entitlements has been severely tested by recent events. Just as problematic as the compromise on financial obligations was the compromise on administrative authority. The House and the Senate passed very different guidelines concerning the respective authority of existing agencies and departments with regard to the regulation of the private pension system. Whereas the Senate wished to delineate clearly authority between agencies, the House's version only generally shared authority between the IRS (Treasury) and the DOL. The compromise solution was to give the IRS authority to regulate the employees' participation in plans, the funding standards of plans, and the rules of vesting in private pension plans that seek federal tax qualification. The IRS was also given authority to waive (in the short term) companies' contributions to their pension plans. By contrast, the DOL was given general authority to make regulations concerning the conduct of plans, and the authority to bring civil and criminal suits in federal court to recover benefits, enforce the payment of plan benefits, and rectify violations of individuals' pension rights. Individuals were also provided legal standing to bring suit to recover, enforce, and rectify violations of their rights. The DOL was also given responsibility for collecting and disseminating information on private pension plans. In all respects, Congress made it clear that ERISA preempted related state laws. Thus, a functional division of federal authority was implemented consistent with the historical mission of the different agencies and departments.

In retrospect, what is remarkable about the debate over this functional model of authority and responsibility was how little attention was given to three issues. First, and consistent with Rostenkowski's claim that the act was primarily intended to regulate existing plans, little attention was given to the issue of which agency or department was to be responsible for the private pension system as a whole. Presumably, that responsibility was left to the DOL, given that so many pension plans were then part of collective-bargaining agreements. Other than indicating that the DOL had general powers to regulate the private pension system, the authority for pension policy remained ill-defined. Second, there was little recognition of the overlapping nature of firms' financial interests in pension plan obligations. That is, by separating administrative functions and authority, little attention was given to how the actions of one agency might flow over into the jurisdiction of other agencies. There was, of course, a presumption of coordination between agencies and departments, but no mechanism for ensuring coordination on policy. Third, and perhaps most remarkably, little or no attention was given to the likely legal authority of ERISA with respect to labor law and bankruptcy law. Indeed, there was very little discussion of the role of the courts in general in administering and policing the act. The financial capacity of workers to go to court to recover benefits or to enforce their rights was never questioned. Presumably, Congress did not anticipate the extent to which the courts would become involved in the private pension plan system.

What dominated congressional debate at the time of passage of the act was concern over portability and the status of the self-employed. The former issue was not resolved to anyone's satisfaction. For many Americans, the lack of portability of their pension entitlements has created a complex array of unrelated plans and benefits. For the self-employed, Congress was more successful: the value of various kinds of individual retirement accounts was enhanced by favorable tax incentives. Again, compromise was the operative solution: in this instance, equity among workers, corporate executives, and the self-employed ensured overwhelming support for the bill.

The Limits of ERISA

Nearly twenty years after passage of ERISA, it is obvious that these embedded political compromises have had a significant impact on the performance of the act. While passage of the act was prompted in part by the impact of corporate restructuring (bankruptcies, plant closures, and mergers and acquisitions) on workers' pensions, no systematic attempt was made to "solve" underlying conflicts of interest. On one hand, companies have a basic interest in minimizing their pension liabilities, an interest that is accentuated during restructuring. On the other hand, workers and the nation have overlapping and reinforcing interests in protecting promised pension benefits. Workers' welfare is at stake, and collectively the continuing integrity of the nation's private pension system is at stake. By implication, Congress believed that there would be relatively few instances of pension plan terminations due to restructuring; it was presumed that the PBGC's insurance pool would be large enough to accommodate those instances. In the worst-case scenario, a number of terminations occurring at once, large claims would be presumably funded out of general revenue. Twenty years later, these assumptions and presumptions are problematic, given the scope of corporate restructuring in American industry and the scale of the federal government's budget deficit (see chapter 2). Notice, though, that these issues of public policy were made more difficult to recognize and resolve by the functional division of authority in administering the act. In this sense, elements of the present crisis of regulation were embedded in the logic of the legislation.

Today, the immanent crisis of regulation is a day-to-day reality in the nation's federal court system. Although the Supreme Court has not made ERISA a subject of special interest, at lower levels in the system "it seems that more and more time must be spent by the federal courts (and, for that matter, by the state courts) on questions arising under [ERISA]" (*Law Week* 60:3125, 1991). Why is law so essential to the functioning and administration of the private pension system? Why is this book so dominated by the law as the object of analysis? These are especially acute questions considering that Congress believed the relevant issues of public policy to be settled by the act. It was recognized, of course, that since pensions is such a technical area (being associated with insurance and risk assessment) revisions to the law were expected and encouraged in accordance with the experience of companies and the PBGC. While revisions to the law have occurred and lawsuits have been initiated in areas of dispute that have required technical resolution, many lawsuits have been on matters of policy and principle. Interpreting the meaning of the law with respect to individual workers' pension rights has been one large, substantive area of litigation. The case study on Continental Can begins with an analysis of the relevant case law concerning Section 510 of ERISA and the rights of individual workers (see chapter 3). Congress expected the federal courts would be involved in these issues, although it also presumed that DOL would take a leading role in such litigation. In fact, individuals (and their unions) have been the source for most related litigation.

On the basis of the legislative record of investigation and debate, what was unexpected was the extent to which the courts have become involved in matters of public policy. For instance, there has been significant litigation about the issue of who (the employer or employees) "owns" excess funds after plans are terminated and all current and expected obligations are met. Litigation in this area could be explained in a number of ways. Since it was not an important problem at the time of passage of the act, it could be argued that Congress did not anticipate its significance and thus (reasonably) did not provide guidelines for its resolution. While the DOL clearly has had a strong interest in the issue, during the Reagan and

Bush administrations the department has not had the political clout to exclude competing opinions about the "ownership" of excess funds from other agencies and departments. And because the issue is bound up with other matters of public policy, such as how to best finance the international competitiveness of American industry, the economic imperatives of corporate restructuring have come to dominate issues of equity and principle. If we add a further institutional dimension to the dilemma—the relative status of pension law with respect to other related and overlapping laws such as labor law and bankruptcy law—it becomes obvious with hindsight why the courts are so involved in ERISA matters. There is little in ERISA by way of a useful recipe for resolving disputes over the relative status of overlapping policies and laws.

The problems of adjudicating the relative status of ERISA in relation to overlapping laws are considered in more detail in the case study on the bankruptcy of LTV Corporation (see chapter 6). Notwithstanding the merits of the argument that ERISA failed to make clear the relative status of related laws, a more general argument can be made about the underlying source of litigation over ERISA. Basically, ERISA was conceived to be a system of rights and obligations. It was deliberately written to reflect the language and logic of the civil rights and antidiscrimination laws of the 1960s. In being so written, ERISA matched in form, if not substance, many other pieces of social legislation of that time. It was part of the "rights revolution" (Sunstein 1990). This is the context behind Senator Javits's claim that ERISA was "nothing less than a pension 'bill of rights' to which every worker . . . is entitled." Indeed, if we took Javits at his word this phrase could be interpreted to mean that ERISA was to have the status of the Bill of Rights of the U.S. Constitution. Still, given that ERISA is a statute, not a constitutional amendment, one might suppose that Javits's intention was to give workers access to the courts as a means of protecting their individual entitlements to pension plan benefits.

The effects of this "bill of rights" were manifold. It made the provisions of collective-bargaining agreements related to pension plans subject to ERISA. Thus, it made the federal courts a forum of review and appeal separate from and superior to the normal grievance appeal procedures of labor contracts. Most generally, it might be supposed that this hierarchical order of rights, where contract rights are made subordinate to statutory rights, was an implied "theory" of the relative status of ERISA and labor law. However, such a broad reading of the effect of ERISA should not be (and has not been) construed to implicate all labor law. Most important, it provided nonunionized workers with a mechanism of appeal independent of the company that employed them. Workers no longer had to belong to a union to obtain a measure of due process with respect to their pension claims. For those familiar with arguments about the decline of the American labor movement, this effect of ERISA fits into a more general argument about the socialization of union benefits. One reason workers have not joined unions as they might have in the past is that the benefits of belonging to a union have been extended to all workers through federal legislation. Workers have had their rights protected in federal legislation on issues such as safety, age and sex discrimination in hiring and promotion decisions, *and* pension benefits over the past couple of decades. But it is clear that ERISA, like so much other new social legislation, encouraged litigation of issues that were otherwise previously undisputed (because there was no means to do so) or arbitrated according to the terms and conditions of collective-bargaining agreements.

It is also clear that the emphasis on individual rights as opposed to membership in collective organizations was quite deliberate, and was encouraged by the unions as a matter of equity and social justice. And it is just as clear in the Continental Can (chapter 4) and the International Harvester (chapter 5) cases that ERISA's pension rights gave unions a useful mechanism by which to act against companies who had subverted the collective-bargaining process in their attempts to finance restructuring. In this sense, it might be argued that ERISA has worked well, even if the scale and scope of litigation are far broader than Congress might have intended. The rights logic of the legislation can be thought, then, to be a valuable means of policing corporate behavior at a time when unions are quickly declining in significance. These linked statements are probably true, but I would suggest that the emphasis of ERISA on individual rights unfortunately privileges form over substance. *If* Congress had been willing to look more closely at the economic imperatives of corporate restructuring and *if* Congress had been willing to make an unequivocal assignment of responsibility for the administration and formation of policy regarding private pensions, then the courts may still have been a limited partner in the regulation of the private pension system. As it is, courts are now essential to the effective performance of the system—witness Judge Robert Sweet's opinion in the LTV bankruptcy case.

The lack of an apparent, congressionally mandated recipe for resolving disputes over the status of ERISA relative to other overlapping statutes has brought some very difficult issues out into the open. With respect to corporate and industrial restructuring, the status of ERISA is contested and disputed. At the most general level, what is disputed is the appropriate balance between the economic imperatives of restructuring and corporations' obligations to their workers and society. Morally, this is a profound issue. It involves questions of ethics and belief, as well as the (contested) definition of socially observed standards of behavior. In chapter 8, I suggest that the question of ethics and behavior are at the heart of much recent litigation over the status of ERISA. This is, I assert, particularly true in the case studies presented in the book. Chapters 8 and 9 argue that many corporate executives subscribe to a very crude, utilitarian, and consequentialist theory of the "good." That is, their actions both with respect to their workers' pension rights and possible legal liabilities under ERISA are justified by the net benefits that accrue to the corporation. This conception of the underlying moral foundations of the law is juxtaposed to others' interpretations of the moral foundations of law, and ERISA in particular. It is suggested that there are profound differences between workers and management in how they understand the moral foundations of ERISA. These differences both contribute to the volume of litigation over the status of ERISA, and the difficulties the courts have had in reaching clear decisions on the relative merits of competing interpretations of the role of ERISA compared to other areas of the law.

Less profoundly, maintaining a clear boundary between the economic imperatives of corporate restructuring and their social obligations is an area of litigation that few courts have been able to easily handle. In both the Continental Can and International Harvester case studies, the courts were faced with arguments from the corporations that their actions were entirely justified by "business considerations." For Continental Can, laying off workers and closing plants were justified by commercial needs given changes in the demand for their products. By their account, the loss of pension rights of some workers was merely an incidental aspect of a larger issue. For International Harvester, the sale and subsequent closing of Wisconsin Steel was none of the court's business. Again, the defense's argument was that the sale, bankruptcy of the steel unit, and subsequent termination of the pension plans were just part of doing business. Of course, both companies failed to sustain their arguments because material was found in their own records documenting the deliberate manner in which both companies went about subverting ERISA. But without such "smoking-gun" evidence, it has proved very difficult to make rules that could reasonably discriminate between corporations' legitimate business interests and society's interest in policing the integrity of the act.

Unfortunately, the lack of a recipe for rationalizing the status of ERISA also means that ERISA is hostage to disputes over the meaning and status of other overlapping statutes. This is best illustrated in the case study of the LTV bankruptcy. Accompanying the recent wave of mergers and acquisitions in American industry, deregulation of a number of major sectors, and the relative decline of many American manufacturing industries has been a wave of corporate bankruptcies. And in some cases, unfunded pension obligations (made possible by waivers granted by the IRS) have precipitated bankruptcy. There is a very real question about the relative status of ERISA claims in bankruptcy proceedings (see chapter 6). But there is also another profound and unresolved question here, a question that has spilled over into the debate over the relative status of ERISA: what is the purpose of bankruptcy? Theorists such as T. H. Jackson (1986) contend that the only purpose of bankruptcy should be as a legal forum for the resolution and collection of debts. By his analysis, ERISA, the PBGC, and workers in general are just creditors like other creditors. ERISA is deemed subservient to bankruptcy law which, according to Jackson, has no higher purpose than the allocation of discounted assets. On the other hand, E. Warren (1987) would argue that bankruptcy must serve a social purpose, must be representative of some underlying conception of social justice. By this account, ERISA may have special status in bankruptcy proceedings by virtue of the special nature of pension entitlements—pensions could be thought as endowments rather than just deferred income (Hovenkamp 1991).

As will become apparent, I tend to favor Warren's interpretation rather than Jackson's. But, personal opinion aside, there is no immediate prospect of resolving the dispute over the proper purpose of bankruptcy. As a consequence, the idealism embodied in Senator Javits's comments at the time of the passage of ERISA has been replaced by a measure of despair and frustration as evidenced by the comments of Judge Sweet in the LTV case. For Judge Sweet, it appears obvious that the law must serve a larger purpose than simply treating all creditors alike. His comments reflect a real concern about the well-being of many thousands of people adversely affected by corporate restructuring. His comments also reflect a realization that the courts are now so intimately involved in the regulation of such issues that any resolution will be a judicial one subject to the vagaries of that process. Indeed, I would suggest that any attempt to rationalize the status of ERISA via a form of industrial policy is bound to be compromised by the nature and styles of judicial policymaking in the federal courts. Policymaking through the "rights revolution" (citing, as an example, the recent plant-closing bill) is a mode of regulation that is unfortunately more general than ERISA and its related statutes (but see Herz 1992).

Crisis of Regulation

All the evidence collected here suggests that federal policy as it relates to corporate restructuring and private pensions is in a state of crisis. In this respect the book is finally a story about U.S. industrial policy: the scope thereof and the costs of being unable to act deliberately and comprehensively in the interests of many millions of people. By default, the managers of corporate restructuring have become the courts and the legal system in general. It should not come as a surprise for the reader to learn that, in my judgment at least, the courts have proved themselves to be ill-equipped to handle the task. This is not to say that the courts are generally incompetent or lack the commitment to social justice that we expect of government officials whose job it should be to protect workers' rights. The problem is that federal judges are not trained for, are not primarily responsible for, and do not have sufficient powers to provide what the federal government refuses to provide—a general blueprint for rationalizing private economic and public interests in the context of dramatic changes in the underlying structure of the modern corporation. Still, we should be circumspect about the scope of my findings. I would not pretend to have exhausted the set of all possible stories of corporate restructuring, or would I claim that the three case studies chosen define the complete character of the current crisis of U.S. regulation. Nevertheless, these stories are in their different ways vital to understanding the evolving nature of regulation and the crisis of regulation in the United States.

It should be apparent that I believe that there is currently no general framework within which to define or enforce private respect for social obligations. In this setting, then, the integrity of the private pension system as it is defined and protected by federal statute must be in doubt just as it is obvious from the case studies analyzed here that many thousands of workers have been illegally denied their pension benefits. At one level, it might be suggested that what I document is an isolated and minor part of an otherwise operating private pension system; and there is some truth to this counterassertion in that the case studies are studies of corporations in crisis, not of corporations able to and committed to funding their pension plans (but see the American Academy of Actuaries 1992). If there are many thousands of companies that continue to operate their plans in accordance with past expectations, the case studies suggest that when operation of those plans conflicts with corporate executives' goals and aspirations, maintenance of a corporation's social obligations will be likely compromised. Thus I suggest here that in instances where economic imperatives and social obligations collide, the regulatory process is neither strong enough (as an institution) nor well enough respected (for its moral integrity) to be adhered to, given the costs and benefits of competing opportunities.

Lack of a general regulatory framework robust enough to protect private pension entitlements from economic imperatives is not just a problem unique to pensions. In fact, it reflects upon the coherence of the U.S. political economy in the sense that it is indicative of a more general crisis of regulation; the crisis of regulation is a crisis particular to certain corporations and industrial sectors but reflects an immanent crisis of regulation in the sense that it indicates aspects of a deep-seated crisis of confidence in the regulatory state. Ironically, it seems that the recent fiftieth birthday of the New Deal regulatory state may be more an epitaph for the passing of an era than a celebration of continuity of an institutional innovation. Apparent in the case studies on corporate restructuring reported here is a profound mistrust of the regulatory state—corporations do not believe that regulations reflect their needs or are responsive to the changing economic environment. Unions and their members believe that the regulatory state has become so politicized that there is no reason to expect consistent application of the rules and certainly no reason to expect a general respect of the underlying logic of statutes such as ERISA. And even the regulatory state is at war with itself; judges decry the lack of effective rulemaking just as regulatory agencies decry the formal legalities of regulation that make any enforcement program a litigation nightmare, instead of a well-defined process of rulemaking and rule enforcement. A profound mistrust of the regulatory process is shared by the targets of regulation, those to be protected by regulation, the agents of regulation, and the adjudicators of regulation.

This mistrust is manifest in many different ways. For example, it helps sustain the argument made by many conservative theorists that statute-based formal regulation should only rarely intrude into the private economic sphere. Those who would argue against industry policy, those who would argue against the imposition of ERISA-type legislation, and those who would argue against the direct enforcement of rules and regulation covering worker safety and the like would also suggest that the virtue of the U.S. political system is its decentralized character. Federal regulation in the form developed since the New Deal is, by this interpretation, anathema to the "proper" mode of regulation in the United States. Case law, common law adjudication, and the maintenance of strict divisions between the private and public spheres are the foundations of this mode of regulation. For its advocates, this mode of regulation relies upon the free market as the ultimate mechanism of sanction and reward. A company that deliberately subverted the trust of its employees, that denied voluntary and agreed-to pension entitlements, would soon lose its reputation as a "good" employer and would thus have to pay a premium in the market to attract workers. Either the wage premium would compensate employees for the risks of working with an untrustworthy employer or the wage premium would so disadvantage the company with respect to the market price of its goods that it would be forced to remake its practices so as to maintain competitiveness. This mode of regulation is thought to enhance the flexibility of local adjustment to new forms of competition, allow for the heterogeneity of local experience, and encourage workers and management to make agreements consistent with their local needs rather than referencing general social standards of need.

As a piece of logic and as an argument for reform, there are many who would believe that this mode of regulation is preferable to the more intrusive statute-based and agency-enforced style of regulation that typified the post–New Deal era (Breyer 1982). And yet, it is an argument without empirical content, being simply an assertion about how the market ought to operate in ideal circumstances.[2] The consequences of a person losing promised pension benefits may be so adverse that no amount of general argument about the ideal operation of the market would be enough compensation. In this setting, social standards are necessary to protect workers who by no fault or decision of their own making are vulnerable to arbitrary acts by corporations. This was, after all, the lesson of the Studebaker bankruptcy—many workers who had invested their working lives with the company (many working over thirty years) lost their promised pension entitlements. Bankruptcy meant that they could not recover their entitlements, and their age meant that they could not start again. Market-based wage-premium penalties on the company were practically irrelevant. Passage of ERISA was premised upon a belief that the market would not be adequate to the task of allocating the true costs and benefits of agents' actions and that the costs of failure were too high for older individuals to absorb. But, of course, the rhetoric of market-based regulation remains and, in an era of apparent regulatory-state failure to police adequately the social obligations that were essential to the passage of ERISA, it promises an alternative to the current mode of regulation. Going from the rhetoric to the current state of regulation provides critics of the current system further reason to exaggerate the mistrust already apparent in the regulatory state.

Rhetoric aside, there are other ways mistrust of the current system amplifies the inability of the regulatory state to police ERISA adequately.

Most critically, there appears to be no common agreement among workers, unions, and corporations about the goals and objectives of the current regulatory regime. For workers, protection of pension entitlements is the essential rationale behind regulation, although even here there may be dispute between older and younger workers. Younger workers may favor a regulatory system that maintains the financial integrity of corporations as operating units whereas older workers might favor a regulatory system that paid out creditors (pension beneficiaries) regardless of the consequences of such actions for the continuity of corporations. In this respect, younger workers and corporate managers may have more in common than younger workers and older workers who belong to the same union, even those who live in the same community and are related by family ties. Lack of agreement about the goals and objectives of regulation (notwithstanding the initial bases of legislation), and lack of agreement about the mechanism of regulation bring to light profound differences about values. Where regulation might properly be thought to be ideally based upon a set of common or overlapping values, in fact the regulatory state has had to operate in a world of conflicting values and beliefs that by their conflict question the very desirability of regulation as an institution. There are apparently few common values that can be used by agencies to forge alliances to thus protect and enhance their credibility. The crisis of regulation in this respect is a crisis of social life.[3]

Summary—ERISA in Context

The integrity of ERISA has been put to the test by the latest round of corporate restructuring and has been found to be wanting. If originally conceived to protect workers' pensions from the economic imperatives of corporate restructuring, on the evidence presented here it might reasonably be suggested that it is not so robust as now needed. This is an often-made empirical argument, well understood in the legal literature. It simply suggests that as circumstances change so too do the power and applicability of a statute (Calabresi 1982). Where it might have been robust enough if applied to circumstances such as those that prompted passage of the act, we might now suppose that current circumstances are somehow now different, more difficult or more complex. This is plausible, as long as we would assume that ERISA was found relevant in the past, if not the present. But, in fact, the case studies analyzed here are some of the very first legal tests of the power of the statute. The suits all began in the early to mid-1980s based upon actions taken by the corporations just after the passage of ERISA (Continental Can and International Harvester) or before any significant tests of the relative power of ERISA in federal court (LTV Corporation). Indeed cases like *Gavalik v. Continental Can* and *Wisconsin Steel* are very important since decisions made about the application of ERISA in these cases will determine the very character and life of ERISA over the long run.

On the basis of the evidence produced here, I argue that some perverse aspects of the U.S. political economy have made policing corporate behavior through single statutes next to impossible. I say "next to impossible" because, as will be seen, the existing regulatory framework is being used to regulate corporate behavior and has been shown to have significant scope and power in the cases analyzed. To think otherwise is to doubly disenfranchise those currently working to protect workers' pensions. It implies that their task is hopeless and that whatever their successes those successes are illusory. More profoundly, it denies the very integrity of the legal-political process as a means of seeking justice—a remarkable claim when we remember how important the legal process is in American society (see Ely 1980). There are, of course, reasons to be skeptical of the possibility of judicial and statute-based solutions to social problems (Clark 1985), but skepticism should not be taken as a warrant to deny the efficacy of U.S. regulatory institutions in total.[4] That being said, the actions and decisions of regulators and federal court judges are not as comprehensive as needed if there is to be a coherent response to the problems of corporate restructuring.

There are four attributes of the U.S. political economy that make any comprehensive resolution of conflict between restructuring and private pension obligations very difficult indeed. Based upon the evidence collected about the practice of restructuring, I suggest that these attributes are evident in the application of ERISA and its relationship to related legislation. At issue here is the *general* coherence (or incoherence) of policy-making. This is what I mean by the previously made claim that the current crisis of regulation is a crisis of social life, involving the logic by which policy problems are normally addressed by the political system *and* is more than a recent phenomenon as if a "proper" redefinition of the scope and powers of ERISA would automatically solve current problems of rationalizing corporations' economic imperatives with their social obligations.

Attribute 1: *The lack of coordination between policies and statutes.* To illustrate the significance of this attribute for rationalizing economic imperatives with social obligations, consider for the moment the various statutes and federal policies embedded in those statutes that are relevant to the adjudication of competing claims for priority status as a creditor in Chapter 11 bankruptcy proceedings. To begin, there is the question of

deciding the relevance of the federal Bankruptcy Code (rather than leaving
the matter in state courts). Assuming a convincing case can be made for
federal jurisdiction, the next step is to consider which part of the code is
appropriate, given both the circumstances of the case and the goals of
bankruptcy, for the company and its creditors. With respect to pension
benefits, younger workers will likely encourage Chapter 11 bankruptcy
proceedings on the assumption that only these proceedings hold the possibility of the firm surviving and thus in the long run paying promised
pension benefits. Older workers, though, might prefer Chapter 7 bankruptcy on the assumption that their immediate interests deserve priority
over younger workers' long-run interests in seeing the company survive.
This kind of dispute about the application of the federal Bankruptcy Code
actually involves at least ERISA (concerning the eligibility and structure
of benefits) and the National Labor Relations Act (NLRA) (concerning
the process of collective bargaining and union representation of those
interests) as well as the possibility of the National Labor Relations Board
(NLRB) becoming involved in adjudication and litigation. As is made apparent in the case study of the LTV bankruptcy, there is no obvious way
of rationalizing these competing interests in the absence of an articulated
industrial policy or some political measure of the rank-order of interests
and social needs. Perhaps such a rank-order is impossible, given the heterogeneity of values. But, without such an explicitly made rank-order, the
courts are forced to fashion their own industrial policy.

Attribute 2: *The tendencies toward litigation.* Without an explicit industrial policy and a regulatory agency for the coordination of competing
and conflicting but relevant statutes, the only forum for a final resolution
of conflicts between economic imperatives and social obligations is the
federal court system. This is evident in so much of our discussion of corporate restructuring. Each case study is a study of corporate restructuring
that has two separate lives and modes of description. They can be first
described as stories of corporate decisionmaking using the terms and tools
of economics and geography; this discourse is dominated by notions of
rationality (the logic of decisionmaking) and the consequences of those
decisions for workers and their communities (see Rose-Ackerman 1991).
They can be also described as legal cases, focused upon competing interpretations of the facts of the cases informed by notions of legal liability
and discretion. Thus, for example, the case study of the closure of Wisconsin Steel begins with an assessment of the economic imperatives of
competition and capital efficiency, analyzes the motives of the relevant
corporate executives, and then analyzes the consequences of their actions
for the plant. In law, though, however relevant this kind of analysis for

determining the circumstances of a case, the bases of adjudication are not normally economic and geographic. Rather the terms of dispute are statutory and constitutional; relating the terms of the case to the law requires a transfiguration of the dispute into legal language and adjudicative practice. For many companies, this process of transfiguration is a means of shifting the focus of the dispute over restructuring from its substantive consequences to its legal justification. At the same time, for those affected, the legal system provides an opportunity to attack corporations using a legal format that is justified by the legal process itself, whereas they may not have substantive grounds to force companies to reconsider the propriety of their actions.

Attribute 3: *The responsive character of policy solutions.* The lack of coordination between policies and statutes, and tendencies toward litigation are clearly connected. Without an explicitly stated rank-order between policies, and without a political recipe that provides a means of generally reconciling competing claims, litigation becomes a very important institution for manufacturing determinancy (Clark 1985). Once understood as *the* mechanism of policymaking, however, it has become a very important arena of political conflict absorbing, though not resolving, disputes over policy goals that might be thought to be normally resolved in Congress. Having had the politics of policymaking brought into court, the judiciary do not have the same legitimacy to impose political solutions to problems of corporate restructuring. Their decisions have to be justified by the language of law. Thus, the courts face an impossible dilemma: making good policy decisions with respect to rationalizing economic imperatives with social obligations requires the tools of political consensus-making, but this is something explicitly denied to the courts (at least in theory) by the value attributed to the formal language of law. Congress has contributed to this dilemma in two ways. First, rather than make comprehensive solutions to problems of restructuring and industrial change in general, a tendency exists to initiate limited statutory responses to narrowly defined problems. Notwithstanding the merits of ERISA as a statute designed to protect workers' pension benefits, its scope was compromised to meet distinct political constituencies. Second, few (if any) policy innovations anticipate new policy problems or are open enough to be integrated with the existing structure of statutes and policies.

Policy formation lurches from one crisis to the next, creating policies that have limited substantive focus and relevance. Lack of coordination and the narrow scope of existing policies sustains the regulatory dilemma of the courts, particularly as the accumulated set of related statutes remains part of the legal framework well beyond the circumstances that initiated their passage. Thus the crisis of regulation is a crisis due to the process of policymaking in Congress and the nature of the legal process that by its very nature gives due respect to competing claims made in accordance with statutory "territory." A more comprehensive solution to problems of rationalizing economic imperatives with social obligations would anticipate the need for statutory solutions to contemporary problems in a way that kept intact a general regulatory framework.

Attribute 4: *The vulnerability of policymaking to special interests*. The lack of policy coordination, the importance of the courts as a forum of conflict resolution, and the responsive character of congressional decision-making all reflect an overarching attribute of the American political economy: its dependence on and vulnerability to special interests. Policies are difficult to coordinate because they are the separate results of intense lobbying on behalf of coalitions of interests organized to achieve narrowly defined results. Thus the problem of coordinating bankruptcy policy with ERISA, the NLRA, and the NLRB is a problem created because of the different interests separately served by the individual statutes and agencies. There are, of course, overlaps between policies and constituencies— the union movement has been able to forge alliances to affect bankruptcy policy, the passage of ERISA, and policymaking by the NLRB. However, this is a fragile kind of overlap—it is an overlap created by a historical accumulation of statutes and policies, some of which the union movement may not now particularly support or be able to influence.[5] Thus, the problem of being vulnerable to special interests is more than a problem of policy formation. It is a historical problem in the sense that coalitions formed for one policy may not be stable over time for the formation of related policy some time later. Consequently, given the vulnerability of the political process to special interests, even Congress may not be able to make the necessary connections between policies passed at one time and subsequent policies. The problem with industrial policy in the United States is its fragmentation between interests, its fragmentation within the political process, and its dependence upon the courts for technical solutions for political problems.

2

Restructuring in Theory
and Practice

All the evidence suggests that the position of the United States in the world economy is more precarious than it has been for many years, perhaps since the Great Depression of the 1930s. The news media is obsessed with the issue, every day ringing the alarm bells about the latest data, be it foreign debt, government bonds' ratings, the trade deficit, or the federal budget deficit. A spate of recent reports on the dimensions of U.S. debt problems have all demonstrated that America has become a much more indebted country, with the scale of debt rising rapidly over the last decade in both the public and private sectors (see Friedman 1988 for an excellent overview). If media comment is at times hysterical in tone and often misguided in diagnosis there are, nevertheless, serious reasons to be concerned about the international economic performance of the United States since it directly affects internal macroeconomic variables such as interest rates and the budget deficit, hence affecting private investment and employment. As alarming as current economic indicators appear to be, the prospects for the United States in the rapidly evolving global economy appear even more problematic. The development of multinational regional trading blocs, the 1992 integrated European Economic Community, and the reopening of Eastern Europe are all threats to the position of the United States in the evolving world economy.

An increasingly hostile international environment is one aspect of current U.S. economic problems. Related, of course, is the increasing vulnerability of local industries to head-to-head competition at home (in domestic markets) and overseas (Thurow 1992). The reasons why local industries are more vulnerable than before will be considered briefly in the next section. For the moment, it is important to acknowledge that both the changing international trading regime and the vulnerability of local industries to overseas competition have so affected the U.S. economy that for the first time since the Second World War fundamental questions are being asked about the appropriate structure, relevance, and capacity of corporations and public institutions to adjust. More particularly, at issue is the economic efficacy of the inherited statute-based relationship between the economic imperatives of competition and the social obligations of corporations. In this respect, drastic changes in the economic environment of many larger U.S. corporations have put increasing pressure on their willingness and ability to respect their inherited social obligations.

Just as current and future pension obligations have become fundamental to managements' design and implementation of restructuring, these same obligations have become vital to the federal government's interest in protecting the integrity of the private pension system. Inevitably, these competing interests have involved workers, unions, corporations, and the federal government in political and legal contests over who should be, and who is, ultimately responsible for the private pension system. Indeed it might be said, as Congress has intimated, that in the context of the harsh realities of international competition the public policy issue has become one of protecting the private pension system from the economic imperatives of corporate restructuring (U.S. Congress 1992).

International Economic Context

Since the early 1970s, the global economy has become both more integrated and more vulnerable to sudden and unanticipated shifts of economic activity originating in one part of the economic system. This is obvious in the significance that must be assigned to events in hitherto peripheral parts of the world (witness the impact of war in the Persian Gulf). It is also obvious that the rate of economic change has increased, measured by the decreasing time between successive phases of investment, disinvestment, and restructuring. It is also obvious that the geographical scope or penetration of economic events has broadened to affect the "four corners" of the globe. More countries are about to join the ranks of the newly industrialized countries' (NICs) club, just as whole regions of the globe (especially Africa) appear to be overwhelmed by the costs of global development. Symbolized by Pres. Richard Nixon's decision to float the U.S. dollar and then the first oil crisis, the early 1970s were watershed years heralding the advent of greater unanticipated volatility in the world economy. That volatility has had profound consequences for corporate structure and the well-being of local economies dependent upon those corporations.

The confluence of three semiautonomous forces over the past two decades or so have together effectively and fundamentally altered the structure of the international economy. The development of the world financial system, initially based on the English pound, then the U.S. dollar, and now based upon intercurrency arbitrage organized through overlapping (in time) but geographically dispersed money markets has been a vital part of the story. The arbitrage process has, in effect, made it possible to transfer capital across the world into and out of physical assets (such as urban office buildings) at a moment's notice. Parallel to development of the arbitrage process has been the accelerating economic strength of Japan in the world economy (a Pax Nipponica in the making? See Leaver 1989) and the later emergence of a number of Third World economies as major centers of production and export. Just as the major cities of the world have become electronically intertwined with finance capitalism, the location of goods production has spread through the world to the very margins of capitalism (herein being the promise of the Pacific Century; see Daly and Logan 1989). Contributing to these geographic integrating processes have been attempts to formally regulate world trade through GATT-based trade policy treaties. These factors have all contributed to a pattern of accelerated global economic change over the last twenty years or so, affecting both the periphery and the very core of the world economy. R. Higgott and A. Cooper (1990) provide a very useful overview of both the evolution of the world economic system in the context of the decline of American economic hegemony and a pessimistic treatment of the problematic future of nonaligned countries in international economic diplomacy.

The geographical implications of these processes can be described in many ways (as apparent from the broad array of papers in Scott and Storper 1986 and Storper and Scott 1992). Of the many related issues, one of the most important in the U.S. context and the developed economies of the world has been the increased vulnerability of both core regions and sectors of advanced economies to foreign competition. In many respects, the U.S. multinational corporate strategy of overseas assembly and production of the 1960s and 1970s has come home with a different national identity—foreign competitors now threaten U.S. corporations on their home turf. One consequence of the international penetration of production and local consumption has been recurrent cycles of global overproduction, particularly in manufactured goods of all kinds and at all levels of technological sophistication. And accompanying overproduction have been recurrent crises of wage and price discounting. Many countries have sought to devalue their currencies in order to reduce the real price of their exported goods, leading to temporary surges in export sales which are then swamped by other countries' pricing policies; this has then prompted further rounds of currency discounting (and so on). This kind of price discounting has flowed over into the cost accounting practices of major U.S. corporations, and have had direct and negative consequences on their workers' pension entitlements.

Another important consequence of global integration has been the realization that distance, the most traditional source of local comparative advantage formalized in location models of production such as Von Thunen's (Hall 1966), is only effective in protecting markets from outside suppliers if and when countries price their products according to the rules of conventional economics. Otherwise, the distance between centers of production and consumption has practically evaporated as a crucial variable in geographically segmenting markets. This does not mean that geography has all but disappeared; rather, its relevance has been submerged in short-run predatory pricing policies and selling practices. Thus dumping has become common practice where, for example, some of the best quality Australian wines are cheaper in Pittsburgh than they are in suburban Melbourne—an example that could be multiplied many times over in all kinds of American cities with many different products from many different countries. Inevitably, and most profoundly, the neoclassical ideal of a stable regime of natural comparative advantage as the allocation mechanism determining what goods countries produce now seems a Chimera, swamped by deliberate state-based strategies of directed investment and disinvestment affecting whole industries, sectors, and communities.[1] Crafting comparative advantage best describes the policy stance of many Asian NICs (Wade 1990).

Few countries can claim in the 1990s that they are so insulated from the pressures of international competition that the external economic environment can be ignored. Those that do so seem to be either erecting quite impossible barriers to external economic forces for reasons more related to maintaining the power of certain political or military elites than for reasons of economic autarky, or are so impoverished that increased international trade is believed to be the only way of promoting local economic development. For those countries in the latter group, World Bank policies and the International Monetary Fund (IMF) have effectively mobilized some important Third World economies to focus on international markets, thus restructuring the internal economies of those countries toward producing goods for export trade and hence toward foreign currency. If we were to read only the U.S. literature on industrial restructuring, however, we might be led to believe that all this is a recent phenomenon— and perhaps it is for the United States. But for many other countries that bore the brunt of postwar growth in multinational production and distribution networks all these trends are familiar, even if now problematic in the context of a stalled General Agreement on Trade and Tariffs (GATT) negotiation process.

Dimensions of Corporate Restructuring

There have been relatively few attempts to analyze systematically the patterns and processes of corporate restructuring in mainstream economics (but see Coffee et al. 1988). Perhaps because of the profound local effects of restructuring, the issue has been more often analyzed by geographers focusing upon a variety of analytical scales—from the global to the local scale. In my own work, using case studies of restructuring in U.S. manufacturing industries, the driving force behind restructuring is presumed to be a combination of declining profitability due to heightened international competition and exogenously driven technological innovation in the domestic markets of large U.S. industrial corporations (see Clark 1986, 1988, 1989a). This is a mode of analysis shared by a number of researchers, including M. Storper and R. Walker (1989), although here I shall be concentrating on issues related almost exclusively to product competition. At one level, competition is simply a matter of price and quality—reflected, for example, in differences in the relative competitive positions of U.S. automobile manufacturers and their Japanese competitors (many of which are now located in the United States; see Mair et al. 1988). At another level, though, competition is also a question of adjustment—the internal or organizational capacity of corporations, industries, and even whole nations to quickly and effectively respond to new opportunities and new competitors.[2]

Looked at in gross terms, international competition for dominance of any one market is inevitably a problem of overcapacity: literally, too much operating capital (located overseas and locally) relative to the size of a single market. In less gross terms, however, international competition is also a problem of differentiation: how corporations can maintain, even increase, their share of a market by distinguishing their products from other competing products on the basis of price, quality, design, and style. To do this, to compete on the basis of gross capacity and product value, normally requires a reconfiguration or restructuring of existing capacity in response to the strategies of domestic and overseas competitors. And in a world of accelerated economic change, restructuring of capacity cannot be just a one-time event for each generation, it must be a process of continual adjustment and *in situ* transformation. This is one definition of flexibility, an organizational capacity not necessarily consistent with the emerging paradigm known as *flexible accumulation* (post-Fordism), relevant to firms and nations. Whereas we might have in the past analyzed firms' production functions as if they had fixed structural coefficients with limited potential for *in situ* substitution (Clark et al. 1986), the ideal type of the flexible corporation is a unit of production that can adjust both its organization of production and its final products in a strategic manner according to changing market conditions.

If this is the ideal, the actual reality is something less and something more problematic in terms of current attempts to restructure firms and whole countries to be competitive in the global context. Restructuring in this context has four different aspects related, nonetheless, to the overall objective of responding to enhanced competition. One aspect is simply the rationalization of productive capacity, which is normally the reduction of overall capacity subject to the inherited configuration of scale and technology. For large corporations, rationalization is akin to portfolio management involving the strategic allocation and reallocation of production within and between plants on a global scale. This kind of portfolio management is not without its costs. Often significant costs are involved in closing plants in the United States, sometimes involving enormous plant-closing pensions. At the same time, there may be costs incurred leaving markets unprotected even if they can only be efficiently served from production units located outside the region or nation. Imagine for the moment the kinds of issues that Kodak's management located in Rochester (New York) must consider in relation to its worldwide network of paper-processing plants. In global terms, the company probably has too much operating capacity and since many of their domestic plants are in all likelihood less efficient and more costly per unit produced than other similar plants in Brazil (and elsewhere), it would be wise to close local plants and serve the U.S. market by imports from other plants in the world. But there are costs in making such a decision, not least of which are the political costs of worker and community dislocation that may translate into barriers to Kodak importing to the United States.

A second aspect of the restructuring process is reduction of the prices of inputs and outputs—the wages and benefits (including pensions) paid to labor and the prices charged to consumers. In many respects restructuring, whether it be at the firm level or the country level, is about reducing the real prices of products given an expected configuration of demand and recurrent global crises of overproduction. Restructuring of production in this sense is always an attempt to increase labor productivity, thus reducing the total stock of labor, and to decrease the fixed overhead costs of labor by making labor more flexible and adaptive to different tasks. On the costs side of the equation, conventional labor costs are measured relative to productivity and discounted according to the prices received by producers for the final product. Most significant now are measures of the real cost of labor that also take into account variations in exchange rates so that the value of labor is measured relative either to international competitors in the local market or to the prices of competing products in foreign markets. Thus, to the extent that corporations can both affect the quantity of labor used and the real prices of their final products, corporations often pursue a dual strategy of wage-cost discounting. It is also apparent that real wage discounting is a common national economic policy—witness the attempts of the federal government to reduce the value of the U.S. dollar relative to European and Japanese currencies.

Discounting the quantity and price of labor inputs relative to the price of outputs is a strategy that describes many corporations' ambitions in restructuring production. The location and relocation of production is part of this mode of operation and might be thought to describe the rationale behind offshore production (see Grunwald and Flamm 1985). But restructuring is not simply a matter of quantities and prices. The value of restructuring for many corporations is the creation of new or alternative social relations of production. Part of the explanation of corporations' interest in using restructuring to remake plant-level labor-management relations could be, in this sense, purely instrumental: if labor is to be more productive, and if labor is to be used more flexibly, the traditional labor contract associated with trade unionism (but which had its origins in Taylor's scientific management revolution) has to become less rigid and more open to renegotiation as events and circumstances change. This is especially important for the introduction of new technology, but is equally important for corporations as they attempt to enhance productivity within their existing network of plants. Less instrumental in the sense of their potential contributions to productivity, and more related to the respective powers of corporation executives and union officials, new forms of labor contracts are often advocated by those responsible for restructuring as a means of overcoming internal resistance to change (Clark 1993).

In a country such as the United States, which has had a consistent, distinct, and differentiated map of labor costs (wages and benefits) and union representation, restructuring has had a profound geographical character. Although not always closely related at the local level, high labor costs and union representation in manufacturing industries have been traditionally associated with northern and midwestern states, whereas low wage rates and minimal union representation has been typical of southern states. For many corporations buffeted by international competition, restructuring has been designed to rationalize capacity around newer southern plants (thereby reducing overall capacity), which pay lower wages at higher rates of productivity (thereby reducing the quantity and price of labor inputs). This restructuring is accompanied by the introduction of

new technologies of production (thereby improving the quality and flexibility of production), with few if any impediments from organized labor
(either no unions at all or at most unions that are dependent upon the
company for continued representation of workers). Paradoxically, this kind
of restructuring strategy has not always resulted in higher overall productivity—the skills, education, and organization of northern workers may
still outweigh the benefits of geographical restructuring—but such a strategy no doubt enhances the power and discretion of senior executives.

A fourth dimension of restructuring relevant to this discussion is that
which concerns changing the literal form and ownership of the corporation.
Much has been written about recent patterns of corporate restructuring
in the finance and business literature (see Coffee et al. 1988). Normally
emphasized in that literature are issues related to the financing of takeovers and role of management in mergers and leveraged buyouts (LBOs)
of corporate units or even whole conglomerates. One reason for mergers
and acquisitions is the need to cobble together fewer units of sufficient
size and efficiency out of the combined resources of a number of companies
so as to withstand increased competition (a strategy documented here in
the LTV case study). The evidence for the success or failure of this strategy
remains open and contested. Nevertheless, F. Lichtenberg and M. Kim
(1989) are of the opinion, based upon their analyses of the U.S. air transportation industry, that mergers do have substantial positive effects on
reducing labor costs and increasing productivity. Recognizing that there
may be economic advantages to mergers and acquisitions, some commentators would nevertheless explain the scramble for control of corporate
assets during the 1980s as simply the product of management greed (Roll
1988). Perhaps the most obvious instance of this phenomenon in the United
States was the RJR Nabisco LBO that involved management and their
advisers competing with a number of outside investment banks for control
of the corporation.

In the context of competition for corporate control, the results of corporate restructuring are normally fourfold: (1) the sale of unrelated valuable units to other corporations so as to finance LBOs; (2) the consequent
rationalization (reduction and consolidation) of capacity by buying companies in related owned industries; (3) the more intensive (exploitative)
operation of the purchased or leveraged units of production burdened by
high levels of debt and few resources for reinvestment; and, (4) the geographical attenuation of sites of production and rationalization from sites
of management and finance of the rationalization process (Green 1990).
Although there has been insufficient research on these aspects of changes
in corporate control, the restructuring of employment, labor costs, and

production processes, and attacks upon labor contracts can be savage and sustained in these circumstances. Indeed, there is a sense in which the financing of corporate restructuring is directly related to the capacity of firms to discount labor contracts, thereby making labor pay for LBOs even if they are not shareholders in the enterprise. There is a real possibility of new regions of prosperity and decline emerging in the 1990s based upon the structure of global finance capitalism and involving whole nations as a result of the competition for corporate control during the 1980s (Clark 1989b).

Corporate Strategy and Institutional Structure

Restructuring has, then, four general dimensions relevant to the performance of corporations in the context of increased international competition:

- capacity reduction through rationalization
- wage and price discounting
- increased flexibility of labor-management relations
- innovations in corporate form and ownership.

The first two of these strategies are clearly apparent in all the case studies documented in this book. The latter two are also apparent, but on a more limited basis (see especially the Continental case study). Geographers are skilled at analyzing the first two dimensions, paying close attention to the effects of restructuring on localities as well as to the intersection between the inherited spatial structure of economies and their constituent parts (a good example of this research agenda is Scott and Kwok's 1989 paper on the structure of the Los Angeles printed-circuits industry). Just as restructuring affects the geography of economic life so too does the spatial fixity of economic life have an affect on the design and implementation of restructuring. This kind of intersection has been well documented. However, it is less apparent that geographers have been as able to work back from local outcomes to corporate strategy in its own right. There is a sense that these dimensions operate as disembodied, autonomous forces separate from the actions and motives of identifiable agents. It is important to recognize that the four dimensions of restructuring noted above are in actuality four different types of corporate strategies for responding to increased international competition. Indeed, textbooks are written for corporate executives emphasizing the malleability of capital in the context of these dimensions (now translated into recipes for nations; see Porter's 1990 book on national competitive strategy).

Once it is recognized that these dimensions of restructuring are nec-

essary elements in any corporate strategy plan, it must be also recognized
that their implementation is often dependent upon the structure and organization of public institutions. In this context, questions about the proper
connection between the economic imperatives and social obligations of
corporations are also questions about the adaptability of institutionalized
labor-management relations to the economic imperatives of global competition faced by corporations. In the United States this type of question
has been asked in many different ways by different agents and interests.
For example, labor relations scholars such as J. Dunlop (1987) assert that
the first and primary responsibility of any collective-bargaining system is
to be consistent with a nation's economic interests, particularly their relative place in the international economy. He accuses the statutory American labor relations system of being too structured, too focused upon parties' formal legal entitlements, and too rigid with respect to the changing
nature of work and production processes. If this sounds like a conservative
manifesto for institutional restructuring, appearances can be deceiving;
Dunlop has for many years supported the interests and institutions of
organized labor in a society otherwise suspicious of any union tendencies.

Dunlop's criticisms of the overly legalistic and too formal structure of
the American labor relations system have been well received by many
unions who now believe that their interests are not served by a system
that has become simply a mechanism for management to delay and obfus-
cate unions' claims (Weiler 1983). Furthermore, it is now generally believed
that the U.S. union movement's future may well depend upon demonstrating that organized labor has a capacity to innovate and respond to
the economic imperatives of foreign competition. Otherwise, given the
rate of membership decline, there may be little left of the union movement
by the year 2000. In fact, it has been asserted that unions may be the only
mechanism by which workers' interests in a just and deliberate labor
relations environment *and* their interests in maintaining and improving
their employment and wage prospects can be simultaneously realized. This
argument does depend, in part, upon another argument to the effect that
union members are more productive and efficient than their nonunion counterparts and that an internally organized workforce is better than a dis-
organized workforce when it comes to the effective implementation of
corporate restructuring (Kelley and Harrison 1990). It is also clear, however, that failure to respond to these imperatives may simply encourage
conservative judicial interests who believe that only an expanded field of
management discretion will save American industry; witness the decisions
of the Reagan NLRB in *Milwaukee Spring II* (1984) and *Otis Elevator II*
(1984). Both of these cases involved the relocation of production within a

corporation to either nonunion or at least lower-wage union-represented plants (described in detail in Clark 1989a). What was most significant about these decisions was the fact that the Reagan-dominated NLRB reversed decisions of the Carter Board, essentially taking sides with management in their contract disputes with unions over the discretion of management to change the site of production without direct union participation.

Notwithstanding arguments and counterarguments about the virtues of unions, in many respects the role and status of the U.S. statutory labor relations system in corporate restructuring has become almost irrelevant to the actual practice of restructuring. In many sectors where union representation is low, and in regions of the country where unions have hardly made an impact in terms of their representation of labor, restructuring has proceeded apace driven by corporate executives' interests and ambitions. And as was noted above, there has been a significant shift toward strategies of rationalizing production around new plants located in nonunion regions implying a belief that maximum management discretion coupled with the latest technology and lower wages will force up labor productivity per unit and force down labor costs per unit to the levels of international competitors. At the other end of the system (in the north and in traditional union sectors such as steel and autos), there have been a number of successful union-based experiments in organized corporate restructuring. These experiments, like their nonunion counterparts in northern industrial sectors, have focused upon building a cooperative and innovative labor relations environment in the belief that only this kind of environment will actually realize the productivity benefits and labor cost-savings promised by new technology and capacity rationalization. No systematic evidence has been collected that would support the general implementation of either model into American industry at large. There are, however, many case studies of experiments in collaborative labor-management relations; see, for example, our analysis of the design and implementation of the joint United Steelworker–National Steel initiative (Clark and Fischer 1987).

In the abstract, it is easy enough to identify how and why individual corporations may be enthusiastic about stepping away from the inherited labor relations system. Rather than being constrained by industry-based collective agreements, if corporations are able to work out their own deal with unions on restructuring, the process may be more efficient and more quickly implemented. Capacity rationalization could be quicker if corporations have the option of shifting labor between jobs, between plants, and in and out of redundancy without having to renegotiate job descriptions or recognize cross-industry wage and benefit scales. Moreover, there is the possibility that with a more efficient process of internal rationalization jobs may be saved by reallocating functions within the company's labor force. In terms of real wage levels, local plant-by-plant agreements may help companies improve labor productivity by instituting reduced staffing agreements, linking wage increases with productivity increases, and even instituting incentive payments for higher rates of productivity. However, to step away from the inherited system may be to also step away from the structure of entitlements and legal protection that unions have been able to formalize in statute regarding workers' (pension) rights. As shall be demonstrated in the next chapter, unions have historically played an essential role in developing public policy protection of workers' entitlements to fair and just treatment.

Thus it is very important to understand that corporations' attempts to discount real wage costs through strategies of pension avoidance and pension cost shifting are strategies that inevitably bring corporations into direct conflict with an inherited institutional structure of social obligations. It is not enough to imagine that real-wage discounting is only a local issue, as if such decisions have no implications for the more general political economy of the United States. In point of fact, just as there have been drastic changes in union-management relations in recent years, and changes in the role of management and labor in the organization of production and financing of corporate restructuring, these changes have affected the integrity of the private pension system. Indeed, given that the growth of the private pension system was closely related to those U.S. corporations now undergoing massive restructuring, it is perhaps inevitable that the forces affecting those corporations also threaten the inherited private pension system.

Pensions and Corporate Strategy

Corporations have sought to avoid their pension obligations in many ways. While it must be emphasized, of course, that many other related strategies are employed by American business, here we will initially focus upon two of the most important strategies, one legal and the other illegal. One obvious kind of corporate pension avoidance strategy involves shifting corporate liability for pension obligations to the federal government. For example, when LTV Corporation declared Chapter 11 bankruptcy in the mid-1980s it attempted to shift its unfunded pension obligations to the federal government's PBGC. The other strategies were not legal.

LTV is a giant conglomerate that began life as a small electronics firm and entered the Fortune 500 list through the acquisition of four companies in the 1960s: Temco Aircraft and Chance Vought Aircraft in 1961, and Wilsons Food and Jones and Laughlin (J & L) Steel in 1967. Steel has played an important part in the growth of LTV, involving the acquisition of Youngstown Sheet and Tube in 1978 and Republic Steel in 1984. These acquisitions (in conjunction with many other factors) also prompted the bankruptcy of the corporation in 1986. In fact, the history of the corporation is one of growth, crisis, and restructuring. In the early 1970s, the acquisition of J & L, the need for special reserves to cover possible losses from the sale of other investments, corporate overhead costs, and subsidiaries' tax payments and dividends put LTV on the verge of bankruptcy. Four of the seven subsidiaries were sold, with business cuts in the remaining three. The sale of assets, cuts in employment, and the retirement of outstanding loans helped the corporation regain financial solvency and access to bank credit. Over just two years (1972 and 1973), debt was reduced by 40 percent and fixed charges reduced by more than 50 percent. Nevertheless, net profits then remained low under the influence of the first oil-price shock, inflation, and the 1974 recession.

In 1978, LTV merged with Lykes-Youngstown (owners of Youngstown Sheet and Tube), then ranked fortieth on the Fortune 500, boosting assets to $3.7 billion. Considered by many as an example of a "merger that worked," the combined Youngstown and J & L saved some $100 million per annum by closing inefficient facilities, combining others, and dramatically improving labor productivity. The merger boosted sales to $2.7 billion by 1979 with a further $826 million rise by 1981, accompanied by $46.4 million in profits from sheet and tube alone. In the 1982 recession, however, sales, profits, and employment were all drastically affected. All integrated steel companies suffered badly during the recession and the very short, lopsided recovery in 1984 did not improve the situation. Major steelmakers continued to suffer from declining demand, a relatively strong U.S. dollar, and fierce international competition until about 1987. Operating losses at J & L in 1982 and 1983 prompted the decision to merge with Republic Steel (ranked fourth in the industry in 1984), also operating in severe financial difficulty, going against LTV's previously stated intentions to decrease the importance of steel to the corporation. Through the merger, management hoped to improve competitiveness by cutting costs (particularly in administration), reducing capital expenditure, improving manufacturing efficiency, and building on the successes of the previous merger. However, the $700 million cost of acquisition of Republic was accompanied by the assumption of $800 million in debt (adding to LTV's existing $1.6 billion debt) and substantially underfunded pension fund liabilities. Although some analysts had predicted gains for LTV from the merger, the combination of debt, pension liabilities, and weak demand forced LTV to bankruptcy.

In filing for Chapter 11 bankruptcy protection in 1986, LTV's actions have highlighted the extent of the crisis in the U.S. steel industry. A number of reasons have been put forward to explain the bankruptcy of LTV, one of the country's largest steel producers. LTV has blamed the precipitous fall in domestic demand, the rise in steel imports, and the lack of government policy to facilitate restructuring. Some steel analysts have also argued that it was a poorly run company. Others blame LTV for their acquisition of Republic and its liabilities and the enormous unfunded pension liability. However, bankruptcy was not the end of LTV. Instead, along with revival in the steel industry, it has allowed the corporation to regain profitability. The cost advantages of Chapter 11 bankruptcy, particularly the transfer of unfunded pension obligations to the PBGC, tax concessions granted to the whole industry by the federal government, and sustained improvements in production efficiency and labor productivity through the bankruptcy proceedings have all improved LTV's competitiveness with USX (the largest steel producer in the United States). The court-led restructuring of LTV, which began in December 1986 with plant writeoffs and the transfer of pension obligations to the PBGC, has been helped by a remarkable transformation in work practices.

LTV's strategy of pension liability shifting was probably one of the more benign of management-designed pension-oriented restructuring strategies. At least it was thought to be legal, even if its consequences were then hotly litigated by the company, the union, creditors, and the PBGC in federal courts. The USWA, which represented its current and retired ex-members (LTV's past workers), argued that retirees deserved more than the PBGC's mandated and guaranteed minimum monthly pension benefits. The PBGC on the other hand claimed, in part, that the company could still pay most of its pension liability if it were to gain more concessions from working members of the union. To that end, the PBGC applied to the courts to return most of LTV's plans to the company; it lost in federal bankruptcy court but prevailed in the Supreme Court (see *PBGC v. LTV* [1990]). It remains to be seen if the PBGC will be successful in this strategy; suits and countersuits have been filed by LTV in federal courts all in an attempt to limit the scope of the Supreme Court's decision (see "First Modified Disclosure Statement Pursuant to Section 1125 of the Bankruptcy Code" dated February 14, 1992, filed with the U.S. Bankruptcy Court *In re Chateaugay Corporation*). Until very recently, perhaps only forestalled by the relative prosperity of the U.S. steel industry in the late 1980s, there was a possibility that the whole steel industry would follow LTV's example by shifting their pension obligations to the PBGC. In the latter years of the Reagan administration, contingency plans were drawn up to rescue the PBGC in the event that the whole steel industry followed LTV's strategy.

Some corporations have sought to avoid their pension obligations by illegally laying off workers before they become eligible for future pension benefits. The lawsuit emblematic of this strategy is *Gavalik v. Continental Can Co.* (later consolidated into the New Jersey *McClendon* case). This case involved the pension rights of workers employed by Continental Can (members of the USWA) who were displaced by corporate restructuring. The company is commonly known as one of the nation's largest producers of container products. From the early years of this century through the first few years of the 1970s, the company focused upon the packaging industry and used that base to diversify into other related production areas such as paper, plastics and glassware, and forestry products. Continental Can's success afforded company strategists the opportunity to experiment with other related investments, including synthetic resins used in fabricating military aircraft parts and a variety of food products. Acquisitions and mergers contributed to the growth of the company, giving Continental a leading role in the market and a recognized name worldwide. Despite its historical success, by the mid-1970s the company had begun to lose its standing as the leader of the packaging industry. Mismanagement of diversified international holdings, external economic and competitive forces, and turmoil within the company about the proper management strategy contributed to the weakening of Continental Can. In this context, the company's attempts to limit and avoid its pension obligations were intimately related to an attempt by senior management to quickly diversify the corporation into nontraditional areas (such as insurance and finance) and hence make the corporation into a multifunctional conglomerate. The aim was to transform the company from one focused on production to a company as a portfolio manager.

Aspects of Continental's corporate strategy are described in more detail in subsequent chapters. However, it is useful to understand how and why pension liability was so important. In 1977, Continental entered the insurance field with the purchase of Richmond Corporation, described by the vice-chairman at that time as "halfway between the insurance giants and smaller, more aggressive companies." Continental's rationale behind the purchase was twofold: an insurance company the size of Richmond required minimal new capital, and Richmond Corporation represented a pool of liquid assets for further acquisitions. Continental also explored resource development by utilizing their forestry land for energy and resources, as well as by purchasing several gas and oil companies. In 1979, Continental acquired a number of energy companies, then consolidated into Continental Energy Corporation, which controlled the Continental Resources Company in Florida, the Florida Exploration Company in Texas, and the Florida Gas Transmission Company in Delaware. Both the diversification of operations and the intensification of investment on foreign holdings were consistent with Continental's managerial style. Historically, Continental believed decentralization would ensure a low U.S. profile in foreign markets, as well as allowing for diverse operations to have adequate independence and autonomy in operation. However, the decentralized managerial style was not successful when it acquired companies unrelated to the packaging industry. The chief executive officers (CEOs) of both Florida Gas and Richmond Corporation resigned their positions shortly after Continental Group took over the companies. While Continental struggled with the managerial control of their subsidiaries, they also had to contend with other competitive and regulatory challenges to the company. For instance, Continental Group was one of fourteen paper manufacturers charged with price fixing; a vice-president and division general manager was sentenced to serve a minor prison sentence.

It was during this period that Continental instituted its secret management policy to limit and control its pension liabilities in its packaging operations. After years of litigation, a federal appeals court found that the company had illegally (in terms of Section 510 of ERISA) denied a group of workers their eligibility for early retirement pensions. Continental's pension avoidance strategy was planned and secretly implemented by upper management of the corporation. Their Bell System was designed to manage Continental Can's unfunded pension liabilities and avoid triggering the payment of early retirement pensions. This system was instituted in the wake of management's plans to rationalize the company's network of plants across the country and introduce new production technology that would radically reduce the need for as many plants and would allow management to achieve another desirable goal: drastic reduction of the number of USWA-represented production employees. Employees close to eligibility for early retirement pensions were identified and permanently laid off. Employees eligible for early retirement pensions were then employed as long as possible to avoid paying their pension entitlements. This strategy was accomplished by closing some departments within plants and relocating production within and between plants.

In another important case initiated in the early 1980s, *In re International Harvester*, the U.S. government took a Fortune 500 industrial corporation to court charging that it had deliberately conceived and participated in a "sham" transaction principally designed to offload a portion of its plant-closing pension obligations. Close to bankruptcy, the company had sold its steel division (Wisconsin Steel) located in south Chicago to another company through a LBO in the hope that it would be then protected from the unfunded pension liability that would accompany any plant closing. To understand the significance of these issues is to look back at the pattern of events that brought IHC close to bankruptcy. The company was founded by Cyrus McCormick some 160 years ago. It has had a long history in the manufacture of trucks and farm and construction equipment in the United States and Europe. As these industries are very sensitive to cyclical upturns and downturns, and are subject to interest-rate and exchange-rate fluctuations, farm incomes, and commodity prices, the corporation has had variable success. Through the 1970s, IHC recorded steady increases in sales and assets, peaking in 1979 ($8.4 billion) and 1980 ($5.86 billion). However, in 1980 and 1981, International Harvester recorded losses of $397 million and $393 million, respectively, mostly the result of a six-month UAW strike triggered by the company's attempt to radically change existing work practices. The strike exacerbated underlying competitive problems in domestic markets characterized by deep recession and high interest rates. The strike-induced shutdown cost some $479 million (with lost sales going to competitors Deere & Co. and Caterpillar), long-term debt increased by $800 million, and interest payments increased from $148 million to $281 million.

In an attempt to save the company from bankruptcy, IHC's management initiated a program of debt restructuring, of downsizing the company to cover businesses, converting $3.5 billion of short-term debts to two-year revolving loans, and giving priority to the management of unfunded pension liabilities (see chapter 5). Three unprofitable plants were shut down, employment was reduced by 5 percent in one year, and prices discounted to win back market share. During 1981, IHC risked default by suspending repayment of principal and reorganized loans. In July, the corporation sold its Solar Division (a profitable manufacturer of gas turbines) to Caterpillar, with the proceeds of the sale hidden in a secret account rather than being used for debt repayment to the banks. Although the economy improved and interest rates moderated in mid-1981, allowing small profits for IHC, by the end of 1981 interest rates again soared to record levels, severely depressing demand, reducing farm incomes and therefore the sale of Harvester's most profitable products, farm equipment. The board of International Harvester sacked the CEO in May 1982. With $900 million in operating losses and $662 million in costs due to shutdowns and asset sales, the survival of IHC was in jeopardy. Further restructuring of the corporation was initiated with the closure of inefficient plants, deeper cuts in overhead costs, reductions in employment, and the sale of construction subsidiaries.

Following one of the biggest losses ever of any Fortune 500–listed company—$1.6 billion—in 1982, restructuring of the IHC began to pay dividends in 1983 and 1984 with increases in sales and net income made possible by economic growth and the revival of the truck and tractor industries. Overall, however, industrial and farm equipment sales continued to decline. In Europe, IHC's performance was also faltering. Market share was being lost in Germany, as well as in France due to high manufacturing costs and overstaffing, which could not be corrected under French legislation. The company lost money in Europe for four years, contributing to International's overall loss again in 1984 when, despite growth in the economy, high interest rates and a strong dollar enhanced foreign competition and reduced domestic demand, sales, and prices. In 1985, IHC wrote off its agricultural equipment business for $479 million, and changed its name to Navistar International, now producing only trucks and engines. Since 1986, Navistar has grown with increased assets and sales, assisted by a weakened dollar. Success continued through to 1989 despite the slowdown in the U.S. economy, greater foreign competition, and a stronger dollar. But with the onset of the recession in 1990, it is unclear how successful the restructured company will be in the coming years.

Gavalik v. Continental Can Co. was a very important case. A crucial test of Section 510 of ERISA, it identified a major corporation as a deliberate law-breaker, and classed as an illegal act corporate restructuring strategies such as the relocation of production, which have as their principal goal avoidance of pension liability. Likewise, *In re International Harvester* was also a very important case with ramifications for how we should understand corporations' public responsibilities, whatever the notional ownership of the assets of a company. In the *LTV* case, the problems of rationalizing competing statutory interests during restructuring have been exposed, but surely not solved. While it is tempting to believe these are isolated cases and that corporate restructuring policies respect and protect the integrity of private pensions, all the evidence suggests that these cases are emblematic of many other corporations' pension-oriented restructuring policies even if these policies often remain undetected (secret) and therefore unlitigated. Pension obligations are simultaneously the object of corporate restructuring plans and barriers to corporate restructuring. These cases are studied in more detail in subsequent chapters.

Pensions and Public Policy

With respect to corporate restructuring and corporate pension obligations, a number of public policy issues warrant close analysis. Corporate decisions both to shift pension obligations to the PBGC and to avoid pension obligations by policies that deny workers their legal entitlements separately and together threaten the integrity of the private pension system. Shifting pension obligations to the federal government threatens the fiscal integrity of the private pension system. The PBGC does not have financial assets that come close to the guaranteed value of the bankrupt pension plans it now administers. Attempts to recapitalize the PBGC by increasing corporate premiums may only encourage firms to terminate more plans, and attempts to limit the value of defined-benefit pension entitlements have drawn tremendous political fire from retirees' representatives. Corporate decisions to avoid (legally or illegally) their pension obligations threaten the integrity of related institutions, especially the collective-bargaining system, which is already quite fragile. Corporate actions designed to avoid pension obligations undermine workers' trust in the U.S. labor-management relations system.

Since the private pension system itself owes much of its development to unions' insistence on bargaining with companies for benefits as well as for normal pay schedules, the current strategies of corporate restructuring involve many aspects of law and social practice. ERISA cannot be clearly separated from the NLRA and the NLRB. Shifting obligations to the PBGC has involved all parties in extraordinarily expensive lawsuits that threaten to take over the normal manner (bargaining and grievance arbitration) in which disputes over pension benefits are adjudicated. As noted in the previous chapter, it is not at all obvious that the court system is capable or experienced enough in handling pension issues as overlapping issues of law and collective-bargaining agreements.

Corporate restructuring strategies designed to avoid pension obligations also raise fundamental questions about the proper scope of private behavior, given compelling public interests. What scope should the United States (as a society and as its own regulators) allow corporations to maximize profits, given the vital public interest in maintaining the integrity of the private pension system? This issue is at the heart of the dispute between LTV Corporation and the PBGC. It was also at the heart of the Continental Can dispute. In court, Continental Can argued that its actions in relocating production and selectively laying off workers were entirely consistent with its policy of maximizing profits. The company also argued that it had acted within the boundaries of its normal scope of power, as representatives of stockholders' interests. At one point the company denied implementing the Bell System. When confronted with internal documents that demonstrated that they had in fact implemented the system, the company claimed that the system was only incidental to its normal business practice. International Harvester mounted a similar defense; its actions were supposedly entirely proper as they were consistent with profit maximization and that their responsibilities for workers' pensions terminated with the sale of Wisconsin Steel. The point at which normal business practice becomes illegal is fraught with many uncertainties—one being how the courts will adjudicate the difference in specific cases. A related uncertainty has to do with the standards chosen to make an appropriate determination of responsibility. It is apparent from the conflicting and contested opinions of the courts in the various cases that there is no settled boundary between normal business practice (maximizing private profit) and the public interest (protecting the integrity of the private pension system).

These issues are all very important to understanding the role of public regulation of private actions. It becomes apparent in subsequent chapters that all elements figure in corporations' actions and legal defenses. But the significance of these issues can be illustrated another way, with reference to one of the most important issues facing U.S. society—the future of the Social Security pension system. According to G. S. Fields and O. Mitchell (1984:xvii), because many "workers are retiring earlier, living longer, and receiving greater retirement benefits," the financial integrity of the Social Security system is at risk. While the system was apparently rescued by Congress from imminent crisis in 1983 through a combination of higher Social Security taxes and reduced benefits, that rescue formula may be illusory. The growing surplus of the Social Security system has been used to reduce the federal budget deficit at a time when the savings and loan crisis has overwhelmed most other domestic funding issues. The juxtaposition of declining national savings rates, projected massive increases in eligible claimants over the early years of the next century, and the current consumption of Social Security reserves is likely to lead to another, perhaps more profound Social Security crisis. This crisis is likely to reduce future economic growth as resources are diverted from investment to pay for Social Security pensions (Aaron et al. 1989).

Given the combined scale of near-term budget deficits and the long-term debt-servicing obligations of the U.S. government, the GAO believes it is unlikely that Social Security reserves will be protected from immediate financial needs (GAO 1989b). One lasting legacy of the recent Republican administrations will be an economic debt burden imposed on the next generation. Notwithstanding these dire warnings, it is difficult to predict future Social Security obligations given the alternatives—especially the future of private pensions and individual retirement plans (GAO 1988a). The Bush administration hoped that in the long term private pension schemes will help offset the Social Security financial burden. These hopes may be, however, wishful thinking, since the integrity of private pension plans in manufacturing industries are themselves currently facing extraordinary financial pressures due, in part, to strong competition and corporate restructuring.

In recent years, many private pension plans have been deemed significantly overfunded, an actuarial judgment made about plan assets relative to the accrued current and expected payments to vested plan participants. Overfunding has been the product of higher than expected inflation rates in the early 1980s, compounded by a rising stock market through most of the 1980s. The GAO (1988f) estimated that private pension plan assets doubled from 1982 to 1986, and even gained in terms of net assets during 1987, despite the October crash. Ownership of excess assets is a matter being litigated in federal courts (some companies contend they own the excess assets because they bear the risks of delivering promised benefits, while some unions contend that since pensions are workers' "wages" excess assets are thus owned by workers).[3] Available data from the PBGC suggests that about 1,900 plans with assets in excess of $1 million or more were either terminated or were pending termination between 1980 and December 1988. These plans covered more than 2.1 million participants and had in total close to $45 billion in assets (see also GAO 1986b).[4]

Termination of overfunded pension plans have been a way for corporations to skim assets and take substantial windfall profits. Anecdotal evidence from industry sources suggests that some corporations have systematically sought out small and medium-sized unionized companies with overfunded pension plans for takeover, closing, and pension plan termination before paying off expected accrued benefits to vested plan participants. The role of pension funds in the recent wave of mergers and acquisitions is difficult to judge given the poor information available on the private pension system (GAO 1988e). Since plan managers' fiduciary requirements are strictly enforced by the IRS, there are few instances of plan managers using their own plan assets to effect the course of a takeover of their client corporation (GAO 1988d). Even so, compelling evidence suggests that pension plans have been an important funding source for hostile takeovers of unrelated corporations (GAO 1988b). Pension plans have often held a significant share of junk bonds offered to pay for LBOs (GAO 1988c, 1988e). Termination and profit-skimming of overfunded defined-benefit pension plans has, however, become increasingly difficult since 1985 (witness the much reduced rate of terminations since the mid-1980s), and could become more difficult in the future if pending bills in Congress were passed.[5]

Nevertheless, two other practices have become evident in the last few years. First, corporations have increasingly sought to convert their defined-benefit plans (which guarantee a certain level of benefit) to defined-contribution plans (which do not guarantee a final pension level), while resisting congressional attempts to reduce the time period for vesting in pension benefits (American Academy of Actuaries 1992). Second, some corporations have sought to shift the financial burden of pension plans by requiring greater contributions by plan participants, while scheming to deny pension benefits to those eligible. These practices have prompted Congress to investigate the extent of bias and discrimination in corporations' administration of their plans, suggesting the need for stricter regulations over issues such as eligibility and vesting procedures (GAO 1987c). One consequence of these strategies has been a leveling off in the numbers of working Americans covered by pension plans.[6] Another consequence has been limitations on corporations' future pension benefit obligations by changing the nature and structure of offered pension plans. And yet another consequence has been a perceived increase in corporate willingness to circumvent ERISA regulations at a time where resources for enforcement have been drastically cut because of federal budgetary pressures (GAO 1989a). In a recent report, the GAO (1991) has suggested that the IRS, for one, must seek ways to improve their enforcement of crucial ERISA provisions. Otherwise, the promise of private pensions will surely evaporate.

If most private pension plans were financially sound and overfunded through the 1980s, a significant number of plans were underfunded. In an analysis of over 14,000 large pension plans, a report by the GAO (1986a) found for 1983 that about 23 percent of plans were underfunded, of which about half had assets worth less than 75 percent of the value of their accrued vested benefits. The GAO also found that nearly 30 percent of plans surveyed in the manufacturing and construction sectors were underfunded and that 84 percent of all underfunded pensions could be found in the manufacturing sector. Because of the historically high levels of unionization in manufacturing and the close association between the collective-bargaining process and the provision of private pension benefits, restructuring of U.S. manufacturing has inevitably affected many pension plans. Indeed in the auto parts, steel, and farm implements industries (to name just three kinds of firms), underfunded and unfunded pension benefit obligations have brought some corporations to bankruptcy. The numbers of underfunded plans have not increased significantly but the scale of debt assumed by the PBGC from bankrupt pension plans has grown to the point where the fiscal solvency of the PBGC is threatened (GAO 1987a).

In part, problems of pension plan underfunding in American manufacturing were exacerbated by the IRS's willingness to waive contributions or allow corporations to delay scheduled payments (see the LTV case study). According to the IRS, rigorous enforcement of pension plan payments might have imperiled the solvency of American corporations at a time of significant economic restructuring (GAO 1987b). The consequences of the IRS's policy for the fiscal integrity of the PBGC have been profound. Over the two-year period 1983 to 1985, 205 bankrupt pension plans were terminated by the PBGC involving $501 million in liabilities. By the 1987 financial year, the PBGC had accumulated $2.2 billion in assets and $3.7 billion in liabilities (PBGC 1987). More recently, the threatened and actual bankruptcy of more industrial corporations (as in the airline industry) have only raised more doubts about the viability of the PBGC (see Delfico 1991 and GAO 1992). According to the PBGC, the actions of companies such as LTV, as well as decisions by the courts, cast grave doubts upon the long-term liability of the (single-employer) benefit guarantee system (PBGC 1991).

Summary

It is quite unlikely that private pensions will cover the expected shortfall of the Social Security system over the next twenty or so years. The real value and scope of solvent private pension plans (and the value and coverage of private medical plans) are likely to continue to shrink.[7] In manufacturing industries where benefits have been relatively more generous, the pressures of restructuring and continuing problems of underfunding will probably lead to further narrowing in the scope, nature, and benefit levels of pension plans.[8] And in industries such as autos and steel, which were so important at the beginning of the private pension system, restructuring—job loss, displacement, and capacity decline, coupled with the lack of portability of vested pensions (GAO 1989c)—will lead to further reductions in the long-term value of pension and healthcare benefits. If this assessment of the current status of the private pension system is accurate, then the future of social welfare for the average citizen is in jeopardy. Most obviously the PBGC, like the Social Security system, will have to rely on Congress to cover the shortfall between assets and liabilities. But most fundamentally, the postwar division of responsibility between public and private responsibility for retirees' welfare is close to rupture.

The current financial problems of the PBGC can be traced to the declining economic fortunes of the largest industrial corporations over the past decade or so. In the absence of a coherent national industrial policy, pension plans have been too often used by corporations as a way to shed excess labor. As a consequence, pension obligations in some union-dominated industries are so enormous that they are barriers to restructuring and barriers to exit from the industry. Thus, there have evolved complex legal and illegal strategies to avoid these obligations and the unions that police corporate actions with regard to those obligations. These vital issues of public policy should indicate to the reader some of the challenges posed by corporate restructuring in the context of the changing world economy. Corporate restructuring threatens the integrity of the private pension system and poses a threat to the viability of pensions given the problems of financing Social Security. Corporate restructuring around private pensions also poses a threat to other valued institutions such as collective bargaining, and corporate restructuring forces us to analyze the scope that society should allow corporations to maximize profits.

As this book seeks to demonstrate, many corporations have come to see their pension obligations as fundamental barriers to economic adjustment. Pensions have become part of the battleground between unions and management. And yet, as will also be discussed, unions are not well equipped to be the agents who keep corporations honest. Obviously, the financial resources necessary to take a corporation through the courts to ensure compliance with agreed-to pension obligations are beyond the means of all but a very few unions. More problematic are the inherent tensions that face a union as it tries to represent the various interests of working employees (union members) and retirees (union members) of the same corporation. It may be in the interests of a corporation and its current employees to avoid paying pension obligations to previous employees so that the long-run jobs and profitability of the corporation are protected. For individual union members, their responsibility for the welfare of past employees is often an abstract ideal. For the union as an organization, this responsibility is a political dilemma. Given corporate strategies of pension avoidance and given the fiscal and political problems that face unions in ensuring that corporations are honest, it may be time to reinvigorate the federal monitoring and enforcing of corporations' pension obligations.

Assuming the private pension system will survive in one form or another, the most important question becomes "what will private pensions be like in the coming years compared to private pensions of the past?"

Society has an interest, but more especially the federal government has an interest, in ensuring that corporate restructuring does not "hollow out" private pension benefits. It would a great irony if, because of the economic imperatives of competition, the private pension system was "saved" by pushing responsibility for the welfare of retirees back to the federal government.

3

Regulation of Private
Pension Obligations

Most studies of the U.S. private pension system focus upon employee compensation packages and emphasize the uncertainty of long-term pension benefits.[1] Analysts such as J. Green (1985) rightly suggest that different types of pension plans under varying assumptions about the age of retirement and death of the recipient imply extraordinarily complex actuarial calculations about the present value of pensions. Similarly, W. K. Viscusi (1985) has noted that vesting requirements (the minimum number of years of service) for pension benefits affects workers' mobility decisions and their expectations about the value of different jobs. By this logic, workers are uncertain about future benefit levels assuming that promised benefit packages are delivered by employers. However, promises may not be honored, just as the law may be subverted. Indeed, S. Rosen (1985:249) observed that Viscusi and others assume "firms are totally passive" where in fact "the testimony surrounding the passage of ERISA . . . [involved] horror stories of workers who were involuntarily terminated prior to vesting." If ERISA was conceived to protect workers from these kinds of "stories," evidence presented here suggests that workers have many reasons to doubt whether or not they will receive their promised pensions. This much is evident in stories told of the suffering of Continental's workers and their families (see Figure 3.1).

The *Gavalik* case was described in previous chapters as one instance of management strategies designed to avoid corporate pension liabilities— a geographically targeted strategy where production was reallocated within and between plants so as to allow the company to lay off workers nearing eligibility for early retirement plant-closing pensions. Whereas subsequent chapters explore corporations' pension-avoidance strategies in the context of restructuring in some depth, we will focus here on Continental's strategy in the context of ERISA. Both the restructuring perspective and the legal perspective are vital to understanding the full ramifications of corporations' actions. By themselves, each perspective is only a partial statement of the scope of corporate strategy. Although social

Laid-off workers tell hardships caused by Continental's illegal scheme

The human toll of Continental Can's scheme to limit its pension obligations was poignantly described at the Washington press conference by three former USWA members and the widow of another former member.

Attorney Daniel P. McIntyre, the former USWA lawyer who initiated the lawsuit, introduced the four and briefly described how they suffered from the layoffs.

Pat Bollinger's husband, Don, contracted cancer after his layoff from Continental's plant in Elwood, Ind. The layoff also meant the loss of health insurance or the disability pension he might have received. By the time of his death in 1987, his medical bills had consumed the family savings and forced his wife to sell their home and furniture.

John Middleton, laid off in 1980 from Continental's plant in St. Louis, Mo., couldn't find another job because employers, knowing he was on layoff, expected he would be called back to work at Continental.

Billie Clark, maintaining a home and supporting her mother and two teenage daughters, was laid off in 1978 after working more than 15 years at Continental's Birmingham, Ala. plant. She had been making nearly $8 an hour. It took her years to find another job at $5.50 an hour.

After Gerald Foy was laid off from Continental's Pasaic, N.J. plant, the loss of health insurance presented him with a grim dilemma. A diabetic condition led to gangrene of one of his toes. His choice: spend down his small savings to qualify for Medicaid to pay for treatment, or treat himself. Foy chose to keep his savings, and induced a doctor to instruct him how to amputate the toe.

McIntyre added that during the months of trial in 1989, Foy attended the court each day, traveling by subway and train from his small and "not very nice" apartment in Brooklyn.

"In a special way Gerald kept us going," McIntyre said. "It was good to have the reality check of Gerald in the room, and to know that we were working for real people."

John Middleton

I lost my home, my car. My wife has muscular dystrophy, diabetes, a heart condition, My stepson has muscular dystrophy, cerebral palsy. The only way we live at the present time is social security and SSI, food stamps and the government. If it wasn't for them, we couldn't go on. I just thank the Lord for these lawyers and the union; I appreciate them fighting for us like they have. I think it was a rotten thing for the company to do. I was ready to devote my life to them, and I would have if they would have done the right thing. But they just decided to do us dirty, and we found it out too late.

Pat Bollinger

I lost our car, our home, furniture, you name it, it was lost. I filed a bankruptcy. To me, in the working class we were always taught you work; you earn your pay. But at that point I felt very, very degraded. Not only had I lost a husband, I lost everything he'd worked for all of his life. And I had to learn to start over within two weeks. And I didn't have much to stand on, just myself, and I'm still trying to stand and walk.

USWA Vice President Leon Lynch describes Continental's plot to prevent workers from gaining eligibility for pension.

Billie Clark

It's devastating to be left without a job. I worked for minimum wage and whatever I could get, and seven years ago I got a job with a food company. It's hard when you get laid off; it's hard for a woman to get a job. And I'm thankful for what everybody's done.

Figure 3.1 The Human Consequences of Continental Can's Pension Strategy
(Source: Steelabor [January/February 1991]: 8.)

scientists may be most comfortable with a simple economic or geographical restructuring perspective, it is important to understand how and why corporations have acted as they have done (often in secret or by subterfuge) in the shadow of the law. To do so requires an appreciation of ERISA as it relates to corporations' restructuring strategies.

The legality of Continental's pension-avoidance strategy in the context of Section 510 of ERISA is a useful beginning point for a discussion for two reasons. First, given the general connection between unions and pension benefits and entitlements, this case allows us to explore the origins of ERISA in the light of changes in collective bargaining over the past forty years or so. Second, after noting the basis and logic of the suit brought by dismissed employees of the company's West Mifflin plant, and the subsequent court decisions regarding the company's legal accountability for its actions, it is apparent that the Continental cases are very important for the meaning and significance of ERISA (Vogel 1987). In the language of contemporary jurisprudence, *Gavalik* is an emblematic case in the sense that it represents corporate pension-avoidance strategies that are at once more common than normally supposed and are necessarily hidden from public view. I would also contend that *Gavalik* is an exemplary case in a couple of ways: in the absence of a set of defining precedents it set the terms for adjudicating subsequent related cases, and it recognized a hidden dispute within law regarding the nature of proof and the limits of causation. In these ways, I aim to provide an introduction for subsequent discussion of various corporate restructuring strategies.

Pensions, Unions, and Collective Bargaining

Comprehensive, reliable data on private pension benefit plans are difficult to obtain (Bodie and Munnell 1992). E. Andrews (1985) estimated that in 1983 50.3 percent of private-sector employees were covered by employer-sponsored pension plans, although only 20.3 percent of such employees were then eligible for future pension benefits. More recently, in 1988 the AFL-CIO estimated that coverage and eligibility rates may have stabilized, perhaps even declined.[2] Most recently, the Bureau of the Census concluded from their survey that 53 percent of all wage and salary workers were covered by an employer-sponsored retirement plan in 1987 (down from 55 percent in 1984) (see Short and Nelson 1991). Just less than 30 percent of wage and salary workers were then eligible for future benefits. Compared to government employees' rates, private employees' rates of coverage and eligibility are low. Andrews estimated that in 1983 83 percent of all government employees were covered by pension plans, of which 47.7

percent were then eligible for pension benefits. The Bureau of the Census estimates that for 1987 95 percent of all government workers were covered by pension plans. The number of private pension plans is at an all-time high. In 1939 there were only 659 IRS-qualified private pension plans; in 1949 there were 12,154 plans; in 1959 there were 54,299 plans; in 1969 there were 199,994 plans; and in 1979 there were about 560,500 IRS qualified plans. From 1944 to 1985 the numbers of private pension plans practically doubled every five years.

Generally, the growth of private pension plans has been most significant in union-represented and -dominated industries. This may seem surprising considering the American labor movement is in decline absolutely (in total members) and relatively (in their share of private employment).[3] Since the Second World War labor unions, especially industrial unions such as the USWA and the UAW, have played important roles in fostering the growth and expansion of coverage of private pensions. These unions played vital roles in establishing pensions as legitimate, even mandatory, subjects for collective bargaining. As well, they were instrumental in developing the political and legal constituencies for the federal regulatory framework (ERISA) that currently protects all workers' (union and nonunion) pension rights. By 1979 (the latest year of comprehensive data relevant to the case studies), the Bureau of the Census estimated that 76.4 percent of union-represented private employees were covered by pension plans compared to 34.9 percent of all private nonunion employees (see Table 3.1). The highest rates of coverage were in those manufacturing industries whose employees have been traditionally represented by unions, especially by large industrial unions. (Note, however, the gap in coverage between union and nonunion workers has closed considerably over the past ten years— in 1987 nearly 90 percent of all unionized employees were covered by pension plans against 60 percent of nonunion workers.)

For example, from Table 3.1 it is apparent that in mining, which was previously dominated by the United Mine Workers, 88.6 percent of union workers and 55.8 percent of nonunion workers were covered by pension plans. In manufacturing, 81.6 percent of union workers and 53.3 percent of nonunion workers were covered by pension plans just as in transportation and utilities 77.2 percent of union workers and 50.7 percent of nonunion workers were covered by plans. In contrast, in retail trade 61.9 percent of union workers but only 19.1 percent of nonunion workers were covered by pension plans. Again with respect to the relevant 1979 data, those industries where union representation was smallest had the lowest rates of pension plan coverage. This is most apparent in eating and drinking establishments where unionization is minuscule and the coverage rate was

Table 3.1 Pension Plan Coverage of Private Union-represented
and Nonunion Employees by Industry, 1979 (in hundred
thousands)

Total/ Industry	Private Employment	Covered Employees	
		Number	Percentage
Total	67,346	30,217	44.8
Union	16,103	12,297	76.4
Nonunion	51,243	17,919	34.9
Agriculture	1,334	165	12.4
Union	47	26	56.1
Nonunion	1,287	139	10.8
Mining	737	504	68.4
Union	282	250	88.6
Nonunion	454	253	55.8
Construction	4,329	1,635	37.7
Union	1,520	1,189	78.2
Nonunion	2,809	445	15.8
Manufacturing	20,785	13,354	64.2
Union	8,008	6,538	81.6
Nonunion	12,777	6,815	53.3
Transportation and Utilities	4,966	3,219	64.8
Union	2,635	2,036	77.2
Nonunion	2,330	1,182	50.7
Wholesale	3,573	1,720	48.1
Union	446	370	82.8
Nonunion	3,126	1,350	43.1
Retail	12,021	2,930	24.3
Union	1,469	910	61.9
Nonunion	10,552	2,020	19.1
F.I.R.E.	4,856	2,334	48.0
Union	304	177	58.4
Nonunion	4,552	2,156	47.3
Services	14,741	4,352	29.5
Union	1,388	796	57.3
Nonunion	13,352	3,555	26.6

Source: Kotlikoff and Smith 1983:45.

as low as 8.7 percent. Conversely, in those industries historically dominated by major industrial unions, such as primary metals (steel), electrical equipment, automobiles, and chemicals (respectively the USWA, the International Brotherhood of Electrical Workers, the UAW, and the Chemical Workers), coverage rates were very high—81.4 percent, 66.4 percent, 79.3 percent, and 81 percent respectively—even if current levels of unionization in those industries have declined in recent years from their postwar peaks. It is not surprising, then, that these industries, the industries under most threat in recent years from corporate restructuring, takeovers, and bankruptcy, are also the industries in which pension obligations are so important in the restructuring process.

The significance of major industrial unions, and in particular the USWA, to the growth and expansion of private pension plans is owed in large part to landmark decisions of the NLRB and the federal courts in the late 1940s. A suit brought by the USWA against Inland Steel Corporation ultimately made pension benefits a legitimate item for the entire economy. The NLRB's decision in *Inland Steel* and the U.S. Supreme Court's decision refusing to review and overturn a lower court's decision in *Inland Steel v. NLRB* (1948) made pension benefits and health insurance benefits mandatory subjects for collective bargaining. Beginning in 1936, Inland Steel had been one of just a few companies to offer a pension plan to qualified (by income) employees. Subsequently, during the Second World War the company extended its plan to cover all employees and then, at the end of the war, developed a trust fund to include those employees who would not have qualified for the plan in the preceding years. Given that the company had already instituted a pension plan covering salary and hourly workers, the dispute between the union and the company was in one sense a minor issue: was the company mandated by the NLRA to bargain with the union over a provision of its pension plan that required employees to retire at age 65?

The company argued it was not mandated to bargain over the terms of its pension plan whereas the union argued that the rules, conditions, and benefit levels of pension plans were subjects that should be construed as relevant to the wages and conditions of employment of union-represented employees. Essentially, the union argued that pension plans ought to be included as mandatory subjects for collective bargaining, invoking language of Section 9 (a) of the Wagner Act, which required companies to bargain with workers' representatives "in respect to rates of pay, wages, hours of employment, or other conditions of employment" (Trussell 1987). Previously, the existence, terms, and conditions of company pension plans were assumed determined at the unilateral discretion of companies. At the time, the company argued that wages ought to be interpreted narrowly as compensation paid directly and immediately to workers upon completion of their assigned work tasks. The company suggested that according to this definition pension benefits were not earned wages but rather benefits due workers according to their length of service with the company. In rebuttal, the NLRB suggested that Congress had used the phrase *"wages and other conditions of employment"* (emphasis in the original) in a generic manner to reflect the terms and conditions of "the entire employer-employee relationship." At issue here was the relationship between employees and employers, not a strict accounting or actuarial definition of variables considered in the legal context as vague and ill-defined.

The board held "we are convinced and find that the term 'wages' as used in Section 9 (a) must be construed to include emoluments of value, like pension and insurance benefits, which may accrue to employees out of their employment relationship. There is indeed an inseparable nexus between an employee's current compensation and his future pension benefits" (pp. 4–5). The board also held that even though pension benefits were not a customary subject for collective bargaining prior to the passage of the act in 1935, there was no basis to believe that Congress had intended "to exclude such plans from the ambit of obligatory bargaining" (p. 10). The NLRB's decision was challenged by the company in federal district court but was upheld. A further challenge in the court of appeals was also dismissed and the Supreme Court refused to reconsider the lower courts' decisions. In the court of appeals, the majority followed the logic and interpretative framework of the board. They dismissed the company's contention that wages should be construed narrowly as they dismissed the company's contention that because pension plans were not referred to in Sections 8 (5) and 9 (a) they were not mandatory subjects of collective bargaining. The court recognized that pension plans were not directly referred to in these sections but went on to note that "this is equally true as to the myriad matters arising from the employer-employee relationship which are recognized as included in the bargaining requirements of the Act but which are not specifically referred to" (p. 251). The court also accepted the board's contention that in other areas wages were construed to mean a wide variety of forms of compensation, including vacation pay and sick pay, as conditions of employment had been construed to include issues such as subcontracting and seniority.

A commentary on the case in 1949 (Note 1949), suggested that the actions of the board and the decisions of the courts had left the matter vague and unresolved ("ad hoc"). In fact, the writer believed that the decisions had favored unions' interest in expanding the limits of legally protected collective bargaining while failing to protect managements' traditional prerogatives. While this idea was of little consequence, the writer also made a perspicacious point of enormous contemporary relevance: "The significance of this decision is less that it called pension plans proper subjects, than it may have started the development of an interpretation of the statute that would define the area of mandatory bargaining" (p. 805). Subsequent decisions of the board and the courts upheld the *Inland Steel* opinion.[4] And, in effect, the postwar growth and expansion of private pension benefits in the U.S. economy was based upon this decision. It provided unions with the legal right to bargain over the provision of pension benefits at a time (*circa* 1950) when their ability to win further wage increases was limited by political concerns. It also provided nonunion employers and sectors a reference point (the kind of benefit that must be paid) in their fight against union representation.

Section 510 of ERISA

Once unions became involved in bargaining over pension benefits, the advent of pattern bargaining and the use of industry wage standards spread pension benefits throughout American industry. Inevitably, the provision of pension benefits spilled over from union to nonunion sectors as nonunion companies used all kinds of strategies to limit the attractiveness of union representation.[5] If the *Inland Steel* case of the late 1940s was an essential first step in the growth and expansion of pension benefits in the U.S. economy, passage of ERISA in 1974 was a necessary second step by the federal government to guarantee workers' pension rights and encourage broader coverage of pension benefits so as to include nonunion sectors. While the IRS had for many years been involved in regulating pension plans and pension funds it had done so in a limited fashion, being most concerned with the tax status of plans rather than the fiduciary performance of pension funds, or the actions of companies with respect to their pension obligations. As noted above, ERISA was passed with the understanding that the federal government would ensure that workers received their promised pension benefits. As well, ERISA set minimum standards for vesting in pension plans, it set standards for pension fund trustee responsibilities, and it established the PBGC as the insurance agency to protect the fiscal integrity of pension funds.

A common interpretation of the overarching public policy purpose of the act is that it was passed to protect employees' pension benefits. This was noted at the time of passage by the Bureau of National Affairs (1974) and is often referred to by contemporary commentators; witness S. Rosen's

(1985) comments on W. K. Viscusi (1985). ERISA also gave workers certain legal rights to due process with respect to their pension claims, rights to information concerning the performance and actions of pension plan administrators, and the right to sue in federal court to correct actions by plan administrators and companies. Whereas in the past union representation, grievance arbitration, and/or collective action in one form or another were the only ways workers could seek redress for abuses by plan administrators, ERISA gave individuals legal standing to pursue their interests, with or without unions. In fact, ERISA's preoccupation with individuals' rights has raised very real doubts about the legal standing of unions to represent their members' pension interests outside of the terms and conditions of collective-bargaining agreements.

The act itself was originally structured into four titles, beginning with Title I Subtitle A, which established the findings and purpose of the act as well as the coverage of the act. Title I Subtitle B then established regulations requiring public reporting and disclosure, minimum participation and vesting standards, minimum pension funding standards, fiduciary standards, and the procedures for enforcement of pension benefit obligations as well as penalties (including criminal penalties) for noncompliance with federal regulations. The other titles set out amendments to IRS regulations (Title II), coordination with other government departments (Title III), and established the PBGC (Title IV). Title I Subtitle B Part 5, Section 510 of the act states in part that "it shall be unlawful for any person to discharge, fine, suspend, expel, discipline, or discriminate against a participant or beneficiary for exercising any right to which he is entitled under the provisions of an employee benefit plan." Section 510 also established that any plan participant or beneficiary could bring a civil action under Title I Subtitle B Section 502 to protect these rights or recover benefits due but otherwise not provided because of discrimination and/or interference with their rights. Another related and important clause was Section 511, which went a step beyond Section 510 by making it a criminal offense to interfere coercively with rights protected by ERISA. However, there have been very few tests of Section 511. For instance, in a rare case, *West v. Butler* (1980), the federal courts had to reach a determination of the right of parties involved in pension-related disputes to use this section in litigation. The federal court of appeals held that since Section 511 was a criminal provision, filing charges was the sole responsibility of the attorney general. There have been more suits based upon Section 510. But as J. Vogel (1987) and T. Collingsworth (1988) note, most of these suits have been of lesser significance compared to the Continental Can cases.

About ten years ago, a test of the scope and relevance of Section 510 came in *Titsch v. Reliance Group* (1982). In a complicated case involving charges and countercharges between the plaintiff (Titsch) and the defendant (Reliance) concerning possible illegal actions by both parties, Titsch alleged that one of the reasons for his discharge had been the company's interest in denying him the chance to vest in the company pension plan. The district court did not accord his Section 510 claim much significance, compared to other issues raised by Titsch. And the court observed in passing that there is no Section 510 ERISA legal cause "where the loss of pension benefits was a mere consequence of, but not a motivating factor behind, a termination of employment" (p. 985). Notice that in this case, as in some other Section 510 cases, the plaintiff was not represented by a union.[6]

A more relevant case (with respect to Continental Can, International Harvester, and LTV) was *Kross v. Western Electric* (1982). There the defendant charged the company with terminating him so as "to avoid continuing to make payment for his company-provided life and medical insurance" (p. 1238). The district court found that he had failed to establish a claim relevant to Section 510 of ERISA, and had failed to exhaust the appropriate pension plan administrative appeals process. However, at the court of appeals level, the court decided that he did in fact have a claim under Section 510 (although it made no determination of the facts of the case) and returned the case for rehearing to the district court. Kross had been discharged during a workforce rationalization action at one of the company's plants. As a consequence of the company's actions, Kross was then not eligible for early retirement pension benefits. In retrospect, it appears that the district court failed to appreciate the distinction between being currently eligible for a set of benefits and the different vesting requirements for more substantial sets of benefits. In their argument against the district court's opinion, the appeals court emphasized that Section 510 demanded a broad, employee-sensitive interpretation. In part, the court noted "Congress would not have adopted such broad and encompassing language had it intended Section 510 to be read as narrowly as the district court in the instant case has construed it" (p. 1242). The court then quoted from a report on ERISA by a House committee which stated, in part, that the act was intended to deal with "malfeasance and maladministration in the plans" as well as broader questions relating to "plant shut downs and plan terminations." The court also quoted a previous judgment of the seventh circuit court of appeals to the effect that "[a] complaint when tested by summary procedures must be given the benefit of every possible implication" (p. 1243).[7] However, on the issue of administrative appeal, the court also held that a matter of "strong federal policy

. . . mandates the application of the exhaustion principle in this case" (p. 1244).[8]

These cases involved individuals and their companies in litigation over employees' rights to due process as construed relevant to Section 510. While the *Kross* case might be thought of as an instance of corporate restructuring (Kross claimed his circumstances were representative of many other individuals' circumstances), perhaps the more appropriate context might be reasonably thought of being related to individuals' employment contracts (as implied by Collingsworth 1988). Union representation was not relevant in these cases. Even so, issues were raised in these cases that remained unresolved and have reappeared in the related *Gavalik* cases and the other two case studies of corporate restructuring (although in different guises). First, how broadly should Section 510 be interpreted? Second, how should the difference be distinguished between the "mere consequences" of other commercial motivations and the possibility that the companies concerned deliberately and illegally sought to avoid their obligations? Third, what is the appropriate mechanism for due process— plan and/or company internal administrative channels as opposed to legal proceedings? As we shall see, the presumption clause of ERISA has effectively meant that legal proceedings dominate other proceedings. However, the other two issues remain widely contested.

A recent case that involved a union (the UAW), corporate restructuring, and Section 510 of ERISA was *Nemeth v. Clark Equipment* (1987). According to a federal appeals court, this case began with the poor financial performance of Clark Equipment (a construction and moving equipment manufacturer headquartered in Michigan) during the 1981/82 recession. Facing a drop of 41 percent in sales between 1979 and 1982 and a reported loss of $234 million in 1982, the company decided to rationalize production (capacity and output) of its construction machinery division. Since it could not close its Ontario (Canada) plant and still remain a competitor in the Canadian market (given trade regulations at the time), the company decided to close its Benton Harbor (Indiana) plant and shift production to its nonunionized and newer Asheville (North Carolina) plant. It is worth comparing this case study with the case study of the relocation of Mack Trucks from Pennsylvania to South Carolina (see Clark 1989a, chap. 3). While many employees were eligible for deferred vested pensions at age 65, many of these same employees were not eligible for plant-closing pensions. Indeed, some were just months short of having accumulated the requisite years of service and age qualifications for early retirement pensions.[9]

Citing *Gavalik*, a group of workers brought suit in federal district court alleging that the company had closed the Benton Harbor plant and relocated production so as to avoid their pension obligations.[10] The district court held that while a case of discrimination under Section 510 had been made, the company's decision to close the plant was not motivated by or based upon consideration of pension costs. The appeals court upheld the decision, even though it noted that the company had in fact given some consideration to the pension costs differential between the two plants. The higher court argued that these costs were not as significant as other costs involved in continuing to operate both plants and that, in accordance with the *Gavalik* decision, since the company had shown that discrimination was purely incidental to other business decisions relating to the best and most efficient location of production, the company was not liable under Section 510. Paraphrasing the court's decision, the company showed to the court's satisfaction that there were alternative and plausible nondiscriminatory reasons for its decisions while the plaintiffs failed to show the "proffered justification" was a pretext hiding an intent to discriminate (p. 903).

This last case raised similar issues to those identified in cases that were about individuals' pensions rights (absent a union and collective-bargaining rights) and is very much related to the case studies in Part 2 of this book. Distinguishing between the "mere consequences" and "motivating causes" behind plant closings was especially difficult for the court. While the appeals court disagreed with the company that the plaintiffs had to show compelling evidence of intent to discriminate, the plaintiffs were unable to show that pension cost considerations were a significant or large part of the company's decisionmaking framework. The court also disagreed with the company's narrow interpretation of the applicability of Section 510; the company had argued that Section 510 could not prevail in circumstances of economic hardship. In fact, as the court pointed out, such circumstances were irrelevant to the intent of the Section, but could be thought essential to the whole purpose of ERISA. Here, the issue of exhausting the administrative appeals process was not raised.[11]

Continental Can in Federal District Court

Many other issues regarding the status and integrity of private pensions have been litigated in federal courts, including the proper role of unions in representing workers' pension interests in concession bargaining,[12] as well as the standing of ERISA in relation to overlapping and relevant states' statutes.[13] With respect to Section 510 cases, it is apparent that considerable confusion exists in federal courts over the scope and appli-

cation of the Section relative to other company actions, as well as confusion
over the appropriate rules for adjudicating Section 510 claims given the
paucity of case law experience in the area. In this context, *Gavalik* and
the cases that have been brought in other jurisdictions related to Continental's actions have been considered by courts, claimants, and commentators alike as leading cases or precedent-setting cases (see Vogel 1987).
While *Gavalik* is considered as the leading Section 510 case, other closely
related suits were filed in federal district court by laid-off USWA-represented employees of Continental Can in California and New Jersey.[14] Like
Gavalik, these suits contended that Continental Can had illegally laid off
employees at its plants just prior to those employees becoming eligible for
early retirement plant-closing pensions. The California (Los Angeles)
cases, *Amaro et al. v. Continental Can Company* and *Payan et al. v.
Continental Can Company*, were settled on August 3, 1987, after the
company agreed to pay the plaintiffs $7 million in damages. The New Jersey
classaction case, *McClendon v. Continental Group Inc.*, was settled in
conjunction with *Gavalik* in early 1991 for $415 million in compensatory
damages.

Although each case was initially tried independently of one another,
case materials from the different cases have been used in the separate
courts.[15] Initially, the federal district court of Central California summarily
dismissed the *Amaro* suit, arguing that an arbitrator's decision denying
a USWA grievance that "Continental's layoff of these employees and its
corresponding shift of production to other plants violated provisions of the
collective bargaining agreement" precluded an ERISA suit on the same
issue. The arbitrator had concluded that the company's actions were a
response to market conditions and, as such, did not contravene the collective-bargaining agreement. The district court's decision was reversed
by the ninth circuit court of appeals. After noting that the grounds of
application for the doctrine of *res judicata* "a final judgment on the merits
precludes the parties from relitigating claims" (p. 749), are not settled,
the appeals court held that an ERISA action to enforce statutory rights
could not be compromised by a collective-bargaining agreement. Citing
Kross, the court said "we are persuaded that in enacting Section 510
Congress created a statutory right independent of any collectively bargained rights" (p. 749), "to hold otherwise would endanger the protection
. . . of ERISA" (p. 750), and the court would not accept the possibility
that "an ERISA claim could be defeated without the benefit of the pro-
tections inherent in the judicial process" (p. 750). Citing a Supreme Court
decision, the court held that arbitrators were not competent to decide
statutory matters.[16] Continental also claimed that the union failed to ex-

haust the arbitration process (similarly citing *Kross*). However, the court decided in this case that all that was required was an interpretation of Section 510, not a ruling on the procedural settlement of a claim that could be settled by arbitration. Again, the court said, "[this] is a task for the judiciary not an arbitrator" (p. 751).

As noted above, the *McClendon* and *Gavalik* cases were settled together in early 1991. Although the first decision of the *McClendon* district court (January 22, 1985) predated the decision of the *Gavalik* district court (September 24, 1985), the *McClendon* case was in the first instance overwhelmed by the defendant's procedural motions. On January 22, 1985, the court dismissed the defendant's motions for summary judgment in favor of the defendant. Judge H. Lee Sarokin held that the benefits at issue were covered by ERISA, that the plaintiffs were not required to exhaust arbitration proceedings, that collective-bargaining agreements do not imply that covered employees waive their judicial rights, and that there was sufficient evidence to proceed with the plaintiff's argument that the Racketeer Influenced and Corrupt Organizations Act (RICO) also applied in this case. On the argument that early retirement plant-closing pensions were not protected by ERISA, Sarokin said, "[it] is wholly without merit" (p. 1499), since ERISA defines employee benefit plans to include benefits relating to unemployment (among other items) also included in Continental's pension plan.

On the other claims, Sarokin followed a line of reasoning entirely consistent with *Amaro*. With respect to the claim that the plaintiffs ought to have exhausted the arbitration process, the company argued that the collective-bargaining agreement required all related disputes to be handled by the grievance process. The court noted that the language of the collective-bargaining agreement was in fact ambiguous on the issue of whether or not disputes *had to be* settled by arbitration. Moreover, despite a strong public policy interest in seeking an arbitrable solution wherever possible, in this case at issue were the plaintiffs' legal rights, not their contractual rights. In essence, arbitration proceedings could not dilute statutory rights (p. 1501). And finally on the same issue, the court cited *Amaro* and *Gavalik* to the effect that Section 510 discrimination could not be reasonably resolved by arbitration given that legal issues were not the appropriate domain of an arbitrator (p. 1503).

With respect to the issue of whether or not by agreeing to arbitrate disputes over pension and other matters the plaintiffs had waived their statutory rights, the court held that ERISA rights were *individual* rights and could not be waived by a union in the same way a union waives the right to strike. Sarokin argued that the right to strike was a group right associated with labor-management relations. In contrast, ERISA rights protected individuals whether unionized or nonunionized—"waiver was neither statutorily permissible nor logically possible" (p. 1505). Other similar procedural motions were introduced by the company's lawyers. The issue of arbitration was considered again and dismissed again on October 6, 1986. The company argued again (citing a recent case) that the plaintiffs were bound to arbitrate the issue. This time, the court noted that the plaintiffs could not be held to an agreement that was fraudulently conceived by the defendant, that the plaintiffs were not forced to arbitrate against their will, and that in any event the plaintiffs were not seeking to resolve a contractual dispute over the level or coverage of benefits, they were seeking recognition of their legal rights.

Continental Can then attempted to implicate the union in liability for the plaintiff's claims. The company argued "if this court holds that Continental violated ERISA, the USWA . . . assisted Continental in doing so by bargaining for and obtaining increased Rule of 70/75 benefits, . . . Rule of 65 benefits, . . . plant-wide seniority knowing that these provisions would lead to large-scale layoffs." In rebuttal, the court noted origins of the *Gavalik* suit in the concern of the union over the plight of laid-off workers. Further, the court argued that the union could hardly be liable for failing to arbitrate the layoffs when the union was unaware of the motivations behind the layoffs. The company did not allege that the union knew about its intentions to deny benefits illegally; rather, the company contended that the union ought to have understood the implications of increased benefits for the livelihood of its younger members. The court dismissed the complaint, noting "Continental's allegations defy logic and common sense. In essence, Continental claims that the union acting legally caused Continental to act illegally, and thus the union should share in the losses occasioned by Continental's wrongdoing" (p. 2408).

Throughout the district court proceedings in *Amaro, McClendon,* and *Gavalik*, the various plaintiffs claimed that they had been denied their pension benefits because of a nationally designed and implemented corporate pension liability–management strategy (described in detail in the next chapter). Through discovery and affidavits, the plaintiffs established that this plan was implemented by senior corporate management in conjunction with their labor relations strategy with the USWA. In fact, individual executives were identified, as was the actual monitoring mechanism used by management to secretly identify and then lay off workers. Against this interpretation, the corporation maintained that it had rationalized production because of serious problems in the can industry. Its strategy of rationalization was argued to be local as opposed to national, and based upon market considerations, not pension liability. Management argued that plant-by-plant rationalization was also based upon the profitability and product mix of different plants leading to the closing of some plants or departments within plants, and the reallocation of production between plants. The company used the testimony of plant managers to validate their argument. The most detailed statement of the company's tactics came with the opinion of the district court in *Gavalik*. Therein the court outlined the pension-avoidance strategy, finding no cause to disbelieve the plaintiff's interpretation of the company's actions.

Judge Alan Bloch found as a matter of fact (#106) that a "motivating factor in . . . [the] decision to close the pail line [in Pittsburgh] was to prevent employees from attaining eligibility for 70/75 and Rule of 65 benefits." This conclusion and the detailed description of the various aspects of the pension-avoidance scheme was accepted by other courts as definitive. Bloch went through the various pension formulas, the benefits costs relative to the standard hourly wage costs, and the added costs due to the negotiated and agreed-to expansion of benefits in 1977. He noted that in 1972 and 1977 employee benefits were about one-half of an employee's average wage package—in 1972 $3,280 on a base wage of $7,152, and in 1977 $8,072 on a base wage of $14,224 (see Table 3.2). The judge also noted the competitive circumstances of the company, including the rationalization of plants and equipment over the 1970s. Without argument Judge Bloch concluded, however, that even though pension avoidance was "a motivating factor" to cap-and-shrink employment in the Pittsburgh plant, the company did not violate Section 510 of ERISA. His opinion derived apparently from an observation that closing the steel pail line, thereby causing the layoff of the targeted employees, was due in large part to business conditions. After reciting the company's position on the competitive status of the pail line, the judge then went through the company argument that the pail line was relatively unprofitable. Specifically, the judge found as fact (#104) that the issues considered by management regarding the future of the pail line were (a) the poor location of the plant in relation to the market, (b) poor and probable declining profitability as the market itself declined, (c) substitution of plastic for steel by customers, (d) the shifting of the market to the Southwest, (e) the high labor costs of operating the plant, and (f) the cap-and-shrink program. By implication, the pension-avoidance program was of lesser significance compared to "other" business considerations.

And yet for all the significance attached to "other" factors, the narrative of the decision focused upon the moves and actions by the company to implement the cap-and-shrink program. Items introduced into the nar-

Table 3.2 Annual Wage and Benefit Costs (Nominal Dollars) of
Hourly Workers at Continental Can Plants Represented by the
USWA, 1972 and 1977

Item	1972	1977
Wages (including overtime)	7,152	14,224
Benefits and Taxes		
Insurance (active)	624	2,300
Insurance (retiree)	192	354
Pension (normal)	480	1,132
Pension (past)	224	281
Taxes	464	1,071
SUB	144	187
Vacation/bonus	448	1,309
Holidays	288	639
EEP	176	408
Shift premium	240	391
Total Benefits	3,280	8,072
Total Labor Cost	10,432	22,296

Source: Finding #35, *Gavalik v. Continental Can Company.*

rative analysis included the motivations behind negotiating plant-wide
seniority as well as the consequences of implementing the program on the
workforce at Pittsburgh. The judge identified by name specific workers
who were terminated just prior to vesting in plant-closing pensions, including Jakub (four months short of vesting), Humenik (two weeks short
of vesting), and Gavalik (just four months short of the service requirement). As in *Amaro* and *McClendon*, Bloch held the plaintiffs did not have
to exhaust the plan's arbitration procedures.

The *Gavalik* Decision Appealed

Neither the plaintiffs (Gavalik and others) nor the defendant (Continental
Can) were willing to let the district court's decision stand. At the third
circuit court of appeals, the plaintiffs argued that (a) the lower court had
made a mistake in not finding that the company had violated Section 510,
(b) the lower court had erred in requiring the plaintiffs to show that the
layoffs were wholly caused by the pension-avoidance scheme, and (c) the
lower court had confused the issues—confusing a concern for liability with
a concern for damages. The company, on the other hand, reasserted their
argument about the necessity of exhausting the dispute through the grievance arbitration system before seeking judicial action. It also claimed that

the legal action was barred by the statute of limitations. The appeals court denied the company's arguments and found in favor of the appellants.

There were some vital issues considered by the appeals court that ought to be recognized before discussion of the next stage of the case at the U.S. Supreme Court. Both the company and appellants raised difficult questions, although the company's questions were more easily resolved than the appellant's questions. Using the lower court's statement of facts and findings the appeals court briefly recited the crucial elements of Continental's pension-avoidance scheme. Whereas the lower court had conceived the narrative opinion from the perspective of Continental's business circumstances, the appeals court's narrative was organized around the design and implementation of the Bell pension-avoidance system. With respect to the company's claims, the appeals court first considered the relevance of the Pennsylvania statute of limitations. The company cited a recent decision of the U.S. Supreme Court which implied that the correct statute of limitations was two years, not six years as assumed by the district court.[17] However, the appeals court found that the company had failed to appreciate the facts of *Wilson v. Garcia:* "the facts of *Garcia* simply belie Continental's contention" (p. 19a). Holding that the Section 510 claim was most consistent with a state employment discrimination suit (an opinion also held by the district court and unchallenged by the company), the appeals court argued that the company had failed to make their legal sources of argument relevant to the extant case. On the issue of exhaustion of grievance and arbitration (collective-bargaining) mechanisms, the appeals court cited *Zipf* (a decision of the same court just one year previous to *Gavalik*) to the effect that Section 510 cases were not required to exhaust arbitration procedures. The appeals court distinguished between issues related to administrative fairness and the protection of statutory rights. Citing the *Zipf* decision, they concluded that "the remedy for Section 510 discrimination was intended (by Congress) to be provided by the courts" (p. 31a).

The opinion of the court on the appellant's appeal was signaled in two ways, even before the court had worked through the arguments. Quoting Sen. Jacob Javits (R-N.Y.), the leading advocate for passage of ERISA in 1974, the court said that Section 510 was enacted "primarily to prevent 'unscrupulous employers from discharging or harassing their employees in order to keep them from obtaining vested pension rights' " (p. 34a). Then, citing the relevant case law and the language of the statute, the court held that violation of Section 510 was "proved" by an intent to engage in proscribed activity, whether this activity was successful or not and whether or not pension benefits were actually denied even in the absence of "smoking-gun" evidence.

On the basis of related employment discrimination cases and statute, the appeals court indicated that there was a five-step procedure for making a determination in a Section 510 case.

1. In the case of a single employee, he or she must demonstrate prohibited employer conduct for the purpose of interfering with the attainment of a pension benefit; in a class-action case the plaintiffs must show that the employer's conduct was standard practice.

2. In the initial stages of the proceedings the burden of proof lies with the plaintiff(s).

3. Once a *prima facie* case has been established, however, the burden of proof shifts to the defendant to demonstrate a "legitimate, nondiscriminatory reason" for its actions.

4. If the employer fails to show such a reason or reasons, then the district court is required to enter a judgment in favor of the plaintiff(s).

5. If the employer raises a plausible reason, then the plaintiff(s) must show that the proffered reason or reasons are not credible.

By this procedure and a brief review of the evidence described and found as fact by the lower court, the appeals court held that the plaintiffs had clearly established Continental's intention to discriminate. Indeed, with the company's internal documents as evidence, the court held that there was no need to proceed beyond the first two steps of the decisionmaking procedure. The appeals court noted that the district court had failed to realize that the company was just as liable for acting to prevent its employees attaining pension benefits as it would have been if it had actually denied employees certain already-vested pension rights. The court also criticized the lower court for requiring a too-stringent standard of proof—the plaintiffs were required by the lower court to show that the affected employees would have been laid off even if business conditions were a consideration.

In essence, the appeals court determined that the lower court should have accepted evidence of "mixed motives" in the decision to close parts of the production process. Mixed motives could include both permissible and impermissible factors; liability was determined by proving an intent to discriminate. The appeals court returned the case to the lower court with a formula for determining damages. Although the case might have then been reconsidered by the district court, the company appealed to the U.S. Supreme Court for review. Three reasons for review were advanced, all procedural and none substantive (in the sense that they might have dealt with the genesis of the case in the structure of pension benefits and the imperatives of corporate restructuring). The company tried common legal strategies of narrowing and stripping the issue of case texture, while "painting" the issue as one of the coherence of law rather than the justice of the extant case. These three grounds were: (1) the circuit courts were divided over the applicability of the exhaustion doctrine, (2) the circuit court's use of a six-year statute of limitations threatened the prompt resolution of disputes and could "chill" the interest of corporations in providing pension benefits, and (3) the plaintiffs should be required to prove without doubt that the proscribed actions would have occurred absent any other actions by the company.

All three grounds of appeal have been considered in depth in the discussion above. None was especially compelling in the sense that the lower courts had failed to consider these issues, or had unilaterally ignored the findings and opinions of other courts. In reply, the brief for Gavalik et al. rehearsed the facts of the case, noting the company's design and implementation of the pension-avoidance scheme, as well as the possible implications of this case for the welfare of many millions of workers. They recognized that there was some confusion over the application of the exhaustion principle but also argued that the confusion had not affected the Continental case, and that the facts as discerned by the courts were essentially uncontested by the company. Lawyers for Gavalik et al. returned to the transcript of debate over passage of ERISA in 1974 to introduce more material on the intended association between ERISA and other antidiscrimination statutes.

Most significantly, the U.S. solicitor general also filed a brief arguing that review of the case ought to be denied.[18] Again the essential elements of the pension-avoidance scheme were reviewed, this time focusing on the cap-and-shrink strategy. The solicitor general sided with the appeals court on the issue of exhaustion, and argued that the courts were the appropriate forum for resolving disputes over legal rights, rather than the use of arbitrators. On the issue of conflict between courts over this issue, the solicitor general argued that those favoring exhaustion were "clearly wrong." As for the statute of limitations, the solicitor general followed the appeals court argument in favor of a longer period rather than a shorter period. And finally, on the matter of proof, the solicitor general concluded the "respondents met that burden by proving the existence of the . . . pension avoidance program and its implementation at Pittsburgh." The Supreme Court denied review on December 7, 1987. After further review at the district court level, the case was then consolidated with the New Jersey *McClendon* case and a decision on compensation rendered in early 1991.

Workers' Pension Rights

I have sought to demonstrate that corporate pension liabilities are a vital "lens" through which to understand the economic and legal dimensions of corporate restructuring. Pension liabilities are barriers to exit in the lexicon of W. Baumol et al. (1988) and may be fundamental impediments to internal reorganization. There have been a variety of corporate "solutions" to these barriers—some legal, others illegal. LTV Corporation declared Chapter 11 bankruptcy and attempted to shift its unfunded pension liabilities to the PBGC. While there has been dispute over the timing and consequences of this tactic in federal bankruptcy court, few commentators would argue that the company subverted or deliberately broke the law. On the other hand, it is apparent that Continental Can's pension-avoidance scheme and perhaps Clark Equipment's scheme (both of which turned on the closing of plants and the reallocation of production) could be reasonably interpreted as strategies designed to avoid their legal responsibilities. In this chapter, I also argued that these schemes were conceived within the context of federal regulations whose statutory purpose is to protect workers' pension rights. Thus, corporations do not have the unilateral power to change, amend, or deny their agreed-to pension obligations—an interpretation of case law made in the context of the NLRA and collective-bargaining agreements more than forty years ago, generalized by statute (ERISA) to cover union and nonunion situations nearly twenty years ago. Indeed, ERISA was passed to regulate the exercise of corporate power given the recognition that corporations could not be trusted to honor their pension and benefit obligations.

Basically, ERISA was passed to limit the impact of economic imperatives; a set of boundaries was established that distinguished corporate actions that were defined as illegal from those that are customarily accepted as legal. Plant closings and the reallocation of production are not illegal. Rather, denying or intending to deny workers' pension rights is illegal. What this chapter also demonstrated, however, is the ambiguity of ERISA in practice. Of course, there is bound to be ambiguity and conflicting interpretations when a law is applied to a new area or in a new way as, for example, when the NLRB extended the NLRA to cover wages and other conditions of employment. There is also bound to be ambiguity when a new law is tested and defined by adjudication as, for example, when the courts have had to determine the meaning and intent of Section 510 of ERISA in the cases considered in this chapter. And there is bound to be ambiguity when the courts have had to determine the application of one law in the context of other presumably relevant laws (as, for example, when the courts have had to place the NLRA in relation to other federal and state statutes). Inevitably, laws are written broadly and the text is open to interpretation. This kind of ambiguity is captured by the hermeneutic style of legal adjudication, even if law is not exactly like literature (that is, completely open-textured; compare with Posner 1988).

If ambiguity was simply an intellectual problem for lawyers and social scientists, we might be less interested in pursuing the matter in the context of restructuring and corporate pension liabilities. However, these are ambiguities that directly affect workers' welfare and are consequently not easily rationalized as an academic exercise. One fundamental question concerns who is to represent those workers affected by corporate pension-avoidance schemes. After the *Inland Steel* decision, unions had the primary responsibility for representing workers' pension interests. The terms and conditions as well as the mechanisms for adjudicating grievance claims of workers' pensions were defined by collective-bargaining agreements, themselves protected by the NLRA. With the passage of ERISA, though, unions' ERISA status was more ambiguous. ERISA was passed to protect individual workers' pension rights, regardless of their union status. Of course, unions may have a fundamental interest in the outcome of an ERISA suit. But they do not have legal standing as the aggrieved party as they might in a suit filed under the NLRA. To extend a suit to cover a group of workers similarly affected by a corporate pension avoidance–motivated plant closing, lawyers must petition for a class-action suit. This is despite the fact that individual worker's pension benefits have until very recently usually originated with a union-management contract and, as in the Continental cases, pension-avoidance strategies may be designed in accordance with workers' specific union affiliation.

As we shall see in subsequent chapters, I would argue that unions are less able to play a role in remedying pension-related corporate-restructuring strategies compared, for example, to their potential role in mediating and representing workers in corporate plant closings and relocations. In fact, workers may be penalized for their union membership. Arguments that workers must first exhaust their collectively negotiated grievance and arbitration procedures before seeking judicial remedies would limit the exercise of workers' legal rights because of their union status but would then ignore their union status when the suit is filed under ERISA. In nonunion situations, where companies have unilaterally established their own plans and plan-grievance procedures, it seems unfair to require workers to exhaust company procedures before initiating legal claims since, unlike union situations, such procedures are not mutually agreed to or negotiated. Some district courts would penalize workers for being unionized and would penalize other workers for being nonunionized where, in fact, union status is irrelevant to ERISA. For workers represented by unions, there is a strong likelihood that their pension rights are systematically violated because of their standing by age and seniority and their location by plant in union-negotiated pension plans. The relevance of these attributes in law is generally unrecognized by ERISA. But it may be precisely those attributes that prompt a company to violate an individual's pension rights. At best, unions are treated as law firms representing groups of workers.

A second important source of ambiguity in workers' pension rights pertains to the definition and enforcement of the boundaries between permissible (legal) and impermissible (illegal) corporate actions as regards their pension obligations. I have already noted that plant closings, the reallocation of production within and between plants, and the introduction of new modes of production in existing plants are all permissible corporate actions. Their rights to do so are generally protected by property rights, limited only by bilateral agreements with labor as regulated by the NLRA. ERISA is nominally irrelevant to these issues. Some courts have held that these kinds of actions cannot be construed to be illegal or in any way evidence of corporate violation of Section 510 of ERISA. This opinion is sometimes evident in the recognition of "mixed motives" (and hence an unwillingness to identify precise illegal actions) and at other times evident in tests of causation like the "but for" test of the *Gavalik* federal district court. By this kind of reasoning, one identifiable class of actions is clearly legal, and another is clearly illegal. However, in actuality it is difficult to maintain such a "bright-line" division between legal and illegal. Depending upon a corporation's intention, relocation of production so as to avoid pension obligations may be thought legal or illegal. There is often a variety of intentions wrapped up in a corporation's decision to relocate production. It is unlikely that a single action could ever signal a violation of ERISA.

As the third circuit court of appeals noted, the alternative is to identify an intention to violate workers' pension rights by way of the relocation of production and to say that the action was against Section 510 of ERISA. The problem here, though, is that once we narrow the focus of analysis to intentions, we depend upon the company and its managers to provide the evidence (or provide an alternative explanation) of those intentions. In labor relations, in many instances illegal union animus cannot be proved because management conducts its antiunion actions (such as relocation) through an informal (secret) code that is not identifiable to outside regulators. There is no reason to believe, Continental Can notwithstanding, that many corporations are not similarly skilled regarding their implementation of pension-avoidance strategies. Moreover, there is every reason to imagine that a plausible alternative intention can be readily concocted in most circumstances where there is no other basis for evaluating the company's claims (that is, absent "smoking-gun" evidence). Given the problems of identifying intentions and the problems of distinguishing between reasonable and unreasonable versions of a corporation's intentions, we should be skeptical of the resilience of the third circuit court's method of determination. An alternative might be to regulate all those actions (e.g., relocation) that are implicated in pension-avoidance strategies. But this kind of regulatory strategy would immediately confront the integrity of corporations' property rights.

Summary—The Promise of ERISA

To analyze the recent experience of workers concerning the intersection between corporate restructuring and the private pension liabilities involved in restructuring requires, in part, an appreciation of the evolution of the U.S. pension system in general. From the decision of the NLRB in *Inland Steel* in 1947 when pension benefits were given the status of mandatory subjects for collective bargaining, the number and significance of private pension funds grew very rapidly. With passage of ERISA in 1974, protection of workers' rights to private pension plan benefits was taken out of the realm of labor-management relations and given a separate legal status—ERISA was intended to protect union and nonunion workers alike. Whereas the origin of Continental Can employees' pension benefits was owed to the union's strength in collective bargaining, litigation over the company's pension-avoidance scheme began with Section 510 of ERISA.

Historically, the level of pension benefits and pension obligations of many industrial corporations has been linked to its union relations. With those relationships have often come industry-wide agreements patterned on developments in the steel and aluminum industries. Throughout the post–*Inland Steel* era the USWA leveraged up pension and related benefits through compromises on wage increases and competition with other unions over industry wage and benefit standards. When Continental came to design and implement its pension-avoidance scheme it set itself against one of the most powerful and innovative U.S. unions. For a union that had fought and lobbied for the passage of ERISA, the suit brought by previous employees of Continental Can (alleging the company had violated Section 510 of ERISA) was a product of the union's interest in policing the administration and integrity of ERISA. On that basis alone, the union's legal campaign against Continental might be reasonably interpreted as an attempt to realize the promise of Section 510. Litigation over Continental Can's pension liability avoidance scheme also gave meaning and significance to Section 510 of ERISA. Prior to *Gavalik* there had been few tests of Section 510 and those few prior applications of the Section had hardly addressed the reach of the Section. *Gavalik* provided the courts, especially the federal third circuit appeals court, with an opportunity to consider questions of the adequacy of proof, the significance of intent to discriminate, and the rationalization of mixed motives. The decision passed scrutiny by the U.S. Supreme Court (in the sense the court refused to review the decision) and consequently has become a leading case in Section 510 litigation.

It was also noted, however, that there may be some fundamental difficulties in applying the court's decision framework to other cases. While the court has provided a relatively low threshold for finding violation of Section 510, experienced corporate managers may be able to circumvent the intention issue by covering its actions with permissible intentions. In *Gavalik* and the related Continental cases the company convicted itself by its own internal documents. In the absence of a "smoking gun," the courts and policymakers need a way of reaching back from observed outcomes to likely illegal behavior. That is, since intentions are so difficult to prove, it may be necessary to first identify the likely circumstances where illegal action occurs, trace actual outcomes, and then mount a rigorous investigation to ascertain whether or not a case exists to be litigated. While some workers may indeed be fortunate to be represented by a union willing to follow through on litigation, as unions decline in significance and the costs of litigation continue to increase without substantive recognition in statute of unions' special status, it does not appear that unions can continue to police Section 510 of ERISA. Indeed, for the vast bulk of Americans not represented by unions, Section 510 may remain an empty promise in the absence of concerted federal investigation.

PART 2

Corporate
Strategy

4

Location and Management Strategy

This chapter is the first of three that document in detail how corporate restructuring affects and is affected by private pension obligations. Each of the chapters makes three kinds of contributions to our understanding of restructuring. First, I aim to show that the connections between restructuring and pension obligations are clearly financial and inevitably linked to the structure of corporations' inherited physical plant and equipment. Documenting this connection provides the rudiments for understanding the origins of identifiable patterns of plant closings and rationalization associated with restructuring. Second, each of the three chapters illustrates in its own way, related to the case at hand, how the financial connection between restructuring and private pensions is also an institutional connection related to corporations' relationships to unions and their workers. And third, I aim to demonstrate that the financial and institutional connections are intimately related to an overarching but hardly well-developed legal framework. In this particular chapter, I work through the corporate restructuring strategy initiated by senior executives of Continental Can. As noted previously, this case material is drawn from litigation and is used to document Continental Can's production and location decisions at its West Mifflin plant during the period 1974 to 1981.[1]

At the outset, it should be acknowledged that the connections between corporate restructuring and pension obligations are not well understood in the literature concerned with corporate location decisionmaking. From a public perspective, more often than not local economic development planners tend to treat pensions as untapped sources of investment rather than sources of enormous private liability. For example, it was estimated for 1988 that the assets of pension plans were worth about $2.5 trillion (Bodie 1990). Some writers suggest that *if* these assets were mobilized for community economic development, private pension plans could fundamentally improve the fortunes of whole regions and their industries; see the seminal argument by J. Rifkin and R. Barber (1978). It is sometimes also asserted that pension plan assets could be (or should be) used to stake employee buyouts of local plants and companies (Bowles et al. 1983) and perhaps management-led LBOs of corporations.[2] In chapter 2, I noted that pension reversions were so used during the mid-1980s. However, this kind of activity has been significantly curtailed by closer judicial scrutiny of trustees' decisions. In fact, despite the rhetoric, the use of private pension plan assets for community development and management and employee investment in their own companies is *strictly* limited by Title I Sections 404, 406, and 407 of ERISA.[3]

With respect to community economic welfare, pensions, plant closings, and corporate restructuring are closely related. Plant closings can adversely affect workers' pension incomes if a plant closing results in termination of a plan and the arbitrary abrogation of early retirement pension entitlements covered by collective-bargaining agreements but not guaranteed by ERISA. Even guaranteed pension benefits may be limited by the PBGC according to their policies regarding maximum benefit levels by age. In this chapter, private pensions are treated as corporate liabilities—current and future financial obligations to vested plan participants differentiated by plant location and the age and seniority of workers. For many U.S. manufacturing firms, unfunded pension obligations are so significant that they represent insurmountable barriers to exit. Thus, various strategies are used to avoid those liabilities, some legal and some not so legal. Here, I deal with an illegal strategy involving the internal rationalization of production.

Deindustrialization and Corporate Restructuring

To begin, it is important to set this case within an appropriate theoretical context. One relevant set of literature is concerned with the patterns of deindustrialization and restructuring. This literature is broadly interdisciplinary, covering sociology (Hill and Negrey 1987), economics (Harrison and Bluestone 1988) and economic geography (Clark et al. 1986). Previously, I noted that industrial restructuring is associated with many different phenomena, including changes in corporate structure, labor practices, the introduction of new technology, and labor-management relations. As well, it is apparent that restructuring is intimately connected to the inherited spatial structure of production within the United States, and between the United States and overseas locations.

In the literature context noted here, restructuring is often paired with deindustrialization. The latter is described by Bluestone and Harrison (1982) as a process of wholesale corporate abandonment (disinvestment, plant closings, and relocation) of productive capacity by industry and region. Both restructuring and deindustrialization can involve massive and geographically concentrated job loss. But it is also obvious that restructuring can involve significant, albeit highly localized, investment and job creation as corporations rationalize productive capacity according to relative labor productivity and the speed of innovation, and diversify production into new locations (products and processes); see the analysis of these restructuring strategies as generally discussed in chapter 2. However appealing the pairing of restructuring and deindustrialization, some important conceptual differences ought to be recognized. These conceptual distinctions play an important role in understanding the motives and behavior of Continental Can. With respect to the firm, deindustrialization describes the accumulated product of separate corporate decisions to exit from an industry or set of industries. By contrast, restructuring describes a process of corporate reorganization—what is produced, how it is produced, and where it is produced—within an industry or set of industries.

With respect to the nation, deindustrialization is sometimes invoked to describe the transformation of the U.S. economy from a manufacturing economy to a service economy (see Rodwin 1989). By contrast, restructuring at the national level may involve reorganization of the nation's institutions, especially the system of labor-management relations, wage-setting practices, and the pattern of private and public responsibility for employees' welfare within and between specific industries. The differences between deindustrialization and restructuring are thus not just semantic. Some firms in the United States can industry literally exited the industry by closing and selling their plants. For example, American Can became Primerica, an insurance and finance company. In contrast, Continental Can Corporation remained in the can industry but internally restructured itself, thereby deliberately challenging the institution of labor-management relations, and the assumption of private responsibility for the costs of restructuring—subverting the collective-bargaining process and illegally laying off employees just before they became eligible for early retirement pensions. In this sense, restructuring is a corporate practice that is intertwined with the formal, institutional, even statutory, division of responsibilities among unions, management, and government.

During the 1960s and 1970s, deindustrialization drastically affected the welfare and economic viability of many communities. One consequence has been the rise of local economic development planning in the 1980s in the absence of concerted federal government public policy (witness the significance attached to the so-called Massachusetts miracle in the 1988 presidential campaign; see Harrison and Kluver [1989] for an analysis of the elements of the growth and decline of Massachusetts). By contrast, restructuring has presented a more difficult problem for national institutions, the responsibility for which is not so easily deflected to the local level. In a society that prides itself on the efficiency and efficacy of decentralized decisionmaking, corporate strategies that aim at circumventing or avoiding statutory responsibilities inevitably raise questions about the continued efficacy of allowing corporations to design their own restructuring strategies without more stringent federal regulations. Such actions also raise questions about the overall integrity, coherence, and administrative authority of institutions; see R. Dworkin (1986) on current legislation and its enforcement.

To illustrate, the case study presented in this chapter is about corporate restructuring at the local level and the intersection between corporate behavior and the fragile, decentralized institutional structure of the American economy. My analysis derives from chapter 2 and is based on four intersecting premises or assumptions that are rarely made explicit in the literature on corporate restructuring. I do not pretend to have synthesized a general theory of restructuring. Rather, the focus of these premises is on the costs of corporate restructuring as a barrier to exit from an industry.

Premise 1: Restructuring is not without cost. Indeed, restructuring can be very expensive, especially at the margin of exiting an industry and/or market locations. One consequence of the high cost of restructuring may be limits on the number of potential entrants to an industry or market, as well as limits on the ability of existing producers to pay for restructuring and leave the industry or market. The costs of restructuring may be due to factors that are the responsibility of the corporation (for example, the write-down costs of plant and machinery). As well, the costs of restructuring may be due to collective-bargaining agreements between corporations and their employees (for example, early retirement and plant-closing pensions), and costs may arise from statutory responsibilities, such as ERISA, imposed by the federal government (for example, adequate funding of private pension plans). At issue is the distribution of the costs of restructuring—among management and stockholders, management and labor, and management, stockholders, and the federal government.

Premise 2: Restructuring is a corporate strategy or response to competition, normally occurring in markets that are in some way contestable. W. Baumol et al. (1988) define a contestable market in terms of the ease of entry of potential producers to a market. This definition has obvious geographical analogues, and may be interpreted to apply to markets segmented by product and place. They also suggest that ease of exit is as important as ease of entry, even though this has received little attention in the literature. The most extreme case, where a market is perfectly contestable (firms can freely enter and leave the market), means that restructuring is a continuous process, designed according to the latest innovation or changes in market conditions. What prompts restructuring in this context is exogenous to the firm, and may involve competition (local, national, and international) from other firms, technological change, and changing configuration of demand.

Premise 3: Restructuring can be a management strategy designed to enhance the value (stock value, asset value, and liquidity) of the corporation. In this sense, I assume management has an internal arena of power that provides it with opportunities to reorganize the firm in ways consistent with management's interests (rationalization, diversification, and ultimately its power). At one level, management discretion is fought for against the power and control of labor (organized and unorganized). At another level, and in the language of contemporary economic theory, management (agents) often acts on its own interests separate from the stockholders' (principals') interests (Arrow 1985). Management's interests need not be counter to stockholders' interests; restructuring that increases the market value of shares may benefit both management and stockholders. On the other hand, restructuring that increases the asset value of a corporation may benefit management more than stockholders in subsequent management-led LBOs. Rarely do such management strategies benefit employees or their communities, although management may forge alliances with some communities against other communities in the interests of localizing the costs and benefits of restructuring (Clark 1989a).

Premise 4: Restructuring is a dynamic process that necessarily reflects and affects the inherited geography or spatial structure of production. Thus, restructuring may be designed in accordance with the history and geography of investment, labor-management relations, and the relative costs of plant closing in one place compared to other places. In this sense, the geography of restructuring is contingent upon other processes *and* may be essential to the character of corporate restructuring as opposed to corporate disinvestment or deindustrialization. Geography matters because it is a strategic variable in the design of corporate restructuring. Corporations' plans are structured and designed at least in accordance with local labor relations environments.

These four premises are used in the following sections to organize and interpret the actions of Continental Can through the 1970s and early 1980s. While I do not intend to prove exactly the reliability of these premises on the basis of this one case study, I do mean to suggest that these premises are a crucial lens for analyzing corporate restructuring strategies and pension obligations from a critical perspective. As has been stressed in previous chapters, this case is of great significance for understanding the process of industrial restructuring *and* the governmental regulation of private pensions in the United States. In subsequent sections, the case study is presented in narrative form following H. White's (1987:45) argument that narrative discourse is a way of transforming events into "intimations of patterns of meaning." As will become apparent, Continental's restructuring of its production system and corporate identity was complicated, involving all four aspects of restructuring (competition, management strategy, costs of restructuring, and the geographical structure of production), overlapping and intersecting at different times and places.

Management Strategy—Diversification and Rationalization

For the sake of interpretation, we begin with Continental's competitive position in the packaging industry in the early 1970s and introduce the then-imagined prospect of changing market circumstances to identify what probably prompted the corporation to begin its rationalization programs. Later in the 1970s, it became obvious that other objectives of the corporation were served by restructuring, including its campaign against the USWA, diversification of the corporation into energy, finance, and insurance sectors, and ultimately its sale to a private company and the subsequent sale of assets to finance the leveraged buyout.

From 1945 to the early 1980s, the U.S. canning and packaging industry was dominated by four major firms: American Can, Continental Can, National Can, and Crown Cork and Seal. American Can was the dominant firm until the mid-1960s, when Continental Can began to emerge as the industry leader through a mixture of new plants (Continental opened forty-one new plants between 1965 and 1970), acquisitions, mergers, and technical innovation. All acquisitions were directly related to packaging processes, packaging materials, and packaging plants in the United States and overseas. In the early 1970s, Continental was able to capitalize on shifting consumer preferences for beer and soft drinks in cans with a new canning system and collaborative deals with the major beer and soft-drink manufacturers for on-site packaging in new or leased plants staffed and operated by Continental employees. Based on optimistic forecasts of further substitution of cans for glass, increasing profit rates, and a surge in sales, Continental was perceived by Wall Street investors to be the canning company with the greatest earnings and growth potential. By 1975, its peak year of output and employment, the company owned over ninety-two domestic plants and properties related to the packaging industry and employed over 15,000 production workers in the United States and Canada. In contrast, American Can (by then the second company in the industry) employed just over 11,000 production employees, National Can employed about 6,000 production employees, and Crown employed just over 4,000 production employees. Continental was the nation's and Western world's largest packaging company with facilities in Canada and Europe. Ten years later Continental only employed about 3,500 production workers. What happened?

In the early 1970s, Continental gained market share by restructuring production *in situ* (within its existing network of plants) and built and leased new facilities around the country in accordance with emerging markets. However, with the growth of the late 1960s and early 1970s came new competitive pressures. Beverage manufacturers, facing severe price competition for the finished packaged product, sought price cuts from the packaging companies just at a time when labor costs were increasing due to a successful strike against the major firms led by the USWA in 1971. About that time, steel and materials prices were increasing but the Nixon administration's price and wage control commission refused Continental's petition for a price increase. Due to the ease of entry of competitors into the industry, the experience of beverage manufacturers in packaging their own products and easy accessibility to new technology, the beverage companies began building and operating their own canning plants. Furthermore, some states passed strict environmental laws limiting the use of nonreturnable cans and plastic containers, two of the product advantages enjoyed by Continental.

Optimistic forecasts of the early 1970s were not realized. By 1975 overcapacity threatened the industry. The beverage companies were now competing with the major firms for contract packaging using up-to-date technology and lower marginal prices. Although the beverage companies did not dominate the market in terms of volume, their capacity and cut-price strategies threatened the price structure and stability of the market. Rather than predicting further growth in canning and packaging shipments, Continental's management forecast declines in shipments. In the mid-1970s, Continental faced four fundamental problems: (1) excess capacity inherited from plants acquired in the 1960s plus the new plants built in the early 1970s; (2) a trend toward new geographical markets and greater localization of production to serve those markets; (3) a need to introduce new technology to remain at the leading edge of the industry; and (4) a need for higher labor productivity given the pressure on product prices. In 1975, the corporation announced a major program of rationalization and diversification.

Diversification was immediately signaled by a change of the corporate name to the Continental Group Inc. From 1976 to 1980, the corporation acquired a major insurance company, two financial services companies, a mortgage company, and a gas and energy resources company. From 1979 to 1983, the corporation sold its flexible packaging division, and sold its Canadian operations including its container plants, carton plants, board mill, and canning facilities. Whether explicitly or implicitly, Continental's management pursued a diversification strategy consistent with the BCG's corporate portfolio and growth formula.[4] The packaging and container groups were treated as "cash cows"—what BCG would describe as businesses in which the corporation had strong competitive positions but that were declining or stagnant with limited investment opportunities. Packaging provided the corporation with a predictable high volume of revenue as long as it could control costs and limit reinvestment in the industry. The long-run competitive position of packaging was sacrificed for the promise of higher returns in the potential "star" performers of the 1980s.[5]

Despite a very difficult period during the 1982 recession when the corporation had to close many of its packaging plants and forestry plants, and sell some assets to maintain cash flow, by 1984 the corporation was once again described by the financial newspapers as a dominant and growing corporation. By then, though, it had become a target for takeover. Sir James Goldsmith (at the time a British takeover specialist) first offered $50 and then $54 per share, and then the Kiewit family group made a successful LBO offer of $58.50 per share (worth a total of $2.8 billion). Continental's management was very much involved in the takeover process. They were obviously concerned about the relative merits of the various bids in terms of the future of the firm. Senior management was also implicated because of stock options they had been voted during the late 1970s.[6] At the time (July 1984), the acquisition of Continental was the largest single LBO of a public company by private investors. To pay off the junk bonds, Kiewit then sold most of Continental's finance, insurance, and energy businesses and voted itself a large one-time dividend payment. In this way it is estimated that Kiewit may have raised as much as $2.5 billion to cover the costs of the buyout.[7]

Ten years after embarking on its diversification strategy, Continental was a much smaller packaging business in an industry still suffering from chronic overcapacity, successive rounds of technological innovation, and depressed product prices. It had gone through a rapid buildup of acquisitions and then disinvestment. The company employed just a fraction of its previous workers. American Can had followed a similar diversification strategy to Continental but had literally become a different company with different products. National Can and American Can's packaging plants were merged into another company, while Crown Cork and Seal remained independent, but small. Continental's diversification strategy benefited management, shareholders, and the banking community. The success of the strategy depended, however, upon maintenance of a high volume of cash flow from the packaging businesses and close control of the costs of rationalizing Continental's canning operations.

When Continental announced its diversification strategy in 1975, it also announced plans to close as many as fifteen plants, write down the asset value of many existing plants, relocate and build new plants closer to their markets, and introduce new technology to enhance labor productivity. Rationalization of productive capacity had begun, though, as early as 1972. In response to the shift of consumers to plastics, low prices, and self-production by beverage manufacturers, Continental decided in 1972 to close and modernize some of its plants, thereby facilitating the introduction of new technology (for example, a two-piece can). To finance rationalization, the parent company created a $231-million reserve termed the "Extra Charge Authorization" (ECA). This reserve was allocated to plant-accelerated depreciation and disposal, labor costs (early retirement pension, health insurance, and severance pay), and equipment transfer and other related expenses (see Table 4.1 for details of its distribution by plant). The ECA reserve only financed the costs of restructuring, not new investment.

In just a few years, the ECA fund was exhausted. Another $100 million was allocated in 1976 for rationalization, this time from the packaging company itself for what was termed the "Plant Utilization Program" (PUP). The PUP concept was a broad policy initiative aimed at decreasing the volume of available productive capacity, increasing plant utilization, and decreasing the number of employees. At a time when the corporation was using assets and cash flow from the packaging businesses to finance diversification into other industries, the ECA and PUP reserves were significant losses to the achievement of overall corporate objectives. The prospect of significantly larger costs of restructuring was recognized by upper management. Officials of the corporation were concerned that closing many of the older plants would incur significant unfunded pension obligations. Reflecting this concern, it was noted at a management meeting in 1979 that plant shutdown liabilities of their oldest ten plants were in the order of $208 million (see Table 4.2). In 1975 and 1976, the corporation moved to limit potential pension liabilities. The PUP program became a "cap-and-shrink" program.

Essentially, the cap-and-shrink program was designed to reduce potential unfunded early retirement pension liabilities by denying near-eli-

Table 4.1 Restructuring Costs by Plant and Union
Status (in millions of dollars)

Plant closings	44.1
Auburndale	2.1
Harvey	12.0
McDonald	6.9
Metropolitan	10.0
Terminal Island	3.5
San Leandro	7.1
Modernization and transfers	46.8
Baltimore	17.4
Clearing	13.9
Houston	4.1
Patterson	2.9
Pittsburgh	2.4
Stockyards	6.1
Accelerated depreciation	60.4
Other modernization	24.5
Other expenses	55.2

Note: All plants listed are USWA, with the exception
of San Leandro.
Source: Document #261 of case file, Federal District
Court of Western Pennsylvania.

gible employees their right to such pensions if the plant in question was
closed. In this way, the costs of restructuring were to be minimized and
shifted from the corporation to individual workers. To implement their
cost-reduction restructuring policy, the corporation needed the cooperation of the union in changing plant-level seniority rules. It also needed
secrecy so that local union officials and management would not recognize
the goals of the corporation, and it required a very sophisticated centralized
management reporting system that enabled senior executives to track the
age and work experience of individual employees by plant location. The
cap-and-shrink policy was first implemented on an experimental basis in
three Continental canning plants, and then broadened to other plants in
other areas of the country.

Design of the Pension-Avoidance System

The following description of the design of the corporation's cap-and-shrink
program is based on documents filed in federal district court in Pittsburgh

Table 4.2 Potential Plant Closing Pension Liability
of Continental Group Inc.'s Oldest Ten Plants by
State, 1979 (in millions of dollars)

Baltimore	24.7
Birmingham	5.3
Clearing, Ill.	29.3
Los Angeles	11.1
North Grand, Ill.	22.4
Patterson, N.J.	30.0
Pittsburg, Calif.	5.9
Pittsburgh, Pa.	32.3
St. Louis	24.5
Tampa	22.4

Source: Document #261 of case file, Federal District
Court of Western Pennsylvania.

and Newark, the bases for court judgments against the company. It is
important to recognize that all parties in the Continental cases (the company, the plaintiffs, and the courts) have agreed on the facts describing
the cap-and-shrink program. However, the company did contest liability,
arguing that (a) its plan was never implemented, and (b) if implemented,
it was of little significance compared to other issues—especially other
(nonpension) business considerations. In the next section, we will consider
its implementation at the Pittsburgh plant.

Understanding the logic of the cap-and-shrink program requires an
appreciation of the structure of benefits negotiated between the USWA
(the union that represented an overwhelming majority of workers in the
can industry) and the company. This union—more than any other industrial
union—was the architect of postwar U.S. private pension benefit standards. As noted in the previous chapter, the right of a union to bargain
for pension and insurance benefits was decided by the NLRB in 1947 and
upheld by the Supreme Court in 1949 in a case involving Inland Steel
Corporation and the union (see Freeman 1985 for a general analysis of the
role of unions in the evolution of American private pensions). Through its
strength in the steel industry, over time the union extended and developed
pension benefits and applied these benefit standards to other industries,
such as aluminum and packaging, in which it had strong representation.
Thus, in many respects the canning industry (including the four major
corporations) followed the pension benefit standards as well as wage and
other benefit standards of the steel industry. By the late 1960s, the canning

industry offered workers normal retirement pensions, health benefits, and early retirement or plant closing pensions comparable to benefits in the steel industry.

To be eligible for an early retirement pension (that is, to retire before the age of 62 and receive accrued benefits) an employee had to have at least fifteen years of continuous service, be at least 50 years of age, and have a combined age and years of service equal to or more than seventy years; or have at least fifteen years of continuous service and have a combined age and years of service equal to or more than seventy-five years—the so-called rule-of-70/75.[8] To be eligible to collect a 70/75 pension, a worker would have to have accrued at least fifteen years of service, be laid off for at least two years or have the company determine within those two years that the worker would not be rehired. Normally, ERISA regulations require that companies must maintain adequate reserves in their pension fund to cover expected long-term pension liabilities—that is, those pension benefits due to workers when they retire at the normal age of retirement. Moreover, the PBGC insures and guarantees those benefits. However, ERISA does not require companies to fund their potential early retirement pension obligations, nor does ERISA or the PBGC guarantee supplemental pension benefits paid to early retirees to supplement their incomes until becoming eligible for Social Security.

Theoretically, Continental's older production workers' incomes (if not their employment) were protected from the worst effects of plant closings. When negotiated in the 1960s in the steel and packaging industries, these benefits were thought important for isolated instances of plant rationalization. Few people in these industries imagined that such benefits would be needed by more than a small fraction of all workers in those industries. Continental did not fund their early retirement pension liabilities, nor did they create a special reserve for potential supplemental benefits. It was anticipated that these liabilities would be paid for out of the corporation's general revenue. This strategy was followed in other basic industries, such as steel and aluminum. During collective-bargaining negotiations with the union in 1974, the company agreed to increase the value of the early retirement pension benefit. And following concurrent negotiations for early retirement benefit changes in the steel industry, in the 1977 round of collective bargaining with the union the company agreed to an additional formula for early retirement pensions—the rule-of-65 (the steel industry settlement agreement was signed in April 1977 and the Continental agreement followed just six months later). Like the 70/75 pension, the rule-of-65 required a combination of age and service to equal at least sixty-five years. However, the rule-of-65 was (and remains) different in a number of respects. To be eligible, employees had to have at least twenty years of continuous service, be at least 40 years of age, and have a combined age and service of at least sixty-five. Whereas the rule of 70/75 allowed for workers to "creep" over two years of layoff to make fifteen years of continuous service, the rule-of-65 required eligible workers to have twenty years service on the day of layoff. If a worker had the required twenty years of service but was less than 45 years of age, the worker was allowed to creep toward the age requirement while on layoff during the subsequent two years. Finally, the rule-of-65 included a clause that an eligible laid-off employee must accept a suitable alternative job offer in the corporation (but not necessarily within the same plant) within a reasonable distance from the employee's home plant or risk losing eligibility for a rule-of-65 pension.[9]

Continental's plans for restructuring their packaging plants brought them immediately against the problem of financing their early retirement or plant-closing pension obligations. As was noted in the previous section, the corporation allocated and spent $231 million and then another $100 million on plant closings and modernization in the early to mid-1970s, and then realized that their potential liabilities were much larger than these funds could handle. Moreover, the company agreed to the rule-of-65 early retirement pension in 1977 after having already spent $331 million on rationalization, and after having realized the potential costs involved in the rule of 70/75 early retirement pension—as well as the added potential costs of the rule-of-65 pension. To control these potential liabilities and the costs of restructuring Continental's packaging company, the corporation designed and implemented in 1976 (one year before agreeing to the rule-of-65) what it termed the "Bell System." In a presentation to senior management, the designers noted that their system could identify plants that had high pension liabilities and shutdown obligations, plants that would have high pension obligations in the future, and individual workers by plant that were nearly eligible for early retirement pensions. Using scattergraphs, the Bell System identified employees who would become eligible for early retirement pensions so that they could be laid off. The system also identified already eligible workers so that they could be employed as long as possible (rather than be laid off, therefore incurring pension liability). The cap-and-shrink program depended on the Bell System to determine each plant's optimum workforce relative to potential pension liabilities (cap) and then determine the optimum reduction in a plant's workforce given local market demand conditions (shrink).

A modified version of the Bell System (Bell II) was then used to instruct plant managers to adjust production to the desired level of employment.

The system could also calculate the potential closing costs of any plant at any given time as well as estimate the savings associated with permanently laying off near-eligible workers at different points in the future. The Bell System provided management with a minimum-cost pension obligation recipe: it capped employment by plant in the short run, and identified the optimal time to close a plant over the long run. Later, in 1977, the corporation introduced what it termed as the "Red Flag" system: an accounting system tied to the corporation's consolidated payroll system that identified employees who were recalled from permanent layoff and were near eligibility for early retirement pension benefits. The corporation would then direct plant officials to again lay off those identified workers. In this manner, senior executives of the corporation tried to keep the Bell System a secret from their own plant managers, and certainly secret from their hourly employees and union representatives.[10]

Implementation of the Bell System

To perfect the Bell System, the corporation selected three older canning plants (Baltimore, Patterson [New Jersey], and Pittsburgh) to be the first plants to test the system. These three plants were called "concept development plants" and were chosen because of their older workforces, their high potential pension liabilities, and low relative labor efficiency. Using December 1979 figures of employment, Continental estimated that these three plants alone carried a potential plant-closing early retirement pension liability of $87 million. The Pittsburgh plant was one of the corporation's oldest plants (built in 1947), designed to produce three-piece steel cans, a technology and product quite outdated by the mid-1970s. In 1975 it was converted to a service center for other plants in the Continental system, producing ends for cans, lithography, and other special items of low volume. It also had a functioning pail-line for making, for example, larger paint and oil cans.

Based on the Bell System, it was determined in 1976 that the plant's ideal cap was around 417 employees (it employed about 940 workers). To achieve this cap, the pail-line was slated for elimination even though it was relatively profitable and located close to customers of the corporation. After considering the possible effects of a rule-of-65 and an increase in the early retirement pension supplement (neither had been negotiated or agreed to with the union at this time; collective-bargaining talks were to begin in 1977), the company decided to cap employment at Pittsburgh at around 436 employees and lay off the near-eligible employees. In a presentation to senior management of the corporation in 1980, it was estimated by the responsible officials that implementation of the Bell System at Pittsburgh had saved the corporation $21 million in plant-closing pensions. The average cost of a rule-of-65 retiree was estimated at about $100,000.[11] At the same presentation, two figures were presented to demonstrate the success of the cap-and-shrink program. Executives were shown the initial (1976) distribution of Pittsburgh plant workers by age and seniority (see Figure 4.1). They were then shown what had happened (by 1980) to those employees under the rule-of-65 line (see Figure 4.2). Just a casual visual comparison between the two figures is enough to convince even the skeptical reader that the program was *both* implemented and highly successful.

By mid-1977 the corporation had decided to close the pail-line and relocate it to a new nonunion site (Fredericksburg, Virginia). In a confidential internal company memo, the logic of this decision was explained as follows: "The most important point associated with this project is the need to relocate this line in order to achieve our PUP action at #72 Pittsburgh" and "The work force management cap associated with the Pittsburgh facility will not allow the proper service of the eastern area and still maintain the work force associated with the pail-line."[12] Just a few months later, the union and company negotiated and agreed to a new contract covering Steelworkers employed by the company in its various plants around the country. The new contract included the rule-of-65 and an increase in the early retirement pension supplement (to $300 per month). The company would not commit itself on the future of the Pittsburgh plant.

To implement the cap-and-shrink program at the Pittsburgh plant, the corporation required a new worker-seniority rule at the plant. Previous to the 1977 contractual agreement, seniority within the plant was based on the time a worker had worked in a particular department of the plant. Thus, a worker who had been employed in the pail-line for twenty-five years would have no seniority rights for employment in the lithograph section. Indeed, a worker with just one year's experience in that section would be able to hold his or her job against a worker with more seniority from another department of the plant. Potentially, this might have meant that a pail-line employee eligible for a rule-of-65 early retirement pension might have to be laid off because of the relocation of the department just as a near-eligible employee retained employment in the lithograph section because the corporation was unable to shift employees around the plant according to plant-wide seniority. The corporation needed such a seniority system if its cap-and-shrink program was to be effective. Coincidentally, the union was also interested in a plant-wide seniority system as part of its new (1977) "Employment and Income Security Program." The ultimate goal of this program was "lifetime job security" recognizing that "most

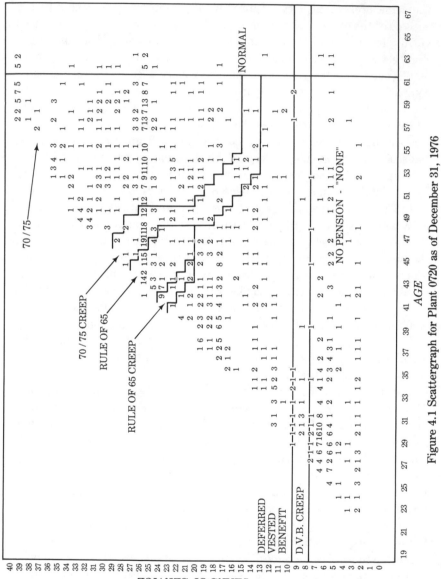

Figure 4.1 Scattergraph for Plant 0720 as of December 31, 1976

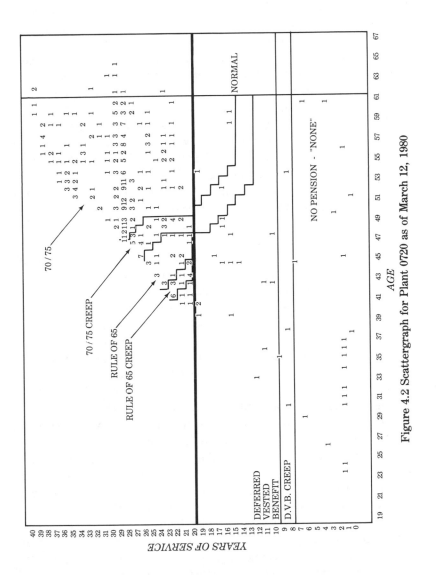

Figure 4.2 Scattergraph for Plant 0720 as of March 12, 1980

employees who work in American industry are highly vulnerable to economic disaster if their plant closes or in the event of a prolonged layoff or
disability."[13] In general, this program was intended to protect the incomes
and employment opportunities of older workers, especially those workers
with twenty or more years of continuous service, in the steel and other
industries in which the union had strong representation.

Plant-wide seniority protected older workers, the union's historical constituency in the industry, from long-term layoffs. Moreover, given the
problems the union had previously encountered in encouraging racial and
sexual integration of their represented plants, the seniority clause may
have also served to encourage greater acceptance of preferential hiring,
and at the same time give existing minority and female employees greater
protection from layoff in the case of departmental closings, which were
increasingly common in the steel industry. It should also be noted that it
was the union that forced through this policy in the steel industry (against
considerable opposition from the companies); the principle of protecting
those workers with at least twenty years of continuous service was tested
by the steel companies in arbitration. In the can industry, the companies
accepted the principle quite readily—in Continental's case it is easy enough
to see why. Once the new plant-wide seniority policy was ratified, the Bell
System was fully implemented. The pail-line was relocated, other departments reduced in size, and employment shrunk to 438. Using the Bell
System, management designated near-eligible employees for permanent
layoff status while arguing to the union that rationalization was needed at
these plants for market reasons. None of the employees laid off under the
Bell System was informed of the permanent layoff status. Most remained
unemployed for two years and thus exhausted their recall eligibility.

Having successfully implemented the Bell System in the three concept-
development plants, the corporation then moved to implement the system
in its other plants. Nineteen plants were identified as having the highest
potential early retirement pension liabilities. Seventeen of these plants
were exclusively represented by the USWA. In Table 4.3 these plants are
identified and located by state. Many of these plants were in the northeast
(Maryland, New Jersey, and Pennsylvania) and the Midwest (especially
Chicago). The other plants were in older industrial cities (such as Birmingham and Los Angeles). The apparent geographical pattern of "capping" reflected the older average age of the plants, the relative obsoles-
cence of production technology and products produced at these plants, and
higher than average maintenance and public utility costs (including higher
than average taxes) in running these plants. Basically, the location of
capping reflected the inherited spatial structure of production and the

Table 4.3 Capped Plants by Region, City, and State
and Union Status, 1975–1980

Atlantic Region
  Baltimore (USWA)
  Hurlock, Md. (USWA)
  Pulaski, Md. (USWA)
  Malden, N.J.
  Passaic, N.J. (USWA)
  Patterson, N.J. (USWA)
  West Mifflin (Pittsburgh, Pa.) (USWA)
Midwest
  Clearing (Chicago) (USWA)
  North Grand (Chicago) (USWA)
  Stockyards (Chicago) (USWA)
  Elwood, Ind. (USWA)
  Mankato, Minn.
  St. Louis (USWA)
  Cincinnati (USWA)
South
  Birmingham, Ala. (USWA)
  Tampa, Fla.
  Houston
West
  Los Angeles (USWA)
  Denver (USWA)

Source: Document #261 case file, Federal District
Court of Western Pennsylvania.

local labor relations between the union and the company.

Although it is unclear precisely when these plants were capped, and
what the savings were to the corporation, in a presentation of the program's success to senior management in 1980 it was claimed that the
program had not only significantly reduced potential pension liability but
it had also reduced the significance of the union in terms of its representation of Continental's production workforce. It was also reported that at
least 1,800 employees had been shrunk (permanently laid off prior to their
eligibility for early retirement pensions) with projected savings of as much
as $500 million. As a by-product of the capping strategy, management also
realized that it could reduce its overall pension expenses by relocating
work to nonunionized or at least non-USWA plants. Pension benefit contributions cost the company $181 per worker per month in USWA plants
compared to $82 per worker per month in younger other-union plants, and

$61 per worker per month in nonunion new plants. Managers of the Bell System also reported that the USWA's representation of hourly employees had gone from 82 percent in 1976 to 64 percent in 1980. They believed that the Bell System had the potential to eliminate totally the Steelworkers' representation of Continental's production workers over the next ten or so years. While perhaps not originally designed to be an antiunion strategy, in effect, because of the USWA's benefit structure and because the union dominated the older packaging plants, the Bell System was targeted on Steelworker-represented plants. We do not need a Machiavellian interpretation of corporate decisionmaking (compare with Clark 1989a, chap. 3) to realize the fundamental nexus between corporate restructuring and antiunion corporate policy—the union's power and benefit policies were the essential target of the Bell System.

The corporation's antiunion strategy was apparent in other ways. When relocating the pail-line from West Mifflin to Fredericksburg the company refused to open negotiations and consider possible concessions from the union that would encourage the company to keep the line in Pittsburgh. It deliberately chose a nonunion setting to forestall the union from gaining local representation. Moreover, it did not encourage laid-off employees to transfer to the new plant even though they might arguably have qualified as a suitable long-term employment (SLTE) opportunity.[14] Whereas the corporation had targeted USWA plants for capping and closing some time in the future, its new plants (at least fifteen were opened between 1972 and 1980) were planned to be at least non-USWA if not entirely union-free. In these ways, the objectives of the Bell System overlapped and reinforced other corporate objectives, notably its interest in reducing the influence of the union.

Allocating the Costs of Restructuring

I have argued that the origins of Continental's early retirement pension-avoidance system are to be found in the corporation's competitive and strategic policies. From the mid-1960s to the early 1970s, the corporation achieved dominance of the packaging industry by acquiring and building new plants and introducing new production technologies. As a consequence of added capacity, the corporation was vulnerable to shifts and changes in the market, as well as to the technological evolution of the industry. *In situ* restructuring was an early response. Later, plant closings and the rationalization and relocation of production within and between plants became the operative solution. Restructuring is in part a response to competition. It is also apparent that Continental's restructuring policies

were shaped and influenced by management's ambitions for the corporation
to become a large and diversified conglomerate. The logic of this management policy is best described by the BCG's strategic management philosophy pioneered by B. Henderson (1979). The corporation's packaging business was treated as a cash cow; revenue and then assets were diverted
to pay for corporate acquisitions in the so-called postindustrial sectors of
insurance and financial services and energy resources. To make the management strategy work, given competition in the packaging business, the
corporation had to simultaneously rationalize its production system and
limit the costs of rationalization. Rather than renegotiate early retirement
pension benefits or try to freeze pension obligations, the corporation agreed
to increased pension benefits *and* set in place an accounting system designed to circumvent their pension liabilities and deny workers their legal
rights.

In these ways, the Bell System was designed to shift the costs of corporate restructuring from the corporation to individual workers. At the
Pittsburgh plant, hundreds of workers were permanently laid off and ultimately denied their pension entitlements. Over the whole corporation,
perhaps four thousand workers were affected by this restructuring policy,
especially those located in older, Steelworker-represented plants. In this
sense, the costs of restructuring were allocated by plant location, the union
representing local workers, and the age and seniority of the plant's workers. By this interpretation, restructuring had a remarkable, differential
geographical impact. However, the geography of production was not simply a passive recipient of the corporation's restructuring policies. The very
design and implementation of the Bell System was based upon the inherited
spatial structure of production. Plants were chosen for the Bell System
on the basis of their location in the labor-management relations system of
the corporation, for their location in the market for containers, and for
their location in the overall cost structure of the corporation. The spatial
fixity of restructuring was determined by the spatially differentiated character and historical sequence of growth of the corporation's productive
capacity, given local labor relations.

For the workers and the communities affected by Continental's restructuring policies, the effects of the Bell System were immediate and long-
term. Workers' incomes and long-term employment prospects were seriously impaired. For the corporation, though, the Bell System saved the
corporation hundreds of millions of dollars. From the initial implementation
of the system in the mid-1970s to the filing of the civil suit in federal
district court in 1981, the corporation grew very rapidly—in asset value,
in revenue, and in profits. The consolidated corporate accounts for the

period show that the corporation nearly doubled its sales (from \$3,101 million in 1975 to \$5,194 million in 1981), more than doubled its net cash flow (from \$167 million in 1975 to \$476 million in 1981), and increased its net cash flow as a percentage of stockholders' equity (from 19.3 percent in 1975 to 30.3 percent in 1981). The LBO of the corporation benefited senior management (who were voted stock options in the mid-1970s), stockholders, the financial community, and the new owners. Restructuring did not benefit workers. They unwittingly helped pay for, and became the victims of, restructuring and diversification.[15]

It is important to draw out the implications of this case for the larger set of policy issues related to the impact of corporate restructuring on American institutions. In particular, we are most concerned about the consequences of these kinds of corporate strategies for the institutional structure of the American economy and the integrity of governmental regulation of corporate statutory responsibilities.

At the outset of this book and throughout chapter 2, I argued that restructuring is assumed to be a private responsibility—an assumption consistent with the official version of the United States as a decentralized economy and polity. Echoing this sentiment, R. K. Weaver (1985) noted that even compared to Canada, debate over U.S. industrial policy presumes that the market, not government policy, is best equipped to decide what should be the response of American business to changes in the competitive environment. This presumption was tested in the last years of the Carter presidency by the Chrysler bailout, and a growing realization that military spending and other kinds of government procurement policies have marked, even deliberate, consequences for technical innovation and growth of American industry, corporations, and regions (see Markusen and Carlson 1989). Nevertheless, these exceptions and procurement policies tend to reinforce opposition to explicit centralized policies rather than extend a mandate for government intervention. This vision of private decentralized responsibility for economic restructuring is reinforced by a set of institutions that were also designed to maximize local discretion. In the context of the Continental cases, the most relevant institutions are the system of labor relations created by the Wagner Act of 1935 and the regulations governing competition and monopoly first conceived in the Sherman Act of 1890 and later extended and developed by the Antitrust Division of the U.S. Department of Justice. Both sets of laws had an economic vision or ideal of America as a decentralized (by geography, sectors, and ownership patterns) but integrated (with trade between states, sectors, and firms) system of commodity exchange. The Wagner Act, in part, envisioned labor representation to a local phenomenon guided by the electoral preferences of workers for and against representation. By this system, neither organized labor nor capital was to dominate the other, rather the individual worker was to be sovereign. Likewise, the Sherman Act envisioned price competition to be between firms rather than dominated by one or a few firms; the consumer was to be sovereign (see Fisher et al. 1983).

The kind of corporate restructuring strategies pursued by Continental from the early 1970s, through to its acquisition and breakup by Kiewit, challenged the integrity of these institutions of decentralized decision-making in a number of ways. The implementation of management's secret plan of pension cost avoidance and limitation depended on hoodwinking the union. Plant-wide seniority was the only way production could be internally rationalized to protect the employment of those already eligible for rule-of-65 early retirement pensions and permanently lay off those close to eligibility. The company used the union's interests in securing the employment prospects of older workers against younger workers. In doing so, the company (and its principal executives) violated (but depended upon) the trust and confidence of the union; trust and confidence are essential for the continuing functioning of the collective-bargaining system. The company's subversion of trust and confidence was apparent in other ways. Although it negotiated and agreed to the rule-of-65 pension and the supplement in the 1977 collective-bargaining agreement, it had already designed the Bell System to avoid its voluntarily agreed to pension obligations. Those near-eligible employees permanently laid off as a result of the Bell System were not the only casualties of the system. The Bell System denied the integrity of the collective-bargaining agreement and the continuing relationship between the company and the union. Most obviously, the use of the Bell System to destroy the union's representation of workers in the company attacks the very notion of the sovereignty of workers' preferences for representation. The Bell System, in effect, penalized workers for their choice of union without offering local workers a chance to reevaluate the terms or conditions of their agreement with the company.

That all these actions were, of course, illegal appears in retrospect to be unexceptional, given other illegal pricing and management strategies of the corporation. Industry spokespersons have noted that the corporation had been involved for many years in price fixing and market-segmentation practices contrary to the Sherman Act and antitrust regulations of the Department of Justice. In this case, price fixing denied the sovereignty of the consumer; the benefits of competition were systematically eschewed in favor of the collective profits of the industry and the dominant firms. The use of the canning business as a cash cow for acquisitions and diversification was not, however, illegal. On the other hand, asset stripping, disinvestment, plant relocations, and leveraged buyouts all deny the interests of the workers involved while fostering the interests of management, the banks, and shareholders.

If the integrity of U.S. institutions of decentralized collective bargaining and price setting were challenged by the actions of corporations like Continental in avoiding their pension obligations, it should be immediately obvious that these same actions more fundamentally threatened the integrity of ERISA and the related pension regulations administered by federal government agencies including the PBGC, the IRS, and DOL. Perhaps, compared to collective bargaining and price setting, the implications of the corporation's actions for the integrity of national pension policy are clearer. After all, with respect to ERISA the corporation deliberately and secretly broke the law. If many other corporations do the same (a real possibility, according to industry and union analysts), the pension prospects of many millions of manufacturing workers are in jeopardy. In this context, I would argue that based on the evidence drawn from the Continental Can cases, the corporate challenge to the integrity of the private pension system need not be imagined as an isolated or unusual case of corporate chicanery. Corporate restructuring may involve the systematic denial of a wide range of laws that protect workers and consumers, as well as denial of their economic and social (nonlegal) interests. To reemphasize, at issue in corporate restructuring is the allocation of the costs of restructuring. This may involve the corporation in a game that cuts across many other institutions and regulations that society values. It is more than just a question of who won or lost in a particular company strategy.

Summary—The Integrity of ERISA

Whereas Peter Drucker (1988) claimed that pension fund *assets* were the ultimate cause of takeover mania during the 1980s, I would argue that corporate restructuring is often designed and implemented according to potential (and actual) pension *liabilities*. Although ERISA protects workers' pension fund assets and their eligibility for pensions, it is clear that pension liabilities are of fundamental concern to corporate strategists. In this case, it was shown in federal court that Continental relocated production, allocated resources, and structured employment on the basis of future pension liabilities rather than the immediate best-use of resources given local demand. Continental can hardly be accused (as American corporations are often accused) of simply maximizing short-run returns without regard to long-run investment opportunities or revenue needs (see Melman 1983). Rather, Continental was more than willing to compromise on short-run returns by utilizing its plant network in such a way that their long-run plant-closing pension liabilities were minimized and their diversification maximized.

For all the debate over the economic and geographical consequences of corporate restructuring, there has been little recognition of the scale of pension obligations and the implications of pension-oriented restructuring for the integrity of American institutions and public policy. For example, D. P. Quinn's (1988) study of restructuring of the automobile industry seems to focus too closely on the macroinstitutions of government and the mix of public/private responsibility for restructuring, ignoring the issues of how difficult it can be to exit an industry, how the costs of restructuring are to be allocated, and how restructuring may cut across corporations' legal responsibilities. On the other side of these issues, D. Harvey's (1988) recent argument that sketches the on-going transition from Fordist production systems to flexible accumulation seems to discount the institutional and legal structure of corporate obligations to their workers, supposing these responsibilities are simply annihilated by economic imperatives. The relationship between corporations' statutory obligations and the economic and geographical imperatives of restructuring is more problematic than his assessment would allow. At one level, it might be argued that this chapter has made Harvey's case for the annihilation of statutory responsibilities by economic imperatives. The evidence presented here implies that many other corporations may be deliberately and secretly subverting their legal responsibilities.

To imagine that economic imperatives simply annihilate social obligations is a tempting response. However, such an interpretation would ignore two essential aspects of this and the other case studies. One, the case study appeared in the first instance as a legal suit brought by the affected workers against the corporation. While it may be too late to return these workers to the circumstances of the late 1970s, if the courts were to enforce significant penalties for violating ERISA the very design and implementation of corporate restructuring relative to corporate statutory responsibilities may be significantly changed. Two, although companies and individuals do many things that are against the law, their responsibility to the law is not simply a matter of adequate enforcement. The laws represent social expectations of appropriate and inappropriate behavior. Violating Section 510 of ERISA was more than a matter of economic need. In doing so, Continental violated social conventions and social institutions that have a separate status and history from the corporation and the economy at large. These conventions and institutions may be valued more highly than economic imperatives. Indeed, as in the case of ERISA, they may have been deliberately designed to counter economic imperatives. Until recently, we have not been accustomed to setting the process of corporate restructuring within such a moral or ethical context. Nevertheless, I will argue that the ethical context of restructuring is crucial for understanding its regulation.

5

Piercing the Corporate Veil

Restructuring is usually considered to be a problem of simple economics. From the locality, to the nation, to the world, whatever the scale of analysis, agents are assumed to be propelled by economic imperatives. Theories of restructuring, like my own disequilibrium dynamic adjustment model (Clark et al. 1986), Michael Webber's (Webber and Tonkin 1990) theory of crisis and intersectoral disequilibrium, even theories of the long run advocated by those who claim to have identified the emergence of a new regime of accumulation (post-Fordism) are all based on such economic imperatives. However useful these theories are (in an aggregate sense) in providing a broad account of the patterns of economic events and local outcomes, they tend to ignore or trivialize human agency, particularly corporate strategy, and the role of law in regulating the process of restructuring. This is despite the fact that most theories of restructuring are based on notions of corporate behavior drawn from other well-developed theoretical perspectives; witness the application of R. Coase's (1960) transaction-cost theory to understanding the geographical structure of production (Scott 1988). In this chapter, the framework introduced in chapter 2 is extended to consider how restructuring intersects with regulation as an administrative process. In particular, the value of regulation theory (the French version) is evaluated with respect to competing notions of regulation as an institutional practice.

Restructuring is here analyzed as a corporate strategy of rationalization, impacting a specific plant and community—in this instance Wisconsin Steel Company (WSC), located in southside Chicago. While this is undoubtedly a partial view, minimizing for the moment the macroscopic geographical character of restructuring, the interest here is in the design and implementation of restructuring as a corporate strategy. The actions of International Harvester Corporation (IHC) in first selling WSC to a small consulting company through a LBO and then precipitating the bankruptcy and closure of WSC by calling in its outstanding loans to the buying company are the essential beginnings of the case study. More generally,

at issue is the logic of corporate strategy in the context of statutory requirements policed by the PBGC, and how subsequent decisions of a federal
district court judge found that Harvester had deliberately and illegally
created a "sham corporation" to protect itself from unfunded pension liabilities.

Throughout this chapter, the focus is upon the intersection between
regulation and economic imperatives. Notice, though, because of the literature context within which the case study is initially situated, regulation
as a concept has two distinct meanings. At one level *regulation,* as a term
used by theorists (notably Aglietta 1979) of the French regulation school,
refers to an ensemble of structures that maintain and coordinate relations
between departments (sectors) of a market economy, ensuring some balance between production and consumption, and thereby allowing for the
reproduction of the existing mode of production. As will become clear, I
also use the term *regulation* to refer to laws and statutes whose logic is
not wholly determined by the economic imperatives of capitalism. In this
sense, regulation is an apparatus of the state and an organized (institutionalized) social practice with rules and customs legitimized by reference
to social norms perhaps deliberately conceived in opposition to economic
imperatives. The reference point here is not the French regulation theory
but the governmental practice, which owes its immediate origins to the
New Deal, of administrative and judicial adjudication of social conflict (see
Sunstein 1987).[1]

A Plant Closing in South Chicago

For most of the post–World War II era, IHC was an internationally diversified company, manufacturing farm implements, self-propelled heavy
machinery and construction equipment, and trucks (among other activities). Prior to its sale of WSC to EDC Holdings in 1977, Harvester had
operated WSC for seventy-five years as a wholly owned vertically integrated steel plant of perhaps 1.2 million tons capacity located on the south
side of Chicago.[2] On March 27, 1980, Harvester declared WSC in default
of its debts to the company and reclaimed its collateral, WSC's mines and
railroads, thereby precipitating the bankruptcy and ultimately the permanent closure of WSC. On the following day, the employment of 90
percent of WSC's hourly workers and 75 percent of its salaried workers
was terminated (some 3,500 workers). WSC filed for Chapter 11 bankruptcy. By May 16, 1980, the PBGC had agreed to the termination of
WSC's pension plans in accordance with Section 4042(a) of ERISA.[3]

As a plant closure, the bankruptcy of WSC was by no means unusual or remarkable, given the extraordinary wave of plant closings that B. Bluestone and B. Harrison (1982) associated with deindustrialization. They estimated (extending Birch's 1979 work) that between 1969 and 1976 as many as 22 million jobs were lost through plant shutdowns and relocations, with many losses concentrated in the midwest United States. Their analysis of the negative consequences of plant closings for communities was especially revealing, matched in this case by the traumatic affects that the closing of WSC had on employment and income in south Chicago.[4] When compared to the crisis of the U.S. steel industry in the late 1970s and early 1980s involving the permanent loss of 300,000 jobs concentrated in just a few regions (Clark 1988), the failure of WSC in 1980 appears as yet another example of deindustrialization. However, the closure of WSC was more than a case of deindustrialization as if WSC as a corporate entity was simply overcome by economic imperatives operating at higher levels of abstraction. Its very creation as a separate company vulnerable to bankruptcy was a vital part of a strategy of restructuring conceived and implemented by IHC's senior management in the mid-1970s.

WSC was created by Envirodyne (the parent company of EDC Holdings) in 1977 through a LBO of IHC's steel division.[5] The sale price was $15 million in cash, and $50 million in secured notes, all of which was financed by outside lenders—especially IHC (a later attempt to involve the U.S. Economic Development Administration in refinancing the deal was too late to save the company).[6] For Harvester, the sell-off of WSC was the way out of a losing proposition. Its antiquated steel division had accumulated before-tax losses of $77 million over 1970–76 and could have cost the corporation as much as $175 million (including $86 million for pensions) to liquidate.[7] Immediate capital needs (just for maintaining the running capital without modernizing the plant) were estimated by a potential buyer to be as much as $150 million. As Justice James Moran noted, the costs of continuing to operate WSC were such that IHC made "a corporate decision to get out of the steel business and to divert that capital to more profitable ventures that were part of its core business" (p. 6).[8] This kind of corporate restructuring strategy, often termed "back-to-basics," was typical of the late 1970s and early 1980s. It was promoted by management consulting firms, the same firms who had led the earlier moves into conglomeration (compare Ravenscraft and Scherer 1987 with Piore and Sabel 1984).

To reemphasize, the LBO of WSC and then its failure was not so remarkable given the general crisis of the U.S. steel industry in the early 1980s. What is remarkable is the way IHC went about the sale of WSC and how those actions prompted the civil suit brought in federal district court by the PBGC against IHC.[9] The PBGC alleged that IHC remained liable for WSC's pension obligations despite the apparent change of ownership. By the terms of the PBGC's suit the sale of WSC was an illegal, "fraudulent," and "sham" transaction designed to evade or at least limit the corporation's legally mandated obligations to its workers. The PBGC charged that the corporation should be held liable for pension obligations arising from the termination of the WSC pension plans. In essence, the PBGC asked the court to look beyond the formal record ownership and "pierce the corporate veil" so as to assign liability to IHC. In his judgment handed down in November 1988, Justice Moran validated most PBGC charges. He contended that the company had deliberately and illegally sought to "evade" its responsibilities for WSC's unfunded pension liabilities (p. 20). Moran asserted that Harvester's senior management, although realizing that WSC had little chance of success, had believed that the sale of WSC and its operation as a wholly independent company would allow Harvester to evade its unfunded pension liabilities. Indeed, Justice Moran suggested that even the timing of IHC's calling-in of WSC's debts was conceived so as to limit its obligations to the PBGC (p. 20). The closing of WSC was the direct result, though not particularly the intended result, of IHC's restructuring strategy which, like other corporate restructuring strategies, had as one of its essential motives avoidance of legally protected but unfunded pension liabilities.

The details of the case will be developed in more detail in subsequent sections. Given the significance I have assigned to the case study, however, it is crucial to understand the way in which the case study is used. At one level, the sale of WSC is a story of corporate strategy and the exigencies of publicly imposed pension obligations. This case and the cases related to Continental Can bring into the open the significance of private pensions in the corporate restructuring process (see chapters 3 and 4). However, the case is not meant to be representative of the normal or average corporate restructuring strategy. Rather, it is meant to be an *exemplary* case that allows for in-depth analysis of issues normally too close to the boundaries of conventional categories. Exemplary cases allow us to identify fundamental problems of and reflect upon the stability of standard assumptions. The case study is also a *leading* case in that it helps define, if not exactly clarify, the legal and public obligations of U.S. corporations in designing and implementing their restructuring strategies. The decisions of Justice Moran have established in a legal sense a distinct and legitimate separation between the economic imperatives of restructuring and public policy interests.

Restructuring and Regulation

Situating the case study within the context of the theory of restructuring would seem to be, at first sight, the obvious next step. However, as was noted in chapter 2, there is no one theory of restructuring. Rather, the literature is dominated by accumulated observations about the dimensions and characteristics of the process. Here, a series of related arguments are made about restructuring as a way of establishing my own perspective on the theory of regulation. Since the case study might easily be thought to be about a plant closing, I begin with the related literature in regional economic development.

Arguably, the theory of regional economic structure was settled two decades ago. Based on B. Ohlin's (1933) pioneering work on interregional trade and G. Borts and J. Stein's (1964) application of neoclassical growth theory to regional economic performance, regions' economic well-being was thought to be the product of comparative advantage mediated by the efficiency of labor. Trade provided the basis for growth and labor productivity determined the local real wage level. This theory was (and remains) static in a temporal sense, being equilibrium-oriented. There is no basis for analyzing the path of local economic change. Indeed, economic change over time is irrelevant compared to metastructural imperatives (compare with Clark et al. 1986). Two decades later, the neoclassical regional economic growth model is in tatters. Scholars have discovered that it was empirically unfounded (although this was apparent in Borts and Stein's original work). As well, the object of scholars' attention has shifted and with the shift of focus neoclassical growth theory has become irrelevant. Whereas neoclassical growth theory provided a recipe for understanding the allocation of capital and labor between regions, scholars have become more interested in understanding and explaining the map of deindustrialization and how restructuring affects particular places. Inevitably, because of the focus on the paths of change and not on the logic of system-wide stability, the literature has become more varied and speculative, involving notions that are at once more contingent or conjunctive in terms of their historical origins, and less analytically tractable in terms of the inherited neoclassical tradition.

It is now difficult to think of just one theory, or one method of analyzing restructuring. Nevertheless, most scholars would readily agree that restructuring is a process of rationalization (rather than simply the destruction of whole industries and places, as in deindustrialization), even if there are many versions of this process. Most would also agree with J. Graham et al.'s (1988) characterization of the dimensions of restructuring, which focuses upon the organization and technology of production, the form of corporation, and the social relations of production (labor relations and unions). These dimensions intersect with, and are determined in part by, the inherited spatial structure. Thus, there is a certain degree of determining "power" associated with the geography of production (using Wolch and Dear's 1988 term), realized in a physical and locational form according to the spatial "lumpiness" of capital (Gertler 1988). Clearly, the inherited structure of production matters in the design and implementation of restructuring. But we must be careful not to overestimate the determining power of structure. Restructuring should also be understood as an organized strategy of corporate change and transformation. As a strategy, restructuring aims to remake the landscape in an image conceived by corporate planners. Thus, the inherited structure of production may be a constraint on that process but it may be also the object of corporate restructuring. Through restructuring, the structure of production is attacked from within.

The significance of my point can be illustrated by critically considering assumptions of the currently fashionable idea of an emerging (or new) regime of accumulation termed *flexible accumulation* or *post-Fordism*. Those who advocate flexible accumulation as the wave of the future suppose the mode of production (in a very broad sense) is being completely restructured so as to be both more flexible *and* technologically adaptive at a smaller economic scale located at fewer more specialized locations. Obviously, this mode of organization has a spatial analogue and implications for the proper organization of the public sector. Strands to the flexible accumulation thesis include the technology-oriented industrial district perspective of M. Piore and C. Sabel (1984), A. Scott's (1988) spatial reagglomeration thesis, through to the French regulation school (Lipietz 1987). To the extent that these approaches foreshadow the emergence of a new regime of accumulation, these authors make, I believe, three basic but unfortunate assumptions.

First, it is assumed that restructuring is a process designed with respect to a desired end-point. Put slightly differently, restructuring is the means (rationalization) to an end (flexible accumulation); in the language of contemporary philosophy this is a consequentialist theory of change. To make this assumption work, though, another often unrecognized assumption must be made about the putative efficiency of economic agents. Specifically, it must be assumed that agents aim at an end-point that is not theirs alone, and that their restructuring policies are designed in accordance with that shared (if unarticulated) collective vision. This assumption presumes the availability of information (undifferentiated by time or space) and the relative efficiency of agents' resource allocation decisions. The third assumption is that structure drives agents' actions and that these economic imperatives are unambiguous (in the sense of well defined) or unavoidable (in the sense of being dominant). These imperatives could be both unambiguous and largely unavoidable.[10]

All three assumptions serve to reinforce theorists' aesthetic presuppositions that the path of adjustment is less relevant than the end-point. It is as if theorists have skipped over the real-time process of restructuring to get to the end of the process and thus the proclamation of a new reality. Unfortunately, analysts have ignored the possibility that the end-point of restructuring is path-dependent, and is thus determined by the interaction among actions, events, and intentions. By idealizing the future, analysts are prone to what I would term a "recognition problem." How do we recognize the significance of current events given uncertainty about the future? If we idealize the future, the recognition problem is circumvented but at the cost of trivializing the present. One is reminded of a recent scientific scandal where it was asserted that cold-water nuclear fusion is possible, but the process whereby such fusion occurs was shown to be inconceivable. More concretely, these three assumptions are entirely consistent with the assumptions of neoclassical regional growth models of a previous generation. Those models were static (non–adjustment oriented), cross-sectional (assuming constant technology and spatial homogeneity), and equilibrium-oriented. By this assessment, the theory of flexible accumulation is nothing more (in an analytical sense) than a stylized version of standard regional economic theory.

The most problematic aspect of the theory of flexible accumulation is its dependence on economic imperatives. By argument and assumption, economic imperatives are thought to be strong enough to annihilate past modes of organization and to restructure the related institutions that regulate the dominant regime of accumulation. Just below the surface of Aglietta's argument is the hoary old idea of the base (economic imperatives) determining the superstructure (social and political regulation). And, like mainstream neoclassical theories, also hidden from view is a general equilibrium model of structural imperatives (an analytical device) only arbitrarily lagged (termed "history") to suggest the passage of time.

The notion that economic imperatives annihilate old forms of organization (social and political) implies a coherence of structure and process that is incredible. It mistakes the end-point, where apparently there will be *one* dominant mode of economic structure, for the process of rationalization. Where there may be contested and countervailing processes of restructuring, the theory of flexible accumulation rationalizes, in an analytical sense, the very processes that are presumed to give it life. And where social and political forces intersect with economic restructuring, it is presumed that those forces are too weak, too compromised by their dependence upon the past regime of accumulation to affect the path of change, or so well organized that they reinforce the path of economic imperatives propelling agents to a new end-point. Restructuring is not so neat or so easily foretold. Nor should it be assumed that economic imperatives are as coherent and well defined as has to be assumed by proponents of the French regulation school. If it is admitted that economic imperatives are actually historically contingent and spatially heterogeneous, then it also has to be admitted that social and political forces (regulation in general) have a life of their own. Discussing the relationship between social and political ideas and economic imperatives, G. Bremner (1983) made a useful point that applies here, even if not related to precisely the same subject matter. Although accepting (and indeed arguing for the relevance of) the importance of economic forces "on the lives of all those whose attitudes they are claimed to form," he also cautioned against allotting "a privileged function to one realm [economic imperatives] of experience, to cast it in the role of cause" without investigating further the intersection between economic imperatives and other phenomena.

An essential theoretical premise of this book is that restructuring is a process of experimentation where the end-point is not known and where the costs and risks of restructuring are considerable. Another premise is that the strategy of restructuring varies according to circumstances, thus affecting the path of change as well as the destination. In one setting, the goal of restructuring may be to be economically competitive with other domestic and foreign firms. In another setting, the goal of restructuring in unionized environments may be to limit, even destroy, the power of unions, thereby broadening managements' discretion and control over production. And in other settings, restructuring may have as its purpose the increased value of shares listed on the stock market just as restructuring may be used to reduce the incentives for hostile takeovers.

Sale of Wisconsin Steel

If IHC's sale and then induced closure of WSC was impelled by economic imperatives, the design and implementation of IHC's restructuring strategy was conceived within a specific historical and legal context. As a corporate strategy, it was neither especially efficient nor necessarily consistent with some theorists' imaginary future. It was, by its very nature, experimental (there being no legal precedent) and risky (there being grave doubts about the capacity of WSC to survive). IHC took a calculated gamble that the PBGC would not hold it liable for or would at least prorate its obligations over time WSC's pension obligations if (and when) WSC failed. That IHC's strategy was designed to overcome federal regulations concerning corporate liability for unfunded plant-closing pensions suggests that the case is an instance of economic imperatives colliding with public power.

Through much of the early 1970s, IHC actively sought a buyer for its steel division. The company contacted as many as eighty firms located throughout the world (including Australia) in its efforts to sell the plant. At a time when the U.S. steel industry was relatively profitable, large and small companies turned down the offer, including Republic Steel, Sharon Steel, Kaiser Steel, Lukens Steel, and Inland Steel. After failing to consummate a deal in 1975 with McLouth Steel that would have rid IHC of its plant for a pretax loss of $65.3 million (and after-tax loss of about $40 million), it was estimated that simply to liquidate the plant would have cost the company nearly $140 million—a sum greater than IHC's consolidated profit for any year since 1966. A combination of accumulating capital needs, warnings from its accounting firm that IHC would have to write down the plant, and the collapse of WSC's secondary (outside) market for steel prompted IHC's senior management to initiate talks with Envirodyne, a small, privately held environmental consulting firm.

At the time of sale, Envirodyne employed about twelve people, had no experience in the steel industry, was itself losing money, and was desperate for cash to roll over a bank loan of about $2 million. After a quick round of negotiations, IHC's board of directors tentatively approved the sale in May 1977. An internal analysis of the benefits of selling the plant to Envirodyne's EDC Holdings estimated that IHC could save as much as $76 million even if WSC failed within two years and if IHC could avoid paying the PBGC its pension liabilities. The sale provided Envirodyne a yearly $1 million "management fee," the payoff of outstanding loans owed to the principals of the firm, and payoff of a loan owed to a bank. The sale also provided that EDC Holdings would assume the unfunded pension liabilities, pay IHC $15 million in cash, and assume $50 million in notes. Chase Bank provided the $15 million in cash (secured by a guarantee of purchase of WSC's iron ore and coal inventories), and IHC accepted the $50 million in notes (secured by WSC's mines and railroads).

In their post-trial position paper to the court, the PBGC summarized the deal in the following terms: "Put simply, the sale was structured so that all the participants, IHC, Envirodyne, Phibro [the company guaranteeing to buy WSC's inventories] and Chase, could be paid from and be secured by WSC's assets, without accepting any downside risk. The down-side risk was to be borne by the PBGC and WSC's employees" (p. 15).[11] Envirodyne protected itself by setting up EDC Holdings and subsidiaries as shell corporations. During the negotiations leading up to the sale of WSC, IHC's management were warned that the deal "appeared flimsy" and could open up IHC to significant legal charges of fraud and evasion of statutory responsibilities. Nevertheless, senior management went out of their way to force the sale.

At a meeting with the PBGC in March 1977, IHC's lawyers floated a hypothetical plan (hiding the magnitude of WSC's pension liabilities from the PBGC) to sell to a "thinly capitalized buyer." Notwithstanding the PBGC's warning of the likelihood of a suit in such circumstances, the general counsel of IHC advised that the company should go ahead with the sale, suggesting that in any event the PBGC would not be successful with such a suit. In mid-May, Cravath, Swaine, and Moore (one of the largest and most prestigious U.S. corporate law firms) warned IHC that the sale of its plant would not provide the company with a "clean break" from its pension obligations. Cravath noted that, given the lack of expe-rience of EDC Holdings and the problems of WSC, there was little like-lihood of operating WSC successfully. And Lehman Brothers (the Wall Street firm brought in at the last moment to blunt Cravath's warnings), advised in mid-June that an EDC-led WSC would not succeed and that the sale was obviously a "sham" whose "main purpose" was to "avoid [and] evade pension and other past service liabilities" (p. 19). Senior manage-ment of IHC either withheld or diluted the thrust of these criticisms; the board gave formal approval to the sale in July 1977.[12]

Almost immediately after the sale, WSC began experiencing financial difficulties. In 1977 (after being forced by IHC to pay the yearly pension installment) it lost $500 million. In 1978 it lost $17 million and in 1979 nearly $44 million. WSC faced a cash shortage affecting its property tax payments, pension and insurance installments, and interest payments to Chase and IHC. And as a consequence of these cash shortfalls, there was little chance of actually investing in modernization of the plant. So as to avoid EDC declaring bankruptcy as long as possible, IHC sought the advice and financial support of the U.S. Economic Development Admin-istration. Without that support, officials of IHC believed that WSC would be unable to meet its mandated pension contribution (the normal quarterly contribution based upon hours worked and defined benefit levels) to the PBGC in September 1979, perhaps signaling to the PBGC the company's immanent insolvency. The IHC issued loan guarantees protecting WSC from immediate creditors (the PBGC included), and in a few instances provided resources for pension fund contributions.[13] Nonetheless, WSC could not be sustained. Early in 1980 IHC was forced to intervene to protect its own assets—the mines and railroads—thereby precipitating the bankruptcy of WSC.

As described in the context of pension liabilities, the economic imperatives (IHC's costs of rationalization) and geographical consequences of restructuring (the sale and closure of WSC) can be readily understood. In order to restructure, corporations have designed strategies around the functional structure of their inherited plant and equipment, paying particular attention to the spatial configuration of their plant-closing pension liabilities (compare with chapter 4). Still open for analysis is an adequate explanation of the LBO: how and why did the buyer participate in this scheme, knowing the chances of success were slim (given the deteriorating physical plant of WSC) and the continuing pension obligations it would be liable for? This question can be asked as an intellectual issue, being relevant to the development of the theory of restructuring, but it has been also asked of the litigants in the PBGC's suits against IHC.

To answer this question requires a more subtle theoretical apparatus than is so far apparent in the analysis of exit costs and corporate strategies (compare with Baumol et al. 1988). Theoretical clues for understanding Envirodyne's (the buyer) and IHC's (the seller) motives can be found in the notions of moral hazard and adverse selection. By S. Breyer's (1982:33) definition, *moral hazard* refers to a situation wherein the buyer does not pay for the full costs of a purchase. Logically, there is a necessary corollary to moral hazard, termed *adverse selection*. By J. C. Coffee's (1988:128) definition, *adverse selection* refers to the selection bias toward financially "shallow" or, as IHC referred to EDC, "thinly capitalized" buyers inherent in transactions where the buyer is in some way protected from the costs of its investment but, if successful, stands to gain significant returns. The connection between moral hazard and adverse selection has only recently been explicitly identified by analysts of the mergers and takeovers boom.

Thus conceived, moral hazard is attributed by O. Williamson (1985) to Frank Knight and by S. Breyer to G. Calabresi (1970). Generally, moral-hazard problems arise in circumstances where economic agents do not bear the costs of their actions, these costs being (in Calabresi's terms) externalized or transferred to others. Implied is an assumption that the market is in some sense inefficient, either because there is no means of imposing constraints on agents' actions relative to overall allocative efficiency and/ or because agents have privileged information that is only revealed after the transaction. This does not mean that individual agents need be thought to function in an inefficient manner; it is easy enough to argue that IHC sought to optimize its use of resources given the circumstances. But in the context of significant transaction costs and asymmetrical information, moral-hazard problems may be endemic to the market (Calabresi 1968). In the context of the regulation of restructuring, moral-hazard problems can occur because authority for monitoring and controlling agents' actions does not exist or, in situations where it does exist, agents keep the relevant information secret, or it is expensive to police actions that would lead to moral hazards.

With respect to the actions of IHC and Envirodyne, the buyer risked practically nothing and, true to the notion of moral hazard, stood to gain enormously from the transaction. The seller also risked very little of its own assets, securing its loan by WSC's railroads and mines. What it did risk was the possibility of a lawsuit by the PBGC. But even here, IHC's legal staff believed there was a good chance of the PBGC being unsuccessful; if the PBGC was successful, they believed that IHC's liability would be limited by the fact that EDC Holdings had operated WSC as an independent company. In the worst-case scenario (if the PBGC was successful in court), IHC still stood to save many millions of dollars of unfunded pension liability. Put crudely, it paid IHC to test the PBGC's power. One consequence of the buyer risking little or nothing in a transaction is that it encourages thinly capitalized agents to take enormous risks. J. Coffee has noted this is especially prevalent in LBO situations, and it builds in the possibility of bankruptcy. Adverse selection occurs, one might suppose, because of what D. Williamson terms *greed*. More concretely, it should be observed that Envirodyne needed short-term cash flow to invest in other non–steel related businesses—greed was mixed with strategic alliances.

Where there is cooperation between the buyer and the seller, as in this case, the costs of the transaction (moral hazard) are not borne by either party, but rather by a third party, often society at large. In this case the buyer well understood the circumstances of the plant. It knew WSC was chronically undercapitalized. Information on the status of the plant was shared between the buyer and seller. As Judge Moran noted, on the basis of this information Envirodyne chose "to agree to a wholly leveraged buyout on terms in certain respects more favorable to International Harvester than the McLouth proposal" (p. 15). Those immediately adversely affected by the collusion between Envirodyne and IHC were WSC's workers, the local community, and ultimately the American public (via the economic burden imposed by the bankruptcy on an already underfinanced PBGC). Cooperation between the buyer and seller often results in the transfer of the costs of a transaction to society at large. This was anticipated by

Cravath, Swaine, and Moore as well as Lehman Brothers. IHC deliberately misled the PBGC about the extent of WSC's unfunded liability and tried to keep their stratagem secret from the PBGC as long as possible.

Piercing the Corporate Veil

When Peter Peterson, then managing partner of Lehman Brothers and later managing partner of The Blackstone Group (the investment company that David Stockman joined after leaving the Office of Management and Budget), briefed IHC's management on Lehman's negative assessment of the sale of WSC to Envirodyne, he not only forecast the bankruptcy of WSC, he also forecast "a series of lawsuits" that would charge that the "transaction was a sham." He suggested that deposition of the parties involved and the evidence extant would show that "a main purpose of this transaction was to avoid, evade the pension and other past service [retirees' and vested employees' medical benefits] liabilities." In making their case in court, the PBGC quoted Peterson time and time again, arguing that the evidence presented in court was consistent with and validated wholly Peterson's assessment. Using more colorful language, WSC (EDC Holdings) also sued IHC charging fraud: that IHC's sale of WSC to Envirodyne was part of "a diabolical and brilliant scheme" designed in part to deliberately mislead the investors about the "true value" of WSC's assets.[14]

Prior to the IHC case, there had been few tests of the "power" of the PBGC in bankruptcy situations. Despite the fact that the corporation had consulted the PBGC in 1977 about its possible liability for unfunded pension obligations if (hypothetically) WSC failed, the PBGC itself had only just begun life as the federal government's private pension regulatory agency—the enabling legislation (ERISA) was passed in 1974 and the PBGC was formally begun on January 1, 1976—leaving open the question of the PBGC's real power in the context of the formal statutory description of its powers. Although a review of judicial decisions regarding the scope of PBGC's powers is beyond this chapter, two particular decisions are useful for understanding the immediate judicial context of the consolidated cases.

In *Nachman v. PBGC* (1980) the Supreme Court upheld an appeals court ruling that ERISA created a right to pension benefits which could not be limited or diluted by other corporate agreements or decisions. Here, the company had terminated its pension plan the day before ERISA went into force and, relying upon a prior agreement with its union to the effect that it would only be liable for pension benefits up to the present value of its plan assets, had refused to pay 75 percent of its promised benefits. The

Supreme Court decided ERISA overrode any (prior) bilateral agreement limiting company liability for promised pension benefits and was designed precisely with this kind of situation in mind. The court also decided that whatever the financial burdens imposed upon companies by ERISA, the act represented the legitimate public policy interest of Congress in protecting workers' pension rights. A more recent decision, *Alman v. Danin* (1986) set the stage for IHC. In that case, an appeals court upheld a lower court decision that had legitimated piercing the corporate veil (looking beyond the formal record of sale and ownership); private company A had taken over another (B), stripped it of its assets, signed an exclusive sales agreement with B, and then negotiated a contract with the union representing its workers (including a pension agreement). After the paper company (B) had failed to pay agreed-to pension obligations, the union then sued company A. The court decided that company A was liable since the intent of Congress in passing ERISA had been to protect workers' pension rights whatever the formal division of corporate ownership. No company could be allowed to evade its social responsibilities, whatever their immediate costs, by simply altering its registered corporate form. To do so would be to forfeit any real ability to police corporate actions—the intent of ERISA.

Of the suits brought against IHC as a consequence of the bankruptcy of WSC, those involving Envirodyne and the PBGC were the most significant. WSC (EDC Holdings) sued IHC charging fraud—that IHC had fraudulently and knowingly overrepresented the value of WSC's assets so as to induce Envirodyne to buy the steel plant. Given the close involvement of Envirodyne's principals and staff in assessing the steel plant at the time of sale, and the fact that two of Envirodyne's staff had actually argued against the sale after investigating the physical plant and assets before being overruled by the company's partners, it is difficult to believe that IHC deliberately misled Envirodyne or that if better information had been available (assuming such information would have been used by the company's principals) Envirodyne would have made a different decision. In his decision of December 1988, Judge Moran observed that (for quite different reasons) both IHC and Envirodyne wanted desperately to believe in the sale; that notwithstanding the actual condition of the plant, the negative advice of outside experts, and the failure of IHC to find an outside buyer in very good economic circumstances, it was in all parties' interests to go through with the transaction. Indeed, not only was there reliable evidence to support this contention, there is a good analytical argument (moral hazard and adverse selection) to suppose in an abstract sense that IHC and Envirodyne colluded in forcing through the transaction.

Before the case brought by WSC against IHC was consolidated with the PBGC case in federal district court, Judge Robert McCormick of the Illinois federal district bankruptcy court decided in 1985 that there was *prima facie* evidence for WSC's fraud case to proceed, although he did not rule on the substantive merits of the case. At the time, IHC had sought to limit the plaintiffs' access to its correspondence with outside counsel (Cravath) and investment bankers (Lehman Brothers), whereas WSC suggested that this information had great bearing on their claims of being duped. In his 1985 decision, McCormick sided with WSC, ruling that the company had to turn over all relevant correspondence. But because McCormick used WSC's submitted mock-up ruling as the basis of his decision without informing Harvester, McCormick's ruling was set aside and the case shifted to Judge Moran's court. Moran also decided that IHC could not protect its correspondence, having selectively used it to rebut plaintiffs' assertions; but he also decided that there was no basis for WSC's claim of fraud.

IHC mounted three arguments against the PBGC's claim that it should be held liable for WSC's unfunded pension liabilities. Generally, all three arguments were premised on IHC's claim that it could not be held liable for the events leading up to WSC's bankruptcy, for actions taken or not taken by WSC, or for the circumstances facing WSC in late 1979; the court could not hold IHC liable for the mistakes or misadventures of another employer. To make this claim work, IHC first asserted that there was a legitimate difference between transferring pension obligations and evading such obligations. It accepted that as a condition of the sale WSC was to take ultimate responsibility for its own unfunded pension obligations. However, drawing a distinction between the act of transfer and what IHC asserted was an unproved claim of evasion, IHC argued that the transfer of liabilities did not per se constitute an offense by the terms of ERISA. By their argument, evasion "occurs only when the parties intend or know that ongoing pension obligations will not be made" (p. 72).[15] Citing related decisions in federal court, the company argued that since it did not enter the transaction to evade its pension obligations and that the transaction had "substantive merit," IHC's transfer of obligations was a legitimate business decision.[16]

Their next argument, that the sale of WSC was a "real" business transaction, logically followed. In their argument, lawyers for IHC went through the company's corporate strategy emphasizing their interest in restructuring activity away from the capital intensive business of steelmaking, toward their core economic interests in truck manufacturing. And repeating the notion of corporate strategy, IHC rehearsed the arguments favoring a related interpretation of Envirodyne's interest in consummating the transaction—nominally the application of technology and environmental engineering in diversified fields of interest. Having asserted that the sale was a legitimate business transaction (there being enough plausible explanations of why IHC sold WSC and why Envirodyne bought the plant), IHC then suggested WSC had a reasonable chance of success. To substantiate this claim, it cited the Economic Development Administration's interest in the plant, the apparent reluctance of the PBGC to terminate the pension plan immediately after the sale of WSC, and the purported confidence of EDC Holdings through much of the 1978–79 period. Nevertheless, IHC recognized that any LBO is risky. But it also asserted that, in the circumstances, the LBO was a worthy risk to take and that making these kinds of judgments was an entirely proper and common business practice.

These two arguments then provided the company with the basis for asserting that IHC could not be held accountable for another company's actions or inactions—that piercing the corporate veil was inappropriate in this case. Citing precedents, IHC asserted that (a) IHC had no ownership interest in WSC after the sale, (b) IHC did not control or directly participate in the management of WSC after the sale, and (c) even if there was such control and domination of WSC, there was no basis for asserting that the sale was fraudulently conceived. Like all arguments of interpretation in law, each of IHC's assertions could be and was challenged by the PBGC. For instance, the PBGC counterclaim stated that due to the arrangement of the LBO, IHC in effect still owned the plant and equipment and the mines and railroads of WSC. Given the claim IHC had on these assets, the only difference with WSC owning these assets was a paper-thin transfer of ownership. Similarly, the PBGC showed that for crucial decisions, including when to pay pension insurance premiums to the PBGC, senior management of IHC dominated the management decisions of WSC. Having countered assertions (a) and (b), the PBGC had to simply return to their already made argument that the actual sale was in fact a sham and that based upon depositions of IHC management, Envirodyne, and outside experts there was evidence to the effect that participants in the sale knew the transaction was very dubious—financially, ethically, and with respect to the meaning of ERISA.

Thus IHC's three-point claim that piercing the corporate veil was inappropriate in this case could be easily turned by the PBGC and used by the agency to prove the need to pierce the corporate veil. Tactically, IHC asserted that the apparent *formal* (and essentially legal) sale of the steel plant to EDC Holdings was enough, and should be enough, to counter the

PBGC's charge that it was responsible for WSC's pension liabilities. The possible success of this strategy depended upon protecting the coherence of the legal distinction between ownership and a more common (but non-liable) interest in the performance of WSC, and the application of legal rules based upon respecting the category of ownership which, when applied in this case, would preempt the PBGC's claims. In contrast, the PBGC's brief was based upon the *substantive* texture of the case: the intentions of Congress in passing ERISA, the motives of IHC in attempting to offload its steel plant, the lack of expertise of Envirodyne, and the very real likelihood that WSC would fail. The PBGC strategy was that piercing the corporate veil was the best analytical method for understanding the logic behind otherwise plausible business decisions associated with the sale of WSC.

There are obvious tensions between IHC's formalist defense and the PBGC's substantively oriented suit. The success of IHC's defense depended upon limiting the terms of the dispute to a narrow reading of the inherited legal categories and applying these categories in a routine manner consistent with customary business practice. Thus, IHC argued a number of times that it should not be held liable for transfers of property or liability, or should it be held liable for the failure of another firm to take the necessary actions to be economically successful. If the court had decided the PBGC suit by this logic, then the intentions of Congress in passing ERISA, the matter of determining IHC's motives in transferring its pension liabilities to EDC Holdings, and the issue of whether or not WSC had a real chance of surviving would have been practically irrelevant. As it was, the PBGC argued directly and deliberately against the formal separation of ownership, justifying their substantive claims by reference to the public policy interests served by ERISA. Indeed, their argument was that in this case customary business practices (such as taking risks or selling property) could not dominate ERISA interests, especially when those public policy interests were instrumental in framing ERISA to deal with precisely these kinds of situations.

In his earlier opinion of March 2, 1988, Judge Moran found that IHC's defense was not plausible. IHC's use of the literal language of the statute (only the employer is liable for unfunded pension obligations) to insulate itself from liability contravened the intent of Congress in passing ERISA.[17] Using a hypothetical example of a company that wanted to escape all its pension liability, Moran noted that the implication of IHC's reading of the statute was that all such a company would have to do is "sell" for nothing that part of its business that had onerous pension obligations to an insolvent "nominee" and walk away: "Even if the nominee only operated the business

for one day before going bankrupt, the employer would have no ERISA liability at the time the pension plans were terminated. Instead, the PBGC's
insurance fund—and so the other employers of America who pay ERISA
premiums—would have to absorb all pension liability. Congress cannot
have intended such a result" (p. 520). And taking the IHC's reading of the
statute to its logical conclusion, Moran suggested that "any employer could
make any pension promises he wished, no matter how wildly unrealistic,
knowing that all he need do to dump them onto the PBGC insurance
program would be to find an insolvent willing to sign a purchase contract"
(pp. 520–21). To back his interpretation of the intentions of Congress in
passing ERISA, Moran then reviewed related statements of members of
Congress speaking in support of the act. He also noted congressional
reports that dealt with sections of the act that were constructed so as to
be relevant to those employers who initiated transactions whose principal
purpose was to evade their responsibilities. In these ways, Moran sought
to show that IHC could not hold to its literal interpretation of the employer.

Limits of Economic Imperatives

Although Judge Moran found in favor of the PBGC with respect to its
argument that IHC is liable for WSC's pension obligations, Moran neither
upheld the fraud claim against IHC, arguing that Envirodyne was a willing
participant in the transaction for its own reasons, nor found that the sale
of WSC was entirely improbable as a viable commercial transaction. It is
clear that Moran favored the PBGC's substantive interpretation of ERISA
over IHC's formalistic defense and for this reason his decision promises
to radically affect the actions of U.S. corporate planners in their design
of strategies to shift the costs of restructuring.

It is not the case, however, that formal defenses always fail when
countered by substantive claims. In fact, a cursory review of ERISA- and
labor-related legal disputes in U.S. federal courts over the past decade
would reveal that formal modes of argument have often held sway over
substantive arguments. One of the characteristic responses of the NLRB
and some federal courts during the Reagan administration was to invoke
formalistic defense of management property rights to counter union claims
of substantive interest in management decisions affecting the location of
production (see Clark 1989a). And while it may be tempting to suggest
that formalistic modes of decisionmaking always favor conservative interests, and substantive claims normally represent progressive interests,
there is no easy way to assign a dependable political interest to either

mode of judicial decisionmaking (see Kennedy 1976). Thus IHC's formalist defense should be understood as a rhetorical strategy determined by the context of the dispute.

So far, the details of the case have been presented and analyzed with respect to corporate strategy and judicial adjudication. The case could be analyzed just as easily in other ways. Consistent with other studies of corporate restructuring and pension obligations in the United States, it could be read as another example of a previously made argument: that the costs of exit (as opposed to entry) can be very high in unionized industries (compare with Baumol et al. 1988). Another related way of reading the case study would emphasize the geographical texture of the case, especially the intersection between the site of production and community-union-management relations, perhaps along the lines suggested by (among others) B. Bluestone and B. Harrison (1982). Yet another reading of the case would emphasize the relative decline of U.S. industry and related communities in the context of heightened international competition (see Lawrence 1984). All these readings would seem to have merit. Certainly one reading would not exclude any other. Interpretations are never exclusive in the sense that data are thought by positivists and some Marxists to provide a conclusive test of meaning (Walker 1989b).

Most essential for a clear understanding of this chapter, the case should be read as an instance of regulation (law) colliding with and dominating economic imperatives (the costs of exit). Reading the case in this manner provides us an opportunity to consider some essential but otherwise neglected issues in regulation theory. In particular the case immediately raises the issue of how robust regulation, represented here as statute (law) and adjudication (judicial review), can be in the face of economic imperatives. While it is obviously impossible to deal conclusively with this issue in the context of one case—although some legal theorists would argue that it is impossible to develop a conclusive argument without the particularities of individual cases, no matter how many cases or examples are cited (see Gordon 1984)—a critical reading of the case with respect to this issue can provide the basis for broader theoretical speculation.

Heretofore the focus of research on restructuring has been on the events and spatial ramifications of economic imperatives; regulation *qua* regulation has been simply appended to economic imperatives on the assumption that the former is determined by the latter (see Harvey 1988). The case study of WSC raises the prospect of the reverse occurring: that regulation determines the design and implementation of corporate restructuring, thereby channeling and molding economic imperatives. Indeed, it might be argued that statutory requirements literally determined the nature of the corporate economic problem.

At this point it may be objected that my case study has simply shown a common and well-known phenomenon: that social considerations may compromise economic imperatives in the short run. In the long run, though, or so the counterargument goes, economic imperatives would *annihilate* any regulation that ran counter to the needs of economic efficiency. This theory of the long run is an argument often made by Marxist theorists (Harvey 1988) and, oddly enough, by those who subscribe to the Chicago school of law and economics (Posner 1986). There are, of course, significant differences between these schools of thought. Presumably, Harvey is making a positive statement in the sense that this condition empirically describes capitalism whereas Posner argues that if economic imperatives are compromised by social regulation, judges ought to ensure that economic imperatives dominate (a normative claim). Although the theory of the long run is well known, I am not convinced that it applies in this case or that it need apply in other cases.

Based upon my critique of flexible accumulation as a theory of restructuring, some simple objections can be raised against the theory of the long-run dominance of economic imperatives over regulation. For a start, this theory presumes a coherence and integration of structure that is remarkable given the apparent reality of fragmentation and incoherence. If the necessary conditions for coherence can be analytically defined, it remains to be shown that these conditions are ever satisfied historically or geographically. The Marxist theory of the long run, like the theory of flexible accumulation, is a theory of the end-point without any notion of how or why adjustment is so organized so as to reach that end-point. In contrast, though, Posner's theory of the long run makes no assumption of what the future looks like but has a process of short-run adjustment to economic imperatives (judicial adjudication) and a rule (efficiency) by which the long run is incrementally reached. However, there is a basic problem with Posner's rule: how can efficiency be maximized without a substantive goal such as flexible accumulation as the target? Either way, by Harvey or Posner, the theory of the long run is incomplete. But another, more fundamental objection to the theory of the long run has to do with the character of regulation as an institution. Regulation is more than just a law or statutory requirement; it is sets of categories, languages, and organized discourses designed to penetrate, just as economic imperatives can penetrate, everyday life. There may well be contests between categories and discourse, but to presume that regulation is so thin that in the long run it just disappears is to deny the very texture of regulation as a social practice. It also denies an essential historical image that regulation of the economy through agencies such as the Interstate Commerce Commission (ICC) literally created the U.S. national economy; the ICC certainly was the basis for the design and development of the modern regulatory state. While we need not reverse the pattern of causality claimed by theorists of the long run (that economic imperatives cause regulation), it is arguable that a historical account of the U.S. economy would properly assign regulation primary responsibility for the current structure of the economy (Hall 1989).

Inevitably, regulation aims to set the terms for social action, either by coercion or by the association of regulation with social aspirations. In this second manner, regulation is more than a social practice, it is a blueprint or idealized notion of society itself. When the PBGC argued in court against IHC's restructuring strategy, it invoked the underlying purposes of ERISA (as stated in Congress) and the necessary limits that must be imposed upon corporate restructuring to be consistent with society's objectives. This substantive argument invoked an idealized vision of the proper relationship between regulation and the economy. Regulation in this sense is, then, also a theory of the long run but one set within the social and bureaucratic practices of the present. While I am unwilling to assign to regulation the role of being the ultimate cause of social structure (therefore always dominating economic imperatives) and would not pretend that these practices are easily rationalized into a coherent whole, theorists of the long run ignore regulation as a social practice.

Summary—The PBGC Victory

The elements of the case study examined and the interpretive framework that was sketched as the basis for understanding the significance of the case study were, by necessity, quite rudimentary and explorative. At one level, analyzing the logic of IHC's corporate strategy was clearly informed by the previous study of restructuring of the U.S. can industry and, in particular, the actions of Continental Can in managing their early retirement plant-closing pension liabilities. This case study of the closure of WSC focused on the design and implementation of restructuring in the context of the theory of social regulation. It is also a case study, though, of corporate restructuring strategies that have had profound consequences for the well-being of American communities.

In older U.S. manufacturing industries dominated by one or more unions, the exit costs of restructuring typically involve corporations in managing the income and employment rights of their workers as well as agreed-to and negotiated pension benefits that are normally written into collective-bargaining agreements and protected by law (by the NLRA and ERISA). Compared to guaranteed pension benefits, the write-down costs of plant and machinery are often very small. In the steel industry, the combined age and technology of most plant and equipment is so old that the single biggest asset is often the on-hand raw materials of production rather than the actual physical capital. Indeed, industry commentators have suggested that the value of the physical capital of an average steel plant is less than the costs of demolishing the plant. It was noted by the PBGC that senior management of IHC believed WSC's plant and equipment to have a negative worth of as much as $20 million.

To close its steel division, IHC would have incurred enormous costs, about half of which were pension liabilities. For its immediate production needs, it could outsource at lower average prices than produced by WSC, its preferred option, given the declining but very competitive market in farm implements and equipment. To innovate, to extend its interests into other sectors, and to shore up its competitive position in the trucking equipment industry, IHC needed to close WSC. When faced with a similar dilemma, Continental Can denied workers their pension rights by laying them off illegally just prior to their gaining eligibility. In this case, Harvester sold its steel division hoping that the new owner would be held responsible in whole or in part for the pension liabilities. In court, their strategy was to apply a formal division of responsibility between themselves as the previous employer and the current employer. More generally, though, the bankruptcy of WSC was the product of corporate imperialism; Harvester presumed that private economic imperatives must prevail over social goals. And so they set about designing and implementing a restructuring strategy that deliberately sought to circumvent what they understood to be the role and status of the PBGC. That they were not successful represents a victory for the PBGC—a victory that also represents the dominance of one theory of society over another.

6

Bankruptcy in the
U.S. Steel Industry

Set within the context of advanced capitalism, its institutions and regulatory apparatuses, J. Graham and her colleagues (1988:488) speak of a "structural transition" of U.S. industry "highlighting the advent of global capitalism and the contemporaneous decline of the monopoly variant." An emerging new map of the structure of production is being created through the process of restructuring that promises to change how we think about the very nature of the modern economy. There is debate over the likely form of the future economy (has Fordism been replaced by post-Fordism?), as there is debate over the logic of change (does flexibility describe the operating principle of successful management?), and over the significance of new forms of production in different communities (are industrial districts the wave of the future or yet another form of exploitation?) (see Harrison 1993).

There can be no doubt about the rate of economic change and structural transformation, driven by what was identified in chapter 2 as "excess competition"—penetration of the protected markets of advanced economies by NIC producers (among others). Nowhere are the consequences of this process more evident than in the U.S. steel industry. Judge Robert J. Sweet, quoted in the epigraph of this book, said as much when he recognized the enormous impact that restructuring has had on the U.S. steel industry. The welfare of hundreds of thousands of workers, their families and communities, has been drastically and adversely affected; the bankruptcy of LTV Corporation in 1986 was one expression of this crisis. But Judge Sweet also identified another issue most fundamental to this book, relating to society in general: how are, or how should, processes of restructuring be regulated in ways consistent with congressionally mandated and legislatively defined public policy? Sweet asks a question that appears to have no immediate answer. Because there is no dedicated regulatory or administrative apparatus whose primary responsibility is industrial restructuring, restructuring is a private responsibility—it is the responsibility of the corporate entity affected by economic change. Regulation in this context is judicial adjudication on a case-by-case basis in response to competing claims for advantage in the restructuring process.

This chapter is the third case study of the regulation of corporate restructuring in American industry. By virtue of the sheer size and impact of the bankruptcy of LTV Steel, this case study has many implications for how we understand the regulation of the restructuring process. Too many theorists, in proclaiming the advent of a new regulatory regime—be it post-Fordism, postindustrialism, even postmodernism—avoid the very real and vital processes of regulation, thereby ignoring the actual logic and implementation of restructuring as a social practice. As in the previous case studies, my analysis here is consistent with a tradition of academic scholarship that sees regulation as dependent upon the events and contexts of leading cases and institutions. Detailed case-by-case institutional analysis is the standard of this tradition (Wilson 1980). Although this tradition can be criticized for being too descriptive, an attempt is made throughout the chapter to situate the case within a broader context. In particular, the chapter should illustrate that this case has very important implications for the legitimacy of the PBGC. Following J. O. Freedman (1978), it is suggested that the PBGC is very vulnerable in situations such as the LTV bankruptcy because of its problematic status relative to economic interests. This case study brings to the fore the contingent nature of its power and the apparent reluctance of Congress to invest the PBGC with sufficient power to override competing claims.

Theories of Regulation

From previous chapters, it should be apparent that my idea of regulation is very broad; it is an organized social practice, an institutional activity, and an administrative set of rules and requirements. For some economists, regulation is simply the political allocation of resources (witness Kahn 1988:2/I). This is too narrow a definition, because it fails to apprehend the instrumentality of regulation as a social institution with agendas inserted within and between institutions. By contrast, those who would follow the French regulation school define regulation as "a structured ensemble of specific institutional forms that not only codify but also steer its economic structure" (Moulaert and Swyngedouw 1989:330). At such a level of generality it is difficult to disagree with such a definition; it encompasses a broad range of interpretations of the relations between economy and society. But it does remain silent on the issue of institutional form. A definition of regulation that comes closest to my notion is to be found in L. Hancher and M. Moran (1989). Therein, regulation "involves the design of general rules, the creation of institutions responsible for their implementation, the clarification of the exact meaning of a general rule in particular circumstances, and the enforcement of the rule in those circumstances" (p. 271). This definition is institution-centered; it is related to the actions of agencies of all kinds, including the courts, but does not idealize the power of rules.

In the social sciences, there is a tendency to treat regulation as an element of social structure outside of the normal context of social behavior. A common metaphor describing the relationship of regulation to social behavior treats regulation as the "floor and ceiling" (the upper and lower bounds) between which agents may act without penalty or coercion. L. Tribe (1989) would term this a Newtonian metaphor of regulation and law in the sense that as the upper and lower bounds of social behavior are assumed to be known, stable, and well defined. Regulation *qua* regulation is simply the background or stage upon which agents act out their own interests and desires. Although it is probably too strong to say that regulation in this worldview is unrelated to social conflict, one consequence of this metaphor is to ignore the intersection between regulation and the formation of social behavior.

The plausibility of this metaphor depends upon a number of assumptions, most of which are hardly ever explicitly recognized. For example, the nature of rules, regulations, and the law is treated in a most naive fashion. It is as if social scientists believe in H.L.A. Hart's (1961) positivist theory of law without recognizing the complexities of that theory regarding problems of recognizing rules and the potential ambiguity of rules. Coupled with this naive conception of regulation as a set of determinate rules is a technical predisposition to analyze social behavior in its simplest form. Apparently, to integrate social behavior with the structure of regulation is to make too complex an otherwise apparently unproblematic connection. Justifying naiveté and technical simplicity is an ideological commitment to the primacy of the individual (or even a social unit such as class) over the state and its institutions. By theory, technique, and ideology, then, there are many advantages for social scientists to assume regulation to be a passive stage for behavior. Some kinds of theorists, notably those of the Chicago school of law and economics, would even suggest that if regulation does affect the actions of agents, the rules of regulation are in some sense inconsistent with the assumptions of individual optimizing behavior and wealth maximization.

Regulation theory as conceived by the French regulation school makes similar assumptions about the nature of rules. Proponents of the regulation approach to understanding late-capitalism argue that the regulatory framework of an economy is vital for the coordination of sectors (departments) of the economy (Boyer 1988; Lipietz 1987). Without a means of coordination, so the argument goes, inherent tendencies towards imbalance (crisis) between production and consumption will overwhelm the stability of interdependent private activity. M. Aglietta (1979) suggested the New Deal model of state regulation of the economy resolved for a time these tendencies, thereby providing a relatively stable regime for growth and development now labeled as Fordism. Once in place, this regulatory framework is treated by theorists as the relevant background against which the actions of economic agents and the state are to be interpreted. Once in place, though, the regulatory framework is assumed uncontested by private agents (although there may be significant conflict between agents) until there is a crisis of that framework—hence the significance of debate over the transformation of Fordism to post-Fordism.

Like many other social scientists, regulation theorists tend to treat the regulatory framework as determinate and complete. It is assumed that once set in place it provides a recipe for social action and a formula for resolving conflicts of interpretation which remains intact until threatened by structural changes in the economy. By analogy, T. Eagleton (1989:37) described the underlying logic of eighteenth-century moral philosophers (including Adam Smith) as one based upon the harmonizing of disparate interests and actions through "a social order so spontaneously cohesive that its members no longer need think about it." Relating this social order to the institution of law, Eagleton noted that "such an internal appropriation of the law is at once central to the work of art and to the process of political hegemony." These paired notions of social order and political hegemony are also central to the French regulation school and are reflected in an idealization of the coherence of regulatory regime once established. Two related arguments of this chapter are that (1) *a priori* defined rules are insufficient as the basis of regulation, and (2) the ambiguity of the rules of regulation, their meaning and application to specific cases, is such that the courts tend to regulate in a pragmatic manner using contested standards of decisionmaking such as fairness and efficiency. One consequence of this kind of regulatory behavior, though, is the significance then attached to specific cases like the LTV bankruptcy. A third argument is that the crisis of regulation is inherent in the practice of rule-based regulation, whether or not there is a crisis of economic coordination.

In French regulation theory there is an implied equivalence of the regulatory framework with an idealized version of the common law. By the language of law, the rules of regulation are assumed to be determinate (unambiguous) and understood with respect to their original meaning.

Once in place, it is assumed that these rules have a integrity and power separate from events of the day. However, as P. Pettit (1990) described it, a plausible model of rule-based social behavior must be able to make coherent heterogeneous expectations, rationalize into one outcome a variety of circumstances, and yet be entirely readable and corrective if behavior does not match with what rules would require. Regulatory regimes cannot be so stable (internally) as supposed. Another problem with regulation theory is its privileging of economic metaimperatives over institutional interests. By Aglietta's logic, the regulatory framework is ultimately determined by the inescapable tensions of capitalism. While there may be epochal variations in these imperatives, only if regulation departs from these imperatives is it (as an institution) of analytical significance. The issue here becomes the relative inefficiency of regulation with respect to economic imperatives. The binary conception of history at the heart of some French regulation models (either the regulatory framework works or it does not—stability or crisis) may be thought to reflect an inability or unwillingness to see institutions and social practices as much more than the reflection of economic imperatives.[1]

This book is premised upon the assumption that regulation as a system of rules should be understood as necessarily ambiguous and contingent upon events and circumstances. Following from R. Dworkin's (1978) critique of positivistic rule-based adjudication, it is assumed here that the principles of regulation intersect with the context of disputes and that, as a consequence, as cases are decided the meaning of regulation affects and in turn changes the behavior of social agents. More concretely, once we accept the intersection between regulation and social behavior as the vital focus of analysis, this chapter will demonstrate that far from accepting regulation as the upper and lower bounds of acceptable behavior, agents contest and challenge those bounds. Indeed, contests over the meaning and application of regulation may dominate legal discourse, involving material interests (of course) but also idealized notions (theories) of the proper relationship between regulation and social action. Notice, though, it is not suggested that regulation is simply a membrane through which more important social interests contest their claims to power. It must also be accepted that regulation is a social institution bound by custom and convention, legitimized by grants of authority as well as constitutional references and imperatives.

Strategic Bankruptcy of LTV Corporation

As we saw in chapter 2, LTV Corporation is a large, diversified Fortune 500 company with interests in aerospace, manufacturing, and steel. Its steel company—LTV Steel Company, Inc.—was formed by the merger of Jones and Laughlin Steel Company, Youngstown Sheet and Tube, and Republic Steel Corporation in the early 1980s. It now is one of the largest steel manufacturers in the United States.[2] In 1988, for example, it shipped 8.9 million tons of steel, earning $4.8 billion in sales and employing over 19,000 workers represented by the USWA. By comparison, the largest U.S. steel company (USX) shipped 12.2 million tons with sales of $5.8 billion, employing over 22,000 USWA members in the same year (see Table 6.1). LTV has, by current standards, one of the lowest labor cost structures in the industry. In Table 6.2, it is shown that the company has negotiated a very low minimum hourly wage rate with the USWA, bettered only by other bankrupt steel companies (McLouth and Wheeling-Pittsburgh) or newly formed companies (like Brenlin). LTV is one of the most profitable U.S. steel companies if operating revenue per ton, profit per ton, and total profit are the bases for comparison. Even so, LTV is bankrupt.

On July 17, 1986, LTV filed for protection from its creditors under Chapter 11 of the federal Bankruptcy Code.[3] From 1979 to 1986, it had accumulated more than $4 billion in debts—debts owed to public electric utilities, mining companies, railroads, municipalities, the banks and the PBGC. In fact, over half of its debts were pension-related. A number of its thirty pension plans (especially four of the steel company plans) are chronically underfunded, being unable to meet current or actuarially forecast, contractually agreed-to pension obligations. Notionally, LTV owes over $2.3 billion in pension obligations, having previously obtained from the IRS a waiver for its 1984 funding obligations. It subsequently was denied a waiver for its 1985 obligations and had its 1984 waiver revoked at the same time (in November 1986). LTV was immediately liable for $350 million in unpaid, past premium contributions. One consequence of this enormous pension debt burden was LTV's notification of the PBGC in December 1986 that it could no longer afford to fund its pension obligations or administer its pension plans. In early 1987, the PBGC brought action in federal district court by the terms of Section 4042 of ERISA for the *involuntary* termination of LTV's pension plans and petitioned to become trustee of those plans.

Of the many possible explanations for the bankruptcy of LTV, two are especially pertinent to the issue of public regulation and pension liabilities. One explanation that has received broad publicity in the media imagines

Table 6.1 Performance of the Seven Major Integrated U.S. Steel Companies, 1988

	Tons Shipped (millions)	Net Sales (millions of dollars)	Revenue per Ton (dollars)	Profit per Ton (dollars)	Total Profit (millions of dollars)	USWA Membership (thousands)
Armco	4.9	2.9	604.4	56.3	276.1	4.6
Bethlehem	10.1	5.5	543.5	52.3	528.0	21.2
Inland	5.5	2.4	443.8	54.1	298.8	10.5
LTV	0.9	4.8	543.8	54.5	488.5	19.3
National	4.9	2.6	522.9	22.5	111.8	7.3
USX	12.2	5.8	476.4	41.2	501.0	22.4
Wheeling-Pitt	2.2	1.1	493.5	78.6	175.7	5.0

Source: Form 10K Annual Report, Securities and Exchange Commission, Washington, D.C., USWA, Pittsburgh.

the bankruptcy of LTV to be an instance of the broader phenomenon of American declining industries: an apparent unwillingness of unions to accept declining real wages during the 1970s and their interest in forcing higher real wages as a payoff for forecast future declines in employment and membership. This end-game scenario, sketched by K. R. Harrigan and M. Porter (1983) and applied analytically and empirically to the steel industry by C. Lawrence and R. Z. Lawrence (1985), supposes that bankruptcy is the extreme but inevitable result of management accepting unrealistic real wage demands in return for continuity of production. Unions are supposed to have significant power in such industries because of the lumpiness of capital in the short run and the lack of plausible options for the future substitution of capital for labor; chronic overcapacity, declining profit rates, and disinvestment in the industry are thought to accentuate these problems. The end-game scenario suggests unions had significant power in the short run because management was captured without investment options. By this logic, union wage demands drove LTV to bankruptcy.

This explanation has the virtue of identifying a villain responsible for LTV's bankruptcy. The PBGC has been particularly hostile to the USWA because some senior executives of the PBGC during the Reagan administration associated the union's wage and pension gains of the late 1970s as the precipitating cause of the collapse of LTV. Although Lawrence and Lawrence (1985) did not consider the relevance of pension liabilities or pension benefits in their analysis, it could be argued that the plant-closing

Table 6.2 Hourly Earning of USWA Workers in U.S. Steel
Industry, 1988

Company	Minimum Hourly Rate (approximate)	Average Hourly Earnings
Acme	$ 9.74	$14.00
Armco	10.75	14.50
Basic Manufacturing	9.80	12.07
Bethlehem	9.87	14.30
Brenlin	8.20	12.40
Inland	10.74	15.03
LTV	9.28	13.80
McLouth	8.00	12.00
National	10.44	16.25
USX	9.88	15.75
USX - Posco	10.75	15.76
Warren Cons.	9.54	13.25
Wheeling-Pitt	8.93	12.50

Note: The minimum hourly rate is that paid to workers excluding
adjustments for vacation pay, benefits, profit sharing or gain sharing. Average hourly earnings is only approximate because many
companies have more than one plant and variations [exist] in hourly
earnings between plants. This figure does not include profit sharing,
but does include overtime. Pension and insurance benefits are not
included.
Source: United Steelworkers of America, Pittsburgh.

pensions, reduced qualifications for pension benefits, and increased benefit
levels agreed to during the 1976 contract negotiations were part of the
end-game payoff conceived by the union's leadership. Moreover, in a public
policy milieu that has often associated the U.S. steel industry with oli-
gopolistic price-fixing practices and antitrust violations, the PBGC's claims
met with considerable support (see Baker's 1989 historical assessment).

Notwithstanding the PBGC's belief in the end-game scenario and R. M.
Solow's (1985:110) suggestion that "there is some substance to the Lawrences' model," there are three reasons to suggest that the scenario is
implausible. For a start, it depends upon union leaders having extraordinary vision (being able to see into the future by as much as ten years)
and remarkable internal power (being able to systematically implement
an unstated desired policy against many competing local interests). While
some union leaders do have impressive vision, this vision is less economic

than it is political and their internal power less totalitarian than it is democratic. A second reason to question the plausibility of the end-game scenario has to do with its complexity. Whereas Lawrence and Lawrence told an intricate story of union power, industry performance, and long-run trends, their indicator of this process was quite simplistic—the relative pattern of industries' average hourly earnings. Evidence for their model, observed increases in earnings relative to all manufacturing from 1970 to 1984, could be, however, easily explained by two unrelated processes: first, the existence of relatively generous cost-of-living-adjustment clauses in steel industry collective-bargaining agreements over this period, and second, continuous retrenchment of employment in the industry (relative to output) over this period and the increase in overtime worked by existing employees leading to increases in average hourly earnings. Third, since the depths of the recession of the early 1980s, the U.S. steel industry has made impressive gains in labor productivity, lowering costs of production, and profit (see Table 6.3), with the cooperation and direct involvement of the union, despite massive losses in employment. The Lawrences' model failed to predict cooperation and recovery from what they imagined to be a terminal game.

Alternative explanations can be found for the bankruptcy of LTV. One would stress the "unfortunate" intersection in the early 1980s of three largely interdependent processes: the rationalization and restructuring of production capacity, the use of early retirement pensions by the company as a means of reducing its workforce, and the rapid penetration of foreign competitors (helped by an overvalued U.S. dollar) into the U.S. domestic steel market. All these factors have exacerbated a secular decline in the demand for steel and the short-run—recession-driven collapse of the demand for steel in the auto, construction, and energy industries. Clearly, all U.S. steel companies have had to face these rapid and profound changes in the demand for steel as they have had to become more competitive (by price, quality, and technical sophistication) with foreign producers.[4] LTV was also a special case, made so by its merger and acquisition strategy.

The merger of three companies into LTV Steel was premised upon the goal of forming a larger, more comprehensive firm capable of competing with USX. The creation of a larger company was thought to be the only way to accommodate deteriorating market conditions, the lack of adequate capital reserves for investment, and the sheer market power of competing firms. It was hoped that the resulting company would have a more efficient, integrated, and diversified production base after allowing for the rationalization of excess assets (see Ravenscraft and Scherer 1987 on mergers strategies in general).

Table 6.3 Combined Performance of U.S. Steel Companies, 1984–1988

Year	Tons Shipped (millions)	Hours of Labor	Cost of Labor	Revenue per Ton	Profit per Ton	Total Profit (millions)
1984	45.5	5.43	$116.0	$513.9	$ 2.5	$ 113.0
1985	47.0	4.94	111.0	478.1	(16.9)	(799.0)
1986	42.0	4.74	112.0	461.8	(39.2)	(1,647.0)
1987	44.5	4.40	104.0	472.1	22.3	993.0
1988	49.4	4.17	103.0	512.0	48.2	2,379.0

Note: Hours of labor and cost of labor are calculated including all production and maintenance staff excluding management. All monetary values are in nominal U.S. dollars.
Source: American Iron and Steel Institute, Washington, D.C.

However, rationalization was deeper and more profound than anticipated by company strategists. Of the sixteen plants operated by the companies as separate entities in 1971, by 1987 LTV had closed eight, two were sold, and one was operating only on a limited basis. Whereas the companies once separately employed about 85,000 steelworkers, by 1987 LTV employed only about 20,000 steelworkers. Retirees were more than triple the number of current employees in 1989. As a whole, the steel industry lost more than 40 percent of its workforce from 1979 to 1988; LTV lost more than 60 percent of its workforce.[5] Although rationalization was anticipated to result in significant costs, the recession of the early 1980s drastically magnified those costs by increasing plant shutdown pension costs while simultaneously reducing revenue and inducing ruinous price competition.[6] Even the largest firm, USX, lost money during this period. For LTV, however, it was not just a temporary problem to be resolved when the market improved. Rationalization added enormous long-term debt, largely the result of having to shed so much labor in such a short period of time, to an already indebted company that had absorbed the debts of the separate companies. As a consequence, LTV could not service its debts to banks, suppliers, or the PBGC. By this explanation, LTV was the creation and victim of an aggressive mergers-and-acquisitions strategy implemented at the wrong time.

It can also be argued, however, that LTV pursued a more subtle strategy than indicated by this discussion of costs of mergers and acquisitions. In essence, a related argument is that LTV deliberately used its pension plans as the means of shedding excess labor (through early retirement and plant closing pension benefits), believing that only this strategy would mollify the union's objections to the massive rationalization of employment. Even if a consequence of this strategy was the bankruptcy of its pension plans, LTV also believed that the PBGC would have to accept the involuntary termination (and hence trusteeship) of those bankrupt plans. It is not suggested here that there was a management-inspired conspiracy to avoid LTV's *legal* pension obligations. Unlike Continental Can and International Harvester, it cannot be reasonably argued that LTV acted in a duplicitous manner or sought to camouflage its real intentions by sham transactions or the like.[7] LTV acted legally in pursuing its mergers strategy, but it did so knowing that the pension costs of this strategy might be ultimately borne by the PBGC. If there is a villain in this explanation of LTV's bankruptcy, it is the company. But unlike other explanations, LTV was neither all-knowing nor wholly in charge of the situation. Its actions were driven by economic imperatives of scale and competition and were contingent on unanticipated events it could not control.

PBGC as an LTV Creditor

For a company such as LTV, Chapter 11 status provides a number of advantages over the normal bankruptcy liquidation-of-assets process. Chapter 11 status gives a company judicial protection from creditors while a plan for payment and reorganization is developed (Cowans 1978, chap. 22). Although the courts do have power to pay off some creditors' pre-petition claims before others, the presumption is that creditors are treated equally and their claims on debtors' assets are held in abeyance until a plan for settlement is accepted by the court and creditors. By convention and judicial precedent, Chapter 11 debtors remain in possession of company assets and operate their businesses consistent with normal business practices subject, of course, to review by the courts. It would be up to a creditor to move in court against this presumption, the alternative being a court-appointed trustee.[8] Perhaps most important, Chapter 11 status provides the debtor with the opportunity "to take advantage of [an] optimum environment for rehabilitation without unnecessary interruption of its business."[9] Indeed, the Supreme Court in *NLRB v. Bildisco and Bildisco* (1983) held that one purpose of Chapter 11 is to facilitate the "successful rehabilitation of debtors."[10] Chapter 11 is a judicial means of maintaining a company as an operating concern while regulating the rationalization of creditors' interests.

Based on Section 4062 of ERISA, the PBGC has a legal and legislatively defined financial claim on any participating employers whose pension plans are terminated. The amount of the claim is to be determined on a case-by-case basis by an assessment of the current value of plan benefits as of the date of termination conditioned, in part by the net worth of the employer at about that time. If necessary, the PBGC has the power to petition federal courts for the imposition of a lien upon employers' assets. Thus, in the bankruptcy court the PBGC could be reasonably treated as another of LTV's many creditors. However, Congress also established the PBGC to police requirements of the act and be the insuring agent for those plans covered by the act. In this context, that is, referencing social responsibilities of the PBGC rather than its immediate legal status as a creditor, the PBGC represents the public interest in maintaining a fiscally sound private pension system, in ensuring that plan beneficiaries receive their benefits on a regular basis, and in protecting workers' pension rights.[11] It is also apparent that the PBGC is more than the agent of public policy as if its agency relationship with Congress was the limit of its power. The PBGC is a financial and regulatory institution governed by formal rules of administrative procedure. These rules provide the PBGC with a great deal of discretion within its general congressional mandate. Thus, it has a measure of autonomy from direct political intervention and immediate economic interests.

The bankruptcy of LTV was a challenge to the PBGC's status and effectiveness, and hence, if allowed to become a precedent, a challenge to its autonomy (power). Financially, the bankruptcy of LTV brought the PBGC itself to the brink of bankruptcy. For example, 1986 was a very bad year for the PBGC; it recorded an accumulated operating loss of over $3.8 billion and a $2.5 billion excess of expenses over income. Two years later, the PBGC was still burdened by an enormous debt on its accumulated operating account, only marginally helped by a positive result on its operating income. From 1984 to 1988 the PBGC had its net number of participants nearly double as it became increasingly in debt. The inclusion of LTV in these accounts (which the PBGC refused pending the outcome of lawsuits) would have added another $850 million in immediate claims. The worst-case scenario planned for by an executive Cabinet committee of the Reagan administration in 1987 was the collapse of the U.S. steel industry and strategic bankruptcy of all companies—this would have added another $15–20 billion in liability to the PBGC's responsibilities. In this context, the bankruptcy of LTV challenged the fiscal integrity of the PBGC and federal government policy.

Less apparent, however, was the threat posed by LTV's bankruptcy to the administrative autonomy of the agency. Despite passage of ERISA in 1974, until the bankruptcy of Wheeling-Pittsburgh and LTV there had been very few legal tests of the PBGC's administrative powers in the area of plan terminations due to bankruptcy—specifically its rules, procedures, and statutory prerogatives governing terminations. As in so many areas of ERISA, only in the early 1980s did the implications of the act for corporate decisionmaking and corporate responsibilities for promised pension benefits come to be recognized. Unfortunately for the PBGC, dispute over the agency's interpretation and application of regulations relating to corporate pension obligations have been normally heard in federal court rather than through an internal administrative appeals process. Though less important in small cases (indeed, most of the PBGC's decisionmaking involves relatively small terminations rather than very large terminations) where the relevant corporation or firm is relatively powerless in the face of agency rules and regulations, just as workers of these enterprises often are not represented by unions or third-party law firms, judicial review is familiar territory for the large companies and large unions. The bankruptcy of LTV immediately put the PBGC into court defending rules and regulations that had rarely been challenged before. The PBGC also had to deal with litigation lawyers whose substantive expertise in matters relating to bankruptcy and labor relations might be thought stronger than the PBGC's lawyers.

One response to the apparent crisis facing the PBGC was an administrative action: the processing of pension plan terminations in accordance with the letter of the law. After review by the federal district court for the Southern District of New York, the PBGC agreed to trusteeship of the plans at its scheduled minimum benefit levels, far below those negotiated between the company and union but not guaranteed by the PBGC. Some early retirement benefits and surviving spouse benefits were lost altogether when the PBGC took control of the plans. An appeal by the union to vacate this order was lost (*Jones & Laughlin Hourly Pension Plan v. LTV Corp.* [1987]). The union then instituted legal action charging that the company had violated Section 1113 of the Bankruptcy Code by failing to provide the full schedule of benefits previously negotiated and agreed to in the collective-bargaining agreement. Section 1113 has had a short but contentious history. Passed by Congress in 1984 as an amendment to the Bankruptcy Code, the Section was conceived as a statutory restraint on corporate bankruptcies whose primary purpose is to avoid their voluntarily agreed-to collective-bargaining obligations (the bankruptcy of Continental Airlines is cited as a precipitating event as is the U.S. Supreme Court decision in *Bildisco*).[12] With the threat of a general strike by the union, a short-term competitive advantage over USX, the declining value of the U.S. dollar, and surging demand for steel in the auto industry, LTV could not afford disruption of production. A new collective-bargaining agreement was signed in 1987 including a profit-sharing plan, wage concessions, and provisions for benefits similar to the previous pension plans and approved by the bankruptcy court.

The PBGC's response to these actions by the union, the company, and the court was to initiate administrative proceedings for the restoration of three of LTV's terminated pension plans. Initially, the logic behind restoration was the prevention of "abuse of the pension termination insurance program." In a review of the LTV situation in August 1987, the PBGC concluded that LTV had established "follow-on plans" with essentially the same benefits, and that LTV's improved financial situation, coupled with its apparent willingness to fund substantially similar pension plans, indicated that LTV should also take responsibility for its terminated plans. A month later, the PBGC issued a restoration order retroactive to January 1987, which LTV refused to comply with, prompting the PBGC to seek enforcement of their order from federal district court. However, the district court denied the PBGC motion, arguing that the PBGC's actions were not supported by the administrative record, that its actions were arbitrary and capricious, and that the PBGC's procedures were themselves inadequate. The district court's opinion was upheld in the appeals court and its motion for summary judgment in its favor denied by Judge Sweet (*Pension Benefit Guar. Corp. v. LTV Corp.* [1989]). Having failed in the U.S. Court of Appeals, the PBGC initiated proceedings with a writ of *certiorari* in the Supreme Court for review of the appeals court's decision (argument was heard on February 27, 1990). There the agency again asserted that the "follow-on" plan was "abusive" of ERISA and that the company could now afford to restore the plans.[13] The court granted the writ, but did so on narrow grounds without making any judgment about the standing of ERISA relative to labor law.

The appeals court based its opinion on a series of propositions derived from a general reading of the objectives of Chapter 11 bankruptcy and the role of ERISA relative to other statutes. On bankruptcy, the court recounted a commonly asserted interpretation that the code is designed to shield a "debtor from the financial pressures imposed by its creditors," thereby treating the PBGC as one of many other competing creditors. In relation to other relevant statutes, the PBGC was accused of failing to "adequately consider the policies and goals of the bodies of law involved in this case and their interaction with each other" and that "this failure renders PBGC's decision arbitrary and capricious." Referenced by the court in this regard was the NLRA, which it believed "must also be accorded due weight." The court also found that the PBGC had "focused inordinately on ERISA" and that "the policies and goals of ERISA must be accommodated along with those of bankruptcy and labor law" (p. 1016). And finally, on the matter of whether or not LTV should or could afford to take on the financial burden of its terminated plans, the court found that the PBGC's calculations were flawed, based upon too short a time period for reasonable projection, and premised upon faulty assumptions. That the PBGC had the discretion to make this assessment was not challenged by the court (there being no statutory direction for the determination of standards for restoration); it did challenge, though, the factual basis and logic of that assessment.

Bankruptcy of LTV threatened the power and autonomy of the PBGC on a number of grounds. The PBGC's resultant precarious financial condition was such that it may have required Congress to bail out the single-employer insurance fund. Even though the company did not succeed in court in having the PBGC's motions for restoration turned over, the Supreme Court's decision may have cost the PBGC an opportunity to protect itself from other LTV-type situations. A precedent has been established allowing bankrupt companies to make deals with their unions consistent with ERISA but outside the direct control of the PBGC. A precedent has been established that requires a "balance" of the PBGC's statutory authority against other competing laws. The PBGC may have been compromised in its attempt to police its desired hierarchical order of statutes that would have privileged ERISA over the Bankruptcy Code and the NLRA.

The Union, LTV, and the PBGC

From the discussion so far concerning the bankruptcy of LTV it should be apparent that the USWA (hereafter "the union") was closely associated with the restructuring of the corporation and subsequent actions in federal court concerning its bankruptcy. From the late 1970s, with the collapse of domestic steel markets and the increasing significance of imported steel to the U.S. economy, the union was active on a number of quite diverse fronts. For example, it played a leading role organizing industry representations in Congress in favor of trade restrictions on imported steel (including support of the 1978–82 Trigger Price Mechanism to protect against dumping by foreign producers and the so-called Voluntary Restraint Agreements of 1984–89) and was very active in Congress in support of plant-closing legislation, trade adjustment assistance, and protection of private pension funds and benefits. This external (to the industry) political role was vital to the industry in the sense that the union was able to forge through its individual contract negotiations a coalition of otherwise competing corporate interests. In many respects, the union sought to stabilize the market for domestic steel, realizing that declining employment was inevitable given the changing nature of the market and the massive rationalization of productive capacity. With an "orderly" decline of employment (membership), and congressionally mandated assistance for displaced workers, the leadership of the union sought to cushion the worst effects of restructuring.

This kind of external political role is relatively recent, at least in terms of the traditional role of the union with respect to federal policy innovations. Though very active in the passage of ERISA and the labor-law reform movements of the 1960s and 1970s, the union has been less involved in attempts to "manage" U.S. trade and industrial competition. The union's more active stance could be in part explained by changes in the leadership of the union. The president of the union, Lynn Williams, came to head the union from its Canadian branch, which has been more active in the party political process in Canada (especially the New Democratic Party) than the U.S. branch over the past two decades. The more active stance of the union could be also explained, however, by fundamental changes in the industry bargaining process caused, in part, by the 1982 recession/depression. The coordinated bargaining committee, involving all major companies and headed by USX management, for many years controlled the contract bargaining process with the union. Resulting collective-bargaining agreements with the union were then implemented and administered by the participating companies. Inevitably, such a centralized bargaining system produced standardized contracts covering wages, benefits, and conditions of work across companies and across the nation. This process also centralized expertise: few management executives and few companies outside of USX were directly involved in the bargaining process. On the union side, expertise was also centralized around head-office bargaining committees.

Breakdown of the coordinated bargaining system in the early 1980s was prompted by the smaller companies' distrust of USX's bargaining stance with the union and a realization by the union and individual companies that increased local discretion was vital if companies were to survive in the new world of price and quality competition. Decentralization of the bargaining process empowered the union in two ways: (1) where USX was once the industry spokesman (as leader of the management bargaining committee), the union could now claim to also represent the industry because it was the only effective means of coordinating information between the competing steel companies; (2) because of the union's continued centralization of its bargaining expertise and organization it had access to all company-specific information, which allowed it to make special deals with smaller, troubled companies and thereby to limit USX's domination of the domestic steel industry. This strategy is sometimes described by senior officials of the union as encouraging a "level playing field" between competing companies. However, decentralization of bargaining brought potential threats to union solidarity. Because of the vital importance now of local issues in decentralized bargaining, maintaining an industry-wide bargaining stance is now more difficult, given competing local issues. In addition, given the greater loyalty of workers to their individual companies relative to the union it is more difficult to organize and sustain industry-wide industrial action (such as strikes). Nevertheless, over the 1980s the union executive was able to maintain solidarity, perhaps because of the extraordinary complexity of concession bargaining and the union's professional expertise.

In this context, the crisis and bankruptcy of LTV presented the union with a real dilemma. At one level, its strategy of negotiating separate collective-bargaining agreements with each company so as to maintain competition in the industry could be used to rescue LTV from immediate liquidation of assets (Chapter 7 bankruptcy). To have one of the largest U.S. steel companies collapse while the union was involved in the 1986 round of collective-bargaining negotiations would have compromised its bargaining position. The union was concerned that its negotiations with USX would be difficult and protracted; it could not afford to have two large-scale disputes at one time. Even before the 1986 bankruptcy of LTV, the union had made significant concessions on wages and conditions of work. The relatively wide (compared to the 1970s) distribution of 1988 standard hourly wage rates noted in Table 6.2 is one indication of the company-specific negotiating stance taken by the union during the 1986 negotiations. Yet for all the concessions made by the union, pension benefits to retirees represented a very difficult political problem, not easily rationalized by reference to its level playing field negotiation strategy. The union neither supported nor encouraged the involuntary termination of the plans. Its strategy was to use the collective-bargaining system to recover what it believed its retirees and members were legally entitled to receive.

Essentially, the bankruptcy of LTV and the termination of its pension plans reduced many retirees' benefits and denied some retirees their supplemental pension benefits due to them when they took early retirement. The PBGC's formula for pension benefits clearly discriminated against early retirees, in some cases did not pay retirees what they had been promised at the time of retirement, and denied some surviving spouses their disability pensions. Although the union does not represent retirees (they neither pay dues nor participate in the political life of the union), in this instance the threats posed by the PBGC and the bankruptcy of the company were such that the union had to become involved in representing their retirees' interests. This representative role was not without its own political tensions. A group of retirees organized against the union and brought suit in federal court, arguing that the union did not represent their interests.[14] At the time, the union was negotiating concessions to keep the company operating (representing the interests of its working members). The union was also in court arguing that the company must pay promised pension benefits regardless of the PBGC's formulas. In this respect, the union based its legal claim upon the notion that the collective-bargaining process deserves as much respect as the PBGC's ERISA claims. Indeed, the union argued before the U.S. Supreme Court that "the PBGC has no business overseeing the kinds of benefit packages that a union and employer may adopt following a pension plan termination." (See Brief for the AFL-CIO and USWA, Case No. 89-390, in the Supreme Court [October Term 1989] undated.)

The union's legal claims were not just a consequence of the special or unique circumstances of LTV. Through 1985 and 1986 the union had been embroiled in a dispute with Wheeling-Pittsburgh Steel (W-P) over similar issues: how the burdens of restructuring or what the third circuit court of appeals cited from congressional testimony over passage of Section 1113 as "the burdens of sacrifices in the reorganization process" were to be distributed (*Wheeling-Pittsburgh Steel v. United Steelworkers* [1986:1091]). Their dispute with W-P concerned the terms of a collective-bargaining agreement with the company which, like LTV, was in Chapter 11 bankruptcy. Over a number of years, the union had agreed to a series of modifications to their existing contract with the company, providing wage and benefit concessions in return for profit-sharing and/or equity shares in the company. With a new contract to be negotiated, the company invoked Chapter 11 as a mandate for rejecting the then-current labor contract and set out the terms of a new contract that, in part, involved further substantial wage concessions, no "snap-back" provisions (profit-sharing or the like), and a mandatory five-year term for the contract.[15] A suit was then brought in bankruptcy court against the union by the company seeking authorization to reject the collective-bargaining agreement. In response, the union charged in court that W-P had failed to respect Section 1113 of the Bankruptcy Code and the integrity of the collective-bargaining process as conceived in the NLRA.

Although the company won permission to reject its contract at the bankruptcy court and the federal district court level, the union won at the third circuit court of appeals. The appeals court denied the company's claims that it had acted in due accordance with its powers as a Chapter 11 debtor in possession. In essence, the court accepted the union's contention that the company had used its powers in an arbitrary and unilateral manner, denying the union any compensation or recognition for its concessions—the company's failure to provide a snap-back provision was indicative of the unilateral nature of the company's actions. Supporting the union's contention that the lower courts had failed to realize the intentions of Congress in passing Section 1113, the appeals court also held that the lower courts had not used proper standards to determine the plausibility of the company's claims relative to the union's interests in a negotiated collective-bargaining agreement. As the court noted, the lower courts had acted more in a manner consistent with the Supreme Court's decision in *Bildisco* than the subsequent modification of that standard by Congress. Of course, this case, coming so soon after the passage of Section 1113, was a test of the application of Section 1113 and as such required a more imaginative treatment than precedent allowed.

Overall, the appeals court supported the union's contention that it was not being treated "fairly and equitably" relative to the debtor and creditors. Specifically, the union had argued Section 1113 protects employees from bearing the entire, or a disproportionate, share of the burden of reorganization and the Section ought to be read as requiring a balance of sorts to offset the company's unilateral actions in determining the union's burden. Notwithstanding the lack of a legislatively defined test of fairness and equity, the appeals court decided that the failure of the company to include a snap-back provision indicated that fairness was denied to workers who were otherwise prepared to provide concessions to help rescue the company from bankruptcy. The reversal of the company's petition to reject the collective-bargaining agreement, and the on-going strike precipitated a crisis at W-P. A creditors' committee negotiated a settlement with the union. This included a new collective-bargaining agreement with wage concessions, profit-sharing, a union representative on W-P's board, and removal of the CEO of the company.

Less than a year later, with the legal suit dismissed and a strike settlement at Wheeling-Pittsburgh agreed to, both provided immediate reference points of negotiation between LTV and the union. As the unsecured creditors noted in their brief to the Supreme Court, "by exercising economic leverage at the bargaining table with a debtor-in-possession, a labor organization may have a disproportionate advantage in the reorganization process" (p. 19). But the union's position has been supported by decisions of the federal court which have protected the collective-bargaining process through Section 1113 of the Bankruptcy Code. Inevitably, the petition by the PBGC for restoration of three terminated pension plans prompted the union to support LTV rather than support the agency. In this respect, the union claimed representation in bankruptcy proceedings as an affected party (members' livelihoods), a participating party in the continuing operation of the company as debtor in possession (their collective-bargaining agreement), and as an "interested" party in the successful reorganization of the company. Whereas the PBGC identified the union as the enemy, believing that the USWA was ultimately responsible for the pending crisis of the whole steel industry, the tensions inherent in the adjudicative process and the contending statutory claims concerning the bankruptcy of LTV were such that the union could claim legitimate standing on statutory bases quite different from that of the PBGC.

Logic of Bankruptcy Policy

E. Warren (1987) began her paper on bankruptcy policy by observing that "bankruptcy is a booming business" and then immediately noted the significance of the LTV bankruptcy for policy and politics. Yet for all the discussion of bankruptcy in theory and practice, the underlying logic of bankruptcy policy as a federal statutory responsibility remains remarkably opaque.[16] Indeed, it is just this opaqueness that Judge Sweet complained about in attempting a reconciliation of competing statutory claims. As currently construed, federal bankruptcy law offers little in the way of a rule or set of rules that would rationalize competing interests around one commonly accepted principle. The competition for advantage in the restructuring process among LTV, the union, and the PBGC is indicative of the uncertainty associated with bankruptcy policy in general.

Since the practice of bankruptcy is uncertain and difficult to rationalize, there have been attempts to develop a more formal, rule-based logic for the judicial adjudication of bankruptcy proceedings. Although denying the ready application of abstract formulas to bankruptcy proceedings, or the possibility of just one principle dominating bankruptcy proceedings, Warren argued that the purpose of bankruptcy is to distribute "an inadequate pie" among competing creditors in accordance with a presumption that all creditors be treated equitably. At the federal level, at issue are the claims made by creditors in relation to one another, given the limited assets of the debtor. Thus, federal bankruptcy protects debtors from creditors but does not guarantee creditors anything more than a fair hearing for their claims. In this sense, bankruptcy does not offer a substantive resolution of creditors' claims (that is, an *a priori* formula for how much money a creditor can expect from a debtor), but rather a forum for having all claims resolved in a manner that does justice to all while limiting the power of any one creditor. Underlying Warren's model of bankruptcy is a distributional nightmare: the court must decide what individual creditors deserve, realizing that no creditor can receive what they were once promised by the debtor. Warren described this notion of bankruptcy as the most commonly accepted model of bankruptcy and the best model for bankruptcy as a policy.

The notion that bankruptcy is a procedural mechanism for resolving competing distributional claims carries with it three subsidiary issues. First, it leaves open the question of the relative authority of other statutory obligations of the debtor and creditors. No claims in the federal Bankruptcy Code rank the relative importance of bankruptcy against other statutes, like the NLRA. Indeed, Section 1113 of the code ensures that bankruptcy cannot be used by companies to deny their customary and statutory obligations to negotiate collective-bargaining agreements in good faith consistent with the NLRA. In a Chapter 11 case, the bankruptcy court actually depends upon the authority of other statutes to maintain the normal operations of the debtor in possession. Second, just as there is no formula for balancing competing statutory claims, there is also no formula for determining fair and equitable distributions. Fairness and equity are not substantive rules, but rather procedural claims for equitable treatment through due process. As Warren noted, the lack of widely recognized or well-defined distributional rules in applications of bankruptcy law to competing creditors leaves the distributional process to the discretion of the courts. Finally, the emphasis on procedure stresses an apparent ambiguity in the bankruptcy process over who is qualified to be heard in the adjudicative process. Although it is often argued that affected employees and communities ought to have a voice in these proceedings, their status depends upon the courts' definition of a creditor. Just as the courts do not protect creditors' claims, the courts hardly protect those affected by bankruptcy.

In the LTV case, these three issues appeared in different guises. The issue of rationalizing competing statutory claims appears inherently and inevitably beyond the scope of bankruptcy law. That the PBGC based its legal strategy justifying the restoration of LTV's pension funds upon ERISA appears both as a miscast legal strategy and as an impossible problem for the court to resolve. The PBGC sought a legal recognition of its claim against the interests of other creditors and affected parties. It made claims in a context where the court was not equipped to make a ruling giving one claimant priority over others. There were no statutory bases for such a priority ranking of ERISA over other statutes, and the court was unable to appeal to any external reference that would have given retirees preference over employees or over other creditors. Either the PBGC made a mistake or, probably more likely, it argued from a rather different notion of bankruptcy law. Perhaps, like many other commentators on bankruptcy procedure, the PBGC recognized that the ambiguities of bankruptcy law are such that an aggressive stance was the only way the PBGC could hope to influence the court.

Warren's analysis of the "dirty, complex, elastic" nature of contemporary bankruptcy law was conceived in opposition to another, arguably more coherent albeit narrower version of "proper" bankruptcy policy. D. Baird's (1987) model of bankruptcy is based upon the Chicago school of law and economics. By the logic of this school, the goal of any law—the rule by which adjudication ought to proceed and the basis for making comparisons between outcomes of adjudication—must be the extent to which an action or decision advances economic efficiency and maximizes economic welfare. Essentially, R. Posner (1986) and others advocate the application of economic analysis to the law, arguing that "the economic theory of law is the most promising positive theory of law extant" (p. 24). Many criticisms of this approach to law and regulation have been made, and it is certainly not my intention here to go back over familiar ground (Clark 1985). It is enough to recognize for the time being that although the Chicago school of law and economics claims a certain virtue in its narrowness and clarity, others have argued that these virtues are illusory and quite philosophically unfounded, being proclaimed at the expense of the complexity of social life that exists outside the confines of neoclassical microeconomic analysis. What is important in the most immediate context of the bankruptcy of LTV is whether or not Baird's model of bankruptcy provides any insight into this particular dispute, especially the claims made by the PBGC and others for special status in the bankruptcy proceedings.

Baird argued that bankruptcy law ought to protect a relatively small universe of affected parties. Specifically, by his logic bankruptcy courts should just protect those who have a claim on the property or assets of the debtor company. Excluded then are unsecured creditors, employees, and the community; in fact, society in a general sense is excluded even though society may bear the costs of bankruptcy. Having narrowed the universe of those eligible to be considered in bankruptcy proceedings, Baird suggested that the evident presumption of Chapter 11 proceedings— rehabilitating the company—is mistaken. Assuming that the sole purpose of bankruptcy proceedings is to maximize the return to creditors, it may well be the case that liquidating the debtor is more consistent with the interests of creditors than saving the debtor in the interests of constituencies not included in the list of proper claimants. Though he did not explicitly address the virtues of cashing in assets, Baird cited case notes that review decisions by the federal courts and the NLRB which have served to speed asset conversion and redistribution (plant closings, the relocation of work, and the protection of management discretion against union collective-bargaining agreements). By the terms of the Chicago school of law and economics, such decisions promote economic efficiency and maximize social welfare. Baird was not unconcerned with the welfare of workers and communities affected by bankruptcy. Quite the contrary. He rejected Warren's implication that his efficiency rule is "the sole standard by which to measure the rights of these people" (p. 824). Rather, Baird suggested that bankruptcy ought to be narrowly understood and applied; workers and communities would be better served by using other statutory instruments (like the NLRA, or plant-closing legislation) to protect their interests.

In one sense, Baird's model is like Warren's—at issue is the distribution of assets between creditors, given a limited pie and the evident inability of the debtor to execute its original promises. At another level, though, there are profound differences between their treatments of bankruptcy. Where Warren would read the category of creditors broadly, including workers and perhaps their communities, Baird would not. Where Warren would argue that bankruptcy serves a complex set of goals, Baird would not. Where Warren would argue that bankruptcy cannot be easily resolved by reference to one rule or one set of rules, Baird suggests that this is precisely the proper domain of an adequate bankruptcy theory. Where Warren depends upon judges to ensure fairness on a case-by-case basis, Baird suggests that to depend upon the judiciary to police the behavior of debtors and creditors is to ask too much. He observed "judges, like the rest of us, are prone to error" (p. 821). In this respect Baird has much sympathy for Judge Sweet's impossible problem. Baird would argue that rationalizing all the statutory and political interests of the competing parties in the LTV case places an impossible burden on the bankruptcy court. Baird would "solve" the apparent problems of current bankruptcy proceedings (who is qualified to be heard, how assets are to be distributed, and how contending statutory interests are to be rationalized) by limiting the claimants, by deciding upon a distribution scheme that maximizes total welfare, and by encouraging contending statutory claims to be heard elsewhere.

The consequences of such a policy would be manifold. The PBGC would presumably have more status as a secured creditor relative to retirees,

the union, and the community (at least). It would not be able to claim
special status by virtue of ERISA, but then neither would the union be
able to claim special status by virtue of the NLRA. The PBGC may or
may not benefit from a distribution rule that maximized total welfare of
all secured creditors. It is clear, however, that whatever the consequences
for retirees of such a distributive rule, they would have no legitimate claim
for consideration in the allocative proceedings. With respect to the existing
workers, they may well be disadvantaged relative to retirees if a Baird-
inspired court decided that maximizing the total welfare of creditors required liquidating the debtor (whatever the commonly accepted logic of a
Chapter 11 petition). In these ways, Baird's model provides Judge Sweet
an answer to his rhetorical question posed in the epigraph to this book:
who is to be responsible for the welfare of those affected by restructuring?
Baird's answer is that Judge Sweet should not be responsible, and possibly
no one is responsible, given the necessary imperatives of economic efficiency. Baird's bankruptcy policy eschews the texture of the extant dispute
for what Warren noted as the supposedly desirable logic of "hypothetical
behavior" and "fixed answers" (p. 777).[17]

Baird's model of bankruptcy policy provides ready solutions to apparently the most difficult problems of resolving competing claims in the LTV
case and other cases. Yet for a federal court judge like Judge Sweet charged
with the responsibility of reconciling diverse interests, Baird's formula
must be disappointing. Baird's rules would limit the power and discretion
of judges in bankruptcy cases, but would also impose on judges a coherent
blueprint for decisionmaking that is relatively insensitive to the magnitude
of claims brought before the court. To suggest, as Baird might, that claims
outside the narrow logic of his model ought to be heard elsewhere is to
suppose there is another "place" for hearing claims made on behalf of those
affected by the current round of corporate restructuring. But that is precisely Judge Sweet's point: there appears to be no forum, no one responsible
for resolving these claims just as there is no explicit federal policy for
corporate restructuring other than that (perhaps) discerned in the patterns
of defense expenditures. Where Judge Sweet identifies great social harm
flowing from restructuring, the proper response according to Baird is to
ignore those issues and treat the matter in the narrowest possible manner.
For Baird, this response has the virtue of limiting judges' regulation of
economic matters that presumably is best left to the market. Baird's bankruptcy policy is a policy of limited regulation consistent with the most
general normative claim of the Chicago school of law and economics—that
regulation only creates more harm than it solves.

Judge Sweet's actions supporting the status of LTV workers, the union, and retirees in bankruptcy proceedings and his insistence upon LTV following through on its collective-bargaining obligations with the union would seem to suggest that Baird's model was not particularly relevant to Sweet's mode of adjudication. Nor does it appear that Sweet was fundamentally concerned with matters of distribution between creditors and the equitable treatment of creditors as a group of claimants. Warren's model, which places a great deal of emphasis on the distributive consequences of bankruptcy, is thus also less relevant in this instance. Whereas both Warren and Baird were concerned that bankruptcy provide a mechanism for the resolution of creditors' claims, Judge Sweet appeared to be as concerned with the rehabilitation of LTV as an operating entity. This does not necessarily mean that Judge Sweet's mode of adjudication was set in opposition to either Baird's or Warren's model. In this instance, it might be the case that creditors' welfare is maximized by the rehabilitation of the debtor and thus Sweet's policy might be consistent with Baird's model. It is also apparent that Warren believed that corporate rehabilitation is a worthy and vital aspect of bankruptcy proceedings. She might still argue that rehabilitation of the corporation must be judged according to its distributive consequences but she might nevertheless support Sweet's policy as being in the interests of all those affected by the failure of LTV, including the community, workers, retirees, and secured creditors.

That being said, there are reasons to suppose that neither Baird nor Warren would especially favor Judge Sweet's policy of rehabilitation. Baird was particularly critical of policies that favor workers and communities over secured creditors. Although not denying the legitimate concerns of those groups affected by bankruptcy, he believed that these kinds of policies redistribute the costs of bankruptcy to creditors who have a much stronger claim on corporate assets than workers do. Warren might also be offended by Sweet's actions that have essentially denied the creditors, and especially the PBGC, preferential standing compared to LTV's employees and retirees in bankruptcy proceedings. Baird might suggest that this case is evidence that judges have too much discretion in bankruptcy proceedings. Warren might argue that this case is evidence of the relative paupacy of current analytical tools for evaluating the distributive consequences of different bankruptcy-policy options. Judge Sweet, however, might argue that rehabilitation of the company is the only "reasonable" option, given "the casualties suffered by a basic American industry that has been battered by intensive and successful competition" and the failure of the federal government to implement or even enunciate an explicit policy for corporate restructuring.

By this interpretation of Sweet's actions, his argument against the PBGC (that it failed to see the significance of other statutory claims) should be understood as a means of protecting the union and the company from outside interference in their negotiations over a collective-bargaining agreement. Given the past experience of the union and the industry in bankruptcy proceedings (Wheeling-Pittsburgh in particular), it should have been obvious to those involved in the LTV bankruptcy proceedings that only cordial labor-management relations could save the corporation. In this sense, Judge Sweet privileged workers and retirees over the secured creditors in the interests of harmonious labor-management relations. The PBGC failed to appreciate either the significance of these considerations in the operations of a steel company or (by its acceptance of the Lawrences' application of the theory of the end-game to the steel industry) the significance of union participation in corporate survival. The PBGC simply pursued the matter of corporate pension liability as a secured creditor concerned only with the distributive consequences of bankruptcy. In this respect, it is doubtful that the PBGC had any interest in the rehabilitation of the corporation; the PBGC, like Baird, would apparently prefer liquidation of the corporation and the distribution of assets if that would be the best means of maximizing returns to secured creditors. But perhaps, unlike Baird, the PBGC is driven both by a concern for equity and by a political concern to maintain its autonomy in the face of congressional doubts about its financial integrity and what it perceives to be (or have been) a conspiracy between the union and the company to "defraud" the public.

Summary—Judicial Pragmaticism

Judge Sweet's predicament was that while there is no statutory guide for resolving competing claims for special status in the bankruptcy of LTV he was nevertheless charged with the responsibility of establishing an adequate decision rule to be fair to the secured creditors and sensitive to the circumstances of the corporation and its workers and retirees. Whereas a federal industrial policy or a corporate restructuring policy might provide such a guide (assuming such policies took precedence over other statutory claims) the judge was left to make policy in the context of competing interpretations of the logic of bankruptcy. His complaint against Congress is quite clearly made in the final pages of his decision of October 17, 1988, wherein he said, "Congress should not wait for reorganizing companies to bankrupt an under funded government corporation already $4 billion in debt, and leave to the courts the task of discerning the congressional purpose with respect to an issue of fundamental importance to the survival of many ailing American industries and the welfare of their employees."

Yet for all of Judge Sweet's dissatisfaction with the operant bases of bankruptcy policy, his actions in formulating a response to the LTV situation was in the best tradition of bankruptcy decisionmaking in U.S. federal courts. Some federal court judges have a great deal of experience in operating at the boundaries of statutory policy. Judge-made law and regulation of private agents' actions in the context of broad but ill-defined statutory imperatives is typical of many fields of judicial adjudication in the United States. Given what Warren and others have noted as the apparent opaqueness of bankruptcy law, Sweet acted in a pragmatic manner to regulate the restructuring of one corporation. And given the significance of the LTV bankruptcy case for bankruptcy case law, Judge Sweet's pragmaticism will have major implications for understanding the propriety of corporate actions in other circumstances in the future. Still, to act in a pragmatic manner is thought by some to be equivalent to acting in an arbitrary or unprincipled manner. This was certainly one of Baird's concerns. He supposed that to act without regard to a set of *a priori* defined abstract principles is to invite judicial error or at least judicial "sloppiness." But in this particular context I prefer Hook's (1974) notion of pragmatism, which I think describes Sweet's solution to his predicament in a methodological sense: pragmaticism is "the theory and practice of enlarging human freedom in a precarious and tragic world by the arts of intelligent social control."

Pragmaticism has the virtue of being responsive and adaptive to new situations, but does reflect a wider problem that goes to the heart of issues in this book. As Sweet implied, pragmaticism is born in these instances by the lack of an adequate legislative framework—the lack of an industrial policy or something similar that would guide the rationalization of competing statutory claims. More profoundly, I would argue that this is inevitable given the style of recent law which privileges rights over substantive policy. In this context, pragmaticism is unavoidable, made so by the role that bankruptcy judges play in administering the restructuring of corporations and the structure of relevant law. If this was an isolated problem, either a one-time event prompted by the sheer magnitude of the LTV bankruptcy (the lack of a legislative framework being irrelevant), or simply a case of limited judicial imagination, then there would be little reason to look so closely at the circumstances and forces at work in this case. But that is not the case.

For the PBGC, the case was also fundamental, though for different reasons. The PBGC is an agency at risk, close to bankruptcy itself (because of corporate bankruptcies that have dumped their pension obligations onto the agency) and in danger of losing its autonomy from Congress and the executive. In a political environment that has been very suspicious of the PBGC, and in a historical setting where independent agencies have often been threatened by Congress for their lack of immediate political and economic accountability (Freedman 1978), the very legitimacy of the PBGC has been shaken by its lack of success in regulating the actions of corporations such as LTV. Judicial pragmaticism is not a solution for the PBGC. Judge Sweet has made the PBGC's job harder in an economic world that deems corporate pension obligations an unbearable burden. If the PBGC is to be effective in protecting pension rights, it will need a stronger claim on bankruptcy proceedings than is currently available. The failure of Congress to provide the PBGC with adequate powers in these situations coupled with a historical suspicion of statutory agencies has placed the PBGC in a double bind: having neither enough power nor enough political clout to carry out its mission of regulating corporations' obligations to their pension funds.

PART 3

Regulatory
Strategy

7

Limits of Statutory Responses
to Restructuring

Corporate restructuring raises the issue of companies' responsibilities to workers and communities, their contractual obligations to unions and suppliers, and their obligations to act lawfully. Corporate restructuring inevitably puts companies on a collision course with laws and regulatory agencies, as well as with social expectations about ethical behavior. Conflict is pervasive. At one level, conflict is between companies and affected groups, between those who benefit from restructuring and those who bear the costs of economic rationalization. As a consequence, community groups, unions, and their representatives in Congress have sought to regulate the process of restructuring, particularly the allocation of costs. ERISA and plant-closing legislation are relevant examples of this regulatory process. At another level, however, it is quite apparent that conflict involves legal and judicial matters. Affected workers and communities have looked to the courts to force corporations to negotiate the design of restructuring, as they have attempted to use the courts to ameliorate the costs of restructuring. The courts have been used by workers and their representatives to force corporations to stand by their legal obligations (see chapter 3). Conflict between economic imperatives and social obligations is conflict over the very shape of society as social and political interests are transmuted into legal claims.

Could such conflict be effectively rationalized by a statute or set of statutes? This chapter makes a series of arguments about statutory responses to the problems of regulating corporate restructuring. For a start, it is suggested that statutes are not *the* solution (in and of themselves) to the problems of restructuring. Although profoundly important as blueprints indicating public goals and objectives, statutes such as ERISA are written in general ways to be interpreted by regulatory agencies and the courts. The predicament Judge Robert J. Sweet faced as he adjudicated the LTV bankruptcy case would not disappear with a new statute. Rather, as has been intimated, a new problem emerges with a new statute: reconciling the new statute with existing statutes—a problem of statutory interpretation and application in the context of particular events.[1] A related argument is that judicial adjudication is an important form of regulation. By virtue of the nature of statutes and the overlapping responsibilities of competing statutes, judicial interpretation is a process of regulation. It should be clear, though, that judicial regulation depends upon social standards regarding overarching policy objectives to sustain their decisions. At issue in this chapter, as well as the next two chapters, is what those standards ought to be—an issue that is strongly contested without any accepted recipe for determining the best standard for policy-making.

In this chapter, these arguments are considered in terms of plant-closing legislation and industrial policy. It is worth pausing for a moment to understand why I have chosen to begin with plant-closing legislation. In many respects, plant-closing legislation combines the essential elements of my argument about the crisis of regulation in general. The plant-closing statute is a statute with an object similar to ERISA: its purpose derives from congressional concern about the community consequences of corporate restructuring. By analyzing the plant-closing bill, I aim to make a strong argument about the nature of contemporary legislation-writing without becoming enmeshed in the intricacies of ERISA. I do believe, however, that the underlying rights logic of the plant-closing bill and the rights logic of ERISA are basically the same. What I suggest by way of analogy and implication is that the limits of ERISA are also in the most recent legislation related to corporate restructuring. The significance of the courts in regulating corporate restructuring is the product of the legislative process.

Plant-Closing Legislation

The plant-closing notification bill, the Worker Adjustment and Retraining Notification Act, became law on August 4, 1988. As with ERISA, passage of the act came at a crucial time in the lead-up to presidential elections. Reagan had vetoed the Omnibus Trade Bill, which originally included the plant-closing provision, in early May of 1988. By most accounts, Reagan was unwilling to exercise his veto and risk a protracted public debate over the merits of a bill, nor was he willing to risk the humiliation of having his veto overridden in Congress by a coalition of Democrats and Republicans (a possibility, given the vote margin by which the new Omnibus Trade and plant-closing bills passed in the House and the Senate; see Tables 7.1 and 7.2). Many commentators believe that had the president rejected the plant-closing bill that action would have been interpreted as symbolic of the Republican Party's (and George Bush's) antipathy to blue-collar labor.

For advocates of the bill, plant-closing legislation represented a necessary response to a pressing national problem—apparent rapid changes in the economy, massive restructuring of basic industries, and unemployment (Ford 1985). Although advocated by many in Congress since at least the oil shock–induced recession of the mid-1970s, the severe recession of the early 1980s (concentrated in manufacturing industries and factory towns across America) further accentuated the need for prenotification (Craypo 1985). B. Bluestone and B. Harrison's (1982) book on deindustrialization was a very important reference for advocates of such legislation. They showed that few workers were given warning of plant closings, and those warned were most often unionized employees in large manufacturing plants. For Bluestone and Harrison, the case for plant-closing legislation was a clear case for equitable treatment of unionized and nonunionized employees alike, for rebuilding the local economic base, and for helping affected workers. The strongest plant-closing bills would have required some form of compensation to affected workers and communities, maintenance of health insurance benefits for a time, transfer rights between plants, and even preferential loans to worker cooperatives to allow them to buy out plant owners. However, none of these bills would have interfered with companies' putative property rights, and none challenged decisions of the Reagan-appointed NLRB in the early 1980s allowing companies to close plants without first negotiating with unions.

The significance of this policy can also be understood in terms of a broader debate in Congress and society about the proper role of government in regulating economic change. Three different positions have been taken on this larger issue, reflected then in the debate over the merits of plant-closing legislation. The most conservative position is advocated by research institutes such as the Cato and Heritage institutes: governments should not regulate economic change since (a) such change is a necessary feature of a dynamic and prosperous economy, and (b) any government regulation would inevitably result in lower rates of economic efficiency, thus (c) leading to greater social costs of economic change in the long run than any costs offset by government in the short run (McKenzie 1981).[2] A more liberal perspective advanced by R. Cyert and D. Mowery (1988) and M. Howland (1988) argues that government can regulate economic change since (a) labor markets are not entirely efficient, and (b) if speedy adjustment can be encouraged, then workers' welfare and the efficiency of the economy will be enhanced, assuming that government policy does not do more than speed local adjustment to global market forces.[3] Bluestone and Harrison do not agree with conservatives and, although agreeing with the

Table 7.1 Votes in U.S. House of Representatives on Passage of Omnibus Trade Bill with (April 21, 1988) and without (July 13, 1988) Plant-closing Provision, and on Plant-closing Bill (July 13, 1988), by Region and Party

| Region/Party | Omnibus Trade | | | | Plant-closing July 13, 1988 | |
| | April 21, 1988 | | July 13, 1988 | | | |
	For	Against	For	Against	For	Against
Midwest						
Democrats	57	1	56	3	58	0
Republicans	17	29	35	13	15	33
North						
Democrats	63	1	62	1	63	0
Republicans	28	13	36	6	29	13
South						
Democrats	78	0	79	0	65	16
Republicans	12	31	38	4	1	41
Near West						
Democrats	11	0	11	0	11	0
Republicans	6	12	11	6	3	14
Pacific West						
Democrats	35	0	35	0	35	0
Republicans	5	20	13	12	6	19
Totals						
Democrats	244	2	243	4	232	16
Republicans	68	105	133	41	54	120
Grand Total	312	107	376	45	286	136

first two liberal propositions, also argue that equity is a vital criterion for public policy intervention over and above efficiency considerations.

The bill that finally passed in 1988 was the product of a coalition between Democrats and northern Republicans (see Tables 7.1 and 7.2)—as such a compromise between those liberals who advocate an adjustment response and those concerned with equity. It provided for sixty days advance notification to workers and communities but was less powerful than earlier versions. Although now targeted at mass layoffs of at least 33 percent of the on-site workforce, as well as plant closings involving at least fifty employees, employers were provided options that were not previously considered matters of choice. Employers can offer affected workers the option to transfer and thus not count those employees as having lost employment; plants can be closed without advance notification and without

Table 7.2 Votes in U.S. Senate on Passage of Omnibus Trade Bill with (April 21, 1988) and without (July 13, 1988) Plant-closing Provision, and on Plant-closing Bill (July 13, 1988), by Region and Party

| Region/Party | Omnibus Trade | | | | Plant-closing | |
| | April 27, 1988 | | August 3, 1988 | | July 6, 1988 | |
	For	Against	For	Against	For	Against
Midwest						
Democrats	7	1	7	1	8	0
Republicans	3	7	8	2	4	5
North						
Democrats	13	0	13	0	13	0
Republicans	6	4	9	1	8	2
South						
Democrats	18	0	16	0	18	0
Republicans	1	7	6	1	1	6
Near West						
Democrats	10	0	10	0	10	0
Republicans	0	12	9	3	3	8
Pacific West						
Democrats	4	0	4	0	4	0
Republicans	1	5	3	3	3	2
Totals						
Democrats	52	1	50	1	53	0
Republicans	11	35	35	10	19	23
Grand Total	63	36	85	11	72	23

penalty if employers reasonably believe that notification could affect the continuity of the business; plants can be closed sooner than anticipated if unforeseen events warrant; and, plants can be closed without notice if a project is completed and labor was on contract. No compensation is mandated for affected workers or communities, and there are no requirements that workers be offered preferential status as possible buyers. However, if an employer violates the sixty-days-notice provision, affected workers can bring a civil action in federal district court for back pay, benefits, or payments previously negotiated up to a maximum determined with reference to wages paid and the days short of the notification requirement. Similarly, local governments can bring suit for limited compensation for failing to advise of a closing or closing earlier than announced.

Whereas plant-closing policy can be argued for on narrow grounds (as

encouraging workers' adjustment to economic change) or broad grounds
(as an equity issue), many would also contend that plant-closing legislation
can be interpreted as a necessary part of any national industrial policy. If
there are to be targets for the path of the economy—the growth and
development of new technologies, new sectors, and reinvestment in older
"core" sectors—there must be also a set of policies that provide workers
a tangible share in the progress made by those development policies given
the burdens of structural change (Obey 1986; Reich 1983). Otherwise, as
was suggested by Judge Sweet in the LTV bankruptcy case, the casualties
of restructuring may be left outside of the benefits of the transformation
process so that their only recourse is litigation. Considerable support exists
for an overall statutory response to restructuring, a response that would
provide judges and administrative agencies with guidelines for allocating
costs, clear policies with respect to workers' and communities' rights, and
clarification of the relative weight to be attributed to economic considerations in relation to corporations' social obligations.

Vote-Trading, Statutes, and Their Meaning

The confidence displayed by advocates of a new statute or set of statutes
is typical of reformers of all political persuasions who believe a legislative
solution is necessary to achieve their objectives. Interpretations of the
role of Congress as the servant of political interests and the evolution of
the process of policy definition and design since the New Deal era have
combined to reinforce the expectations and confidence of reformers in
statute-making. If these expectations are of relatively recent origin, there
is doubt that public policy and statute-making are now thought so syn-
onymous that G. Calabresi (1982) suggests the adjudicative process is
"choked" on the accumulated statutes. Concomitant with the "age of statutes" has been the development of the administrative state: the public
bureaucracy responsible for implementing policy (statute), regulating private actions, and policing the implementation of policy.[4] Administrative
agencies such as the NLRB and the SSA are the most obvious and well-
known administrative apparatuses. However, it is quite apparent that
there is a myriad of other agencies, including the federal court system,
which also implement, regulate, and police policy by virtue of their constitutional powers of review.

Set within the context of the administrative state, the effectiveness of
any policy depends upon the process of policy design and implementation.
If Congress was to pass a comprehensive industrial policy, that policy
would have to be allocated to some administrative agency for implemen-

tation. This assumes, of course, that the bill itself is written in a detailed manner, that its provisions are clearly specified, and that an agency is identified to implement the policy according to the statute's specifications. So, for example, in the case of the plant-closing bill, the provisions of the policy—the requirements placed on employers with respect to their social obligations—were specified, and the federal courts were identified as the review body responsible for determining whether or not employers had complied with the provisions of the act and whether or not they should be penalized for failing to meet certain provisions. That was a small statute, in terms of page length (fewer than six full pages). By contrast, ERISA is gigantic, running for hundreds of pages, containing many different titles and provisions, as well as subsequent revisions and additions. Nevertheless, even in that case, Congress identified a number of agencies responsible for the implementation of the act and also identified agencies responsible for policing and enforcing provisions of the act. After passage, the focus of public policy shifts from the statute to the effectiveness of regulatory agencies vis-à-vis the implementation of policy.

While I am not disavowing the significance of that kind of analytical assessment, a prior set of considerations must be taken into account: the value of statutes as policy and legal documents. That the value of a statute is at issue in these terms may come as a surprise to some social activists. There is, at times, a tendency to treat statutes as coherent and complete documents, their integrity guaranteed by the fact that they originated in Congress. But as I suggested in reviewing the origins and logic of ERISA, skepticism is increasing about the value of statutes, what they provide in the way of authoritative statements about the goals and objectives of policy, and the extent to which they are deliberately written to be vague about the nature and standards of regulation required to attain stated goals and objectives.

To illustrate, Rubin (1989:369) began his assessment of the status of statutes by observing that "policy formation has displaced the diffused and incremental operation of the common law as our primary means of social regulation." Notwithstanding the significance of the judiciary as interpreter of statutes, he went on to argue that policy formulation by Congress has itself been displaced by administrative agencies. And notwithstanding the assumed equivalence between statutes and the law as a definitive set of "rules governing human conduct" (p. 371), he also suggested that statutes are rarely as assumed; administrative agencies are normally the origin of rules and regulations, not the legislature. What are statutes then? Rubin's answer was that statutes are "a set of public policy directives that the legislature issues to government implementation mechanisms" (p. 374).

By his assessment, statutes normally contain three types of information: statements of broad policy goals, standards by which administrative agencies are to design and implement policy, and identification of the agencies responsible for the design and implementation of policy. However, Rubin argued that most statutes are intransitive, meaning that until the relevant administrative agency acts, "the ultimate target of the statute cannot know what behavior the statute will require" (p. 381).[5]

There appear to be two plausible explanations for the intransitivity of statutes. The most general explanation (referencing Wittgenstein and Derrida and deconstruction) is that statutes (like language in general) are indeterminate by nature (Clark 1985). This suggests that intransitivity is a property of both statutes and the rules and regulations of administrative agencies, and that what Rubin and others identify as the open-textured nature of statutes is typical of all text-based discourses. At issue in a fundamental sense is the inexact (or slippery) relationship between language (its terms and labels) and reality (their presumed objects) (Searle 1983). This is, in all probability, too abstract an issue for the immediate concerns of this chapter. Nevertheless, by the logic of deconstruction it would be said that determinacy is only reached momentarily and in the context of some event or situation that provides a reference point for fixing meaning. However important this observation is about the inevitable hermeneutic nature of law (Goodrich 1986), there is a further problem of intentions: statutes may be deliberately written by Congress in order to use this property of language whereas administrative agencies normally do not intend that their rules and regulations be intransitive. Why should legislators deliberately write opaque statutes? Here a number of explanations may help to answer the question.

Public-choice theorists believe that intentional intransitivity is a product of legislators' interest in and need for reelection. R. E. Barnett (1987:288) noted that "the vagueness of today's statutes . . . enables politicians to support particular legislation that pleases certain constituencies without alienating others. This deliberate vagueness shifts the battle over a statute's meaning away from the legislature into the administrative process and the courts." Vagueness is thus a strategy for coalition-building, sometimes termed *log-rolling* or *vote-trading* (garnering political support from related interest groups through broadly written and interpreted statutes), while minimizing the risks of organized political dissent (Mueller 1989). At the same time, intransitivity shifts the burden of fixing the meaning of a statute and its constituent rules and regulations to agencies and the courts that are not directly responsible to political interests. The costs of this strategy for agencies and the courts can be considerable. Not only are the decisions of administrative apparatuses subject to extraordinary scrutiny, the lack of direct political accountability for policymaking may prompt questions about their legitimacy. These tensions are further exacerbated by an apparent willingness of the legislature to pass statutes of dubious constitutionality. Not only is the administrative state then embroiled in policy disputes distant from their own bureaucratic interests, their legitimacy is further weakened by doubts about the constitutional integrity of their actions in implementing or refusing to implement policy.[6]

Another explanation of the intentional vagueness of statutes comes from those interested in the institutional evolution of Congress and the increasing significance of congressional staff. P. Strauss (1989), while agreeing that public-choice theorists have an entirely plausible explanation, suggested that the fact that Congress has become so large means that staff now play a crucial role in organizing legislators' activities.[7] One consequence is that congressional representatives are often isolated, their claims muted by staff concerned to maintain a place in the bureaucratic hierarchy. This argument implies that staff are more risk-adverse than legislators, often more permanent in the bureaucratic system than legislators, and have career paths in Washington, D.C., that depend more upon the established political structure than legislators. By this argument, statutory debate serves either of two functions: it allows for the trading of votes and favors and/or it allows for personal statements of support or dissent in terms of particular local constituencies (a related argument advanced by Mikva 1983). In either instance, legislators' votes are deployed by staff as ambit claims for future considerations.[8] This organizational perspective builds upon and extends the public-choice argument. Like public-choice theory it sees voting as a strategic activity, made more valuable by vague statements of policy rather than well-defined statutes. But unlike public-choice theorists, advocates of this perspective "explain" behavior with respect to the interests of the bureaucracy.[9]

How is this shift of responsibility from Congress to agencies and the courts for the interpretation of statutes accomplished and sustained? From an organization perspective, the answer is very simple. Unlike congressional staff, judges and agency officials are most often professional, not political appointees. Their career paths are tied as much to their external profession as they are tied to internal employers—their performance is oftentimes evaluated with respect to professional standards. Most important, their organizations are handicapped by structure: their mandate is given to them by Congress and/or the Constitution. Formally, their powers are derived either from express instructions from Congress or from general propositions derived from the Constitution. These structural imperatives allow Congress to delegate and direct, but leave no room for negotiation or refusal. The only option for the courts is to embarrass the legislature by finding as unconstitutional their passed statutes. But this is a delicate issue, made so by the judiciary's and agencies' essentially undemocratic position in the polity (Clark 1985, chap. 3). If the structural division of powers is not enough, the language of democracy is so centered upon Congress that there are practically no options for agencies or the judiciary to invent a role for themselves that can avoid responsibility for what Congress refuses to define (the meaning of statutes).

Given these explanations of the intentional vagueness of statutes and the inevitable need for further determination of the meaning of passed statutes by agencies or the courts, what does all this mean for a corporate restructuring policy? Let us first consider what happened to the plant-closing bill. Clearly, it had a difficult passage through Congress and was caught up in presidential politics. The bill represented a strategic threat to established political networks but was an opportunity to reinforce the loyalty of northern blue-collar workers to the Democratic Party. Even so, it had little in the way of statements of principle, and began with titles, definitions, and exemptions, not general claims of policy. This is unusual, but on the other hand, given the political tensions surrounding the act, it was entirely predictable. In its various original forms, the bill sought to establish the terms and conditions for compensating workers and communities affected by closings. As well, advocates of the bill believed that companies should provide extended health-care coverage, provide buyout options for workers if they desired it, and allow for transfer rights between plants. The version passed and ultimately signed into law made compromises on these terms and others; compensation is not a right but a possibility if the company concerned failed to provide adequate notification. Even this was conditional upon wages paid, and could be denied by a court if it believed the company had acted in ways consistent with the intentions of the act.

If in the abstract the bill was contentious and politically divisive, in its final written form the bill was neither. Moreover, it contained vaguely defined reasons for exemption from what are now the weakest notification requirements. For instance, companies can be excused from notification requirements if it "reasonably and in good faith believed" such notification would adversely affect the prospects for investment [Sec. 3(b)]. As well, companies are not liable if they fail to provide notification in cases where business conditions "were not reasonably foreseen" or in cases of "natural disaster." Labor hired for a certain time under contract is also exempt from the notification requirements, and nothing in the act is deemed to violate or invalidate NLRA provisions concerning the replacement of workers during a strike or lockout. These criteria for exemption, based generally on "reasonable standards," are to be adjudicated by the courts (no administrative agency was charged with that task). Consequently, definition of those standards, their application to specific instances, and their regulation (policing and maintenance) are the responsibility of the courts. This is not a *policy* in a conventional sense; rather it is a license to litigate. By Rubin's terms the bill is intransitive. And by the terms of public-choice theory, bureaucracy theory, and state theory, its deliberate intransitivity is to be expected given the political contentiousness of the bill as well as the ability of Congress to shift to the courts the responsibility for defining standards of performance. It would seem clear that this is the fate that awaits any industrial policy, or any other policy that addresses the relationship between economic imperatives and social obligations.

Prospects for a Restructuring Agency

Imagine an industrial policy statute was passed, collecting together otherwise disparate statutes such as the plant-closing act, the worker adjustment and training provisions of the trade bill, the provisions of ERISA that protect workers' pension rights, and the tax incentives provided for worker-owned buyouts of companies. Imagine also that this bill was passed by a coalition of northern liberals (Democrats from Atlantic and Midwestern states and some Republicans) and western Democrats (principally from California, Oregon, and Washington), and was reluctantly signed into law because of Republican pressures to do something for communities adversely affected by military base closings. This is a plausible scenario, matching the geography of congressional support with other recent congressional initiatives such as labor law reform, as well as the lobby for southern economic growth, even though the notion of an industrial policy is anathema to many conservative Republicans (Clark 1989a).

Assuming an industrial policy, conceived in part to speed local adjustment to restructuring as well as to ameliorate the worst affects of restructuring, how would such a policy be implemented? One option is to establish a new, dedicated agency for designing and implementing provisions of the new statute. Taking the hypothetical statute one step further we could imagine that a federal administrative agency was proposed, a political gesture referencing the need for federal planning and the protection of local workers' welfare. As originally conceived, such an agency might be called the Community Adjustment and Recovery Agency (CARA), its name being deliberately associated with the NRA of the invalidated National Industrial Recovery Act of 1933.[10] As recommended, CARA would be responsible for administering retraining grants, relocation assistance, monitoring plant closings and notifications, and for seeding grants and technical assistance for local private development initiatives.

Now all this is hypothetical. I do not mean to suggest that a real administrative agency must exist for a policy to be implemented, or do I mean to have exhausted the possible tasks and functions of such an agency if it were established. I do mean to suggest that this is an option for any government contemplating the implementation of a new policy, but at the same time I would also suggest that it is an unlikely option. Clearly, a new statute would not be protected from the problems noted above about the vagueness of statutes in general. But more particularly, for a variety of reasons Congress would not establish a new agency to implement an industrial policy. Even if it were established, the president need not agree. Any Republican president would use the establishment of an agency such as CARA as an excuse to veto the enabling legislation.

Notwithstanding the nostalgia of some liberals for a New Deal–inspired administrative agency for implementing industrial policy, there are two important reasons for believing that Congress would not establish such an agency. First, and without regard to the possible merits of an agency in this particular instance, over the last decade or so Congress has sought to limit the discretion of established agencies. Strong claims are made in Congress and elsewhere that administrative agencies are out of control, and that their relative autonomy has enabled the strongest agencies to circumvent and avoid the scrutiny of Congress and the executive.[11] That many of these agencies are operating in a political realm of contested values, policies, and priorities has further convinced critics that the powers of agencies need to be reviewed, even restricted. There is a certain irony, of course, in these attempts at institutional control; as noted above, Congress itself has been unwilling to provide strict statutory guidance to agencies in the form of detailed rules and regulations. If administrative agencies are out of control, their powers are enhanced by the deliberate vagueness of passed statutes and the apparent unwillingness of Congress to articulate clearly political choices in ways that would provide agencies with an external measure of responsibility to congressional intent. Even so, administrative agencies have "failed to serve as vehicles for democratic aspirations" (Sunstein 1989:429).

Another reason why Congress would be reluctant to establish a new agency is that many existing agencies are thought unsuccessful. There seem to be a number of different versions of this argument. Some commentators suggest that in terms of economic regulation, administrative agencies failed to adequately design their rules and regulations in a manner consistent with, or related to, sound economic principles. This is a sweeping generalization. It argues for an assessment of regulatory practices based on an abstract theoretical notion of economic efficiency (measured by reference to private actions with and without government intervention). Moreover, this argument suggests a clear and unequivocal rule regarding the proper relationship between economic imperatives and social obligations—the latter must be designed so as to be consistent with the former (Breyer 1982). This assessment is contested by those who argue that the role of regulation is more complex than this reductionist formula: in many respects, administrative agencies were conceived so as to accommodate a "balance" between economic imperatives and social obligations. Even so, it is indicative of the dissatisfaction of many groups with administrative agencies' performance that Breyer's formula is thought by many to be a useful means of reasserting control over agencies' actions. Other commentators have suggested that administrative agencies are too bureaucratic and too cumbersome for innovation and responsiveness to local needs (Salamon 1981).

Nostalgia for the past aside, it is doubtful that any new industrial policy statute would be accompanied by a new dedicated administrative agency responsible for the design and implementation of industrial policy. There is little prospect of a Japanese MITI-like industrial and community adjustment agency. With all this in mind, the options are varied.[12] C. Sunstein, commenting on the postwar performance of U.S. administrative agencies, notes their "pathologies" and argues for "new initiatives," particularly "a system of aggressive legislative, judicial, and executive control" (1987:429). Thus we can imagine, like L. Salamon (1981), that some adjustment policies will be implemented by "third-party" governmental organizations, by existing organizations (such as the DOL, which is currently responsible for disbursing worker-adjustment stipends), and even local voluntary organizations who compete for funding from the federal government for projects to assist displaced workers. But, assuming that Congress remains disinterested in detailed statutes, there also will be increasing pressure to involve the federal courts in adjudicating the applicability, on a case-by-case basis, of general standards of "reasonableness"—affected workers and their communities will be provided rights to bring civil actions in federal courts to establish their entitlements. In this respect, the courts will, and have become, an important mechanism for designing and implementing policy.

With respect to administrative agencies and their regulations, the federal courts are normally thought to provide a necessary bulwark against the arbitrary and capricious use of power. In this context, the courts have three related roles. First, they ensure that agencies act in accordance with the law, not just their enabling statutes, and other laws that protect individuals' rights in a most general sense. It is important that agencies be responsible to an institution of review that is directly responsible for the monitoring of agencies' actions. Nominally, the legislature is such an institution. Practically, though, the courts are the only real option for most citizens. The danger is that agencies become a law unto themselves, with their own internal review systems that do not allow for an outside perspective. Second, it is thus important to ensure that regulatory agencies act in a manner that is consistent, deliberative, and considered. That is, there is an identifiable process of decisionmaking that is neither arbitrary nor capricious. The third role derives from the other two: that the courts provide citizens with a forum for review and redress. These roles are consistent with those that describe both the role of the American judiciary in society and a court system that is ideally both outside the process of governmental decisionmaking and removed from any personal, professional, or institutional interest in the outcomes of the proceedings (Richards 1989). By contrast, administrative agencies and their officials normally have considerable personal, professional, and institutional interests in seeing disputes resolved in their favor.

Recognizing the practical importance of doubts cast on administrative agencies by critics in terms of their democratic and policymaking failings, and recognizing that Congress has looked to the courts to be the bulwark against bureaucratic power, it is not surprising that the legislature should circumvent agencies in favor of courts as the ideal agency for policy implementation. With respect to the plant-closing statute, Congress has sought to establish an institutional framework whereby legal rights are the mode of regulation. For example, Section 510 of ERISA protects workers' pension rights by virtue of general language assigning pension entitlements priority over corporations' economic interests, buttressed by a right to civil litigation if corporations fail to act in accordance with those requirements. This method of regulation is also embodied in the plant-closing statute. Section 5 provides workers and their communities a right to judicial review if corporations fail to act in accordance with provisions of the act. And rather than have penalties for noncompliance set by statute, the courts have become the assessors and adjudicators of economic harm.

Judges as Policymakers

To readers schooled in contemporary social science theory it may appear odd that the judiciary is treated here as an institution of regulation. No doubt readers are familiar with analyses and evaluations of individual judges' decisions—this kind of textual analysis is the basis for most case studies in law and social science and is the basis of the analyses of the consequences of corporate restructuring and for workers' pension rights. In the U.S. context, at least, this kind of analysis is crucial if we are to understand the pattern of recent events in corporate restructuring. That being noted, it is also vital that we step back from individual decisions and consider the role of the judiciary in general as regulators of government policy. Here, the analysis is couched as if the judiciary is an institution ideally governed by rules and modes of conduct that could be equated with what might be expected of any organization. While it may be tempting to treat each judge and his or her decisions as separate events unrelated to a broad institutional arrangement of power and order, in a sense romanticizing and idealizing the individuality of judges compared to administrative agencies, in fact judges are bureaucrats in much the same way agents of administrative agencies are bureaucrats: they process claims, they make decisions, and they fulfill functions designated by the legislature in relatively routine ways according to criteria established by others.[13]

Arguing that judges are bureaucrats is not the same as arguing that they have no distinctive qualities of value to the legislature, and to society in general (Atiyah 1983). It was noted above that judges' relative isolation from partisan political interests (relative to the legislature) provides the legislature with a convenient place to locate potentially divisive issues of interpretation. Given their apparent isolation from (and some would say ignorance of) the terms of political debate, the judiciary is argued by some to have one fundamental quality over and above any other quality shared by related administrative apparatuses: a rule-based, formal method of decisionmaking.[14] Formalism is a quality normally attributed to the institution of law, and is thought to be a most desirable and valuable aspect of Western democracies. While I do not necessarily believe some of the more extravagant claims made historically for the virtues of the rule of law (Dicey 1885), it is apparent that the ideal of rule-based decisionmaking is a vision supported by many theorists who would argue that the judiciary has a superior mode of decisionmaking compared to the legislature (Unger 1986).

Summarily defined, formalism is a desirable attribute of legal decisionmaking that can be "analyzed in isolation from the substantive issues that the rules or standards respond to" (Kennedy 1976:1687). Ideally, formalism has three virtues. First, to the extent to which rules are clearly articulated they provide an unequivocal basis for directing certain kinds of actions. Kennedy terms this virtue *formal realizability:* given a criteria of applicability, the appropriate set of rules determine action. Put succinctly, if conditions *a, b, c,* and *d* hold then does *X.* A related virtue of rules is their *generality:* a level of abstraction that is inclusive of a broad set of unspecified possibilities and contingencies. These two virtues then imply a degree of imprecision regarding particular issues, broad coverage in application, minimal discretion on the part of the judiciary in terms of choosing rules for circumstances, and a minimum number of exceptions, gaps, or events not covered by those rules. Rule-based adjudication or regulation has one other virtue. To the extent that rules are general and formal, as opposed to particular and substantive in design, then the fact that these rules include many different circumstances implies that rule-based adjudication is *indifferent* about the worth (moral or otherwise) of private actions that fall within those parameters. Even if judges have certain prejudices or beliefs that they would like to apply to cases, because rule-based regulation requires judges to apply formal rules to categorically defined cases, there would be no opportunity to do so and no basis for evaluating the correctness of rule-based adjudication.

Formal rule-based decisionmaking is thus a desirable aspect of the judiciary. Indeed, it might be argued that only the judiciary is so virtuous, the legislature being dominated by narrow interests and administrative agencies dominated by an inherent interest in, and control over, the rule-making and rule adjudication process. If these are its virtues, these virtues are also used as a defense against those who question the expertise of the judiciary in matters of public policy. For many commentators, especially those concerned with corporate restructuring, industrial relations, and enhancing the competitiveness of the U.S. economy, the judiciary lacks an adequate knowledge of the substantive issues requiring regulation (see generally Morris 1987). Furthermore, it is also oftentimes asserted that the judiciary, and even specialized adjudicative agencies such as the NLRB, lack an adequate appreciation of the realities of corporate management and the decisionmaking processes of corporations, thereby suggesting that the judiciary is probably an impediment to decisionmaking at the local level. To those who would argue that the judiciary are singularly ill-equipped to make relevant decisions, formalism is invoked to defend the judiciary. Where lack of substantive expertise might be interpreted as a limitation, advocates of the judiciary as "formal" regulators suggest that ignorance is a virtue: it supposedly enables disinterested decision-making, encourages limited intervention in local events, and encourages the application of general rules rather than involvement in every situation.

What do federal district judges know of the substantive realities of corporate restructuring? Recognizing that the adjudication of workers' claims progresses on a case-by-case basis, judges are unlikely to gain more than a passing knowledge of the causes and consequences of plant closings except in specific situations. Recognizing that such claims would be a mere fraction of all claims made before the courts, it is very unlikely that judges would know anything more than the crude rules of applicability of the statute (the numbers of layoffs and the proportion of plant workforces). At this level of generality, there is little need to go into the privileged backgrounds and elite social status of federal judges in order to realize that at a personal level few federal judges have had experience working in manufacturing plants of any kind. Similarly, there is little need to go into the particular ideological and educational qualifications of recent appointees to the federal courts to realize that federal judges are probably quite unmoved by the plight of laid-off blue-collar workers and their communities. There is every reason to imagine that federal judges would depend upon the expertise of corporate managers rather than the expertise of union officials and their representatives; by training, they are predisposed toward the opinions of the managerial elite. The views and opinions of workers and their communities appear to rate very low in the order of argument.

If it was just a case of applying the rules as laid down by the legislature, assuming that formal techniques of judicial decisionmaking apply, there need not be significant concern about the lack of substantive expertise and privileged background of the judiciary. We might legitimately wonder about the value of such decisions; nevertheless, there would be more interest in the design of the rules by the legislature. But, of course, that is just the problem: the legislature has deliberately avoided setting down rules for adjudication and has passed standards as the basis for adjudication. This is precisely the problem for judges in interpreting ERISA. It would be a problem for any industrial policy statute that provides those affected with the right to bring suit in district court for compensation but then also requires courts to adjudicate those claims with respect to reasonable standards. If the legislature deliberately avoids definition of those standards, what is needed for stable judicial policymaking is a recipe or formula for a common interpretation of those standards across cases and between jurisdictions.

By convention, a well-tried formula has been identified for determining the meaning of a statute and its provisions. Judge Frank Easterbrook (1988:59) describes the formulae as having the following steps:

> First look to the language of the statute; if that is clear then stop; if it is not clear then turn to the legislative history; if the legislative history is not clear then do whatever the agency says; and if none of the above is clear then either go with the values underlying the statute or put in a hypothetical question. Ask what the legislature that passed this bill would have done had the issue been put before it explicitly. This rump legislature, sitting in the mind of the court, then gives the authoritative answer.

Easterbrook is scathing in his criticism of this method of settling the meaning or interpretation of a statute. He is particularly critical of the presumed powers of judges to "read" the minds of legislators, sarcastically referring to judges as the legislature's "oracles." He would trust and only use the words of a statute, depending upon the expertise of the "skilled, objectively reasonable user of words" (p. 65).[15]

Judge Easterbrook's argument is just one against the mainstream of contemporary judicial practice. Given the routine nature of most judicial decisionmaking, it would be naive to imagine that his critique has been especially effective in changing judicial practice; the formula he so aptly describes has been the dominant rationale for decisionmaking for many years. At the same time, while I do not agree with his alternative recipe for statutory interpretation, it is apparent that the conventional formula is quite inadequate in relation to legislative practice. Just consider its potential failings if applied to the plant-closing bill. As has been noted a number of times, the bill basically allows for companies to close plants before the sixty-day notification period has elapsed if there are "reasonable" grounds to do so. Determination of the reasonableness of companies actions will, however, inevitably end up in court as those affected seek damages and clarification of the meaning of "reasonable." Since the notion of "reasonable" is a standard, not a formal rule (according to the distinction made by Kennedy), the judiciary has a great deal of discretion in interpreting its meaning in different settings. This is not to suggest that "reasonable" has no inherited meaning or reference point from which to apply a customary interpretation. In fact, "reasonable" refers to a common law tradition of interpretation based upon community standards of what is fair and reasonable (Goodrich 1986:152–53).

Can the customary four-step formula help resolve the meaning of "reasonable"? The first step would be to investigate the language of the statute for clues about its meaning. The plant-closing statute, though, does not provide the reader (however skilled or reasonable) with a definition or set of definitions that would make the interpretive puzzle any easier to resolve. The legislative history of the bill is more problematic. That history could be read any number of ways, emphasizing the equity concerns of some congressional representatives, as well as the concerns of others for facilitating the adjustment of workers and their communities to economic change. Presumably, it could be read as a history of equity interests being dominated by other efficiency-like interests notwithstanding the origin of the statute in the liberal left of the Democratic Party. Since no expert agency would then offer its own interpretation of the meaning of "reasonable" (a deliberate choice made by the legislature to leave the issue to the courts), and given the fact that the courts' own substantive expertise on the matter is next to nonexistent, there is little prospect of a substantive interpretation of the statute in a manner consistent with the experience of American workers in different situations. If then the court asks the question that Easterbrook so despises—what would the August 1988 legislature say about the meaning of reasonable in the particular case in question?—the answer would be hardly dependable and surely contested by all kinds of claimants who could offer their own entirely reasonable interpretations of "reasonable."

The indeterminacy of interpretation is obviously a problem for judges making decisions about the meaning of statutes and their provisions. It is also obviously a problem for those affected by corporate restructuring; having a statute that was presumably enacted to cover certain situations becomes a legal riddle providing little or no protection for American workers. Union expectations about corporations' responsibilities to their workers and communities may be a product of the lobbying that went into enacting the bill, but are as much the product of the interpretive contest fought out in the courts about the language by which the statute was written to accommodate many diverse views. Thus, the meaning of the plant-closing statute, and any industrial policy statute that had a similar construction, would involve a contest among efficiency (and its various meanings), equity (and its meanings), and whatever else could be identified as a motivating force behind the passage of the act. Presumably, the judiciary would even hear arguments from the Chicago school of law and economics that would claim that the only plausible interpretation is that which maximizes the welfare of the whole society. The result may be that, if the court follows such an argument, plant closings are encouraged and formal notification requirements are rarely enforced because "reasonable" grounds are interpreted in a manner consistent with macroefficiency, not local equity.

At the very least, with such a range of interpretations possible, and many conflicting arguments about corporations' social responsibilities (given economic imperatives), those affected by restructuring will pursue a more cunning legal strategy than perhaps previously thought necessary. That is, rather than take the risk of having a claim for damages denied by a judge or court that followed a conservative (pro-efficiency) interpretation of "reasonable," workers, communities, and their representatives would search out judges and courts that were more sympathetic to an equity interpretation of "reasonable." For instance, compare the federal appeals courts in Pennsylvania and Illinois. The latter is now intellectually dominated by Reagan appointees with a vested interest in the application of Chicago school law and economics efficiency principles, whereas the former remains sympathetic to the equity implications of claims brought before it in labor-oriented disputes. It would appear that a plausible legal strategy for a sympathetic consideration of workers' claims would involve a strategic (re)location of those claims in Pennsylvania, if at all possible (or for that matter relocation to the Manhattan federal bankruptcy court). Inevitably, forum shopping would become the most appropriate response to the problem of statutory vagueness and interpretive indeterminacy.[16] Just as inevitably, the Supreme Court would be asked to adjudicate competing interpretations, but unfortunately the grounds of resolution might be so narrow that the statute itself would lose its usefulness—rounds and rounds of litigation would result. This is, I believe, the fate that awaits any industrial policy.

Summary—Against Conservatism

I have argued that a federal statutory response to the impacts of corporate restructuring in the form of an industrial policy will not achieve the goals of its staunchest advocates. This does not mean that an industrial policy is unwarranted. All the evidence presented here about corporate restructuring points to a problem of significant individual and community proportions. It should not be surprising that judges and others are so concerned about determining the proper rationale for allocating the costs of restructuring. The numbers of workers affected, pension benefits jeopardized, and the communities at risk to restructuring are enough to suggest the need for a national policy response. Nor should we be complacent about the future; those corporations bought and sold through leveraged buyouts financed with "junk bonds" during the 1980s now threaten the solvency of many other communities over the coming decade. However, the failure of Congress and the executive branch to establish a formula or mechanism for rationalizing economic imperatives with corporations' social obligations has left policy in a shambles. Ad hoc policymaking by the courts has been one result, only tangentially informed by existing but unrelated statutes (such as plant closings, pensions, labor relations, bankruptcy, and company law).

So why be pessimistic about the value of such a statute if passed? Here, three different but related reasons were advanced concerning the limits of a statutory response. Drawing upon the example provided by the plant-closing bill of 1988, a statutory response may be so compromised by the vote-trading that goes with the passage of bills in Congress that its provisions end up as merely guidelines for judicial decisionmaking. Indeed, where we might expect a set of provisions establishing the proper relationship between economic imperatives and corporations' social responsibilities, all that may be passed are standards for judicial review. In fact, there are good reasons to believe that federal public policy in this area simply encourages affected citizens and communities to seek their own redress through civil suits. Drawing upon the plant-closing bill once again, it is very unlikely that a new agency would be established to regulate restructuring. The lack of accountability of administrative agencies, coupled with their potential powers of design and implementation (given deliberately written vague and general statutes) have all prompted the legislature to look to the courts as the apparatus of public policy.

The legislature's current distrust of administrative agencies is surprising given the importance of these agencies over much of the twentieth century. Since the New Deal era, the design and implementation of policy has been the raison d'être of the administrative state. The tendency of the legislature in recent times to pass intentionally vague and ill-defined statutes has only served to increase the powers of the administrative state. This ironic turn of events emphasizes the profound significance of the current impasse in Congress on matters of economic policy and regulation. The shift toward the courts as the preferred regulatory apparatus is a remarkable but disturbing aspect of the internal incoherence of the legislature. Despite the confidence of the legislature in judicial decisionmaking, the federal courts are by no means well equipped to handle this task. Their lack of expertise and the likely generality of the rules and standards of an industrial policy are such that there may be little prospect of a common interpretation of policy. All a new statute for industrial policy may do is encourage further litigation and forum shopping.

These conclusions about the limited value of a statutory response to corporate restructuring are based upon observations about the nature of the legislative process. Whether inspired by public-choice theory, a sense of the relationship between legislative staff and legislators, or more radical state theory, the argument presented above presumes that the legislature is so enmeshed in vote-trading that meaningful statutory solutions to pressing national problems are quite unlikely. The significance of federal courts in implementing public policy is then the unfortunate combination of a fragmented legislative process and deep suspicion of the power of administrative agencies. I would suggest that this is doubly unfortunate for national policymaking: it reduces the options for policymaking and policy reform, implying a consistent lack of concern for monitoring the policy design and implementation process; and, it places extraordinary pressure on the judiciary to act in innovative and politically sensitive ways that simultaneously capture the middle ground of an otherwise fragmented polity (interpreting the meaning of an industrial policy statute) and also to respond to the interests and needs of those affected by restructuring (adjudicating the case at hand). This kind of responsibility exposes the judiciary, quite deliberately, to political pressures that the legislature are unable to rationalize. Abdication by Congress of the responsibility for comprehensive statute-making (as opposed to statute-passing) has simply transposed the terrain of policy debate.

For some liberals, these conclusions may appear to be a conservative argument in disguise. What has been suggested, albeit by implication, is that the courts should not have to intervene as much as they do in the policy process. That they do so in cases of corporate restructuring is more a reflection upon the decisionmaking (in)capacity of the legislature in designing statutes, rather than a reflection of the courts' decisionmaking abilities or special expertise. So far this is not obviously a conservative argument, but there are hints of a conservative refrain. For example, some conservative bankruptcy specialists would argue that the involvement of many bankruptcy judges in designing the rationalization of corporations often goes too far and should be constrained by tighter rules of procedure and a more restrained interpretive stance (suggesting that the courts are not qualified to pass on complex economic matters and ought to be held accountable to rules of economic efficiency; see Baird 1987 and chapter 5). Personified by the raucous debate over the proposed appointment of Robert Bork to the U.S. Supreme Court, at issue are the limits of judicial responsibility for public policy. Even so, their arguments for limits on judicial involvement in policy matters are, in general, different than mine. Conservatives like Bork would argue for judicial practice to be based upon a narrow reading of history emphasizing the original conception of judicial roles and responsibilities. I do not share that view, nor do I think that judicial intervention can be so easily ruled out by returning to a world that has totally passed by.

The apparent failure of Congress to fashion comprehensive rule-based policies relevant to the experience of the average American worker represents a threat to policymaking that is more substantial and of longer-term significance than the antigovernment sentiment that has been with us now for more than a decade. Such sentiment may be durable in the sense that it appears and reappears in many debates about the desirability or otherwise of industrial policy. However, as the example of plant-closing policy demonstrated, the mainstream liberal argument for government intervention to speed individual and community adjustment to economic change remains well entrenched. On an issue-by-issue basis it can garner enough support from both Democratic and Republican liberals to be the dominant public policy perspective in Congress. When supported by those seeking intervention for equity reasons, it can carry the passage of a bill. However, it is apparently unable to be the basis of an articulated public policy that would define industrial policy in a substantive sense. Perhaps one reason for its weakness lies with the compromises necessary to make it a mainstream policy perspective. Perhaps another reason for its substantive weakness is its apparent lack of direct relevance to substantive moral issues—about who is, and who should be, responsible for the welfare of workers and their communities.

8

Ethics and the Strategies
of Subversion

How are the actions of corporations in an era of economic and geographical restructuring to be interpreted? What are the relevant behavioral variables? What logic would usefully distinguish between claims of ethical and unethical corporate behavior? Case studies of corporate restructuring presented in previous chapters demonstrate that many corporations have designed restructuring strategies in response to the pattern of their pension liabilities and the risks of incurring sanctions and penalties for abrogating legal obligations to their employees and the PBGC. Although these case studies were not explicitly interpreted in the context of a theory of the firm as profit maximizer, it is apparent that the costs of restructuring have significant implications for how firms act and how they evaluate the desirability of alternative competitive strategies. Corporate restructuring strategies, especially those that have as an objective exit from an industry, can be understood as being part of the more general phenomenon of industrial competition and market structure; just as entry to a market can be thought to drive corporate strategy, so too can the costs of exit from an industry be thought to determine the geography of firms' decisions (*pace* Baumol et al. 1988).

Notwithstanding the virtues of this approach for the theory of restructuring there are limits to its efficacy. While perhaps obvious, the language of analysis is confined to the logic of price theory and the consequences of rational (constrained) maximizing decisionmaking. Yet running parallel to, but submerged below, this analysis of corporate restructuring and pension liabilities is another set of concerns having to do with more contentious issues; the ethics of corporate restructuring is one such issue, especially where corporate strategies are deliberately designed to break the law or at best are designed to circumvent legally mandated and protected corporate obligations to employees. Also at issue are the motives and the personal ambitions of corporate executives: greed, a lust for power, and a flagrant disregard for social norms of proper behavior may be the most appropriate terms for characterizing the motives of executives of International Harvester Corporation, LTV Corporation, and the Continental Can Corporation, respectively. These are not the customary or conventional terms of analysis used in case studies of corporate strategy, but this is changing (see Shubik 1988).[1]

This chapter is about the ethics of corporate restructuring. Whereas most case studies of corporate decisionmaking in the social sciences make no distinction between different modes of private behavior on the basis of social criteria of right and wrong, we will here explore the logic necessary for making such judgments. If corporate restructuring was simply a private matter, involving only those with an interest in and control over the process, the morality of such decisions would be relatively unimportant (except, perhaps, in a philosophical sense).[2] The fact is, however, corporate restructuring has many adverse effects, often prompting legal disputes involving those affected and their claims for protection and special status relative to those who initiate changes in corporate structure and management. Many disputes are about fair treatment, due process, and equity— topics that are not the standard fare of studies of market structure or industry performance. But these ethical notions are of vital importance in law, and in society in general (as the case studies have demonstrated), and are based upon public, albeit contested, notions of proper behavior. Indeed, it might be said that "ethics emerges" in this context "as a defense against the violence of human relations" (to quote Siebers's [1988:95] felicitous phrase).

Relevance of Ethical Judgments

We shall begin discussion with the dimensions and consequences of corporate restructuring. This departure point is enveloped within the language of economics: the costs and benefits of social action. This is inevitable, one might suppose, because of the significance of the economic language of litigation.[3] The court cases involving Continental Can, International Harvester, and LTV Corporation were dominated by economic considerations, including the costs and benefits of disputed actions. It can be shown, however, that this language is related to a specific kind of ethical theory often invoked as a defense against litigation, just as the terms *greed* and *management hubris* appear to reference another kind of ethical theory. The aim of this chapter is to expose the bases of these competing ethical conceptions of proper social behavior. It is not intended to adjudicate in any fundamental sense their philosophical plausibility; this is best left to philosophers whose analytical tools and temperament are both more general and abstract than the problems at hand (see Parfit 1984 as the paradigmatic example). While I do have my own inclinations regarding the virtues or otherwise of contemporary ethical theories, the focus here is on the logic by which others make ethical judgments in the context of corporate restructuring.[4] Because this research is intended to explain the actions of corporations in formulating and implementing their restructuring policies, their actions and the responses of those affected by restructuring are the primary objects of analysis. If corporations then defend their actions in court by appealing to certain standards of social conduct, union officials and their legal representatives (and workers and their communities) have quite different notions of proper social conduct. These agents have, summarily speaking, very different ethical theories.

The previous case studies of corporate restructuring emphasized the significance of pension liabilities in corporate strategy. Though obviously bound up with broader recipes of competitive strategy—for example, the use of "cash cows" to finance diversification, mergers and acquisitions, and rationalization around core economic activities—it is apparent that implementing these competitive strategies has been contingent upon managing the associated pension liabilities. To accommodate these liabilities and yet remain consistent with chosen competitive strategies has required what some commentators might term "innovative techniques." The courts have observed in all instances that the companies concerned developed quite remarkable techniques to control their current and potential pension liabilities. At the same time, these techniques have required the use of deception, secrecy, and even outright lying (in two cases), all in the interests of achieving corporate goals thought unattainable if pension management techniques were designed and implemented with the full knowledge of those targeted. If the ends dictated the means—the goals of competitive strategy dictating the need for secrecy and deceit—and were the basis for justifying *ex post* the logic of corporate restructuring, not everyone has accepted the necessity of these actions. In fact, there is a sense that union-initiated (USWA) and PBGC-initiated litigation over corporate restructuring has been driven by fundamental disapproval of the means of restructuring, even in cases where litigation has been framed in accordance with the relevant statutes and precedents regarding the integrity of pension benefits and funds. At issue (in part) is a disagreement over ethics, given unions' genuine concern for protecting the economic welfare of those workers affected by corporate restructuring.

Litigation by affected unions, workers, and the PBGC against corporations for their pension-oriented restructuring policies could be easily explained as attempts to recover benefits due to workers or funds due to the government that were illegally denied through corporate restructuring. This explanation of litigation has the virtue of being immediately related to the legal process; it references notions of due process and the enforcement of individual rights that are at the heart of American jurisprudence (Richards 1989). It is also plausible that litigation has been prompted by a concern to redress the harm done by restructuring, if not completely or adequately for those affected then at least for those who might be the targets for corporate restructuring in the future. Both the USWA and the PBGC cannot afford to allow such actions to go unchallenged considering the potential universe of possible similar actions by other companies in difficult economic circumstances. But just as plausible as recovery and redress are as explanations of litigation, so too is a litigation strategy of retaliation. That is, workers and the PBGC could be thought of as pursuing a strategy designed to punish companies for betraying their trust and cooperation. Retaliation is not as easily measured as the recovery of benefits might be measured or as redressing the harm might be conceived; retaliation could be measured by the costs of litigation but is more simply (and profoundly) an unqualified attack upon the veracity of the relevant corporation. Retaliation has been an important element in litigation (as much as recovery and redress) and has been prompted by union and PBGC officials' belief that companies have violated their trust, thereby acting unethically. Most specifically, I would assert that secrecy and subsequent deceit by management in their pursuit of lower cost rationalization has offended unions' and PBGC officials' unstated but firmly held moral beliefs.

To suggest that the basis for legal retaliation is a sense that the companies concerned have violated union and PBGC standards of ethical behavior is not a common or, more to the point, a conventional argument about social agents' motivations. Like arguments about greed and hubris, what is being referenced are notions of morality rather than standard assumptions about profit (utility) maximizing behavior. Conventionally, it is thought to be enough to analyze corporate behavior with respect to goals and objectives—desired outcomes—and to assume that actions, the means by which desired outcomes are achieved, are chosen in accordance with their efficiency in achieving those desired outcomes. Providing chosen actions do not violate legally defined requirements or agreed-upon (impersonal) constraints, there would seem to be no legitimate basis for retaliation. By this logic, outcomes legitimize actions. But this is just one moral claim. Although vital to conventional economic theories of social action, a focus on outcomes does not exhaust or deny the efficacy of counter ethical claims that place great significance on judging the virtue or lack thereof of social actions in their own right. That being said, it must be also recognized that judging actions with respect to ethical standards is a very contentious issue within philosophy and jurisprudence. Some moral theorists such as S. Kagan (1989) suggest that judging actions by reference to social standards of behavior, and thereby denying outcomes their primary status, is indicative of "ordinary morality"—intuitive notions about the right and the good. He also acknowledges that even if intuitive notions are an essential attribute of ordinary morality, it is just as apparent that such intuitions are based upon theoretical propositions regarding the status of personal constraints on actions, and the allowable options for behavior.

Secret-keeping, Lies, and Deception

A common definition of *secret* suggests that it is something kept private, information not generally disclosed to the public or an audience. Often the term is used conditionally, describing an attribute of something else, as suggested by the phrase *secret ballot*. While secrecy and privacy are obviously related (the latter enabled by the former), it is important to recognize their differences in terms of behavior (Bok 1984). When used in the context of a person's actions, to hold a secret is often thought to suggest that something, most likely information, is concealed from others' knowledge. On this point, K. L. Scheppele (1988:12) defined a secret as "a piece of information that is intentionally withheld by one or more social actor(s) from one or more social actor(s)." She asserts that secrecy is about the distribution of information (thereby distinguishing *secrecy* from *privacy*), arguing that intentionally withholding information from parties who would have an interest in that information is the raison d'être of secret-keeping.

As all agents operate under conditions of uncertainty, it is neither rational nor efficient (assuming that information has a price and that agents have limited resources) to attempt to collect all relevant information. What makes a secret a secret, then, is that information vital to a person's actions or expectations is purposefully and unevenly distributed, advantaging the secret-keeper and disadvantaging the target. Thus, it is the pattern of information in a relationship that determines if any piece of information is a secret or not. Scheppele values this definition because it allows us to see secrets as strategic devices, rationally conceived for gaining advantage in social relationships. This definition has the virtue of discriminating between information being unavailable by accident or by position and information that is a strategic variable in relationships between agents. By this logic, information is neither benign nor epiphenomenal. This definition has one other important implication—secret-keeping is a relational category; evaluating the significance or otherwise of a piece of information

depends upon situating the analysis in the context of a particular relationship. Scheppele's theory of secret-keeping is thus context-sensitive,
and is based upon what individuals expect in terms of their treatment by
others, not simply their individual interests unrelated to social relationships and social obligations.[5] In many respects this is a deontological perspective.[6]

With respect to the strategic value of secret-keeping, Scheppele identifies three related conditions that must hold for secrets to have significance. First, the interests of those concealing information and those who
are the target of concealment should not be "completely coincident"
(1988:45). That is, there must be some advantage to be gained by the
secret-keeper from the target by virtue of the secret. A relevant example
drawn from the case material on corporate restructuring would be the fact
that Continental Can was able to reduce its restructuring costs by keeping
secret its pension-avoidance strategy. The company systematically reallocated and relocated production within and between plants so as to shelter
workers eligible for plant-closing pensions and laid off near-eligible workers. This policy was kept secret from the affected workers and many of
the company's staff. If those affected by this strategy had known of the
company's actions at the time of its implementation, the union would have
immediately stopped the company from implementing its policy. Another
condition is that the information concealed is such that, if known by the
target, he, she, or they would change their behavior. That is, it is not only
important that the target not know the relevant information, it is also
important that the target not know information that would change the
relationship between the secret-keeper and target. Again, with respect to
Continental Can, the fact that the union was unaware of the corporation's
actions in implementing their Bell System pension cost-reduction program
meant that the union did not appreciate the ramifications of agreeing to a
plant-wide seniority system. The final condition is that "the secret-keeper's
pay-offs must be dependent on the choices of the target of the secret; but
the reverse need not be true" (p. 47). In essence, the secret-keeper is
better off keeping the target ignorant of the true circumstances. For example, in the Continental Can case, the company might have gained as
much as $500 million in savings from its secret restructuring policy.

Scheppele's notion of secret-keeping implies that the beneficiary of a
secret behaves on at least two levels—with the target of the secret as if
nothing has changed in their relationship, and outside of the target by
taking advantage of the fact that the target knows nothing of the secret.
Inevitably, operating at both levels involves the possibility of contradiction
(between stated goals and secret agendas), confusion of purpose (exter-

nally and with respect to the target), and discovery (of the hidden agenda). In the International Harvester case, the company sold its steel division, hoping to avoid or at least substantially discount its responsibility for plant-closing pensions, simultaneously maintaining to the PBGC that its actions were consistent with normal business practice and its liabilities significantly less than were actually the case. To ensure that the local union supported the sale, International Harvester undertook to support the steel division's pension plans even though it had little intention of honoring those undertakings. To forestall actions by the PBGC to review the merits of the transaction, the company misled the agency about the magnitude of its pension liabilities and the ability of the new owners to support the pension plans. Throughout the court proceedings, the company made every effort to limit the scope of information available to the PBGC and the union concerning the true motives of the corporation and the advice it had received when packaging the transaction. It hoped that the sale of the steel division on the grounds of business expediency would be sufficient to legitimate the transaction, covering up apparent contradictions of stated purposes and actual outcomes, thereby limiting discovery of the extent of the plan. In a general sense, keeping secrets necessitates lies, deceptions, evasions of the truth, and conspiracies of silence and action, all in the interests of limiting discovery.

Economic agents are not unaware of the potential of deception. Suspicion of agents' motives and actions and conflicting interpretations of the logic of observed outcomes promotes distrust of official (company) explanations. In the Continental Can case, union lawyers for laid-off workers discounted company explanations (again business considerations) for the pattern of observed layoffs (which were dominated by workers close to attaining eligibility for plant-closing pensions), and through the legal system sought to establish the facts of the case. The company itself did not trust its own line managers with the real reasons for layoffs; plant managers were told to rationalize production in their plants in accordance with company objectives of cost efficiency and market penetration but were also required to hire and fire certain "flagged" workers regardless of those general corporate objectives. Distrust of local managers meant that the company had to centralize the administration of personnel hiring and narrow the audience for the secret strategy, setting in motion apparent contradictions in objectives and confusions of goals between staff at different levels of the corporation. For those managers able to piece together elements of the (secret) strategy, their exclusion from the design and implementation of the strategy was interpreted as corporate disloyalty to them and their employees—rumors within the company about the strategy then became part of the initial set of leads used by union lawyers to begin legal proceedings. Even in the legal proceedings, however, the company attempted to limit the possibility of discovery. Internal documents were altered, records misplaced, and parts of original documents not included in submissions to the court, all in an attempt to keep the secret. When it was finally exposed through the discovery of an internal company document detailing the design and implementation of the Bell System, the company denied the veracity of the document.

Agents must accept the risk that their secrets will be discovered. Indeed, the case studies of corporate restructuring analyzed here all depended upon discovery of documents detailing secret corporate strategies (Continental Can), the exposure of corporate lies and deception (International Harvester), or the argument that collusion between agents was apparent even if collusion cannot be documented (LTV Corporation). These case studies suggest that corporate restructuring may often involve secret stratagems, even illegal stratagems. A corporation contemplating a secret rationalization program must weigh the advantages to be gained against the risks of being caught. Simply calculated, as International Harvester appeared to do, the benefits of a secret strategy could be the sum of plant-closing pension payments avoided evaluated against the costs of litigation and liabilities imposed by regulatory agencies and the courts once the secret strategy is exposed. Given the lack of legal precedents in this area, and the possibility of avoiding all penalties, the economic returns to a secret strategy could be very high. A more sophisticated cost-benefit analysis would include the higher costs of labor-management relations once the secret is exposed (disruptive negotiation tactics, strikes, complex contract language, rejected ratification votes) associated with deceived employees. Of course, if the secret is kept long enough, allowing the company to complete its rationalization program, it may be able to avoid all labor-management relations costs.

Ethical Judgment in Theory

Cost-benefit analysis of keeping secrets can certainly identify important aspects of corporate decisionmaking. There is little doubt that International Harvester deliberately considered the likely financial returns of deceiving the PBGC, the time period over which to maintain the sham transaction so as to gain maximum benefits from the strategy, and the likely penalties if found out or if the transaction failed over the short run. However, to limit the analysis of secrets just to the costs and benefits to agents of keeping secrets is to remain limited to, or embedded within, a very simple version of economic (utilitarian) *consequentialism:* that is, the only value or measure of worth attributed to secrets is that derived from agents' own objectives in keeping secrets, and the costs of keeping secrets again measured with reference to agents' individual circumstances. It is this simple version of consequentialism that I now analyze in detail.

Philip Pettit (1989:117) defined *consequentialism* as the doctrine that holds "that the right option in any choice is that which promotes the realization of the relevant valuable properties." In the context of utilitarian theories of social action or behavior, consequentialism suggests that the right actions (means) are those that promote the best outcomes. Sometimes counterposed to this notion of consequentialism is the deontological argument that "the right option is that which honors a relevant value by exemplifying respect for it in this [a] particular instance" (p. 117). Put slightly differently, the deontological argument is that some actions are wrong even though those actions might produce the best overall outcomes as consequentialists might measure them (see Scheffler 1982). Deontological theorists argue that the means to an end must be judged according to more general social standards than simply their contribution to the attainment of some individual's personal satisfaction. At this point it might be argued that this is a strong realist thesis—transcendental social standards are vital here in evaluating the virtue (or otherwise) of individuals' actions. Though deontologists may be strong realists, I am not. Social standards may be contingent and local in the sense of their claimed relevance to certain events.

To illustrate, recall the argument made by the PBGC against LTV Corporation and the USWA. The agency has suggested that the company and union colluded in the design and implementation of restructuring. By its interpretation of events leading up to the involuntary termination of LTV's pension plans, the company strategically entered Chapter 11 bankruptcy in order to shift its pension liabilities to the PBGC and had sought an agreement with the union to provide similar benefit packages to those terminated in return for industrial peace. The PBGC essentially claimed that their collusion is wrong even though the net effect may have been to rescue LTV from Chapter 7 bankruptcy, thereby saving the jobs of current employees, the welfare of retirees, and the investment (albeit heavily discounted) of stockholders. By virtue of the distinction made above between consequentialism and the deontological view of ethical behavior, the PBGC might be thought to have used a deontological argument against collusion, whereas the company might be thought to have used a consequentialist argument for the outcomes of their policy to justify their actions in seeking termination of the pension plans (this was the argument accepted by the federal district court). If this latter kind of interpretation appears overly abstract or possibly unreal, the Chicago school of law and economics follows a consequential line of reasoning when arguing in favor of actions in the legal context that maximize social welfare, discounting or denying the relevance of deontological considerations of proper conduct (see, for example, Baird [1987], who argues that the scope of bankruptcy policy is limited to those actions that maximize total welfare). By this logic, secret-keeping may be entirely justifiable if the terms of judgment include analysis of the relative consequences of secret-keeping as opposed to complete openness.

At issue are the grounds for deciding what actions are right and what actions are wrong. The claims made for deontological reasoning hinge upon two notions: (1) that the importance of ethical values is not immediately reducible to the simple economic metric of cost-benefit analysis, and (2) it appears that the Chicago school is unwilling to make judgments about the value of individuals' actions separate from the relative significance of possible outcomes. To emphasize this point, critics of utilitarian consequentialism note a logical implication of the theory that maximizing total welfare could involve denying the well-being of a small group of individuals in the interests of the whole of society (see Hardin 1988, section 7). While no doubt a plausible public policy, such a policy may violate other firmly held moral claims (such as due respect for peoples' well-being) not counted in the analysis of outcomes. Hardin suggested this type of criticism of utilitarian consequentialism is more often than not based upon impossible examples, so "contrived and fanciful" that it is impossible to draw any reasonable moral inferences.[7] However, the case studies on corporate restructuring noted in this book would suggest that protagonists in legal disputes over corporate restructuring are as much concerned with deontological considerations as they are with the economic consequences of actions. The USWA was as much concerned with the unethical actions of Continental Can in implementing its Bell System as it was with the consequences of that corporate policy for the well-being of affected workers. Understanding the motivations of the union in pursuing the company through the courts requires that recognition and due respect be given to deontological reasoning.

Deontological reasoning does not reject the relevance of the consequences of actions; what is rejected is the simple-minded consequentionalist notion that only the best (maximum) outcome determines the weighting of options. A crucial but often unrecognized distinction between utilitarian consequentalism and deontological reasoning has to do with the significance attributed to social standards of ethical judgment. For many economic (utilitarian) consequentialists, social standards are not the basis for judging individual actions; it is enough to work from desired outcomes back to enabling actions without overlaying a set of standards that are important for other reasons. Of course, not all consequentialists would accept such a theoretical practice. D. Parfit (1984) noted that individuals acting alone could be "collectively self-defeating," thus necessitating a *social* criterion of the "best" outcome that would fundamentally order individuals' actions.[8] But such a philosophical claim is not often readily recognized in economic (utilitarian) consequentialism. In this sense, ethics as a social practice may be more closely related to deontology than to consequentalism. Indeed, for many economic consequentalists the social norms of proper behavior are quite irrelevant. For most social scientists the study of ethics is simply a matter of politics, assuming that social standards of behavior are nonobjective and therefore vacuous as objects of inquiry, unverifiable or testable in practice, and either just rhetorical (purely linguistic) or subjective (personal) or both. This kind of realism, where the only things that count are directly measurable, is quite extraordinary, implying a ready-made world in which *the* true theory of morals, and by extension the rules of social conduct, corresponds with the underlying structure of *the* world. This kind of realism denies the plurality of views, and the social construction of expectations concerning proper behavior.[9]

Such an economic consequentalist might also argue that concern for the ethics of corporate restructuring is misplaced since agents' actions can be well enough understood using neutral economic principles (such as the theory of contestable markets) without resorting to more complex notions of proper conduct. So, for example, it could be argued that International Harvester sold its Wisconsin Steel division to maximize its cash flow, an action entirely consistent with expectations derived from profit-maximizing models of the firm. That the corporation used this explanation as a means of justifying what the PBGC believed to be a sham transaction conceived by the corporation to circumvent its legal obligations would add unnecessary complexity to a story well enough explained. Defenders of economic consequentalism would presumably argue that it is better than deontological reasoning because it is, methodologically speaking, more aesthetic (compare with Pettit 1991). To accept such an argument would be to ignore essential social criteria by which agents' decisions are often evaluated, which is not a problem if the audience for analysis is a narrow academic discipline, but surely a problem if the analyst hopes to be responsive to the complex problems of social regulation and adjudication (Hollis 1990).[10]

Ethics is more than a concern for methodology; ethics as a form of deontological reasoning is concerned with questions of how society and, in particular, how individuals in society ought to live and conduct their affairs (Brown 1987). In summary terms, Marcus Singer (1989:168) noted "an ethical person is one who, completely by instinct or training and without reflection on the consequences of his or her actions, does the right thing." By comparison, "an unethical person . . . is either one who pays no attention whatever to the ethical ramifications of his conduct, or else one who, knowing the moral dimensions of his conduct, is not moved by it." This pair of definitions of ethical behavior, one positive and the other negative, implies a set of assumptions or claims about the nature of ethical reasoning. It is apparent that the "right thing" is not determined by a person's interests or the consequences of different options of behavior. The "right thing" is socially conceived, thus denying an often-made argument by utilitarians that the bases of observed social action are ultimately to be found in the personal desires of individuals. Denial of this kind of reductionism is also to be found in the notion that there is a distinction to be made between ends and means. In utilitarianism, there is a sense that the means are justified by the ends. Though it is argued that this crude amorality could be controlled by invoking rules of behavior that all rational agents would agree to in the interests of their continued individual integrity (see Gauthier 1986, for example), Singer suggests that an ethical person is more than an economic utilitarian; ethical behavior is such that the right kind of action is chosen regardless of the individual consequences of those actions. Like S. Scheffler (1982), Singer presumes that individuals use social standards to judge the virtue or otherwise of their actions, standards that go beyond the circumstances of any one individual. To summarize, Singer's pair of definitions, ones that are central to this chapter, are nonconsequential, nonutilitarian, and fundamentally social.

For J. Rawls (1971) and many other moral philosophers, the essential terms of deontological ethics as a field of study are the *right* and the *good*. Both terms are extraordinarily vague (as is the related term *justice*). Much of moral philosophy is devoted to explicating their meaning(s), working from different and competing vantage points (for example—natural language theories, empirical tests of their use, and even jurisprudential notions of original meaning and precedent). Analytically, however, both terms have the properties of being transcendental and transparent. That is, the right and the good are thought to have superior status relative to other competing notions of proper behavior, irrespective of circumstances, and are thought to be transparent in the sense that their meaning is not contested by agents who may have quite different locations in society. In the absence of an accepted method of fixing the meaning of these two ethical terms—natural language theories, empirical tests, and legal techniques being themselves contested and disputed concerning their standards of veracity—it has become apparent that no rule-based test of the right and the good can hold the confidence of all citizens (respecting people's honest differences of opinion), returning the issue of meaning to the political arena for determination. Rather than continuing to assert that such "thin general terms" are the bases of ethical judgments, increasing attention is being paid to "thick" ethical concepts such as lying, stealing, cheating, and (in this case) secret-keeping that is designed to deceive and use the honest intentions of others.[11]

The distinction between thin and thick ethical concepts (a distinction often attributed to John McDowell and Bernard Williams; see Arrington 1989) is one of degrees and methodology (how to best approach ethical problems), rather than being necessarily a distinction of fundamental philosophical significance. Those who advocate the use of thick ethical concepts do not deny the bedrock importance of the right and the good as important reference points for discerning morality. The notion that lying and stealing are unethical is owed in part to a claim that such behavior is inconsistent with the right and the good. However, it is also claimed here that thick ethical concepts can not simply be reduced to those metaethical concepts. It is through the analysis and assessment of unethical conduct such as lying and deception that metaethical concepts achieve some explicit definition and meaning. Thus the relationship between thick and thin ethical concepts is recursive and reflexive, where the latter depends upon the practice of ethical evaluation for substantiation (Hurley 1985). Likewise, where I have argued that secret-keeping (deliberate deception) by corporations in the course of restructuring is unethical, in part I am referencing broader standards of the right and the good—trust and the willing cooperation of others. The value of thick ethical concepts is that they can be directly attributed to the behavior of social agents. By contrast, the charge that corporate actions are amoral has neither the emotional charge of accusing a company of deliberate deception nor the legal significance of accusing a company of negotiating in bad faith or employing unfair tactics. Thick ethical concepts are less abstract than their thin cousins, they can be directly applied as evaluative criteria to persons' actions and behavior, and they are empirical terms relevant to social relationships.

Despite the value of thick ethical concepts for making social judgments, these notions can be contested for their meaning and for their application to events and agents. Using thick ethical concepts does not remove the need for adjudication or absolve the analyst from making normative judgments. Ethical practice, whether of the thick or thin kind, is judgmental. When the USWA brought actions against Continental Can in federal district court for violating Section 510 of ERISA it did so not only to protect the interests of its members but also to punish the company for deliberately violating the union's trust and cooperation. In court, both the ethical issues and the apparently more technical legal issues interact with one another, with the former providing the grounds for assessing the intentions and behavior of the company and the latter providing the terms for prosecution and retaliation by the union. There is a very real contest for power in the definition and application of thick ethical concepts to social disputes.

Significance of Dirty Secrets

The previous sections of this chapter were devoted to establishing the social relevance and theoretical foundations for making deontological ethical judgments. The point of this analysis has been to establish the plausibility of others' (especially the USWA's and the PBGC's) claims that companies have behaved unethically in attempting to avoid their pension obligations. Working through this analysis has brought into the open two preliminary conclusions that are used to inform subsequent analysis: first, although companies' actions can be judged in relation to their consequences, the conduct or behavior of corporations in pursuing their objectives can be entirely sufficient as grounds for disapproving of the ethics of such conduct (the deontological ethical claim); and, second, some social standards of behavior have stronger claims for recognition and respect than others, especially those standards directly attributable to social agents and their relationships with others (the thick ethical claim). The advantage of this analysis is that it provides identifiable empirical criteria for ethical judgment, even if contested or disputed by those involved. Ethical judgment should not be idealized as somehow consensual in substance or form. These two analytical claims help us to understand the moral logic by which unions and the PBGC have objected to companies' actions. By this logic, legal retaliation is more than a form of personal vendetta—such actions are sustained by defensible philosophical claims.

To appreciate the significance of these claims in the context of this chapter and in the context of the actions of corporations concerning their pension liabilities requires further elaboration. In essence, the problem is more complex than initially imagined. If secret-keeping is unethical, referencing deontological and thick ethical reasoning, how do we (or should we?) distinguish between secrets, presuming that some secrets are more important than others? Put slightly differently, in the context of the relations between unions and corporations, the question becomes: why are some secrets between labor and management forgivable whereas others are not, and some are so significant as to prompt retaliation by organized labor?

There are probably two kinds of answers to this question. At the most general level (that is, in an abstract philosophical setting), deontological ethics supposes that any identified violation of the social norms of behavior is evidence of unethical behavior. Thus, we would not want to distinguish between levels of secret-keeping, rather the decision rule would be to judge all of that kind of behavior as unethical and therefore morally inappropriate. Those analysts who advocate the significance of thick over thin ethical concepts would then suggest that by violating social norms of trust and cooperation (by keeping secrets) corporations have done significant damage to their integrity. Yet any experienced labor negotiator would immediately protest that such moral judgments are too harsh. It must be realized that all parties to labor contracts or agreements keep secrets from one another and that all kinds of social relationships are based on an implicit acceptance of the existence of conflicting interests and their hidden agendas. By this logic, experienced labor negotiators would suggest that any broad-based conclusion that secret-keeping is itself unethical would be both unrealistic *and* unrelated to the context of decision making in social relationships. Thus a more detailed specification of the problem is needed. Realizing that secret-keeping is inevitable (indeed, a recognized part of any negotiation strategy), why then are some secrets more offensive than others? Why do some prompt retaliation whereas others are simply accepted and factored into the expectations of parties to any relationship?

From an abstract ethical level, then, it is necessary to move to a more context-dependent analysis to understand the reasons for retaliation. I would suggest that secret-keeping prompts retaliation when such behavior attacks the bases of long-term relationships—that is, when secret-keeping attacks the bases of trust and cooperation of one agent or set of agents in another agent or set of agents. What this suggests is the existence and importance of deeper thick ethical criteria for judging behavior, criteria that are the inverse of secret-keeping. If secret-keeping involves lies, deception, and cheating (necessary elements of any strategy of secret-keeping), it also can be argued that such behavior violates the trust and cooperation of related agents (necessary elements of any long-term relationship). One way of evaluating the significance of a secret is to consider whether or not such an action threatens the long-term continuity of a social relationship.

In the case of Continental Can's secret strategy of plant rationalization and pension avoidance, the union's trust in and cooperation with the company was used quite deliberately and in an entirely rational but unethical manner by the company to ensure the efficient implementation of the Bell System. Once exposed, however, the secret strategy became a very real and major impediment to collective bargaining between the union and the company. The union has little reason to trust the company, and even less commitment to the company's more recent concerns to improve efficiency through a new collective-bargaining agreement. Retaliation in this context is a form of punishment, but is also a strategy of redefinition—a legal device aimed at establishing the dominance of the union over the company, thereby redefining through a third party and on legal grounds the terms of a relationship previously only loosely defined because of the existence of trust between the parties. There cannot be any doubt that a narrow legal definition of parties' responsibilities to one another is an unsatisfactory way of regulating a relationship over the long run. For one party, or all parties, such binding relationships become inevitably too restrictive and unresponsive to the exigencies of events and unanticipated opportunities. Nevertheless, some secret-keeping is so significant that such action betrays the essential moral order that makes self-regulated cooperative action possible. Just recall for the moment the relationship between the PBGC and International Harvester. When considering their options, the company approached the PBGC for an off-the-record preliminary assessment of its likely liability if it sold Wisconsin Steel to another company. Trading on its previous good relationship with the agency, the company deceived it with imperfect information and then used its preliminary opinion to push through rationalization that the company hoped would allow it to avoid much of its liability.

The continuity of a relationship is an important criterion for judging the significance of secret-keeping, but so too is another criterion—the extent to which secret-keeping threatens the viability of the relationship. If avoidance of pension liabilities was the ultimate goal of Continental Can, a subsidiary and related goal was to limit the power of the USWA by reducing its representation of workers in the company. Whereas the union had a set of expectations about its relationship with the company, based upon a series of past contract agreements and negotiations over issues of mutual interest, the company aimed to change fundamentally those expectations and, by the terms of the union, the viability of the union's role in the company. Thus retaliation could be seen to be more than an attempt at regulating a relationship, it could be also understood as a means of ensuring the viability of one party (the union). There are two ways of understanding the notion of viability: at one level, it refers to the relative power between agents in a relationship, and at another level it also refers to the internal cohesion of any one agent relative to the other agent (or agents). So far, the first meaning of viability has been emphasized. But it is important to recognize that for a union, at least, internal cohesion is vital if a union is to maintain collective solidarity. Any company that breaks the trust and confidence of a union also threatens the internal solidarity of a union—that is, the trust and confidence of its members in the union's leadership. In this context, legal retaliation for unethical conduct is a necessary response to protect members' welfare *and* to demonstrate the leadership's willingness and capacity to act against company betrayal.[12]

Related to the criterion of viability is another, more fundamental criterion—institutional integrity. As was demonstrated in the LTV case, the PBGC has been under considerable pressure to demonstrate its effectiveness and vitality in this era of corporate restructuring. By design, the agency is inherently compromised because of its dependence upon Congress for legitimacy; being neither democratically elected nor directly related to an organized political constituency, its institutional integrity depends upon proving its administrative capacity. In instances where secret strategies by corporations to avoid their mandated pension obligations are exposed, an immediate question is raised about the PBGC's administrative capacity. In instances where companies have obviously used the PBGC, either by misrepresenting the extent of liabilities (as in the International Harvester case) and/or by dumping unfunded liabilities on the agency (as in the LTV case), the agency has a vital interest in retaliation. Again, the trust and cooperation of parties to a relationship are at risk when companies take advantage of an unknowing party. It is just as apparent that the viability of a relationship is threatened when secret strategies are exposed. But perhaps most critically for the PBGC, secret strategies threaten its political or institutional integrity. The only way to redress the situation in a strong public manner is a lawsuit, even if the odds of winning are negligible.

The significance of secret-keeping must be judged in relation to the continuity and viability of social relationships, and the harm done (or not done) to agents' institutional integrity. If secret-keeping does not represent a threat to the continuity of a relationship, then its significance is limited even if notionally unethical. Likewise, if the viability of a relationship on the terms negotiated and inherited from the past is not threatened by secret-keeping, then (again) its significance is limited. Clearly, threats to agents' institutional integrity can be the most serious effects of secret-keeping. But notice as well that the essential foundations for judging the ethics of behavior remain the trust and cooperation of parties to a relationship. Whatever the consequences of such actions, there is an *a priori* defined standard or set of standards for behavior. These attributes of social life—social norms as defined by J. Elster (1989, 1990)—can be both resilient and flexible and thus capable of absorbing all kinds of strategic actions (ethical or otherwise), or quite fragile and inelastic and thus very vulnerable to the least provocation. Determining the significance of secret-keeping outside of the context of a particular dispute is thus fraught with many indeterminacies. As suggested by Scheppele (1988), it is apparent that judging the significance of secrets must be sensitive to the context of behavior; otherwise we are left with strong ethical standards that may be so general as to be unrealistic and irrelevant.

Public Contests of Morality

Much of the discussion about ethics and the standards of ethical behavior in this chapter has focused on understanding the bases of such judgments by unions and government agencies in the context of corporate decision-making. I have sought to show legitimate grounds for making ethical judgments about agents' actions that do not reduce, in the final instance, to an economic cost-benefit analysis of potential outcomes. In doing so, though, there is a sense in which the analysis has tended to take the side of the unions and the government agency as if they were obviously in the right and the corporations obviously wrong. Even if this were true, recognizing that my analysis largely supports their perspective, such an analysis would be too partial for the scope of the problem. However persuasive the logic of previous arguments, it must be acknowledged that the corporations concerned have fought back with their own interpretations of motivations and quite different standards of behavior. They have sought to show that unions' (and the federal government's) ethical standards are at best irrelevant, given legitimate legal bases for corporate decisionmaking, and at worst quite disingenuous and misleading, given the true motives of the protagonists.

The case studies referenced earlier sought to analyze how and why corporations responded to their pension obligations in the context of rapidly evolving management-led competitive strategies, and to analyze the moves and arguments made by those corporations in court in order to limit their legal liability. Rarely if ever have the corporations made explicit reference to union- or government-based ethical standards; their defensive posture has remained almost exclusively legal in its technical sense (that is, concerned with procedure and the formal grounds for liability). Nevertheless, just as the unions and government have used the courts to, in part, punish the corporations for transgressing their ethical standards, so too have corporations used the legal process to attempt to identify a sphere or arena of activity in which its actions and motivations are isolated from or distinguished from others' social standards of behavior. In summary form, three arguments have been raised by corporations in defense of their actions: (1) their adversaries ought to have known that participation in aspects of the corporations' competitive strategy would involve rationalization costs (indeed, perhaps they did know, implying that current litigation is just cynical political face-saving rather than evidence of superior ethical standards); (2) there is a legitimate and entirely necessary distinction between public and private interests (a distinction between ethical standards and unrelated economic imperatives); and (3) if ethical standards are to be applied to private actions it should be recognized that not all standards are equally virtuous (since corporate restructuring advances total societal welfare, any transgressions of social standards of behavior made in achieving that goal ought to be judged as comparatively minor and of less significance).

The argument that unions and the PBGC actually knew what the companies intended by their policies is largely about the ethical virtue (or lack thereof) of the protagonists. In the Continental Can case, the company argued that the union must have known what would happen when they pressed for introduction of the rule-of-65 plant-closing pension plan. Likewise, International Harvester has argued that the PBGC must have realized the true situation when giving advice on what company lawyers described as an otherwise hypothetical situation. In the LTV case, the PBGC has suggested that the company misled the public and acted in collusion with the union, all the time pretending to be unaware of the inevitable consequences of their actions in maintaining pension benefits during bankruptcy.

This kind of argument implies a degree of familiarity by the unions and PBGC with company pension goals and objectives which is quite extraordinary. But if this argument was true, an observer might wonder why Continental Can and International Harvester sought to maintain the cloak of secrecy (in and out of court) for so long. Why bother with a complex web of lies and deception if the target of the secret knew all along? Alternatively, it might be supposed (as the companies have intimated) that the union leadership (in the Continental case) and the PBGC executive staff (in the International Harvester case) knew what was likely to happen but informally colluded with company management against their common enemies—the union's ordinary membership and the company's line management in the former case, and the public in general in the latter case. This is exactly the argument suggested by the PBGC against the company and union in the LTV bankruptcy; it supposes a degree of sophistication on the part of union leaders and upper corporate management undreamt of when considering ordinary workers and line management. At the heart of this argument is an unstated claim that if corporate managers are to be indicted for unethical conduct, so too should union leaders, and even staff members of the PBGC. By implication, it is argued that union leaders and the PBGC knew or should have known if they had taken the time to ascertain the facts of the case. Either way, neither the union leaders nor the PBGC deserve greater respect than the companies, and they certainly don't have the ethical right to accuse the companies of behavior that is inconsistent with common standards of right and wrong. By this logic, legal retaliation by the unions and PBGC is a cynical exercise and should be dismissed and sent back for renegotiation.

An alternative line of argument would have it that the companies should not be held accountable to public ethical standards where in fact their actions are consistent with a separate sphere of action known as "business considerations." Here it is not argued that the union and the PBGC actions are similarly tainted by unethical considerations. Rather than making a judgment about the veracity of their ethical stance, it is suggested that their ethical stance is irrelevant in the context of other legitimate criteria. No doubt "business considerations" are respected by the courts, and have been accepted as grounds for corporate decisionmaking in other instances. Both Continental Can and International Harvester placed great faith in the significance of this defense. The former corporation suggested that business considerations were such that those workers laid off would have been unemployed whatever their eligibility status, while the latter company has argued that the sale of property is wholly the right of the corporation, and cannot be compromised by reference to others' social or ethical considerations. In the LTV case, both the union and company have argued that they also have a sphere of legitimate action that should not be compromised by the PBGC; in this instance, it is not a private property right but a claimed right for respect of the collective-bargaining process that is invoked. One way or another, what is being claimed is respect for a principle that transcends ordinary morality or some other standards of decisionmaking. To make the argument work, a distinction is drawn between parties' private interests and those of the public. On the basis of this distinction, private interests have priority over public concerns—the latter may be entirely reasonable, but of secondary concern with respect to the fidelity of private rights.

The public-private distinction is well known and common to liberal theories of American jurisprudence (Unger 1986). It relies upon two problematic assumptions. First, it is assumed that private interests exist (logically) before public interests; and, second, it is assumed that public interests have lower status than private interests because the latter are in some sense natural, whereas the former are only determined on a case-by-case basis and thus do not have the transcendental virtue of the latter. Now it is true, of course, that liberal judges (and liberal theorists) are willing to compromise principles in instances of compelling public interest. But that is indeed a strong claim to be made, especially where what is claimed as worthy of protection are the virtues of trust and cooperation—notions that appear as relatively intangible compared to corporations' private property rights. As I have noted elsewhere, the claim that the LTV's and Steelworkers' collective-bargaining agreement deserves such protection is weak at best. There is nothing intrinsically private at stake in that relationship (at least in the sense claimed by Continental Can and International Harvester)—the PBGC could equally claim to have a special relationship with the corporation. Nonetheless, the public/private distinction is a form of morality, a form of social anthropology, which legitimates private sentiments over public standards. Public ethical standards may be plausible, but their relevance is in doubt once we accept such a distinction.

While public ethical standards are perhaps plausible in theory, there are those who would argue there is nothing natural at all in privileging private interests over public interests. Indeed, the whole distinction has been argued to be a convenient fiction; it makes sense neither sociologically (how can a private sphere exist without being constituted by the public?) nor historically (the private sphere has only a logical status in theory, and is not an historical reality). In this sense its critics would argue that it is an arbitrary distinction, justified only by its utility in abstract theoretical philosophy of the utilitarian kind. More trenchant critics like Jameson (1981) would also argue that the distinction is deliberately fabricated in the ideological apparatus of the state legitimately to mark off as out of bounds the actions of private agents whose primary purpose is capital accumulation. It is, by this reasoning, an intellectual device conceived for the sole purpose of reproducing private property rights, protecting those rights from the ethical claims of the majority disenfranchised from ownership and control. Jameson's ethics are entirely materialist in origin, and bespeak a world in which ethical philosophy has a close and intimate connection with economic power. Here, the logic of capitalism demands a formal justification with reference to nature; the division between public and private in this sense is not natural but ideologically constructed and therefore vulnerable to attack from counterclaims. Thus, the reference to a private world is a reference to *both* an ethical claim and an institutionally protected defense against the intrusion of anticapital ethics.

If the unions and PBGC were not aware of the corporations' motives in seeking agreement on certain provisions relating to pension obligations, and if they had no way of knowing (at least at the time of implementation), there is every reason to deny the veracity of the first kind of management defense of their actions. While we can never be completely certain of anyone's true motivations, all the evidence suggests that the unions and PBGC were deceived by Continental Can and International Harvester. No evidence exists that they knew or should have known of the corporations' true motivations until it was too late. Furthermore, however significant the distinction between private interests and public morality for the maintenance of property rights, it is apparent that the courts have generally denied the transcendental power of that claimed distinction. In the Continental case, although the district court found favor with that distinction, the appeals court and Supreme Court found it a flimsy defense in the face of overwhelming evidence of unethical and illegal corporate conduct. The bases of their decisions are not explicitly ethical—concern for the case record, evidence, and the meaning of Section 510 of ERISA dominated the proceedings. On the other hand, it is clear that the courts have favored *public* standards of behavior as opposed to what is clearly a rationale for action that simply justifies, but does not defend, unethical behavior. The court in the International Harvester case went so far as to suggest that there is nothing sacred in the public/private distinction, and that the private sphere must be penetrated in the interests of public justice. If, by using this language, the court signals respect for the distinction, in practice the distinction evaporates as public standards of behavior come to dominate the discourse.

A defense of corporations' private interests has come from an unlikely source—academic mainstream economists in the form of the Chicago school of law and economics. R. Posner (1986) argues that the judiciary ought to decide issues so that economic efficiency is enhanced (the means) and social welfare maximized (the ends). Although not denying the existence of other forms of ethics, Posner has suggested that this judicial rule is in fact the only reasonable rule, justified by what it can achieve for society as a whole (but see Levinson 1991). To the extent that other ethical rules are consistent with outcomes that would result from its application, there is no conflict between the efficiency rule and ethics in general. However, it is apparent that the rule would conflict with union and PBGC sentiments. That is, the Chicago school would argue that to the extent Continental

Can, International Harvester, and LTV Corporation achieved lower cost, more efficient rationalization of productive capacity through their secret policies, then social welfare is enhanced. If, on the other hand, social welfare would have been greater (measured by dollars and cents) and if rationalization had been a cooperative venture with the unions and PBGC, then the *best* procedure would have been cooperation, not secrecy. Indeed, secrecy would have been unethical (and irrational) in this context. Notice how utilitarian and consequential this ethical standard is, and notice how contingent ethical judgments are when the reference point is a calculated outcome, not some *a priori* standard.

Although argued for in the context of firm relocations of productive assets and the rights of unions to represent workers in those situations during the Reagan administration, economic efficiency has not met with great enthusiasm as a judicial decision rule. Nor has it met with great enthusiasm as a plausible ethical standard (see Dworkin's 1980 compelling critique). While many may find its ethical calculus crude and uninspiring, what seems most incredible is the strong claim made on behalf of the transcendental virtues of efficiency. And why maximum social welfare should be so virtuous compared to other ethical standards seems hardly explained. In the cases under consideration here, the corporations concerned never raised economic efficiency as a defense for their actions. Although it might be thought as being consistent with a defense of the public/private distinction, there has been no attempt to calculate the *social* benefits of secrecy in such a fashion. The social reference point has been defined and controlled by the unions and the PBGC. In this sense, the corporations have been forced on the defensive with the moral ground occupied by their protagonists, and a judiciary unsympathetic to claims of imagined collaborators and an implausible distinction between public and private morality.

Summary—Ethics of Regulation

The ethics of social action is a problematic topic in the social sciences. As a research topic it appears too subjective, being often a topic of great controversy wherein customary modes of analysis are unable to resolve conflicting claims of the moral correctness of actions, as well as a topic of incredible imprecision in that the terms of reference used to make ethical judgments are themselves contested and deeply disputed. By contrast, it is often held that the best kind of social science is that which eschews normative judgments for the empirical realities of observable actions, structure, and events (therein mimicking the natural sciences; see Roth's

1987 critique). The methodological simplicity argued to be so virtuous and indicative of this kind of social enquiry is no doubt idealized. Even so, this recipe for social analysis is often buttressed by a shared belief in the integrity of data and a shared distrust of social standards of value. Social scientific arguments against the study of ethics are, by this analysis, less an issue of substance than an issue of the apparent inherent inadequacy of ethics as a field worthy of systematic study.[13]

This proclaimed distinction between the worlds of ethics (full of conflict and dissent over principles) and a certain kind of social science (characterized by stable values and consensual agreement on the terms of human association) can be taken too far. This chapter has sought to demonstrate that ethical disputes typically have identifiable and substantial theoretical foundations. To imagine that ethical disputes are just subjective disagreements over intangible notions that have no coherent or logical form is to egregiously miscast an essential and vital part of social life. That there is conflict between theoretical foundations is not disputed. What is disputed is the often asserted idea that ethical conflicts are basically groundless, being simply exercises in rhetoric rather than substance. Failure to apprehend this point could lead social researchers, for example, to ignore vital explanatory clues for understanding the logic and motivations behind union and federal government litigation over corporate restructuring. And failure to apprehend this point would lead some researchers to conclude that justice has been done once compensation has been arranged for those workers affected by corporate restructuring where in fact litigation provides unions and others an opportunity to retaliate against corporate actions for violating essential social norms of trust and cooperation. Compensation is important. But that is just one rationale for social action, itself being based upon an ethical theory normally termed *consequentialism*. Another ethical standard is at work when unions retaliate against companies for breaking social norms; a form of deontological reasoning is the most appropriate reference point in this context. Ethical reasoning is an organized discourse, providing intelligible clues for social analysts wishing to understand the complexities of law and society.

On the other side, social science is less coherent and certainly less consensual in logic than often acknowledged (just as the natural sciences are more hermeneutic than commonly acknowledged by social scientists; see Toulmin 1982). Moreover, it could be argued that the application of social science methods to issues of moral conflict can do significant harm to the integrity of the latter. When social scientists attempt a rapprochement between ethics and techniques of social analysis, there is a tendency to reduce one to the metric of the other. Thus, the translation of conflict over the terms of social association (and the terms of judicial adjudication) by the Chicago school of law and economics into the imperatives of economic efficiency and the goal of maximum social welfare makes two basic errors. First, it would appear that the very texture of ethical conflict—dispute over the appropriate standards to judge the virtue of social action—is lost in an attempt to rationalize conflict under one metalogic. If useful for the efficacious application of social science methods to ethical disputes, there is a sense in which the metalogic is inadequate in the face of social pluralism. We often judge the health of a society by its ability to tolerate divergent opinions; in its most extreme version, totalitarianism is the imposition of just one ethical standard. Second, what are claimed as being the consensual standards for making ethical judgments are often just one form of ethical reasoning imposed over others. Social scientists by training are (normally) utilitarians and their rules of justice often reflect a commitment to judging actions by their consequences. While this is no doubt an entirely plausible theory of ethics, it is not enough either to understand social action or to make policy determinations on the bases of litigation.

Secret-keeping in the context of corporate restructuring and companies' responsibility for pension liabilities should be understood as an important ethical issue. Favoring a deonotological perspective, once exposed, secret-keeping in corporate restructuring attacked fundamental social norms: the trust and cooperation of unions and the federal government in the veracity and integrity of the companies concerned. Based upon recent developments in moral philosophy, there are plausible reasons for believing (as the unions believe) that lies, deception, and secret-keeping are all unethical actions. This does not mean, though, that all secrets are so significant. While it is tempting to make such grand, all-encompassing philosophical claims, evaluating the ethical significance of secret-keeping in the context of corporate restructuring requires an appreciation of the context-dependent nature of making such judgments. Put slightly differently, I here sought an answer to the following question: if everyone keeps secrets, why was secret-keeping in this context unethical? Basically, the answer had two parts: first, by keeping secret their true intentions, corporations used the trust and cooperation of unions and the federal government to subvert their legal obligations; and, second, by keeping secret their true intentions, corporations sought to undermine the power of unions with respect to their ability to represent workers' legitimate interests. Summarily stated, the corporations used secrecy as a strategic device against their unions and the federal government while using the trust and cooperation of those organizations to further their programs of economic restructuring.

It might be supposed that as much as a concern for ethics is an interesting and, in some quarters, a fashionable topic its public policy significance is nevertheless relatively small. This kind of opinion presupposes that ethics is a private matter—if not wholly subjective, then, at best only a matter for dispute between the interested parties. However, such a limited reading of the significance of unethical behavior in the context of corporate restructuring would fail to appreciate the origin of such disputes and their possible implications for public institutions. In many respects, what has been identified as unethical behavior from the perspective of the unions and agencies involved are simultaneously legal disputes concerning the integrity of the laws governing the private pension system. If the courts do not adequately penalize corporations for their attempts at avoiding pension liabilities, and if the federal government does not adequately police corporate decisionmaking in the context of corporate restructuring, then the very integrity of the private pension system is at risk. Failure to penalize adequately such actions would encourage corporations to view penalties as simply another cost to be incurred in restructuring, just as failure to adequately police legal obligations would encourage corporations to view breaking the law as a worthwhile risk to take in the face of regulators' indifference. One implication of a failure to adequately penalize and to police the actions of corporations would be further attacks upon the rights of workers to private pensions. If this behavior was systematic across many industries, then the whole private pension system would be put at risk. In this context, unethical private behavior may have, as consequentialists would argue, drastic public consequences.

9

Status of Corporations' Social Obligations

Attempts to enact laws to protect workers' pension rights have been informed by the evidence of corporations' behavior and the recurrent phases of economic expansion, contraction, and restructuring. In this respect, the recent plant-closing bill can be read as a political response to recurrent problems of accommodating restructuring (see chapter 7). Always at issue in debates over new policy initiatives is the proper relationship between economic imperatives and corporations' social obligations, especially the proper boundaries between the two: what is admissible corporate behavior, given their economic imperatives, and what is inadmissible behavior, given the expected social obligations of private agents. Although hardly ever considered in an all-encompassing manner, this issue appears and reappears in all debates over public policy design and implementation. Nevertheless, there are strong expectations that those boundaries are to be respected by corporations' management, whatever their economic costs. Even so, there is considerable evidence that many corporations either openly or secretly deliberately violate the integrity of those boundaries. Corporations appear to routinely work through benefit-cost analyses of respecting legal boundaries—the costs of regulation versus the benefits of breaking the law discounted by the probability of being caught, the cost of litigation, and the probable penalties if found liable.

Notwithstanding the notional ideal separation between economic imperatives and social obligations embodied in statutes such as ERISA, in practice corporations would want those distinctions blurred in favor of the primacy of their economic imperatives. This is evident in many ways, most obviously when they argue in the courtroom that they must be allowed to violate social obligations when economic imperatives warrant such actions. This argument is expressed either in terms of an invoked warrant they believe is provided by "business considerations" or is the product of an expansive reading of the boundaries of economic imperatives and a narrow reading of the boundaries of social obligations. Either way, corporations argue that their responsibilities toward shareholders and creditors (and themselves) take precedence over all others and want the courts to treat those affected by their actions as just another set of claimants for scarce resources. In this sense, workers' legal rights are summarily reduced to just another set of economic costs, and economic efficiency is idealized as a benefit to all. This chapter explores the intellectual logic used to sustain such arguments, referencing in particular the theory of rational choice behavior. In doing so, two general claims are advanced. First, however plausible such a theoretical perspective is in explaining behavior, when used as a defense of corporate behavior it delegitimizes the role of regulation and ultimately reduces its overall effectiveness. This kind of theory is not simply a means of explanation, it is most profoundly an argument that justifies a certain form of social life. In this context, to maintain significant status for public regulation requires a reassessment of the terms and ideal relations of economic life. The second general claim of the chapter is that moral sentiments must be reintroduced into public discourse over the logic of regulation. Only moral sentiments (of a certain type) have sufficient status for regulatory regimes to withstand the twin evils of economism and reductionism so prevalent in the theory of rational choice behavior *and* the practice of corporate restructuring.

Logic of Corporate Restructuring

The case studies of corporate restructuring which form the core of this book have all been in basic industry and manufacturing. The logic, determinants, and patterns of restructuring observed in these case studies can be generally explained as being a product of three interrelated economic conditions: first and most simply, the necessity to reduce excess productive capacity; second and perhaps more problematically, the need to increase labor productivity or at least decrease per-unit costs of production; and, third and most fundamentally, the maximization of corporate managers' strategic options. These three factors could be thought to depend upon one another. For example, to increase labor productivity it may be necessary to first reduce excess productive capacity (a necessary condition, not a sufficient condition for higher rates of labor productivity).[1] Similarly, if corporate managers are to have any discretion in choosing strategic options for growth (rather than declaring Chapter 7 bankruptcy and liquidating all assets), they must first reduce excess capacity (reducing the operating and financial costs per unit of production) and increase labor productivity (increasing the return per unit of production). Reduced capacity and higher labor productivity are necessary conditions for greater internal financial liquidity, itself a condition for strategic innovation.[2]

The experience of the companies studied here suggests that excess capacity is often the result of a combination of factors made critical to the survival of the corporation by unanticipated economic events. For many corporations, growth in demand over the post–World War II era was accommodated by the addition of new plants and equipment to the existing stock of capital. Changes in the configuration of domestic demand were responded to on an incremental basis; the inherited economic landscape is thus patterned by plants whose age and technological sophistication reflect both geographical shifts in population and shifts in consumption patterns. The advent of significant international competition in the 1970s in combination with the following deep recession of the early 1980s made the inherited networks of plants and facilities grossly outmoded. Thus, rationalization of excess capacity became imperative and has had three different elements: the closing of aged and technologically outmoded facilities; the closing of facilities making either the wrong product (or products) or located in regions of stable and declining demand relative to markets experiencing significant growth; and the closing of facilities whose output or product is duplicated by other more productive facilities. Not surprisingly, capacity rationalization has had a rather special geography, concentrated in regions whose economic history is the history of corporate growth and development.

Having cut excess capacity back to a core set of plant and equipment, corporations have sought ways to increase labor productivity. In some instances, new forms of work practices and new types of labor contracts have been introduced in cooperation with unions. In many other instances, production has been shifted to sites where such practices are part of a new technological configuration of production (flexible manufacturing) rarely involving unions or their representatives.[3] It would be a mistake, though, to imagine that these strategies are only designed to increase labor productivity. What some corporations have sought is not only more efficient utilization of labor and capital, but also reduction in the costs of production *and* rationalization, by deploying their labor in ways that improve overall financial liquidity. While it may be thought that the relocation of production to newer and more efficient plants improves labor productivity (which it often does), it sometimes also decreases the costs of rationalization. Relocation of production may facilitate the transfer of liabilities incurred in rationalization from the corporation to a group of workers or even to the federal government. This was the net intended result of Continental Can's and International Harvester's attempts to re-locate and outsource production and close plants, thereby facilitating shift-ing of pension liabilities to others.

As so written, corporate restructuring appears to be a simple problem of strategy design and implementation. But how are these actions to be understood in an intellectual manner? Many years ago it might have been said that the objective of management was to operate their business as efficiently as possible, thereby maximizing profit.[4] However, with company conglomeration and increasing scale has come a more complex agenda for management. For middle-level, subsidiary-based managers the goal may still be very much the ideal of efficient "local" operation but managers are now also subject to meeting requirements imposed by corporate manage-ment regarding achievement of certain revenue and profit levels set in accordance with the overall objectives of the corporation. In many respects subsidiaries are increasingly treated as sources of finance rather than just as production units (that is, as fixed assets). When the Wisconsin Steel division of International Harvester failed to meet the corporation's ac-ceptable levels of performance, the division became increasingly vulnerable to rationalization and, ultimately, sale. Likewise, when executives in the Continental Group sought to diversify and extend the range of operations outside their traditional packaging sectors, available revenue from canning subsidiaries was transferred to corporate headquarters to help finance acquisitions.

Since at least the late 1960s and the widespread implementation of the Boston Consulting Group's notion of switching income from stable and/or declining sectors ("cash cows") to growth sectors ("stars"), corpo-rations have been increasingly treated by their senior management as portfolios of assets and liabilities to be manipulated in accordance with profit opportunities (see Hax and Majluf 1984). And since senior mana-gers are typically rewarded according to the overall short-run perfor-mance of the corporation, individual units have become part of a larger jigsaw puzzle of income and potential costs that together affect levels of management compensation. It is not surprising, then, that corporate executives have been so aggressive in shifting the costs of restructuring. Executives' interests are implicated in the design and implementation of restructuring since lower costs increase disposable revenue, enabling greater management discretion and ideally higher returns; executive power is a product of the assets available for deployment and the returns realized from those deployed assets (see Roll's 1988 theory of executive behavior).

Over much of the 1970s and most especially through the 1980s, a succession of different recipes was advocated for corporate portfolio management. The BCG model of diversification through the diversion of internal funds was a popular recipe, leading to enormous conglomerates composed of many different and unrelated operations. However, only those corporations with sufficient unleveraged funds could go the BCG route; other corporations already adversely affected by declining demand and increasing competition found it practically impossible to move outside of traditional sectors (witness the heavy costs of the LTV Corporation's strategy of consolidating its position in the U.S. steel industry). Notwithstanding the BCG's enthusiasm for conglomeration, as a corporate strategy it is now thought by many commentators to have failed. The argued-for efficiencies of common management and financial control and decentralized operation were apparently difficult, if not impossible, to realize in most situations (see Ravenscraft and Scherer 1987). Thus, beginning in the late 1970s there were many attempts to rationalize back to core business interests, as was illustrated in the study of International Harvester's attempts to rid itself of its steel division (and other less-related businesses) and focus its talents on farm equipment and transportation units. The increasing popularity of this model of corporate management was one reason for the enormous sell-off of assets in the 1980s, precipitating the growth in significance of leveraged buyouts. The experience of Continental Group over the 1970s and 1980s mirrors these events; from conglomeration and diversification to its sale in a leveraged buyout and hence the stripping off of unrelated businesses to finance the sale, Continental's workers were the victims of changing tastes and fashions in corporate management.[5]

Interests of Corporate Executives

This brief sketch of management objectives is obviously incomplete in that it is based upon a limited set of case studies drawn from one segment of American industry. There may well be significant differences between industry groups, even between countries; see N. Wrigley (1992) on the restructuring of the U.S. and U.K. retail industries. On the other hand, this sketch describes a world familiar to many analysts of corporate behavior, especially at the level of corporate strategy. The intention here is not to repeat more extensive analyses of corporate strategy (see for more details Porter 1980). Rather, the purpose of this discussion was to establish three general claims that will be used in subsequent analyses about the liability of corporate executives for the consequences of restructuring. These claims have to do with the motives of corporate management and can be summarily stated as:

1. Senior corporate management are motivated by a complex set of overlapping interests, operating at a variety of scales within their corporation, all informed by the economic environment in which they function.

2. Corporate managements' interests may well be consistent with stockholders' interests (although this is not always the case) but are always related to their compensation.

3. Over time, managements' strategic response to economic conditions may change as circumstances change, given their overriding interest in maintaining and increasing their levels of compensation.

Notice that these three general claims are all related to the economic environment in which management operate; in the rest of this section, these motives will be associated with the economic imperatives of restructuring.

These three general claims are also consistent with models of the firm that assume that agents maximize profits or some measure of economic rent subject to constraints. Put more abstractly, it is assumed here that corporate managers are *rational* in the sense that they choose "the best *means* to achieving a given *end*, goal or objective" (Harsanyi 1983:231, emphasis in original). This is, of course, the simplest definition of *rationality*. In the context of corporate restructuring, more complicated versions of rationality are appropriate, including those that would consider the costs and benefits of different actions in relation to stated goals and even those versions that would allow for a variety of possible goals, the final choice being dictated by an assessment of the relationship between stated goals and overall preferences (a comparison drawn between so-called manifest preferences and underlying true preferences; see Harsanyi 1983:233). More precisely, what is assumed here is that management assesses options with respect to their causal effectiveness in achieving desired goals, accepting for the moment that there remain unanswered questions about how managements' uncertainty and strategic interaction with others affects the process of rational choice.

It must be stressed at this juncture that by describing corporate managements' actions as rational in these terms, I am simply making a judgment of how they appear to have acted in the cases analyzed in this book, and how they tend to act in general. R. Brandt (1983:144) would in all probability suggest that this is a judgment that is act- or agent-appraisive about actions that were taken in the past. This does not mean, however, that I endorse those actions. Just because corporate managers are rational in this restricted sense does not mean to imply that their actions are in any sense morally correct (compare with Gibbard 1983). Indeed, what has been identified in the discussion above about the actions of corporate management is that their behavior is understood in the first instance to be relative to their economic environment. Other criteria to judge their actions include the extent to which they act in accordance with their social obligations. In the previous chapter I argued that other criteria utilized by affected agents would suggest that such rational behavior is in fact unethical. Beginning with managements' economic interests does, in one sense, assign priority to those interests relative to their social obligations. But it is not meant to be implied that this is the necessary priority between economic imperatives (first?) and social obligations (second?), although some courts seem to suggest that this is the correct ordering (see the reversed opinion of Judge Bloch in *Gavalik v. Continental Can*). Essentially, I am making an analytical connection and an observation about behavior, justified by evidence culled from the case studies on corporate restructuring.

Thus, it is assumed here that corporate executives maximize their compensation, accepting that this has an identifiable monetary value and is positively and proportionally related to their control of corporate assets, their status, prestige, and power (over fellow executives and employees). Based again on the case study evidence, it should also be understood that executive compensation has two related temporal dimensions; in the short run it is the performance of the corporation that determines executive compensation. But notwithstanding the often-made claim that this time frame has severely disadvantaged American industry, planning takes place over longer time frames than just the short run.[6] Maintenance of labor-management relations, the competitive standing of corporate units, and the flow of revenue for investment all demand planning over a longer term horizon than implied by measures of short-run performance. I would expect a rational corporate executive plans for compensation over both the short and the long run since actions taken in one time period could have either positive or negative consequences for compensation in the next period. Assuming executives maximize, there is no logical reason that executives would deliberately and knowingly compromise subsequent compensation levels by short-run actions that would lower their future returns.

The notion that executives plan their compensation over the longer term in the context of short-run economic imperatives is a useful device for understanding the logic of corporate restructuring. However, as so stated, it is still too simple to capture the whole picture of corporate restructuring. Three complicating issues are hinted at in the previous discussion. First, if corporate executives do plan over the longer term they do so under great uncertainty—it is often not clear what the *best* means are for achieving desired goals. Thus, their plans are always partial in the sense that they may be changed if better information is found about the relative value of different options, and their plans are always being hierarchically reordered with respect to achieving their overriding interest in maintaining and expanding current compensation levels. Further complicating this issue is a realization that making partial plans is not a costless exercise—there are nonrecoverable sunk costs associated with implementing a plan just as there are opportunity costs in not following alternative options (see chapter 5). Corporations that have significant revenue resources thus tend to experiment with a number of options simultaneously while less well endowed corporations have to take their chances. Inevitably a great deal of learning is involved in implementing plans, although some of the lessons may not be as valuable as others if corporations are unable to capitalize on those lessons (compare with Bratman 1987, chap. 3).

A second complicating issue is the realization that the implementation of plans, even the *best* plans (if identifiable), are dependent upon the cooperation of others. This is most apparent in corporate restructuring where labor unions are often heavily involved in the design of restructuring, changes in work practices to facilitate the success of plans, monitoring of plan implementation, even the financing of restructuring (see Clark 1989a). In instances where cooperation is not desired, as in cases where corporations believe that unions or their representatives would frustrate their plans, the design of restructuring must nevertheless take into account the likely actions and counterresponses of those affected. In this sense, all corporate planning related to restructuring involves strategic interaction with other parties. Such interaction may or may not be predictable— without prior knowledge of parties' interests and motives, such interaction could be very risky and uncertain in effect. Over the longer term, though, strategic interaction may in fact become quite predictable—the product of mutual learning from one another based upon sequences of decisions that involve all parties over a range of different kinds of issues. In these cases, initiating a new policy may be made more difficult by expectations (positive and negative) built up over time through the accumulated set of past actions and interactions.

Clearly important in all planning is information—about the best options, about the actions and responses of others, and about the economic environment in which planning takes place. This third complicating issue is probably the most problematic for corporate planners. Without adequate knowledge of these factors and others, corporate planners may be tempted either to not respond to changing circumstances and thereby risk both short-run and long-run compensation, or to respond by minimizing short-run affects leaving the longer term consequences of their actions to others in the corporation (labor unions) or outside of the corporation (shareholders). We can imagine, then, that a profound lack of knowledge about how to realize their overall interests may encourage corporate executives to leave for other opportunities. In this sense they may simply cash out of the situation (for example, the company or the particular unit of production).

To illustrate the implications of these assertions about rational decisionmaking, it is useful to consider a series of hypothetical cases working from the simplest to the most complex situation (see Figure 9.1). Represented in these hypothetical cases is a choice that faces executives time and time again as they respond to the economic imperatives of competition and innovation—simply the choice between continuing to produce, recognizing that this option entails significant obligations in terms of meeting their on-going commitments to labor (as well as governmental agencies and their regulations), *or* cashing out of production in that particular industry or sector and diverting derived revenue to other opportunities. This kind of choice is that which has faced all corporations studied in this book; from Continental Can, to International Harvester, and even the LTV Corporation. Summarily stated, and in the language of game-theoretic analysis, the choice is between cooperation and noncooperation (the latter being understood in this context as cashing out).

The simplest case (Case 1) is the initial choice at time t made by a corporation about whether or not to invest in an opportunity—this is a choice between the available opportunities (including the opportunity costs of not investing) with respect to executives' overall interests in maximizing returns and, hence, their compensation. Although stated as an investment decision, it is also a decision about whether or not to cooperate with labor and the concomitant obligations that would go with a collective-bargaining agreement or contract.[7] At this point, not to cooperate is tantamount to not investing, therefore passing up the opportunity for potential profits and the payment of wages and benefits. The payoff is represented in Figure 9.1 as (0,0); the first value measuring the corporation's return and the second value being workers' compensation.

Having decided to cooperate at time t, the next opportunity for the corporation to consider the value of their investment comes at time $t +$ *1*, perhaps the end of the financial year or perhaps the end of the production cycle but most often the end of the collective-bargaining agreement with labor. In this case (Case 2), the time between the initial decision to co-

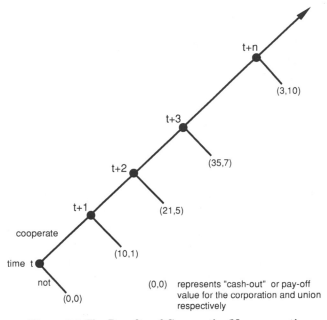

Figure 9.1 The Benefits of Cooperation/Noncooperation

operate and the point of reconsideration is relatively short; I assume that investment has been limited to necessary plant and equipment and the accumulated obligations to labor are of less importance than the wages paid to labor. Assuming that both parties have gained from cooperation, again the choice is whether or not to cooperate, given the now-limited costs of cashing out and the availability of other opportunities (10,6). Again assuming cooperation, we could imagine a whole sequence of these decisions over time from t to $t + n$ involving analyses of the costs and benefits at the end of each time period of continuing to cooperate set against the value of competing opportunities. Each time, if the payoff remains positive and greater than the returns of other opportunities discounted by the costs of cashing out of the relationship, then we would imagine that it is rational to continue cooperation. This represents the corporate decisionmaking process as if the only relevant factors in decisionmaking are short-run costs and benefits.

But now imagine (Case 3) that over a sequence of cost-benefit calculations associated with the choice between continuing to cooperate and the value of cashing out it becomes apparent to management that their likely return from cashing out is increasing over time. As represented in Figure

9.1, their cash-out value increases absolutely and proportionally from time t to time $t + 3$. Assuming that the short-run returns of cooperation are positive and at least stable from one time to the next, then the long-run potential cash-out value becomes an inducement to invest and reinforce their commitments to the production unit. But now (Case 4), having noted that the corporation is increasing its commitment to the unit at each decision point, the labor union begins to demand greater short-run benefits at each renewal of their contract, thereby leading to a squeeze on short-run returns to the corporation (beyond time $t + 3$). And recognizing that the potential value of cashing out is also increasing for the firm, the union now begins to demand higher pension benefits and, in particular, plant-closing pension benefits.[8] Thus at time $t + n$, when economic events force the corporation to reconsider their portfolio of investments, its executives face a very difficult choice: to continue to cooperate may still reap short-run benefits but at lower rates than alternative options. On the other hand, while cashing out may have in the past reaped a significant one-time benefit and would have allowed diversification into other opportunities, the benefits of this option is now heavily discounted by the costs of cashing out, specifically the plant-closing pensions (3,10). It is rational for the corporation to cash out into other options, but it is limited in doing so by the costs of that policy.

What can the corporation do in these circumstances? From the case studies developed in this book a series of legitimate (legal) options is apparent:

1. A rundown in investment and capital replacement over subsequent time periods as the corporation slowly diverts revenue to other more attractive options.

2. Selective branch and departmental closings within production units as employees retire and are not replaced.

3. Closings of other units not so locked into long-term contractual relationships with labor unions.

4. The sale or transfer of production units to other corporations.

All these strategies and others are used in corporate restructuring. But there is another option, not legitimate but nevertheless considered. Why not cash out as originally planned but in such a way that the plant-closing pensions the company is obligated to pay labor are at least minimized, if not totally avoided? This is, after all, the most rational option since the other options are too slow in their implementation, may never recoup the once-anticipated cash-out value, and take the corporation into a downward cycle of disinvestment and reduced competitiveness. This option will only work, however, if the union and others affected never suspect or have reason to believe that illegally cashing out is the corporation's intention. But given the sequence of prior decisions taken by management to continue cooperation, there may be little cause for the union to suspect management of such a strategy. And if the union has different criteria by which it judges the actions of others—emphasizing ethical, legal, or social commitments to others—then what may appear rational for one agent may not be readily "seen" by another agent.

Compliance and Deterrence

So far, as described above, corporate executives have been assumed to be narrowly self-interested in maximizing their compensation. It is apparent, of course, that to do so requires executives to maximize other indicative variables such as corporate profit rates and shareholders' returns (and other variables; see Roll 1988). Presumably, executives' compensation levels are directly and positively related to variables; if there is any real difference between compensation and these indicative variables, for the sake of this argument I will assume that such differences do not matter. Emphasized in this discussion has been the rationality of corporate executives, whether in pursuit of their compensation goals over a sequence of events and time periods or in their strategic interaction and cooperation with other agents who can directly affect corporate performance and, hence, executive compensation levels. As so described, a corporate executive is assumed to be (in the language of Gauthier 1986:167) a *straightforward* maximizer: defined as "a person who seeks to maximize his utility given the strategies of those with whom he interacts." For executives so disposed, the world is a simple place dominated by their expectations regarding compensation and how their actions and strategic interactions with others further those expectations. In the terms of rational choice theory, an expected level of compensation is the *end*, and corporate executives' actions and interactions are the *means* to that end. (Of course, it may be true that uncertainty over the extent to which a set of means contributes to executives' compensation may make the choice of means problematic and fraught with doubt about the efficacy of possible actions and interactions).

The previous analysis of corporate decisionmaking was set within a rather special context: a version of a more general issue of whether or not the corporation concerned ought continue to produce and operate plant and equipment given expected returns *and* the expected value of foregone opportunities discounted by the costs of closing. Put in terms of game theory, or more precisely the logic of rational-choice theory, the options are respectively to continue to cooperate with the union or break off that cooperation and establish new relationships in other fields of production. However, cooperation has two possible meanings in this context. It could refer to a willing agreement with another agent (in this case the union) to act together according to the terms of a joint arrangement based upon the expected value of cooperation compared to the value of noncooperation. Or, it could refer more simply to a contractual agreement with the union that advances their separate interests rather than their collective interests. The former idea of cooperation is more subtle than the latter idea; the latter simply assumes that corporations make strategic alliances (that is, cooperate) when it suits them (the expected value to the corporation of an alliance is greater than acting alone) whereas the former idea of cooperation implies the possibility of a *shared* goal distinguishable from, and more important than, the separate interests of contractual partners. I assume here that as straightforward maximizers, corporate executives value cooperation in the simplest form—for its efficacy in achieving executives' compensation goals rather than for any more complicated notion of a shared enterprise.[9]

Are union officials straightforward maximizers, just as corporate executives are assumed to be in this chapter? If we were to accept without reservation the dominant economic model of union behavior, the answer to this question would be quite simply—yes (see Hirsch and Addison 1986). Based upon the pioneering work of J. Dunlop (1944) many years ago, it is now assumed that union officials maximize their members' wages and benefits (their indicative variables), and hence their own levels of compensation. There are some problems with this assumption in that officials' compensation is more often determined by members' dues payments rather than being directly related to members' wages and benefits. Nevertheless, for the purposes of this argument it is a useful beginning point. Notice rationality (the means-and-ends type) is easily accommodated within this logic as is the prospect of making strategic alliances with corporate executives so as to best achieve desired goals. But it is also possible that union officials, more so than corporate executives, have a complex set of motives. Consistent with the ideology and social values associated with belonging to a union in American society, union officials might be just as well described as being *conditional* maximizers; that is, "disposed to cooperate in ways that, followed by all, yield nearly optimal and fair outcomes, and does cooperate in such ways where she [*sic*] may actually expect to benefit" (Gauthier 1986:177). Our choice is to model behavior as if their choice is either to act as a straightforward maximizer and simply maximize workers' wages and benefits in the context of competing corporate strategies of profit maximization, or to be a conditional maximizer and maximize the collective welfare of both groups even if this may mean compromising workers' individual interests at the margin relative to collective interests.

I do not intend justifying here, at least, my opinion that union officials have a more complex set of motives and reasons for action than corporate executives. While it is easy enough to treat union officials as being straightforward maximizers on the assumption that business unionism has replaced old-fashioned idealism, in point of fact there remain many instances of union officials acting in a conditional maximizing manner (Clark 1989a). More interesting than extensively debating the point is to understand the implications of making this assumption for corporations' strategic behavior. To begin with, D. Gauthier (1986) makes a number of relevant observations in this regard, starting with a brief characterization of conditional maximizers. Whereas a straightforward maximizer would only choose to act in a manner consistent with his or her optimum, a conditional maximizer may well join a collective project that results in outcomes only *close* to his or her optimum when the resulting outcomes are characterized as fair and equitable in an overall sense. Whereas no straightforward maximizer would sacrifice utility in the interests of collective welfare, a conditional maximizer may do so *if*: (1) there is an expectation of benefit flowing from that action; (2) there is a reasonable likelihood that others would act in ways consistent with the interests of the collective project; and, (3) the expected benefit is greater than the overall benefits flowing from non-cooperation. It is assumed that there is a tangible reward in a collective sense of individual actions that may fall short of their very best expected personal benefit. By this logic, agents willingly choose cooperation not only according to the individual benefits of strategic alliances but also according to the collective benefits of a shared enterprise—business unionism is consistent with strategic alliances, old-fashioned idealism is consistent with shared projects that result in fairness and equity.

For the sake of argument, it is assumed here that union officials are conditional maximizers in that they are "disposed to cooperate" with corporate executives in shared projects that result in greater overall benefit than if they acted singularly with respect to their own utility in strategic alliances. To illustrate with reference to union bargaining policy: union officials might be thought of as acting as conditional maximizers when they agree to collective-bargaining agreements that increase labor productivity in the interests of advancing overall welfare in a just and equitable manner, whereas union officials might be thought to be acting as straightforward maximizers when they would only accept collective-bargaining agreements

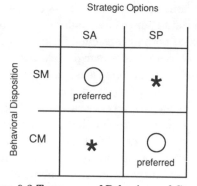

Figure 9.2 Taxonomy of Behavior and Strategy

that increase workers' wages and benefits regardless of the consequences of that claim on overall welfare. On the other hand, I will assume that corporate officials are straightforward maximizers in the sense that they are disposed to maximize their compensation, given the strategies of others. As so written, it is apparent that there may be an unfortunate asymmetry between union and corporate expectations—union officials would prefer shared projects that result in overall greater welfare in a just and equitable manner, whereas corporate officials may be less interested in shared projects and more interested in strategic alliances that advance their own compensation, whatever the consequences of such behavior for overall welfare. This asymmetry is represented in Figure 9.2: straightforward maximizers (SMs) prefer strategic alliances (SAs), and conditional maximizers (CMs) prefer shared projects (SPs). Note, though, that SMs could pick SPs as a strategic option, and CMs could be reduced to SAs if the circumstances are right.

To work through the implications of this asymmetry of dispositions and preferred strategic options, let us return to the scenario sketched in the previous section. At time t, the corporation decides to cooperate with labor in producing a commodity, moving on to time $t + 1$ when, having cooperated, expected benefits are realized and another set of decisions is taken to continue cooperation over a finite horizon. To make the analysis more complicated, I will assume that at time t, union officials and corporate executives are unaware of one another's precise behavioral disposition, but are aware that on average union officials tend to be conditional maximizers and corporate executives tend to be straightforward maximizers.

It may be protested at this point that union officials would not willingly enter into cooperation in these circumstances, given inadequate knowledge of their partner's behavioral disposition. But I think it is more than possible union officials would do so, assuming that they would put in place a set of monitoring devices to scrutinize corporate behavior and perhaps some potential penalties to deter corporate executives from taking advantage of their idealism. Of course, I do assume that union officials would not enter into any agreement if they were not convinced of the possibilities of benefiting from the arrangement. The question unanswered at time t or even time $t + 1$ is whether or not they have entered into a strategic alliance (an option often preferred by corporate executives) or a genuine shared project (union officials' preferred strategic option). Corporate executives would optimize their interests with the former option but, to convince union officials of their willingness to collaborate in a full and complete manner, may promise to act in a manner consistent with a shared project.

From time t through to time $t + n$, it may be very difficult for union officials to discern whether or not corporate executives are acting in ways inconsistent with their promise. Since expected future benefits from cooperation are positive and larger than the corporation's immediate cash-out value, there is no reason to conclude that executives are acting in ways inconsistent with their promise—at this point in time there is a close, perhaps one-to-one relationship between the current and expected benefits of a strategic alliance and the behavior consistent with a shared project. Moreover, since union members benefit in terms of wages and supplementary rewards close to their ideal of a fair and equitable return, there is no reason for union officials to think otherwise. However, union officials are aware of executives' general dispositions toward straightforward maximizing and strategic alliances. Even though corporations continue to act in ways consistent with conditional maximizing and shared projects, with each decision period t to $t + n$, it becomes increasingly obvious that the benefits to corporate executives of breaking their promise and returning to a SM/SA mode of behavior are increasing (the cash-out option comes into play). How is the union to ensure executives' compliance with their promise? What options are available to unions to deter corporations from breaking their promise? Here are a set of possible strategies that the union could pursue split between compliance and deterrence. None of these strategies has any *a priori* guarantee of success, or should we imagine that they are exclusive of one another in their implementation.

Compliance

Increase monitoring of executives' behavior

Reinforce expectations of behavior consistent with a shared project at each point of renegotiation of the collective-bargaining agreement

Test executives' behavioral dispositions in contract negotiations by varying terms of settlement relevant to both strategic alliances and shared project options

Continue to emphasize the moral component inherent in making a promise, notwithstanding the economic terms of the initial agreement

Deterrence

Introduce through the collective-bargaining agreement a grievance procedure for penalizing noncompliance

Threaten lawsuits for violating the terms of collective agreements, possibly according to notions of unfair labor practice

Threaten to revert to straightforward maximizing/strategic alliance behavior and thus increase the costs of production, whatever its consequences on long-term competitiveness and employment

Tie aspects of the collective-bargaining agreement to legal/statutory requirements, thereby threatening to directly involve the federal government if the corporation violates its promise

Threaten to expose the acts of individual corporate executives to public scrutiny if they break their promise

This list of possible strategies of compliance and deterrence is not meant to exhaust the set of all possible strategies. Moreover, it is apparent that their relative significance is practically impossible to determine without particular information about union-management relations in actual corporations. However, the list is useful in another way—it illustrates that there are three broad ways of ensuring compliance and deterring noncompliance. In a summary fashion, unions can use internal procedures (internal to the contractual relationship between unions and corporations), such as the negotiation process or the grievance arbitration process, to reinforce their claims and expectation about proper corporate behavior. Unions can also use prices (wages and other components of labor cost) to test compliance and penalize noncompliance. The threat of arbitrary wage increases unrelated to corporations' expected benefits may deter noncompliance. And unions can use external reference points (social and legal) to ensure compliance and invoke as a deterrence factor. So, for example, the possibility of "shaming" executives who break their word, invoking social standards of moral obligation associated with the notion of promises in contractual relationships (Fried 1981), and using legal sanctions derived from federal statutes are all possible "external" strategies. Whereas these social standards may not have costs directly attributable to the costs of operating a company, "shaming" may have a cost in terms of the reputation of an executive, just as breaking moral codes may have a cost in terms of acceptable social behavior. Legal sanctions may have "real" costs (literally monetary penalties), but may also involve the unacknowledged costs associated with damaged reputations and broken promises.

If this is plausible as a list of strategies and as a set of options, it seems also apparent that compliance may in any event be difficult to ensure in the face of a determined protagonist. As we have seen in the case studies that form this book, corporations may act with calculated duplicity, using the notion of a shared project and a willing conditional maximizer to advance their own interests in cashing out of the relationship. Detecting this kind of behavior is difficult when corporations may in fact act in a manner consistent with a shared project, and only over time switch intentions (but not apparent behavior). Being aware of this possibility is not enough; nor does it appear that sanctions for noncompliance have been particularly effective. Retaliation for noncompliance, invoking promised penalties, may or may not be effective if the very entity being threatened is itself transformed by corporate restructuring. In these circumstances no amount of internal monitoring of compliance will make a difference. Again it might be protested that if agents were to act in these ways, they would only be able to do so once—their reputation as an untrustworthy straightforward maximizer would ensure that they only attract like (if any) collaborators. But, of course, nothing is ever quite so simple: a damaged reputation after the fact of discovery does not compensate those adversely affected, and those affected do not necessarily have the option of not contracting with such agents in the future. In such cases, by virtue of previous experience, all agents would be reduced to acting explicitly as straightforward maximizers.

Status of Public Regulation

The previous discussion of the motivations and rationale behind corporate restructuring was, in one sense, rather abstract. I have deliberately rewritten an accumulated set of observations about the behavior of corporate executives derived from a set of case studies into a more general theoretical framework that emphasizes the rationality of individual behavior taken over a sequence of events. As written, it mimics conventional notions of corporate strategy, doing so in the context of a strategic "game" with organized labor. The analysis could be written, of course, from the perspective of labor. But to do so would run the risk of suggesting that labor plays the "game" with corporations as an equal. In point of fact, the reason why such games should be (more often than not) written from the perspective of senior corporate management is that management has the initiative power in these situations. Labor unions can respond and do, as I have attempted to demonstrate. But again, more often than not, their options are limited to counter response (attempts at closing off options) and threats of retaliation (such as increasing the cost of options) rather than new initiatives outside the parameters set by management. In essence, it is assumed that management's control over property in all its forms (plant and equipment, as well as finance and revenue) provides it with the initiative power, if not the controlling hand in a game of power.[10]

If there are certain analytical advantages in so describing the actions of executives in corporate restructuring, there are also some profound limitations that accompany such methods of analysis. Clearly, this kind of method allows us to strip away many of the complicating issues involved in restructuring, and thus understand the essential rationale of corporate executives. And, it demonstrates the problems faced by union officials who have to both anticipate the long-term ramifications of short-run agreements, and act in the short run in ways that facilitate the continuity of contract relations. On the other hand, this kind of analytical treatment carries with it significant limitations: because of its parsimony it lacks the scope of more complex treatments and inevitably introduces gaps in our understanding of the complex interaction among agents, events, and interests (compare this treatment with the detailed analysis of the LTV bankruptcy in chapter 6). These are, perhaps, the problems of a certain aesthetic nature as much as being the empirical limits of method of enquiry. More profound is another kind of limitation: as written, there is little recognition of the significance of public regulation except in an assumed equivalence regulation as a constraint, just like union contracts are constraints. The implication of this assumption is that regulation can be treated by corporations just like any other environmental factor—in terms of its costs and benefits to the corporation.

There can be little doubt that many corporations treat regulation as just another variable with a price. This much has been demonstrated by the various case studies of corporate restructuring in this book. And if we were to limit analysis to just the framework noted above, it is apparent that there are good analytical reasons to treat it as such. Indeed, corporate executives, when seeking a means of justifying their actions in court, often retreat to this kind of framework, suggesting that to have done otherwise would have been to act essentially irrationally and betray their obligations to shareholders to maximize returns. This framework is, then, inherent in any defense that depends on "business considerations" being a separable and distinct domain of executive power. Here, I want to suggest three limitations to this analytical framework. In doing so, part of my intention is to demonstrate the analytical limits of this approach. But more important, I want to indicate how and why regulation is more than just another cost to business. Indeed, I aim to show that this kind of interpretation, that regulation is just another cost, is fundamentally immoral.

In the first instance, a most obvious limitation of this framework is the apparent relative isolation of agents from broad social standards of proper behavior. To the extent that there is any recognition of the interplay between agents' actions and the interests of others, the decisionmaking calculus remains agent-centered, albeit adjusted in a strategic manner to the anticipated interests of others. This does not necessarily mean that social standards are irrelevant to agents' decisionmaking; individuals may choose to abide by social standards, presumably assuming that those standards are instrumental in achieving agents' long-term interests (Gauthier 1986). But this kind of acceptance of social standards is purely voluntary and dictated by a person's interest or lack thereof in abiding by common social standards of decisionmaking. Crudely described, agent-centered decisionmaking models treat people as profoundly selfish and egocentric. Moreover, the instrumental nature attributed to social standards belittles accepted notions of moral virtue, the role of law in representing collective interests, and the significance of social obligations (formal and informal). All this would not be a problem if the issue was only one of theoretical precision and logic built around a simple behavioral assumption. However, in the public policy domain egocentric models would apparently deny the integrity of social institutions that are valued for more than mere instrumentality. As a defense of corporate restructuring, the egocentric model has been appropriated from its intended purpose (which was to analyze the bases of individual and collective action) to now being the basis for arguing against the integrity of social obligations.

Egocentric behavioral models portray individuals as rational, self-serving calculating agents—this is their virtue (for analytical purposes) and this is their vice; such models come at a heavy cost. By their nature they ignore peoples' emotional commitments to others, and deny the social obligation of citizens to participate in civic life as a forum of moral discourse about the proper parameters of individual behavior (Barber 1989). Attempts to reconcile these issues within egocentric models only serve to emphasize their tendencies toward economic reductionism. Take, for example, passage of ERISA in 1974. It might be said that its passage was the result of many plant closings around the country, just like the closing of Studebaker in South Bend, Indiana. The actions of corporations in closing plants could be reasonably described by the analytical framework noted above; indeed, a general appreciation by lawmakers of the terms and logic of that analysis was in all probability the basis for passing laws to rule out as illegal those kinds of actions in the future. That is, having recognized the economic imperatives of corporations in restructuring production, Congress also sought to establish a boundary between admissible actions and inadmissible actions. Perhaps this is the kind of example that best illustrates M. Hollis's (1987:47–48) point that "institutions can emerge as the unintended sum of intended consequences." In essence, regulation is a collective enterprise prompted by the separate intended actions of individual corporations. By these terms, regulation is not just another instrument for achieving the interests of egocentric individuals; it represents a social interest in protecting the collective welfare of society and thus is more than what companies or individuals would otherwise willingly construct or agree to in its implementation.

In the discussion so far of the analytical assumptions of the rational-choice behavioral framework, I have identified two basic limitations. First, the relative isolation of agents from social standards of behavior means that models dependent upon this framework cannot account for presumably nonrational behavior that respects peoples' social obligations and, worse still, provides an analytical logic that would justify corporations breaking laws that do not facilitate their interests. Second, the idea that institutions, social norms, and the like are only valued to the extent that they are instrumental in achieving individuals' interests strips those institutions of any moral or collective value derived from a sense of social well-being and ignores the possibility that institutions are the direct (but unintended) result of egocentric behavior.

My third point is that these kinds of models seem only to reward (in a payoff sense) those actions that result in the best consequences for individual agents. Winning the game is everything, whether in terms of the formal analytics of behavioral analysis or in terms of the actual attitudes and moves of the corporate executives involved. Again, the logic of the model reinforces and justifies the notion of winning at minimum cost—included in the structure of costs are all kinds of social values and institutions, even the rule of law. Pricing the effects of social institutions and the rule of law is a necessary part of the formal analytics of the framework.

Doing so, though, reduces social obligations to *just* a money value and thus allows executives to cynically reconceptualize moral rights and wrongs as merely costs and benefits. The moral force of peoples' obligations to others is thus lost in a crude transfiguration of the terms of social life. It is one thing to imagine game playing by these rules; it is an entirely different matter to make the norms of an analytical game the basis for justifying antisocial actions in court or elsewhere. One can only suspect that the popularity of these kinds of game frameworks in U.S. business schools has encouraged corporate executives to play out for real "winning" moves and countermoves regardless of social interests (compare this analysis with Braithwaite's 1989 observations about patterns of crime and the theoretical models of many U.S.-based criminologists).

These three limitations of the rational-choice behavioral framework are not unknown to theorists who work in this domain (see Gauthier 1986), or would they be a surprise to agents whose behavior is conditioned by living in this kind of economic world. Demonstrating the theoretical logic whereby agents would move from their own narrow interests toward a just social contract has preoccupied many political philosophers, including most significantly J. Rawls (1971). And it is just as clear that agents often recognize the limits of this framework in their negotiations with others and thereby attempt to broaden the terms by which decisions are made and enforced. (Just consider, for example, the importance attached by unions to decisionmaking criteria like "just wages" and the writing of formal contracts of agreement to protect workers' pensions from corporations' strategies of economic restructuring.) Nevertheless, as a general framework for decisionmaking it can be reasonably suggested that rational-choice theory *both* increases the cost of regulation *and* decreases its effectiveness in individual cases. The rationale of this argument is developed in more detail below. What I mean to suggest (as Braithwaite [1989] points out in relation to the regulation of crime) is that by placing a premium on the interests and actions of individuals, as rational-choice theories do, social albeit informal (nonlegal) standards of behavior are so neglected that only state coercion (in the form of regulations and their enforcement) is left to protect social welfare. And, unfortunately, this is not enough.

Without accepted informal social standards of behavior, it would seem logical that corporations would be disposed to:

a. not comply with regulations that have little moral or social force separate from the deliberate actions of the state; thereby,

b. encouraging corporations to act with duplicity and secrecy in relations with other agents; thus,

c. requiring more intensive monitoring by the state of corporate actions and intentions; implying,

d. the need to protect internal "whistle-blowers" who would expose actions otherwise deliberately hidden from view.

From assertion *a* through *d*, the argument is simply that once corporate behavior is separated from well-accepted social standards of behavior, economic imperatives dominate. By that logic, there may be little benefit in complying with regulations, and certainly a great deal of benefit in hiding actions from view which deliberately subvert those regulations. Without a relevant social basis for judging behavior (that is, an on-going process of public scrutiny), the only way corporate actions can be held accountable to social interests is if the state invests a great deal of resources in "watching" their behavior.

This logic can be extended through a series of further steps once we recognize that monitoring must be just the initial step in ensuring compliance. If corporations can be shown to break the law, there must be:

e. a significant capacity for the state to bring suits in court to redress those illegal actions; further implying,

f. that there be appropriate penalties for noncompliance, since,

g. there are often well-defined economic returns for noncompliance; although,

h. there may be also very high economic returns from delaying and undermining the integrity of the legal process.

From assertion *e* through *h*, the argument begins from the assumption that corporations will continue to act illegally if the risk of detection is low, or hide their actions if the state intensively monitors actions and intentions. If, once these actions are detected, the state has little capacity to institute legal proceedings and if, once brought to court and found guilty of illegal actions, corporations are faced with only limited penalties for noncompliance, it will continue to benefit corporations to break the law. If significant penalties are pending, it may also pay the corporation to use the legal process against itself by delaying and attacking the integrity of adjudication procedures. What is most alarming about this scenario is the likelihood that corporations become so skilled at "gaming" regulation and the regulators that no amount of state capacity and penalties for noncompliance will deter the determined corporate executive. In this sense, the costs of regulation will inevitably increase but the rate of compliance may, at the same time, actually decline.

Perhaps all this sounds far-fetched, at least in the abstract. But in the context of corporate restructuring, and given the examples of corporate behavior developed in this book, it should be clear that these assertions describe common-enough corporate strategies. Take, for example, Continental Can. Notwithstanding social obligations to act in good faith when negotiating with the United Steelworkers' union, and notwithstanding their legal obligations to respect the boundary between admissible and inadmissible economic actions with respect to workers' pension rights, the company instituted a systematic program to subvert its social obligations to the union and avoid its legal obligations to its workers. Without strong social pressures to respect the bargaining and negotiation process, subversion of its relationship with the union was yet another example of a profound antiunion sentiment that pervades the U.S. collective-bargaining system in practice and in law (Weiler 1983). And without a precise definition of the legal obligations of corporations to their workers with respect to pensions, and without a statutory definition of the penalties of noncompliance with ERISA, the company obviously believed it would benefit from its policies of subversion and avoidance. To make it all work, the corporation acted with duplicity and secrecy, believing then that the chances of being caught by the government were negligible and, if caught, the likely penalties would be small relative to the economic return. Only the actions of the union (with help from within the company) made noncompliance a legal issue, and even then, the company was nearly able to subvert the legal process by falsifying documents.

Moral Imperatives of Regulation

Regulation—its logic, rules, and penalties—unrelated to moral sentiments becomes just a game that the public cannot finally win. It might be said, of course, that the case studies that form the core of this book prove just the opposite—that these cases are instances of regulation "at work" even if the outcomes are not as desirable as I would want. But to argue so would be to conflate the legal-regulatory *process* with the *substantive* content of regulation. In all three cases, regulation has come a poor second to corporate objectives. Even though Continental Can was found liable for violating Section 510 of ERISA, deciding an adequate set of penalties has been stymied by a campaign of legal delay by the company, but in any case this has been rendered practically irrelevant by the fact that the company has now little capacity to pay penalties, given its current debt structure. Despite the fact that International Harvester was found liable for its "sham" sale of Wisconsin steel, the company clearly gained so much more from its actions than it is likely to pay in penalties. And finally, the

PBGC's case against LTV Corporation has failed to advance much beyond the conundrum of balancing off bankruptcy law with ERISA. In all cases the legal-regulatory process has been turned in against itself. Even if these cases were successful, it is clear that the regulatory process is a very blunt instrument for promoting public welfare—the workers affected and the corporate executives responsible have long since departed.

Perhaps another argument against this account of the limited power of regulation would suggest that a different set of cases could return a different verdict. There is no doubt that the entire book depends very much on three cases. Yet when these cases are linked with rational-choice theory it should be apparent that their significance goes beyond the circumstances of individual events. The logic of that kind of theory in the context of corporate restructuring dictates a certain conclusion. But this need not be the only conclusion if a broader view is taken about the proper foundations of regulation. A deliberate distinction between benefit-cost analyses of lawful behavior and expectations of corporate behavior could delegitimate the logic that would otherwise justify such behavior. Essentially a way must be found whereby corporate behavior with respect to public regulation is evaluated according to terms that do not in the final instance reduce to prices (benefits and costs). Reasserting the relevance of moral sentiments would be one such strategy, realizing that at the moment there is little in the way of "hard" evidence to prove the efficacy of such a strategy. The first step to implement such a strategy (and the only step we will take in this chapter) is to identify a moral standard for application.

It is immediately obvious that this is a topic of immense scope and complexity. Whereas the relative value of competing moral imperatives including justice, equality, and efficiency (centered on, respectively, Rawls 1971, Dworkin 1985, and Posner 1981) could be debated, as well as debating the merits of various instruments of moral authority such as "shaming," I will consider just one crucial aspect—the moral imperatives inherent in contractual relations between agents. In many respects the institution of contracting goes to the very core of the disputes central to this book. Continental Can used their collective-bargaining agreement (contract) with the USWA to subvert their public obligations—by this interpretation the company induced union cooperation through the contractual process all the while never intending to honor the intent of the 1976 contract. Similarly, International Harvester obtained the willing cooperation of their union in the sale of Wisconsin Steel by claiming to stand by their contractual obligations while intending to off-load those agreed-to pension obligations onto the "shell" corporation (at best) or the PBGC (at worst). In the LTV case, the company has apparently gone to great lengths to

honor its contractual obligations with the union but at the cost of subverting its obligations to the PBGC (the regulatory agency's interpretation
of events). All these actions and responses can be interpreted from a moral
standpoint, and have been so interpreted.

C. Fried (1981) makes the case that contractual relations are, in the
final instance, dependent upon moral sentiments. In particular he suggests
that making a contract is equivalent to making a promise and, as such,
carries with it a social obligation to live up to the terms of the contract.
Why is this a *social* obligation, rather than being just an exchange between
two private agents? Fried references the social conventions that go with
promise-making: the promisor intentionally invokes " a convention whose
function it is to give grounds—moral grounds—for another to expect the
promised performance" (p. 16). In the context of corporate restructuring,
where union officials recognize the temptations facing corporate executives
to cash out the value of cooperation, to make a contract to provide pensions
to workers (as in the Continental Can case) is akin to *inducing* union
officials to put aside their reservations about likely corporate behavior.
Moreover, in circumstances of apparent restructuring (the International
Harvester case), to promise to stand by previous contractual obligations
is to deliberately invoke social norms of *trust* and *honesty*. As Fried goes
on to remark, "to renege [on a promise] is to abuse a confidence that he
[the promisor] was free to invite or not, and which he intentionally did
invite. To abuse that confidence is like (but only *like*) lying: the abuse of
a shared social institution that is intended to invoke the bonds of trust."
To deliberately induce cooperation through a contractual agreement including pensions or any other benefit while never intending to stand by
the terms of that contract not only harms the welfare of those affected, it
also brings into question the integrity of a fundamental social institution.
In this sense, the harm done is private *and* public, just as making a promise
involves private calculations of benefits and costs and public sentiments
about expectations of behavior. For the PBGC in the LTV case, the bankruptcy of the company appears to the agency to trade on the social obligations of the company to the society as a whole.

The centrality of moral sentiments, particularly the notion of promise,
to Fried's conception of contract resonates well with the arguments made
above and elsewhere about the strong moral content apparent in legal
disputes over corporate restructuring. Moral sentiments in this conception
provide an essential social rationale for ensuring compliance with regulations. Such social claims do not, however, exclude the possibility of
subsidiary claims reinforcing the importance of moral sentiments. For
example, the fact that union officials and workers relied on the promises

made and the contract signed providing for plant-closing pensions suggests that Continental Can is responsible for the welfare of affected workers over and above the immediate loss of income. In the absence of inducements and promises of cooperation, workers may have sought out other jobs, made different kinds of claims for compensation on the company, and generally changed their behavior to protect their long-term welfare. The fact that the company's actions promised long-term benefits to the workers through cooperation would also seem to suggest that the whole calculation of whether or not to cooperate in terms of likely benefits depends in the final instance upon the levels of trust and respect between the contracting parties. In these ways, the promise principle argued to be essential to the institution of contract facilitates other actions that may be both more personal *and* self-interested. Thus it is crucial for making strategic alliances and it is essential for shared projects—in the absence of trust how could or why would agents believe calculations of their likely benefits?

At the same time, Fried would also argue (and I would accept) that it is not simply the benefits of a promise that make it important that promises be observed; rather, it is the fact that contracts are built upon moral expectations of social behavior that make it vital that promises be respected. In this respect, Fried makes a basic distinction between a "simple" market transaction and an exchange relationship based upon contractual obligations. This is not a distinction that is widely shared in the economics literature, although it does have some support in the legal literature, albeit in an abstract form. For writers such as R. Posner (1981), there is nothing special in a contract. By his logic, contracts only formalize voluntarily agreed-to cooperation that results in gains to both parties (strategic alliances). If the terms or circumstances that prompted the signing of a contract change then, according to Posner, contracts should change or be voided to reflect the new circumstances. Whereas he would likely agree that Continental Can, International Harvester, and LTV Corporation had no business in agreeing to contracts they had no intention of honoring, neither should they be held accountable for contractual financial obligations that overburden the companies. In this respect, compensation ought to be limited and be calculated so that these costs do not restrain companies from pursuing their best economic interests. Overall economic welfare, by this logic, demands a flexible and noncoercive model of contract law in its definition and adjudication. For some critics of Fried, like P. S. Atiyah (1981), this is already the case, notwithstanding the arguable merits of Fried's proposal. For others, such as Dworkin, the putative hegemony of economic efficiency as a normative ideal remains a contested and (thankfully) only partly realized conception of human relations.

By noting Fried's conception of the moral foundations of voluntary contracts, I mean to suggest that there are good reasons for contesting egocentric models of benefit-cost calculations of the integrity of social regulation. Once it is realized that individual action both references collective and moral expectations of behavior and is responsible to the public for its consistency with those expectations, we transcend the narrower logic of the costs and benefits of individual action. As such, it is an alternative in a theoretical sense to Gauthier who would *derive* moral sentiments from individuals' calculations of their benefits and costs of collective action. Moreover, it is an antidote to those writers concerned with the logic of judicial adjudication who would assign priority (in a nominative sense) to only those actions that contribute to maximizing economic welfare. With respect to notions of ethical conduct, in part the distinction is between deontological and consequentialist reasoning—concern about the virtue of individual actions in relation to moral foundations being a deontological issue, whereas the derivation of moral agreements based upon their economic effects is a consequentialist issue. Even so, it must be acknowledged that Fried's "contract as promise" was framed as a deliberate counter-response to more collectivist notions of contracting which would apply more rigorous social standards of evaluation for judging the performance of agents to a contract (Kronman 1981). For Fried, contracts provide individuals with the necessary institutional context for finding their best welfare. This is not simply a functionalist conception of the ideal of contract, it is also a social institution that literally provides the basis for a procedurally just society. Thus it is a liberal antidote to liberal claims that the value of regulation can be only judged in relation to individuals' assessments of its benefits and costs.

Summary—Economic Imperatives

Throughout this chapter I have considered the status of regulation according to the terms and logic of rational-choice theory. This strategy was used for two reasons. First, understanding corporate decisionmaking requires an understanding of the dominant language in which decisions are made about cooperation/noncooperation, the boundaries of regulation that define admissible and nonadmissible actions, and the degree to which corporations respect their contractual commitments to others. This is the language of business management, but is also a language in close accord with traditional liberal ideals of individual volition and welfare. It is easy enough to contest the internal logic and consistency of that language, but to neglect it altogether, or to dismiss it as obviously and only ideology, would be to fail to appreciate how and why the status of regulation is so problematic in corporate restructuring. A second reason for considering the status of regulation in these terms was to show how and why different expectations of behavior often translate into policies of subversion on one hand (corporations) and policies of deterrence on the other hand (unions). At the heart of the problem are very different motives and conceptions of collective well-being.

Despite radical asymmetries of intention and belief, cooperation must nevertheless be sought if corporations are to make a profit, and workers are to be employed. Within this necessarily tense relationship, the ideal of the contract emerges as an essential reference point for agents' actions. The question is then whether or not contracts are only a means to an end (corporations' ideal) or a social institution embodying first moral sentiments and then instrumentality that exist separately from their utility in specific cases (the union's ideal). This is also the question that must be asked by public agencies if they are to sustain the integrity of their regulatory regimes. Given the force of economic imperatives, a social reference point for behavior must be maintained, one that depends upon moral sentiments, not simply upon the costs and benefits of observing certain kinds of regulations.

There can be no doubt that the economic imperatives behind corporate restructuring are powerful and ever-present. If these imperatives are apparent in media comments about the relative position of regions and countries in the global economy, they are also at the very core of executives' compensation. Thus, another aspect of the restructuring process that I have tried to demonstrate is how structure (the logic of competition and innovation) intersects with agency (the rationale for individual action). This should not be interpreted as suggesting a one-to-one relationship between structure and agency wherein the former determines the latter. Through this hypothetical set of scenarios and the analysis of agents' motives and intentions, I have also tried to demonstrate that responding to economic imperatives can take many forms, some of which may clearly result in cooperative shared projects that transcend the separate individual interests that drive strategic alliances. Which particular strategy is employed depends upon many variables. Important in this context is regulation, and not just its instrumental efficacy in policy behavior. Most important, the logic of regulation becomes a crucial reference point for agents' actions—does it simply police strategic alliances, and therefore run the risk of being factored into corporations' assessments of the costs and benefits of competing options, or does it deliberately represent certain essential moral sentiments such as trust and honesty, which should not be immediately reduced to costs and benefits? The former option is unfortunately an often chosen path.

The analysis of economic imperatives and the status of public regulation offers, however, an interesting contrast in styles of reasoning and logic. In terms of economic imperatives, it is apparent that what drives behavior is a rational means/ends calculation of the best outcome. By the logic of theory, and by the patterns of experience, corporate behavior is reducible to a "simple" calculation of benefits and costs. This apparent connection between economic imperatives and methodological simplicity stands in contrast with the logic argued to lie behind public regulation. If regulation is, in the terms of economic imperatives, a form of constraint on behavior or a price on unwanted outcomes, regulation is similarly reduced to a simple economic calculation. But if regulation is grounded in moral sentiments, methodological simplicity gives way to more complex notions of social institutions and perhaps deontological ethical reasoning. In this respect, reductionism is not the operative solution; the complexity of moral sentiments as evident in our expectations of others' behavior serves to distinguish and protect moral claims from being immediately recalculated into benefits and costs. Whereas the analysis of economic imperatives tends always to reduce to a realist account of unavoidable necessity, the analysis of public regulation from a moral sentiments perspective tends toward an idealist image of complex social norms of behavior. The difference may appear to be one of methodology, and to some extent it is. But a more profound difference derives from the quite separate normative assumptions that underpin the analyses. As written here, the interpretation of economic imperatives is a egocentric conception of society, whereas the interpretation of public regulation from a moral sentiments perspective derives (in my case at least) from a communitarian, or what J. Braithwaite and P. Pettit (1990) would call a republican conception of society. Maintaining this difference is the only way that public regulation can retain its distinctive status.

PART 4

Conclusions

10

Crisis of Regulation

A creeping crisis of regulation exists in the United States. Through the evidence presented in this book, the crisis is apparent in the inability of the federal courts and statutory corporations, such as the PBGC, to fashion and maintain stable and well-defined arenas of public authority relative to corporations' economic interests. Whereas recognition of this crisis in the media is more often than not limited to the circumstances of particular events, the current crisis of regulation is to be found in many U.S. industries and sectors. For example, even though the pension and related bankruptcy problems of the Texas Air Corporation (the recent parent corporation of Continental and Eastern airlines) are often explained by reference to the actions of individual corporate executives, the available evidence suggests that Texas Air's financial problems are similar in origin to many other unionized companies in other industries with entitled-to defined benefit pensions. In this respect, the crisis of regulation in the private pension system is a crisis of accommodating economic change in the context of previously agreed-to and statutorily protected pension benefits.

At one level, it might be said that this crisis is basically administrative. It reflects, as suggested in the Introduction, Congress's inability to design coherent sets of rules and regulations to be implemented by the bureaucracy. If this explanation is immediately relevant to issues of regulating corporate restructuring, as well as industrial policy and economic development, C. Sunstein (1990) for one suggests that the New Deal administrative state is itself in decline. While the origins of this decline could be traced immediately to the attitudes and actions of recent Republican administrations, its decline could be due as much to issues that relate to the internal coherence of the administrative state as it could be due to an incipient ideological shift to the right. At a step removed from the administrative state, policing rules and regulations has become more difficult over the past fifteen years or so—for example, P. Weiler's (1983) data on the rise in unfair labor practices since the early 1970s. Notwithstanding

235

the problems of maintaining the coherence of rules related to collective bargaining in the face of significant shifts of policy by the NLRB (comparing the Carter Board with the Reagan Board in cases such as *Milwaukee Spring I* and *II*), it appears that unfair labor practices were on the rise for a number years prior to the conservatives' tenure at the NLRB. Of more immediate relevance, it can be observed from the findings of the General Accounting Office (GAO 1992b) and from the case studies of this project that policing ERISA has become difficult because of the willingness of companies to subvert the law.

The crisis of regulation, reflected in problems of administrative incoherence and the policing of corporate behavior, is a vital part of contemporary economic life. It occupies governmental institutions, companies, and unions in extraordinarily lengthy and expensive legal and political contests of power. At this level, where the practice of regulation is an essential rationale for social action, any argument about a creeping crisis of regulation may appear to be quite removed from the exigencies of real events. Nevertheless, as the courts have suggested in cases related to pensions and corporate restructuring, any understanding of the genesis of these contests for power and any appreciation of the reasons why such contests are not easily resolved with respect to current statutes require a broader assessment of the status of regulation. One aim of this chapter is to summarize and refine what I believe are the essential dimensions of the current crisis of regulation. What we are witnessing is the crisis of an ideal—the ideal of the administrative state as custodian of the public interest, buttressed by expertise and the instruments of law but in effect denuded of significant political power because of an unresolved conflict between democratic interests and institutional authority.

Crisis of Regulation I—Essential Arguments

Throughout this book, the issue of corporations' pension obligations has been used as a vital lens through which to view and understand the problematic intersection between regulation and economic imperatives. It could be reasonably suggested that other, perhaps more important, issues demonstrate the unresolved tensions between economic imperatives and public regulation. The savings and loan crisis, the problems encountered in regulating insider trading on Wall Street, even the apparent inability of the two branches of government to effectively reform the federal budget process so as to reduce the federal deficit could be identified as equally important vantage points of analysis. While recognizing their significance, and recognizing moreover that the crisis of regulation in American industry is both more pervasive than case studies can indicate and is deeply embedded in contemporary society, I would also suggest that the issue of pensions is of profound importance to millions of workers and to the federal government. In an era of severe financial crisis where the federal government now depends upon the Social Security surplus to fund a portion of its budget, the prospect of a generalized devaluation of the private pension system must be viewed with alarm. If carried through to their logical conclusion, the case studies suggest that American industry would renounce their pension obligations in the face of competing economic imperatives. In effect, the private pension system may be so compromised that in the future retired workers may have to return to an impoverished public sector. This added burden, plus the likely future problems of again funding Social Security, are bound to shift the burden of the current budget crisis to the next generation.

By the logic and incremental sequencing of various chapters, this book advanced a set of related arguments. As there is a certain sequential logic to the chapters, there is a sequential logic to the introduction of these arguments, beginning with the simplest notion and moving on to more contentious issues. In summary terms these arguments can be described as follows.

Argument 1: *The response of corporations to changing economic conditions is fundamentally structured by their social obligations—most obviously those embodied in statutes but also those obligations embodied in informal social norms.* There were two parts to this argument, one empirical and the other theoretical. The empirical argument is entirely straightforward. Notwithstanding the enormous economic pressures on corporations to restructure in ways that would most efficiently enhance competitiveness, corporations have designed their restructuring strategies with respect to their social obligations to maintain and protect the integrity of workers' pensions. Sometimes restructuring has respected the virtue of these obligations, and sometimes restructuring has been designed to deliberately circumvent these obligations. At one level, these obligations are strictly legal, as illustrated by statute-based contests for power between the PBGC and corporations. But I think I have also shown that obligations may be more than just legal; obligations may be evident in social norms, including agents' ethical expectations of trust and honesty in contractual relationships. One way or the other, corporations obviously do not have a free range of options in economic restructuring.

More theoretically, it was also suggested that corporations' behavior is necessarily structured by their inherited capital stock (and attendant social relationships) arrayed across the economic landscape. This was illustrated by reference to corporations' capital stock, the utilization of labor, and the nature of contractual agreements between management and unions. And it was also shown that the inherited logic of corporate structure has great implications for the welfare of specific workers and their communities. This list of "landscape" variables can be extended, however, by including variables that relate to social norms and expectations as well as the legal context of decisionmaking. To imagine that corporations *should* have a free range of options (as some legal, economic rationalists would argue) or *do* have a free range of options (as some corporations have contended in court) is to ignore the necessarily bounded rationality of agents' decisionmaking. Abstract theorizing about firm behavior as if there were no relevant landscape variables or if those variables should not be relevant is hardly relevant when the courts are being asked to make judgments about proper behavior in a social or geographical context (compare with Rose-Ackerman 1991).

Argument 2: *Regulation is a distinct sphere of social action, relatively autonomous from economic imperatives and justified by ideal conceptions of social life.* As in the first argument there were two parts to this argument, one empirical and the other theoretical. Throughout the book, the process of regulation has been made an essential element of the story of corporate restructuring. Here, we have been most concerned with the logic and character of regulation as an institutional practice, hence the concern for the process of adjudication and the pattern of institutional boundaries placed on the restructuring process. One consequence of this empirical strategy has been exposure of the uncertainties and dilemmas of regulation, principally as a mode of discourse but also as an institutional arrangement of power. Take, for example, the question of the responsibility for regulation. On issues such as pension termination and pension funding the PBGC is a leading federal agency responsible for ensuring compliance with statutory obligations. But the PBGC is not alone in that responsibility. Like so many other federal agencies, it depends upon the courts to enforce its decisions as it (and the IRS) depends upon Congress for its warrant of power. Empirically, each institution has its own policy agenda. Some are narrower than others, but all are conceived with respect to their own interests in the context of others' powers. To imagine that regulation of pension entitlements is an integrated whole, organized with respect to overarching economic imperatives (as some theorists of regulation are wont to imagine) is to be simply ignorant about institutional structure, and to be naive about institutions' interests in furthering their powers relative to other related institutions. This empirical argument says nothing about corporate restructuring—but that is precisely the point:

one of the most profound problems of the current regulatory framework
is its internal, institutional incoherence reflected in the competition for
power between institutions.

More theoretically, again, if we take seriously this kind of empirical
observation there is no reason to suppose that economic imperatives (or
any other extrainstitutional motivating force) need dominate or have priority in the administration and implementation of regulation. In this sense,
the public rationale for regulation (even that expressed in the preamble
of statutes) may serve an important legitimizing function, but in other
ways (in determining the pattern of jurisdiction, the role of an institution,
or the definition of rules and regulations) it may be less important than
competing institutional interests in determining actual behavior. This also
suggests that a theory of the state must be an essential part of a larger
explanation of regulation in contemporary societies. At this point the
reader should remember that my own perspective on this issue is state-
centered and stresses the relative autonomy of state administrative units
(see Clark and Dear 1984). Thus, inherent in all this discussion of data
and opinion is a theory of the state that denies the supposed virtues of
assigning priority to economic imperatives as the ultimate or metatheo-
retical device for explaining all social phenomena.

Argument 3: *Regulation can be only effective in controlling corporate
restructuring when linked explicitly to ethical standards that reference
fundamental social expectations.* All the evidence drawn from the case
studies presented in this book suggests that regulation is contested, subverted, and disputed. Regulation does not appear to command corporations' respect in and of itself; regulation just because it is done by public
agencies does not justify itself. Indeed, by the narrowest and most economically oriented criterion, regulation costs money and opportunities.
Given the cloak of secrecy that shrouds the actions of corporations as well
as legal standards that deliberately partition corporations' actions into
public and private spheres of life, monitoring those actions is a vital and
necessary function of government. Otherwise, economic imperatives dominate and regulation becomes a mirage idealized by many but hardly respected by any.

A further observation is warranted, though, about the robustness of
monitoring. Because corporations have come to expect and have adapted
to government monitoring of their behavior, the only really effective response to corporate abuse of regulation is a system of surveillance that
encourages reporting by employees and community members. In this respect, the connection between regulation and ethical standards needs to
be deliberate and explicitly made for all social agents to appreciate. Indeed,

one of the empirical lessons of this project has been the realization that litigation and the monitoring of corporations' actions is closely connected in many workers' minds with ethical standards. Unfortunately, many rules and regulations deliberately eschew ethical considerations for a legal language stripped bare of the motives that initially prompted passage of the related statutes. If legal modes of regulation are to be effective in a social sense in providing a means of publicly censuring agents whatever the outcomes of specific legal suits, regulation itself has to be more closely allied in language and effect to public standards of correct behavior.

In theory, to overcome corporations' tendencies to reduce regulation to mere accounting costs and benefits, a personification of corporate action is required. Too many arguments made in court about corporate responsibility appear to deliberately avoid finding individual agents as being responsible for the actions of corporations. This kind of argument has a long history in law and commercial contract; it references a legal fiction made in common law between juristic and natural persons (Coleman 1974, and see Horwitz 1992). Juristic persons have advantages, of course, for transacting and exchanging commodities. But in many instances, as evident in the case studies presented in this book, it is simply a convenient fiction to hide behind when corporations are held accountable for observed actions. In theory, what is required is a repersonalization of the corporation so that ethical standards can be applied to particular individuals even if at another level those same individuals are indemnified in terms of their personal liability for financial transactions. This kind of exposure of corporate agents to public standards of behavior will require a reassessment of the underlying and inherited theory of the corporation and the roles and responsibilities of its agents (see the American Law Institute's [1988] reworking of its principles of corporate governance).

Crisis of Regulation II—Economic Causes

With respect to workers' pension rights and corporate restructuring, no project on regulation can afford to ignore the significance of economic imperatives. Indeed, it might be reasonably suggested that this whole project began with economic imperatives; corporate restructuring has been shown to be the inevitable result of responding to at least shifts in market competition (new markets, new products, and new competitors) and changes in the technology of production (affecting the price and configuration of production). For example, the process of rationalization within Continental Can was prompted in part by changes in consumer demand and the development of new ways of packaging beverage products. In the case of International Harvester, the company rationalized production in an attempt to meet new overseas competition in its core activities; rationalization was a means of simultaneously improving the quality of production and decreasing the price of finished goods in line with the price structure of new entrants to the market. The issues of price and quality were also significant for the LTV Corporation—only lower prices at higher levels of quality could provide LTV with a place in the newly competitive U.S. steel industry. The economic imperatives of competition have driven these firms, and others in American industry, to find ways of improving efficiency in the context of their inherited structure of production. By corporations' assessment, regulation is just one more cost to be rationalized: the crisis of regulation is also an economic crisis whose parameters now do not fit the new economic regime.

Modern explanations of the evolution of law, the most relevant and formal version of regulation, often stress the significance of economic forces in determining the nature of regulation. Since at least the New Deal era, which is now normally interpreted as a watershed moment when economic imperatives forced regulation into a compliant and functional role with respect to economic stability, a rough connection is often made between economic needs and regulatory efficacy. For R. Posner (1986) and the Chicago school of law and economics, this rough connection is still too elusive in particular cases, given their formula for economic efficiency. By their account, judges are too often seduced by claims of justice that have unfortunate consequences for efficiency, or are in other ways simply ignorant of the virtues of economic efficiency relative to other competing but inferior bases for judicial decisionmaking. Nevertheless, the connection is clear and the logic of this order of concepts rarely disputed in academic circles. Indeed, any reading of realist accounts of the evolution of law would find, I think, a strong thread of agreement with this putative order of concepts. C. Beard's (1935) classic study of the design of the U.S. Constitution makes this connection and order of concepts *the* essential reference point for understanding the logic behind debates over the Constitution's form and purpose.

If economic imperatives are the motor of history, the force behind the structure of regulation, how does regulation change? There are two related answers in the literature. One answer would be simply that as new situations arise, new law (rules and regulations) are introduced to cover those situations. Over time, when the need for those regulations fades, their application to new events declines and finally disappears. G. Calabresi's (1982) explanation of the "age of statutes" as well as the apparent life cycle of statutes is an instance of such an explanation. In the common law tradition, M. A. Eisenberg (1988) argues that regulation does not change incrementally in response to each new event but paradigmatically, referencing T. Kuhn's (1970) theory of scientific revolutions. By itself, each "new" economic event is not enough to prompt a response in the form of new regulation but "if anomalies persist and accumulate" a crisis results, and a new regulatory regime is then introduced to rationalize the new reality with the old economic structure. The same causal connection is retained as is the order between economic imperatives and regulation, the differences between Calabresi and Eisenberg being a question of timing and the short-run possibility of retaining the coherence of a regulatory regime relative to separate economic events. Notice that these two models, Calabresi's *incremental relevance* model and Eisenberg's *parameter-shift* model, are representative of more general arguments made in various literatures about the nature of regulatory change.

Assuming a causal connection and rank ordering between economic imperatives and regulation, how useful are these two models of regulatory change in the context of corporate restructuring and pension obligations? It could be argued that Calabresi's incremental relevance model can usefully explain the passage of ERISA in 1974. If we begin analysis of the origins of the act with an assessment of the significance of the Studebaker bankruptcy and plant closings in the mid-1960s, I have argued that this case and similar cases in other regions and sectors of American industry prompted Congress to initiate hearings and research to ascertain how to protect workers' pension rights. This ultimately led to the passage of ERISA. The incremental relevance model provides a clear recipe for interpreting the significance of ERISA: its origins are in an economic event, and its value is judged with respect to its relevance then and its relevance now. One implication of the incremental relevance model is, however, the possibility that as economic events change (say, for example, American industry is now fighting for its life and cannot afford to pay previously agreed-to but legally binding pension benefits), so too should regulation be changed (corporations, by this logic, should be relieved of dysfunctional financial burdens). This simply suggests that the question of relevance is very contentious, disputed by the parties affected and by no means such a simple recipe for "explaining" regulatory change as may be implied by a first reading of Calabresi.

Assuming laws (rules and regulations) to be a functional response to current needs presents Calabresi (and anyone else who would make the rough connection between economic imperatives and regulatory efficacy) with a problem. Once new regulations become "middle-aged," when their utility is not so well defined and their relevance is of less significance compared to more pressing needs, they may lack credible "majoritarian support." The obvious solution is to repeal the now outdated regulation and institute a new, more relevant one in its place. But at this point, Calabresi recognizes a simple but powerful fact: "getting a statute enacted is much easier than getting it revised" or repealed (p. 6). Statutes represent political interests, not just systematic economic-functional needs. And with political interests go questions of moral value and ethical commitment. To suppose that the raison d'être of regulation is only its economic functionality is to so limit the terms of analysis that the moral or ethical issues leading to the passage of ERISA (for example) are forgotten in a rush to canonize its functional successor. Any analysis of the passage and significance of ERISA must also recognize the significance of claims made at the time for protecting the welfare of American workers. There is no reason to believe that the relevance of this concern has diminished over the past few years; in fact, on the evidence presented here, the need for a strong ERISA is more important than ever before, given the economic imperatives of corporate restructuring.

The incremental relevance model of regulatory change provides an explanation of how and why new regulations are introduced. But its dependence upon economic functionalism means that it is weak when it comes to explaining the relative significance of one set of regulations compared to others, as it appears incapable of recognizing the resilience of regulations as normative manifestoes. By contrast, Eisenberg's parameter-shift model provides a more convincing explanation of how and why regulatory regimes change, accepting that individual sets of regulations may well be introduced for reasons consistent with the incremental relevance model. The question then becomes whether or not the parameter-shift model is useful for explaining the more general crisis of regulation which is argued to be endemic to capitalism in the late twentieth century (Aglietta 1979).

To adequately answer this question requires, in the first instance, a brief excursion into the history of what A. Chandler (1990) calls "managerial capitalism" but what is sometimes also referred to as Fordist capitalism (Lipietz 1986). Chandler's massive study of the rise and evolution of capitalism in Britain, Germany, and the United States, with reference to patterns of economic structure and organizational innovation in a number of related industries, is not a study of regulation per se. Rather, it is a study of the development of managerial conventions situated in the context of an emerging world economy. If his story has a certain coherence and logic over nearly a century, at the very end of his book he looks briefly at the character of post-1960 managerial capitalism and asserts that this period may be a new era. In particular, Chandler identifies six changes in the modern corporation which he believes have no historical precedent. In summary terms, Chandler believes that corporations are now: (1) moving into markets in which they have no apparent competitive advantage (measured in terms of production); (2) separating corporate management from line management, treating the productive units of a corporation as a part of a larger portfolio of resources and opportunities; (3) engaged in a process of buying and selling units as a form of business in its own right; (4) divesting operating units as a matter of course; while (5) financing portfolio management through external debt; and (6) using new capital resources, particularly the pension fund economy.

If this template is taken as a lens through which to evaluate the actions of the three corporations that make up the core of this project, it becomes apparent from Table 10.1 that it is useful for understanding the context in which corporate restructuring has occurred since the mid-1970s. Listed are company strategies consistent with Chandler's conception of the "new" managerial capitalism in the order listed above (1 to 6). Also included, though, is the strategy of internal debt financing which remains of vital significance to American corporations. Continental Can, the one company among the case study firms that followed through the BCG formula for competitive strategy, most closely fits Chandler's template. Less closely related is the LTV Corporation, and even less closely related is the International Harvester Corporation. The precise recipes for corporate competitiveness and the moves made by executives to rationalize their operating units in ways consistent with those recipes are described in detail in previous chapters. The point is that what Chandler describes, and what I would assert is evident in the case studies of this book, could be taken as evidence for what Eisenberg might call a paradigmatic shift in the underlying structure of managerial capitalism. We would expect, then, a related parameter shift in the regulatory regime so as to be consistent with the new economic imperatives.

The most obvious and, I would suggest, the most profound question to be asked in this context is whether or not there has been a paradigmatic shift in managerial capitalism. Recognizing the empirical significance of the six dimensions of change identified by Chandler and recognizing that they each have relevance for understanding corporate restructuring do not require us to accept the existence of a paradigmatic change. At best, I am agnostic about the reality of such a shift. At worst, like many other researchers in allied fields, I remain very skeptical of the plausibility of this claimed shift in the whole structure of managerial capitalism. There are three particular issues to be stressed in this regard.

First, how can we distinguish empirically between incremental eco-

Table 10.1 Major Corporations' Competitive Strategies

Strategy	Continental Can	International Harvester	LTV
New markets	Yes	No	Yes
Division of management	Yes	Yes	—
Mergers/acquisitions	Yes	—	Yes
Divestiture of units	Yes	Yes	Yes
External debt financing	Yes	Yes	Yes
Internal debt financing	Yes	No	Yes
Sensitivity to fund managers	Yes	No	No

Sources: Chandler (1990) and author's case studies.

nomic change and the paradigmatic shift argued to be characteristic of current circumstances? To justify the idea of a paradigmatic shift requires a means of empirical discrimination that so far has not been demonstrated in these circumstances. Second, what reason (or reasons) is there to suggest that the identified changes are a coherent whole, representing a structural shift rather than being simply a loosely associated group of factors that have been organized together by corporate strategists and business consulting companies? Any reading of management strategy texts would suggest that consulting companies have been deeply implicated in the rate of corporate restructuring. And third, what evidence is there of a shift in the regulatory regime? Or, recognizing that some advocates of a parameter shift in regulation would assert that this is still to be resolved, what evidence is there of a causal connection between economic imperatives and regulation that runs from the former to the latter? Recent analysis of factors encouraging leveraged buyouts during the 1980s would suggest that federal tax policy was an especially important determinant of corporate restructuring, not the other way around (see generally Shoven and Waldfogel 1990).

The assumptions made above that there is a causal connection and rank ordering between economic imperatives and regulation and that regulations are a functional response to current economic needs must be questioned. In particular, and on the basis of the arguments presented in this book, I would assert an additional set of arguments.

Argument 4: *While economic events are often important in prompting the introduction of a new regulation or set of regulations, they are by no means the exclusive determinant of regulation.* This is a simple empirical argument, given substance by the case studies of restructuring discussed in this book but also given credibility by an observation that many regulations begin life as a moral response to an economic event, not only a policy response to an economic problem to be fixed. It is vital that a separate sphere for moral issues be retained independently of concerns for economic efficiency. Otherwise, the possibility of protecting workers from economic exigencies will be lost in a misplaced effort to create an aesthetically pleasing and thus simple account of regulation.

Argument 5: *Regulation may first appear as a response to economic events but may itself be a response to problems of coordination and policy design in and between.* It is a mistake to imagine that the economy is an integrated whole, and that regulation as an institution necessarily reflects this "wholeness." It is important to remember that regulation is always partial and additive, hardly ever comprehensive and integrative with the inherited regulatory apparatus (witness ERISA). In a world of regulatory complexity and overlapping jurisdictions, the practice of regulation is always a process of accommodation with competing institutions rather than a simple response to an obvious problem, be it in the economy or in the policy arena.

Argument 6: *The relevance of a regulation may be in the first instance determined by an economic event. In the long run, however, the resilience and integrity of regulation has much to do with the partisanship of regulators and the strength of their political constituencies in ensuring the maintenance of the regulatory apparatus.* The fact is that the "power" of ERISA relative to the economic imperatives driving corporate restructuring has only been tested in the past decade. Its continued relevance is owed to the actions of unions and the PBGC, mediated by the policies of adjudication pursued by the courts. Federal judges may in fact follow an economic-functionalist line of reasoning, as the Chicago school of law and economics suggests. But this is not guaranteed in any way. Indeed, based on the evidence in this book, the significance and resilience of equity-oriented modes of legal reasoning stand as a barrier against simply economic functionalism.

Crisis of Regulation III—Institutional Factors

Economic events are important, precipitating causes of the introduction of new regulation. Whether as single events (Calabresi's model) or as a set of accumulated disturbances to an established order (Eisenberg's model) economic events often provide Congress with due cause to respond. This implies, though, that economic events may only rhetorically legitimize deeper (equity-based) conceptions of the need for regulation. There are, then, other less functional explanations of the status and significance of regulation. Here, it is argued that these explanations can be often linked to ideal conceptions of the rule of law as a formal device for rationalizing conflict, to moral conceptions of the proper relationship between economic imperatives and social obligations, and a belief in the power of the administrative state to provide what the market cannot—a blueprint for social action. To simply assume economic functionalism and dismiss the ideal of regulation as just ideology legitimating class interests is to impoverish social analysis. As E. P. Thompson (1975:262) says, "For class relations were [sic] expressed, not in any way one likes, but *through the forms of law;* and the law, like other institutions which from time to time can be seen as mediating . . . existent class relations . . . has its own characteristics, its own independent history and logic of evolution."

To appreciate the problematic role and status of regulation in American society over the past decade or so requires, in the first instance, a recognition of the campaign for deregulation that began with the Carter administration and was given full flight by the Reagan administration. In so many areas of government policy, deregulation was the watchword for the past fifteen years or so. Beginning with a concerted review and analysis of the consequences of regulation in the airline and trucking industries in the last years of the Carter administration, the movement for deregulation and self-regulation was sponsored by the Reagan administration in areas of more recent federal regulatory concern, such as occupational health and safety, environmental assessment, and product safety. Along the way, traditional areas of federal regulation, such as antitrust, interstate commerce, and financial institutions have come under scrutiny, leading more often than not to either deregulation (as in the savings and loan industry and the airline industry), reduced regulation and new forms of competition (as in the areas of environmental assessment and interstate telecommunications), self-regulation through self-reporting by private firms to the federal government in areas previously monitored by government agencies (as in mine safety standards and occupational health and safety), and a general process of decreased monitoring and surveillance of private industry. The consequences of this process for workers' safety, the financial integrity of many major U.S. institutions, and the actual prices paid by consumers for products and services once only provided by government-regulated monopolies or oligopolies (for example) have yet to be systematically counted. It is obvious, though, that in the 1990s, there will be concerted moves to reregulate given the excesses of the past decade.

Even so, whatever the costs of deregulation, it was a movement that many policymakers from the left and the right of the political spectrum thought justified, given the historical performance of regulated industries. In particular, two types of claims against regulation were made at the time by those close to the congressional regulatory review process (see Breyer 1982). One type of criticism focused upon the costs of regulation, an issue most often ignored or relegated to a secondary consideration relative to the benefits of regulation for certain segments of the public. Referencing the airline industry, this issue was raised with respect to apparent and unexplained fare anomalies between different jurisdictions (state and federal) and between different geographically paired service routes. Oddities of pricing structures and often variable standards of service provision unrelated to pricing rules conspired to question the validity of administrative decisionmaking. A second type of criticism, related to the first, concerned what critics argued to be typical of regulated industries: a consistent lack of choice for consumers and an unwillingness (or inability) on the part of regulated companies to do anything that would respond to consumer needs. Whereas regulation was once thought to be the best means of protecting the public from the market power of large private organizations, critics of regulation in the late 1970s accused regulatory agencies of sheltering those organizations from consumer demands while imposing on consumers an unnecessary financial burden that in effect was a subsidy to those organizations to continue providing an inefficient service. In effect, those agencies charged with the responsibility for regulating industry had become partners with those industries restricting consumer choice while charging too high prices for a poor level of service.

Since the New Deal, but more particularly since the 1960s, regulatory agencies have been thought of as the means of protecting the public and the best means of ensuring a rational process of decisionmaking in areas of strong policy concern (Sunstein 1990). The process of agency establishment peaked in the early 1970s with the creation of agencies such as the PBGC in 1974 and OSHA in 1973, two agencies charged with administering and ensuring the compliance of companies with new legislation concerned with workers' retirement welfare and their on-the-job physical welfare. Being two of the last regulatory agencies created by Congress, they embodied many of the features that critics such as Breyer later came to identify as essential causes of the failure of regulatory agencies to provide adequate public service. Three characteristics of the modern bureaucracy draw particular notice and argument.

First, the most progressive and more recent federal government agencies provide a broad array of channels for public participation in agency decisionmaking. At first sight, it might be imagined (as Congress certainly intended) that openness to public participation is a virtue rather than a vice. There can be little doubt that the newer agencies have made this aspect of their organization an important rationale justifying their decisionmaking capacity. However, in practice, openness to public participation has brought with it some unfortunate consequences. The hearings process has become heavily formalized, based often on a quasi-legal format referencing notions of "procedural fairness" "due process" and the "public interest." This format has then encouraged an adversarial relationship between agencies and affected and regulated parties, has made representation of opinion an expensive and cumbersome process, and has encouraged advocates to frame issues with respect to the procedural logic of agency decisionmaking rather than the substantive merits or otherwise of the proposed or contested set of regulations. More particularly, the process of representation and deliberation has isolated the public from those parties directly involved in the regulation process by shifting the terms of discourse from the measured outputs of a policy or set of regulations to the nature and manner of agency decisionmaking. Agencies' dependence upon this process has been further encouraged by the fact that appeals of their decisions typically go to the federal courts. The courts normally evaluate the logic of those decisions with respect to the process of decisionmaking rather than the substantive merits of the case.

According to Breyer, adherence to formal proceduralism makes for poor regulation. He blames (if "blame" is the right word) the agencies themselves for this problem, even if agencies are reasonably very sensitive to the decisions of the federal courts. If proceduralism is a problem for substantive regulation, it might be also interpreted as a response to the actions of those parties immediately affected or regulated by those agencies. That is, it could be also argued that formalism is a response to the conflict engendered by the imposition of regulation, and that without such formal mechanisms for controlling conflict the integrity of agency decisionmaking would be challenged in Congress and the courts on a regular basis. For Congress, the establishment of an agency to regulate a specific part or sphere of private activity could be also understood as a response to political conflict; agencies by this interpretation are created to absorb and isolate conflict from the mainstream political process. For an agency to be unable to contain conflict would, by this interpretation, deny one of its essential reasons for being. Unfortunately, by formalism the process itself has become the terrain for dispute. Hence the following argument.

Argument 7: *In this sense, the process of regulation has been turned against itself, subverted by those willing and able to use legal proceduralism against the regulators.* Without strong support from the political process, and given the immediate judicial audience for their decisions, it is little wonder that agencies have sought refuge in proceduralism.

A second, and what Breyer might describe as a profoundly conservative characteristic of contemporary regulatory agencies is their bureaucratic nature. To some extent this characteristic is related to the first in that formalism, even its more recent legal sense, is a traditional mechanism for organizing the structure of a bureaucracy. Indeed, Max Weber (1978) in his now classic studies of bureaucracy goes to some length to describe modern bureaucracies in terms of formal, legal structures defined by rational sets of rules that enable the transference of authority up and down the hierarchy. For Breyer and others, the existence of internal rules of responsibility and power, as well as formal rules of initiation and response to policy issues, indicates the inherent limits of agencies for making policy-relevant decisions. Historically, this type of formal structural division of power and responsibility was thought to enhance the process of systematic decisionmaking, limiting the possibility of arbitrary action on behalf of any one bureaucrat and limiting the possibility that groups of agents could take over by corruption or other means the substantive design of regulations. In this sense, formalism was thought to provide organizations with a certain level of objectivity or independence from the interests of either agencies' agents or external clients.

Formalism and objectivism are certainly two desired attributes of agency decisionmaking, desired by Congress on one hand because it is supposed to isolate political conflict over competing interests, and policed by the courts on the other hand as necessary attributes of legitimate agency decisionmaking. If idealized as such, many critics would assert that agencies become so self-interested in their own power vis-á-vis competing agencies, overlapping jurisdictions, and those enemies who would support curtailment of their powers that the substantive mission of regulation is secondary to self-preservation.

A great deal more can be and has been written about the motivating interests of bureaucracies. Here I want to suggest that the internal focus of many agencies coupled with a concern to demonstrate to the outside world their objectivity regarding issues of substantive interest has in effect led to a paralysis in the capacity of agencies to make strong decisions on matters of regulatory principle. Take, for example, the issue of the proper boundary between economic imperatives and social obligations—the issue that goes to the very heart of the current problems of protecting workers' pensions in the process of corporate restructuring. Whereas this is both a large issue, crossing many agencies' possible jurisdictions and affecting many levels of the political process, the interests of many agencies is in policing their own power even if this means that substantive issues are left to fall between agencies or left to one agency in particular that cannot garner the cooperation of others. Because agency power is in part legitimized by reference to formalism and objectivism, the prospects of an agency making a deliberate choice to side with either corporations' needs vis economic imperatives or with unions who would want corporations' social obligations enforced must be understood as limited.

Notwithstanding the merits of economic efficiency, there remains a strong political interest in Congress for policing corporations' social obligations. Caught in between are regulators whose legitimacy is not based on making value choices but in making expert decisions. At this point regulators, understandably, often retreat to technical expertise thereby obfuscating the policy issue. Thus, Argument 8: *Regulators would prefer to leave issues of normative judgment unresolved than make a decision that is sure to antagonize some parties affected, and thus involve them in political conflicts that spill over into Congress.*

A third characteristic of the modern administrative state that Breyer and others would argue mitigates against effective regulation has to do with its inability to innovate beyond the realm of inherited bureaucratic practice. Essentially, agencies are the creatures of the rules and procedures that were promulgated at the time of their statutory establishment. This does not mean that those rules and procedures are so tightly written that there is no room for discretion or opportunities for innovation within the context of the enabling statutes. In fact, the possibilities of agencies with such wide discretion has from time to time concerned Congress and the executive branch. But this discretion appears more often in its potential than its realization, for three reasons. One, any agency is in effect constrained by conventions of formalism (narrow interpretations of rules and procedures) and objectivism (technical expertise rather than normative claims). The second reason involves their association with other agencies— that is, new agencies mimic old agencies' practices, thereby maintaining the careers of civil servants and limiting the potential for open conflict between agencies about how decisions are made. The third reason for limited use of discretion goes to a concern expressed earlier about the problems of overlapping jurisdictions between agencies and between agencies and the courts. Innovation would threaten agreements made between agencies to respect one another's turf, just as innovation would invite the courts to scrutinize those actions with respect to other agencies' claims of power and responsibility.

In effect, agencies are conservative by nature as well as in their actions. Whereas many issues demand an aggressive and innovative regulatory response, agencies tend to limit their actions to those that can be defended on the grounds of convention and precedent. Whereas many issues require normative judgments about the proper boundaries between private action and the public interest, agencies tend to avoid such decisions, recognizing that to be implicated in defining those boundaries is to step directly into the political process. Whereas many issues require a commitment to an integrated, even cooperative, policy response combining the jurisdictions of other agencies, those same agencies tend to narrow their responsibility to issues that can be resolved internally. Whereas Breyer and others would suggest that regulatory agencies are apparently unable to make good regulation, the reasons for this seem to do more with the relationship of agencies to the political process than any inherent lack of expertise or lack of adequate training in their areas of jurisdiction.

The crisis of regulation with respect to the question of corporate restructuring and private pension obligations is a crisis of institutional structure—the division of responsibility between Congress and the many agencies that together overlap and compete for jurisdiction in areas related to corporate restructuring. This crisis is particularly acute in the general area of industrial policy and corporate competitiveness. To be effective in responding to the economic imperatives associated with new forms of competition from overseas would require the coordination of at least the PBGC, the IRS, the NLRB, and OSHA. In many ways, these agencies intersect with one another at the point of the contractual relationships between management and labor. If there is to be an industrial policy that would rationalize workers' pension obligations in the context of other contractual obligations involving wages and conditions of work, all agencies would have an interest in any regulatory actions taken to rationalize the whole. However, if we take seriously arguments made above about agencies' motivations and incentives, it would seem obvious that no agency would have an interest in joining with others to create a new boundary between economic imperatives and social obligations. Indeed, all agencies would seem to have incentives to do just the opposite. To design a new boundary between economic imperatives and social obligations would require a normative blueprint that would hierarchically order currently divided agency responsibilities into a coherent whole (perhaps the U.S. needs an institution such as France's Council d'État that would have a general coordination role between federal policies and agencies expanding upon Judge Easterbrook's comment in *Roll Coater, Inc. v. Reilly* [1991]).

If this all seems far-fetched it should be recognized that this is precisely what some courts have argued for in their attempts to rationalize bankruptcy law with other competing statutory obligations of firms. The problems of reconciling competing statutory interests in the LTV bankruptcy case have much to do with the fact that there is no coherent statement from Congress on how to define the proper boundary between economic imperatives and social obligations. To expect agencies to do what Congress appears unwilling to do is to ask the wrong set of institutions to rationalize what are, after all, extraordinarily intense and highly competitive political interests. This, then, leads to Argument 9: *Without political resolution in Congress, the crisis of regulation will blunder on from case to case without any prospect of final resolution.*

Reinvigorated Regulation

Corporate restructuring is a process of economic and geographical rationalization that has overtaken the capacity of American regulatory institutions. Whether this was accomplished by stealth or by the inability of related regulatory agencies to respond coherently to the consequences of restructuring the regulatory process is in a shambles. As this project began as a project of analysis and description of the patterns of corporate restructuring, its initial focus on the intersection between restructuring and workers' pension entitlements has broadened somewhat to be replaced by a concern about the proper relationship between economic imperatives and social obligations. It also broadened to argue the case for an arena of regulation legitimized by normative notions of an ideal relationship between economic imperatives and social obligations rather than an apparently easy, but fundamentally mistaken, notion of economic functionalism. As such, the project is an argument for a reinvigorated system of regulation, even if conceived in rather different ethical terms than is currently the case.

Along the way, and as part of a process of documentation and description, the project concentrated on the actions and performance of three major U.S. industrial corporations. By access to confidential company documents, we have been able to peer closely into the very logic of corporate decisionmaking. A picture of corporate strategy has been built up by detailed analysis of events and actions of three corporations that have gone through a remarkable, and in each case different, process of reconstruction. Because each of these companies has had to replay its actions through federal court, our understanding of the intersection between regulation and action has been greatly enhanced. Beginning with the actions of Continental Can in the mid-1970s, it has become apparent that a vital and yet heretofore little understood factor in the restructuring process has been the problem of funding previously agreed-to private pension obligations. These obligations are an important barrier to restructuring, and as such a significant barrier to exit from an industry. The very process of industrial economic change by corporations has been designed and implemented with these obligations in mind. To better understand the processes of change requires an appreciation of the role of regulation in a modern economy. No corporation has the freedom to act simply according to its own best interests, even if that corporation would argue that this ought to be the case. A more sophisticated theory of corporate behavior is needed that makes this insight an essential part of the story.

If this story had been written in the early 1980s, there would have been considerable disagreement about its substantive thesis—that understanding the process of restructuring in the context of regulation is important. The debate at that time was dominated by the question of deindustrialization, prompted by B. Bluestone and B. Harrison's (1982) work but enlivened by a more general debate over the prospects for an American economy dominated by service industries, not manufacturing (see Lawrence 1984). Reconsidering that debate ten years on, from the vantage point of empirical work on the process of corporate restructuring it appears to me, at least, that Bluestone and Harrison were more in tune with the emerging restructuring process than Lawrence. If we were to rewrite Bluestone and Harrison now, we might emphasize the issue of corporate strategy as opposed to the question of deindustrialization per se. Lawrence's argument would now be better understood if framed as a question of overall global competitiveness rather than being framed as a question of the process of sectoral growth, decline, and succession.

But even if the argument was rewritten, there are two substantive differences between their approaches reflected in my own understanding of the corporate restructuring process. First, and most obviously, Bluestone and Harrison chose to base their argument upon case studies of deindustrialization at the local level. This approach, like my own, gives an immediacy and relevance to understanding the process of economic change not matched by macrosectoral studies. Following their strategy here has allowed us to see the process of change more directly and to understand the problematic nature of regulation. Second, emphasis on the geographical dimensions of corporate restructuring has helped us also understand how and why the process is so intertwined with the relations between labor and management. The case studies presented here are significant by virtue of contractual agreements between labor and management, sustained and enforced by the federal courts. The macrosectoral approach, although recognizing the significance of reforming the American labor relations system, is not so able to appreciate the structural power of that system in the design of local economic change.

Once beyond the documentation stage of the project, and once the point had been made about the problematic intersection between economic imperatives and social obligations, the next phase was to reconsider the rationale for regulation. Here I emphasized time and again how important ethical considerations are both for contractual relations and for providing a defensible logic of the existence of regulation separate from economic functionalism. It is too easy to reduce ethics and related normative claims to mere economic consequences. Although justifiable as an exercise in the aesthetics of model building, it is hardly sufficient as an explanation of social behavior unless what is being advanced is a normative claim that ethical considerations ought to be denied equal status with economic imperatives in the design of social institutions. This is an agenda for some legal and economic theorists (Posner 1986). But it is still only an agenda item; aesthetics aside, many still believe that regulation carries with it a moral force that transcends economics. For those concerned with protecting regulation from economic functionalism, the ethical dimension must be reintroduced to the argument. This means, of course, a reevaluation of the dominant social science practice of excluding such issues from serious analysis.

In terms of protecting regulation from economic functionalism (protecting workers' private pension entitlements from corporate restructuring), I would argue that a reinvigorated regulatory regime is essential to the survival of the private pension system. In the first place, a deliberate effort must be made to reestablish the legitimacy of regulation in the face of severe economic pressures being brought to bear on U.S. industry. This can be done, one might suppose, by indicating in some way how respect for social obligations maintains the stability of the general system of social and class relations even if it adversely affects some particular corporations. This would be an argument of economic functionalism with a difference— instead of regulation serving restructuring it would serve the reproduction of the social order. However appealing this strategy is in the sense that regulation is legitimized by reference to the "enemy" albeit transposed, the argument reduces regulation to another version of economic imperatives. What is needed is an argument that deliberately preserves the integrity of regulation separate from economic functionalism. The only way I can see that being accomplished is if the terms of discourse are moral as opposed to economic. This is to idealize moral claims at one level, but to also realize that this is its charm for many people in the wider community. This does not mean that people are necessarily "mystified by the first man who puts on a wig" (Thompson 1975:262) (assuming regulators are judges as well as agency bureaucrats). Rather, it presumes that regulation is given its force with reference to those aspects of economic life that the average citizen finds abhorrent.

More specifically, and on the basis of studies of regulation made in this project, I believe it is vital to rethink the design of regulation with reference to desired social action. Take, for example, the issue of penalties for noncompliance. All the evidence culled from this project suggests that many corporations view penalties imposed by the courts for violating regulations as an avoidable cost of restructuring. In response, the cost of penalties could be increased, making them so severe that their application would threaten the very viability of the corporation found guilty of transgressing regulation. This type of response could have two affects: (a) it could force companies to become more law abiding, but would be more likely to (b) encourage companies to engage in even more subtle and secret strategies of noncompliance, and if caught, companies could be encouraged to engage in legal tactics akin to guerrilla warfare. It seems more than obvious that many companies now consider the regulatory process as just an expensive legal charade. Regulation so conceived is thought by many corporations to lack economic legitimacy; by their interpretation draconian penalties would only reinforce their distrust of the regulatory process. In any event, I find it difficult to imagine that a federal court would today enforce such severe penalties that (even on a one-time demonstration basis) would actually bankrupt a company. If such a court was so brave, it might simply encourage more companies to seek shelter in the bankruptcy courts from paying their legal obligations.

Higher penalties applied to corporations will not achieve the best results, no matter how serious their transgressions of regulations. There may be a significant return for applying harsher penalties if regulators identify individual corporate executives as the targets of their enforcement procedures. It is remarkable that in the years since the passage of ERISA in 1974, the Justice Department has not used Section 511 of the act to sanction corporate executives' behavior. That Section, coming immediately after Section 510, which holds in part that it is unlawful to discharge an employee so as to deny his or her right to pension benefits (the basis of the *Gavalik* suit), holds that it is "unlawful for any person through the use of fraud, force . . ." so as to deny a person their rightful pension benefits. Unlike Section 510, which allows for civil damages suits, Section 511 would allow for fines and imprisonment of those executives found violating workers' rights. Given the very high rewards that many executives have received for participating in and designing pension-avoidance strategies in the course of corporate restructuring, attributing criminal penalties to them (as opposed to attributing them to corporations) may make enforcement of regulations an easier job for regulators. Such a strategy would, of course, depend upon a level of monitoring and surveillance that heretofore has been rarely initiated by the Justice Department outside of their organized crime units. But morally, what is the difference between criminals associated with crime syndicates and corporate executives who deliberately violate workers' pension rights for their own gain and their organizations' gain? One answer to this question may be that the difference is to be found in the legitimate economic interests of company shareholders. But this response is absurd economic functionalism: moral right and wrong is to be reduced yet again to an economic rationale.

Once we take seriously the notion of applying criminal procedures against corporate executives, it is not too significant a step to take to use criminal procedures to publicly humiliate those executives found to have sabotaged public regulation. At issue here is not simply applying criminal penalties to executives (which, if these penalties are monetary, could be paid for by their corporations or by anonymous benefactors), but using the public regulatory process to identify and ridicule those who transgress regulations. What I have in mind is a process of public sanction similar to the disbarment procedures of many Western countries' medical, accounting, and legal associations. What these boards do are two things: they clearly and deliberately apply their associations' ethical standards to the actions of individuals and hence judge their professional integrity; and they strip those individuals so sanctioned of a capacity to earn a livelihood as members of their particular profession. There are no similar corporate executive associations. But the courts could function in effect in an analogous manner by humiliating those found to have transgressed regulations so that their employability as a corporate executive is seriously jeopardized in most legitimate enterprises. By virtue of the increasing role played by pension fund managers and shareholder associations in the internal affairs of corporations, it is very unlikely that so-labeled corporate executives could again find employment in major public or even private companies. All this argument depends, though, on maintaining a public moral imperative to regulation. Otherwise, if regulation is so debased by economic functionalism, the average citizen may legitimately imagine that public humiliation of corporate executives is simply a cynical exercise of power of one elite group over another.

If there is to be a concerted, systematic response to the current regulation crisis, the structure of institutional responsibilities needs to be redesigned. In particular, I would advocate a fourfold realignment if institutional innovation is to be relevant to the dimensions of corporate restructuring identified in this book. First, Congress must regain authority over the regulatory process. Most obviously, Congress must take responsibility for the political choices involved in rationalizing economic restructuring with social obligations. Clearly, agencies will not take that responsibility, and the federal courts are not equipped (theoretically or practically) to make the choices they are currently forced to consider. Second, Congress also must make explicit its desired hierarchical rank-order of principles and policies. The current crisis of regulation is partly a result of a failure to make explicit a political hierarchy of statutes relevant to the issues addressed in the courts. Third, agencies must have also enough power and scope consistent with their "place" in a newly defined hierarchical rank-order of principles and policies. These powers ought to go beyond the right to impose financial penalties. Agencies must have powers, consistent with their relative positions in the hierarchy, to go beyond regulating juridical agents (corporations) to actual corporate executives. Lack of trust of agencies, coupled with their most conventional powers of penalty and deterrence, have simply made agencies ineffective with respect to corporate executives' motives and behavior. One way to go forward is to encourage agencies to identify culprits within private organizations and to use moral sanctions based upon relevant (to their mandates) community standards to penalize corporate executives' actions.

Asking Congress to make explicit their hierarchical order of principles and policies may not favor workers over corporations, or does such a hierarchy need to bolster social obligations with respect to economic imperatives. Nor do I believe that such a chosen hierarchical order would be fixed over the long run. We may well find that the rank-order changes significantly over time in much the same analogous manner as suggested by the notion of a paradigm shift—the logic of regulatory regime changes suggested by M. Eisenberg. I do think, though, that such a rank-order is the only way to solve the present crisis of regulation and responsibility. It would provide Congress with another means of evaluating agencies' actions and a rationale for allocating and policing their functions. For agencies, such a rank-order would clearly favor some agencies over others. But it would also provide a formal structure for a division of powers that could encourage both confidence in their mandates and even cooperation between different levels of agencies. For the courts, though, there may be less reason for judicial policymaking; that is, rationalizing competing and undifferentiated (in terms of their relative priorities) principles and policies may be less important in specific cases. Nevertheless, such a rank-order may allow the courts to take the moral imperatives of specific statutes seriously. At present, the confusing mix of relevant principles simply forces the courts to look elsewhere for a recipe to rationalize moral claims (hence the seductive claims of economic efficiency). A rank-order with a well-defined set of principles connected to agencies may allow the courts to follow Congress rather than make up what Congress has failed to do. This, then, is the fourth step necessary for a comprehensive realignment of institutional powers.

Notes

Chapter 1. ERISA and the Crisis of Regulation

1. There is great debate over the costs and benefits of mergers and acquisitions. Some analysts suggest that mergers and acquisitions have often benefited productivity and competitiveness even if in some instances such strategies have not realized promised benefits (Paulus and Waite 1987). Identified as a positive aspect of mergers and acquisitions is the efficiency discipline imposed by heavy debt burdens and the stake that management often have in LBOs. On the other hand, there are those who would argue that this kind of corporate strategy does nothing more than enrich a select group of corporate executives, lawyers, bankers, and stockholders at the expense of employees and the public in general (Roll 1988). I do not intend to make an assessment of these arguments here; what evidence I have suggests that mergers and acquisitions and related LBOs have been used as needed to enhance the market value of the corporations concerned.

2. A critical assessment of this argument applied to an area of regulation is provided by L. I. Boden and C. A. Jones (1987). Their study of remedies for occupational diseases (notably asbestos-related diseases) analyzes the role that labor-market wage premiums may play in providing an incentive to control occupational hazards outside the normal channels of regulation. Their conclusion is that "workers' compensation and compensating wage differentials should be supplemented with additional interventions to reduce the social costs of asbestos-related disease to the efficient level" (p. 342). They argue that a lack of adequate information about occupational risks and a lack of reasonable alternative employment make it unlikely that wage premiums will provide sufficient incentives for market-based regulation.

3. A good example of this sentiment is provided by Oliver Hart (1984:184). Commenting upon critiques of neoclassical economics, Hart suggests that advocates of neoclassical logic do not necessarily believe a *laissez-faire* world would "work particularly well in practice" but do believe that "it seems superior to the alternatives, e.g. planning." This assessment is based upon his review of recent theoretical developments in the literature that stress the asymmetries of knowledge and market power but suggest as well that regulation is the worst solution. Such theoretical pessimism has infected the polity, providing both analytical reasons to distrust political solutions to economic problems and a rallying ground for those who have an economic interest in less regulation and less enforcement of existing regulations.

4. This is, I think, the lesson to be drawn from N. MacCormick's (1990) friendly critique of the Critical Legal Studies (CLS) movement, particularly of M. Kelman (1987) and R. M. Unger (1986). It is clear that CLS and the allied developments in literary criticism relating to the theory of deconstruction have demonstrated that the determinate meaning of law that many mainstream lawyers have claimed to exist cannot be sustained (see also Levinson 1991). Instead, the "reality" of law is its indeterminacy and the inevitable conflict over apparently equally plausible interpretations. Accepting that this is the case (see Clark 1985) is not the same as suggesting that the legal enterprise is a total fraud. At issue is the power of competing interests to control interpretation. In this respect, since unions have had a great deal of influence over the interpretation of ERISA legislation (as they were instrumental in the passage of the legislation) there is every reason to believe that the legal enterprise can be used to advance workers' interests in the process of corporate restructuring.

5. This argument about the fragility of coalitions of interest is most relevant to the post-1970 era. It reflects the decline (in terms of representation and in terms of relative significance) of traditional democratic networks involving the unions and progressive alliances in general. These networks were able to forge and maintain relatively stable coalitions over many years (see Sanders 1987). But now, they have been supplanted by professional lobby groups whose interests are both more narrow and more opportunistic.

Chapter 2. Restructuring in Theory and Practice

1. While I have emphasized the role of government policymaking in structuring the patterns of trade, it is important to acknowledge that intracorporation trading over national borders has also come to play a major role in displacing natural comparative advantage as the geographical sorting mechanism of production. The world car is an obvious instance of this phenomenon. Less obvious but no less important is the trade in components affecting all kinds of manufactured goods, even producer services (see Thurow 1992).

2. There are, of course, other modes of analyzing the dynamics of capital accumulation (see Webber and Tonkin 1990) just as there are forms of competition based upon scale, product quality and innovation, design and marketing—aspects of competition all too apparent (for example) in the changing range and styles of automobiles sold overseas and in the United States.

3. In a recent decision, *Firestone Tire and Rubber Co. v. Pension Benefit Guar. Corp.* (1988), Judge Oliver Gasch of the U.S. Federal District Court for the District of Columbia noted that until 1984 ERISA provided no formula or rule for dividing excess assets between employer contributors and vested pension plan beneficiaries. And it was certainly the case that few if any plans contained within them or within their associated collective bargaining agreements any formula for dispersement. The PBGC's rules for dispersement have been tested in recent years by companies (like Firestone) unwilling to accept the PBGC's ruling that their share of excess pension fund assets is less than 100 percent.

4. The PBGC estimated that in the early 1980s there were about 110,000 insured

single employer–defined benefit pension plans, covering about 30 million participants (GAO 1986b).

5. Senator Metzenbaum (D-Ohio) (in conjunction with Rep. William Clay [D-Mo.] of the House Subcommittee on Labor-Management Relations) introduced a bill in early April 1989 that would in effect penalize firms that terminate their pension funds for the purpose of asset skimming. By the provisions of the proposed bill, corporations would have to re-fund (in fact overfund) their terminated plans at a higher rate, make cost-of-living adjustments to retirees' benefits, and pay a tax of the amount of reversion. Some industry commentators believe that such provisions would make it impossible for companies to go through on pending reversions (four hundred of which were suspended by the IRS in 1988), and initiate new reversions (see *Employee Benefits Alert* 1[4] April 14, 1989).

6. Compared to nominal wage costs, employment benefits costs (including pension costs, health insurance costs, and vacation costs) increased very rapidly during the 1980s. As of 1988, benefits accounted for as much as 32 percent of the value of total compensation in the goods producing industries and the management classes. Even in retail and service sectors, traditionally low wage sectors, benefit costs account for as much as 20 percent of all compensation (see Bureau of Labor Statistics *News* 88-293 [June 16, 1988] and 88-361 [July 26, 1988], Washington, D.C.).

7. The GAO (1991a) reports many corporations are now very sensitive to the escalating costs of funding health benefits to retirees.

8. There is a great deal of ignorance about the value of private pension benefits in manufacturing industries. Currently a retiree from the steel industry receives a pension in the order of $400 to $800 per month. For a blue-collar worker, this is a relatively generous pension. Many other retirees, however, receive much less than this; evidence presented at congressional hearings on underfunding and overfunding of pension plans suggests that a retiree could receive as little as $61 per month after a lifetime of employment with an employer (U.S. Congress 1988:153).

Chapter 3. Regulation of Private Pension Obligations

1. Uncertainty over the value of pension benefits varies by the type of pension and the party involved (McGill 1984). For example, defined benefit pension plans essentially fix the future nominal value of a pension benefit. However, these types of plans rarely fix the future real value of such a benefit to an employee just as the real cost of providing such a benefit by an employers may also be unknown. See Gustman and Steinmeier (1988) for a detailed empirical assessment of the sources of uncertainty of the future value of pension benefits. They use perhaps the only reliable source of national data on the dimensions and significance of pensions for households, the 1983 *Survey of Consumer Finances*.

2. See *Labor and Investments*, published by the Industrial Union Department of the AFL-CIO (8[7], September 1988).

3. Clark (1989a) provides detailed information on the decline in the number of union-represented employees, the rate of unionization, and the significance of unions

in the U.S. economy. Union representation of private nonagricultural employment has gone from about 43 percent in the mid-1950s to about 14 percent in 1987. Recently, the union movement has lost a further 6 million members, so total union membership is now about 16 million, down from its peak of about 22 million in the mid-1970s.

4. Close and immediately related cases were *General Motors Corporation* (1949) and *Cross v. NLRB* (1949). In the former case, the company had unilaterally changed aspects of its group insurance program without consulting the union (UAW). The board concluded that the company had "refused to bargain . . . based on the erroneous legal premise that there was no statutory obligation to bargain as to insurance" (p. 781). The board cited the Inland Steel (1947, 1948, 1949) and Cross cases as evidence that pensions and insurance were mandatory subjects for bargaining. The Cross case was also concerned with the right of companies to act unilaterally with regard to the terms and conditions of group insurance programs. The court, citing Inland Steel, argued that "Congress did not intend to restrict duty to bargain collectively only to those subjects which up to time of enactment of act had been commonly bargained about" (p. 875). A more recent case, *Pacific Coast Association v. NLRB* (1962), made it clear that there was nothing special in pension plans that distinguished them from other subjects for collective bargaining.

5. The more powerful a union and the more protected the domestic market, the better the coverage of workers and the better the level of benefits. Notice that to the extent that these unions were able to fashion industry-wide master contracts, geographical variations in coverage and benefit levels were minimized. The most important instances of this phenomenon were the USWA's contracts with the steel, aluminum, and canning industries; geographical disparities in wages, benefits, and employment rules were systematically attacked by the union from the early 1950s. It is also apparent that few unions were able to exert such pressure as the USWA. The American union movement in general was unable to penetrate the south. Thus there were, and remain, systematic geographical disparities in pension coverage and benefit levels between regions—disparities that are patterned on the relative success or failure of the union movement to gain representation (Clark 1989a, chap. 2).

6. This particular case was cited as compelling in *Watkinson v. Great Atlantic & Pacific Tea Co.* (1984). There a discharged employee brought suit against the company, alleging it had terminated his employment so as to prevent him from attaining additional pension benefits. The court held, citing *Titsch v. Reliance Group, Inc.*, that denial of benefits was a "mere consequence" of the termination decision.

7. *Schaefer v. First National Bank of Lincolnwood* (1975).

8. A similar case to Kross was *Zipf v. American Telephone and Telegraph Co.* (1986). Afflicted with chronic arthritis, Monica Zipf was terminated by AT&T the day before her service with the company would have entitled her to extended long-term disability benefits. The district court summarily dismissed her Section 510 claim without considering the merits of her claim because she failed to exhaust the company's administrative procedures. The appeals court rejected this argument,

holding that there was no implied exhaustion requirement in ERISA and that "suits alleging violation of substantive rights conferred by ERISA can be brought in a federal court notwithstanding an agreement to arbitrate" (citing *Barrowclough v. Kidder, Peabody & Co.* [1985], p. 892).

9. Early retirement pensions were available to those employees who had (a) worked at the plant for thirty years or more on the last day of service, or (b) had a combined age and service (assuming a minimum of ten years service) of eighty-five years. The average age of its Benton Harbor employees was fifty-two years of age and the average years of service was twenty-five years. The plaintiff with the most years of service had accumulated twenty-seven years. Thus, even though most employees had vested in their deferred pensions, a much smaller group of employees were close to attaining eligibility for early retirement pensions.

10. The company had also denied most workers a chance to relocate to Asheville on the basis of interplant transfer clauses of the collective bargaining agreement. Spokespersons for the company defended this decision by arguing that the transfers would have adversely impacted the financial status of the Asheville plant's pension plan.

11. One reason for lack of consideration of the relevance of the grievance and arbitration mechanisms of the collective bargaining agreement between the union and the company may have been the fact that when the local union refused to sign the plant-closing agreement negotiated between the International union and the company, the International decertified the local (compare with my case study of the internal political struggles within the UAW over rationalization of production within the AMC corporation; Clark 1989a, chap. 4). For an instance where the relevance of grievance and arbitration mechanisms was considered in an ERISA context, see *Graphic Communication Workers Local 680 v. Nabisco Brands* (1987).

12. See, for example, *Parker et al. v. Connors Steel Co.* (1988).

13. See *Pilot Life Insurance Company v. Dedeaux* (1987).

14. Another suit was filed by USWA-represented employees in Alabama (*Mason III et al. v. Continental Group, Inc.* [1983, 1985, 1986]). This suit was not, however, originally based upon Section 510 of ERISA. Instead the plaintiffs filed under a state fraud statute, charging the company had misled them by promises of continued employment where in fact the company had had no intention of honoring those promises. Only later, after an initial hearing on the fraud issue, was the complaint amended to include the Section 510 charge. In this case, the district court dismissed the complaint, holding the plaintiffs had failed to exhaust grievance and arbitration proceedings on the issue of their termination. This opinion was also extended to the ERISA charge, and was affirmed by the appeals court. The plaintiffs appealed to the U.S. Supreme Court, but were denied a hearing. In a minority opinion, however, justices White and Brennan argued the lower courts had clearly erred on the exhaustion issue (citing *Amaro*) contending "the court should grant certiorari in this case in order to resolve the uncertainty over the existence of an exhaustion requirement in cases of this kind" (p. 864).

15. In August 1982, Judge Alan Bloch of the Federal District Court of Western Pennsylvania (the Gavalik judge) issued an order prohibiting the plaintiff's counsel from using Continental's documents in other law suits. The irony is, though, the

Amaro documents were more powerful than the "smoking gun" sought by the plaintiffs' counsel. Continental Can fabricated parts of the documents it produced in the Gavalik suit.

16. *Alexander v. Gardner-Denver Co.* (1974).

17. *Wilson v. Garcia* (1985).

18. Given that Charles Fried, the U.S. solicitor general, was appointed by the Reagan administration and was thought to be a supporter of corporate interests against workers' interests (see Note 1987 and compare with Fried 1991), it may seem surprising that his office sided with the Ninth Circuit Court of Appeals (compare with Caplan 1987). However, there are reasons to imagine that Fried would have found the Ninth Circuit opinion compelling—it was based upon "smoking gun" evidence, it was based upon respect for judicial authority in matters of legal rights, and it held as a matter of principle that intended discrimination was illegal. Considering that C. Fried (1981) has promoted the moral virtues of contracts as promises, it might also have been possible that he was offended by Continental's subversion of its collective bargaining agreement.

Chapter 4. Location and Management Strategy

1. It should be acknowledged that it was difficult to research and analyze this case. H. R. Northrup (1984) provides an example of a case study analyzed in similar circumstances. For a variety of reasons, Judge Alan Bloch of the Federal District Court of Western Pennsylvania directed that lawyers for the union and plaintiffs, as well as lawyers for the defendant, could not discuss the case with anyone not directly a party to the dispute. Moreover, the judge directed that all documents relating to the corporation's business strategies remain closed to the public. This prohibition was only recently lifted.

2. There is considerable debate over the role of pension plan assets in management-led LBOs and corporate takeovers. For example, Peter Drucker (1988:71) claimed that "pension funds are the ultimate cause of the explosion of hostile takeovers in the last few years." Even so, from 1985 to 1988 there were only about seven occasions where the DOL had to intervene to protect the integrity of plan assets and plan trustees (GAO 1988g). According to some economists, the recent wave of mergers and acquisitions was prompted by changes in the corporate tax code in 1981 (see Auerbach and Reishus 1988; Shleifer and Vishny 1988) and the depreciation of the U.S. dollar (see Williamson 1990 for a general review).

3. See A. Harris (1987) for the amended ERISA code. Sections 404 and 406 require (in part) that plan fiduciaries must discharge their duties "solely in the interest of the participants and beneficiaries, . . . with the care, skill, prudence, and diligence [of a prudent man] . . . by diversifying the investments of the plan" (404). Section 406 also holds that it is not admissible to "transfer to, or use by or for the benefit of, a party in interest, of any assets of the plan." Section 407 generally limits plan investments in their companies to just 10 percent of the "fair market value of the assets of the plan (Section 407[a][2]) and since December 1984 a plan may not hold more than 10 percent of its assets determined as of January 1975 in the company. These limitations are ceilings; it may be determined that even a 5-percent holding violates the fiduciary (prudence and diversity) responsibility of

plan trustees. While the DOL does not believe it has adequate authority to police the issue (GAO 1988g), it has recently formalized civil penalties under Section 502(i) of ERISA for Section 406 violations (transactions between a plan and "a party of interest"). Section 502(i) of ERISA allows the secretary of the DOL to impose civil penalties of up to 5 percent of the value of the prohibited transaction and, if not corrected within 90 days, as much as 100 percent of the value of the prohibited transaction (for details, see the *Federal Register* 53:37473, September 26, 1988).

4. In fact, this strategy was widely discussed in the financial newspapers in the early 1980s. Continental's spokespersons were quoted as saying that they were seeking to raise as much as $500 million from its packaging and canning business (through the sale of plants and diversion of funds from this business) for investment in energy resources. As late as 1984, Continental acquired another major energy corporation through this strategy. Diversification was a common corporate strategy of the early 1980s, fostered by the success of BCG in corporate rationalization, and the very high finance and energy prices of the period 1979 to 1982.

5. A. Hax and N. Majluf (1984) described "star" businesses as those in which a corporation has a strong market position, characterized by high rates of sales growth, but which need significant and continuing investment so as to maintain and capitalize on their market position. In this instance, it is debatable if Continental's investments were truly "stars" or more likely BCG "question marks"—those businesses that appear very attractive because of their high rates of growth, even though the corporation has not achieved significant market share. The "question marks" may be the potential "stars" of the next generation.

6. The role of Continental's management in the buyout appears very complex and difficult to disentangle. For instance, it is difficult to know whether or not management initiated the buyout, that is, whether or not the buyout was a hostile act or promoted by management. J. Gordon (1990) observed that management often has a superior position in a buyout because it knows more about the value of corporate assets than outsiders and may, if their interests are protected, help the market and stockholders value competing bids.

7. It is privately estimated that Continental's assets (95 percent of which were packaging plants) were worth about $2 billion in 1986. Even if the sale of these plants realized only one-half their estimated value, it is obvious that the LBO was a very good deal for Kiewit. Details of the company's assets and sale of businesses are available, in part, from the Securities and Exchange Commission 10-K Form (K585770), Washington D.C.

8. An employee who did not have the required years of service or was not of the minimum age but had still worked for at least ten years is deemed to be vested for a normal pension at the standard retirement age of 62.

9. This clause is termed the Suitable Long-Term Employment (SLTE) program. Despite its apparent theoretical significance, few employees within the packaging industry were offered SLTE jobs that took them away from their "home" plants and even fewer accepted such offers.

10. Senior management limited access to employee files so as to shield line managers from knowing the Red Flag status of their employees. Special user ID codes and passwords were necessary to access these files. At the same time, senior management recognized that there were likely to be morale problems if line man-

agers became aware of management's willingness to compromise on "traditional considerations such as efficiency, quality, service, and productivity" (see Document No. 165 of the case file available from the Federal District Court of Western Pennsylvania, Pittsburgh).

11. For details see Document No. 28 dated May 15, 1977, filed in the case material at the Federal District Court of Western Pennsylvania (Pittsburgh).

12. Document No. 162 of the case file, available from the Federal District Court of Western Pennsylvania (Pittsburgh).

13. A detailed description of the goals and objectives of this program is in the 1977 Steel Settlement Booklet No. PR-229, available from the United Steelworkers of America, Pittsburgh.

14. Of course, SLTE opportunities were only relevant for workers moving between Steelworker-represented plants. Thus, in practice it would have been very unlikely that workers in the West Mifflin plant would have been required to move *if they had been requested*. Normally, the relevant SLTE plants covered by the Steelworkers for Pittsburgh employees were located in Indiana, Illinois, and New Jersey. Details of the location of SLTE opportunities by plant are to be found in a document prepared in March 1980 explaining the Continental pension program available from the United Steelworkers' Union, Pittsburgh.

15. Notice that while few people in these industries initially realized the potential long-run financial consequences of their early pension agreements, by 1977 the union was quite aware of the potential burden of their rule of 65 pension. In a briefing to steel industry members, the union noted

> the rule of 65 pension and pension supplement, and the related programs contained in the new contract would impose an extremely heavy financial obligation on a company for the shutdown of an old facility. It [the rule of 65] is intended to encourage companies to take the other option—and use the money to modernize the old plant. To the extent it accomplishes this goal it will protect the jobs of young and old alike.

See 1977 Steel Settlement Booklet No. PR-229 available from the United Steelworkers of America, Pittsburgh.

Chapter 5. Piercing the Corporate Veil

1. For a related discussion of regulation theory see M. Piore and C. Sabel (1984). They are uncomfortable with the economism of the French regulation school, preferring instead to see regulation as part of the state or even equivalent to the state. Unfortunately, although they argue against treating regulation as just government intervention, as most economists would, their own notion of regulation remains so vague that it is quite impossible to distinguish their approach from the French regulation school except by virtue of their proclaimed difference.

2. At the time of sale, only one of the plant's three blast furnaces was operating (the two nonoperating furnaces were built in 1908 and 1914, while the operating furnace was built in 1929) and only one coke battery was being used. A basic oxygen furnace (installed in 1964) worked but its continuous caster (installed in 1966) was practically inoperable. WSC's "blooming mill" (hot rolling mill) was also in poor

condition, was very inefficient compared to other firms' mills, and required massive investment to make it reliable. It was estimated that the plant operated at only about 50 or 60 percent of capacity through the 1970s, providing bars and special shapes to Harvester's manufacturing works. See the PBGC's "Proposed Findings of Fact and Conclusions of Law," dated July 14, 1988; Civil Action Nos. 81 C 7076 and 82 C 6895, U.S. District Court for the Northern District of Illinois, Eastern Division.

3. Section 4042(a) of ERISA was designed to protect plan assets and prevent further deterioration of a plan's financial position. It may be invoked by a corporation when it is unable to pay plan installments on its pension liabilities, when it is unable to pay benefits, or when the corporation has little chance of continuing as a viable entity.

4. For an in-depth social and economic analysis of the impacts of the closure of WSC on south Chicago see D. Bensman and R. Lynch (1987). Not only do they provide a "richly textured" analysis of the plant and the community (including discussion of local union politics and Democratic Party politics in Chicago), they relate the closure of WSC to the closure of U.S. Steel's South Chicago plant at about much the same time. While interesting, their perspective is centered on the community, and neglects the strategics of the corporation that are the basis of this chapter.

5. The standard definition of an LBO is "a business practice wherein a company is sold to a small number of investors, typically including members of the company's management, under financial arrangements in which there is a minimum amount of equity and a maximum amount of debt." See *United States v. Tabor Court Realty Corp.* (1986), p. 1292. LBOs are often financed by the seller (as in this case), junk bonds (noninvestment-grade certificates), or the sell-off of assets by the buyer. Normally these financial arrangements are secured by mortgages on the assets of the new corporate entity (see generally Bebchuk 1990).

6. By recent U.S. standards, the LBO of WSC in 1977 was a small transaction (compared with the LBO of RJR Nabisco for $21 billion). Nevertheless, it was important at the time because there had been few such transactions involving a major Fortune 500 corporation selling off part of its business in such a manner. In 1981, there were only 91 such transactions, valued in total at $3.1 billion. By 1986, there were 308 LBOs valued at $40.9 billion, and LBOs transacted in 1988 were worth in total $65 billion (excluding the RJR Nabisco deal) (GAO 1989c).

7. Estimates made by the PBGC (and not contested by International Harvester) in their "Memorandum in Opposition to Harvester's Motion to Dismiss," dated December 9, 1987; Civil Action Nos. 81 C 7076 and 82 C 6895, United States District Court for the Northern District of Illinois, Eastern Division. Harvester preferred to count the losses of their Wisconsin Steel Division in after-tax terms. By their reckoning, the division lost $8.6 million over the 1971–76 (inclusive) period. See their "Answer to Amended Complaint," dated October 14, 1983; Civil Action No. 81 C 7076, United States District Court for the Northern District of Illinois, Eastern Division.

8. There are many different estimates of the costs of continuing to operate WSC, estimates made by the company and others, including steel consultants. One consultant in 1974 estimated that it would take $217 million to simply integrate

the operations of the plant and another $1 billion to rebuild the plant into a nationally competitive plant capable of competing successfully with the best steel manufacturers in the U.S. (see PBGC's "Proposed Findings of Fact and Conclusions of Law").

9. Other suits were brought against IHC by parties affected by the bankruptcy of WSC. The union brought suit as did Envirodyne, which charged IHC with fraud in the initial sales agreement. For the purposes of this chapter, the focus is reserved for the PBGC suit.

10. S. Scheffler (1982) termed this kind of theory as "act-consequentialist." It depends upon some *a priori* ordered ranking of desirable end-points such that one (post-Fordism) dominates all others and that all agents act in such a manner consistent with the achievement of that end-point. Notionally such end-points are thought desirable for reasons of economic efficiency and/or social justice. In this instance it appears theorists assign priority to post-Fordism because they suppose (I imagine) that it is the unavoidable end-point, determined by the immutable economic imperatives of capitalism.

11. See transcript of PBGC's post-trial position paper in *Consolidated Litigation Concerning International Harvester's Disposition of Wisconsin Steel*, No. 81 C 7076 and 82 C 6897, Chapter 11 Proceedings No. 81 A 0442, U.S. District Court, Northern District of Illinois, Eastern Division, dated July 14, 1988.

12. Even after the board gave formal approval to the deal, IHC's outside labor law counsel advised the company in August 1977 that despite the sale it would remain contractually liable for the pension benefits bargained and agreed to with Wisconsin Steel's independent union. Indeed, just one month later, IHC reached an agreement with the union to the effect that it would provide a pension increment to WSC's workers if, under special circumstances, EDC Holdings declared bankruptcy and the pension plans were then administered by the PBGC.

13. According to IHC's legal counsel, Harvester advanced approximately $50 million in concessions to keep WSC going. This included $9 million as a loan guarantee for the EDA project, $12.5 million in advances for sales of steel never delivered, $20 million in emergency credit, and $3 million in expedited payments for steel components. IHC has claimed that it never advanced monies for WSC's pension contributions. See "Navistar's Detailed Proposed Findings of Fact," dated July 14, 1988; Civil Action Nos. 81 C 7076 and 82 C 6895, U.S. District Court for the Northern District of Illinois, Eastern Division.

14. See "Navistar's Summary of Position," dated July 14, 1988; Civil Action Nos. 81 C 7076 and 82 C 6895, U.S. District Court for the Northern District of Illinois, Eastern Division.

15. See "Navistar's Trial Brief," dated May 6, 1988; Civil Actions 81 C 7076 and 82 C 6895, U.S. District Court for the Northern District of Illinois, Eastern Division.

16. See *Dorn's Transp. v. Teamsters Pension Trust Fund* (1986), *Flying Tiger Line v. Teamsters Pension Trust Fund* (1987), and *Cuyamaca Meats v. San Diego & Imperial Counties Butchers' and Food Employers' Pension Trust Fund* (1987).

17. By his interpretation of Congress's intentions in passing ERISA, "Congress did not intend that an employer should be able to defeat his ERISA liability merely

with private contractual provisions." See *In re Consolidated Litigation Concerning International Harvester's Disposition of Wisconsin Steel* (1988:520).

Chapter 6. Bankruptcy in the U.S. Steel Industry

1. Notwithstanding disclaimers to the contrary, what R. Walker (1989a) calls "pure windowdressing," I believe functionalism and an unfortunate Althusserian inspired economic-driven structuralism—characterizes applications of the French regulation school. A good example of this kind of analytical practice is D. Drache and H. Glasbeek's (1989) paper on the "new" Fordism in Canadian labor relations. Although eschewing the pronouncement of a new regime of accumulation (neo-Fordism), they do argue that there is a new global economic reality that will transform the Canadian labor relations system. See also D. Drache and M. Gertler (1991).

2. Although Judge Robert Sweet considered LTV to be the second largest steel company in the U.S., data on employment, production, and profit shown in Table 6.1 suggests in fact that Bethlehem Steel Corporation is the second largest. LTV may well have been the second biggest company in about 1984 or 1985—before rationalization was completed. It is also apparent that Bethlehem and LTV are of very similar size, at least relative to USX.

3. Chapter 11 bankruptcy is designed to protect the corporation or entity at risk of default on all its debts from the immediate actions of its creditors while it reorganizes so as to meet those debt obligations (Cowans 1978, chap. 22). Keeping a company operating is normally an appropriate policy when it is worth more as a functioning entity than its separate assets when sold, or when there are no outside buyers with sufficient resources or information to make a buy decision (Bebchuk 1988). Robert Clark (1981) describes Chapter 11 as the "sale" of the company to its creditors—although this sale is hypothetical, it is nevertheless a move to benefit creditors over shareholders with respect to their "shares" of assets of the reorganized corporation.

4. While I would also accept that high relative wages were a great disadvantage to domestic steel producers through the 1980s, I do not agree with R. W. Crandall (1989) and others that high wages were the precipitating cause of the decline of the U.S. steel industry. All the evidence of the past decade shows that when challenged to become more competitive the union negotiated lower real wages, give-backs, and lower benefit levels in return for profit-sharing.

5. Over this same period, all manufacturing lost just 12 percent of its 1979 employment. See Supplement to Employment and Earnings (June 1986 and August 1989), U.S. Department of Labor, Bureau of Labor Statistics, Washington D.C.

6. D. Carlton and R. Gertner (1989) demonstrated that in durable manufacturing there are inherent tendencies toward price competition, even in industries dominated by one or more firms. Even without the 1980–82 recession, there are reasons to believe that the LTV merger would have been affected by significant cost-revenue squeezes.

7. Commenting upon the PBGC's case against LTV, Judge Sweet said in the strongest terms, "There is no factual or legal basis for the PBGC's finding that LTV has abused the pension termination insurance system."

8. See U.S. Code Annotated (1987), Pamphlet Number 1, page 245, Note 10a, citing In re. Cole, Bkrtcy.E.D.Pa., 66 B.R. 75, and in 1986 see page 284, Note 10a, citing In re. Paolino, Bkrtcy.Pa.1985, 53 B.R. 399, West Publishing, St. Paul, Minn.

9. See U.S. Code Annotated (1986), Pamphlet Number 1, page 285, Note 1, citing In re. Air Vectors Associates, Bkrtcy N.Y. 1985, 53 B.R. 668, West Publishing, St. Paul, Minn.

10. The U.S. Court of Appeals for the Third Circuit noted in the same case that an "underlying" legislative policy of Chapter 11 is "to provide opportunities for a debtor . . . to return to financial viability" (p. 77).

11. See *Pension Benefit Guar. Corp. v. LTV Corp.* (1988) for a discussion of Congress's intentions in establishing the PBGC. Therein the U.S. Appeals Court for the Second Circuit denied the PBGC's motion to restore three of four LTV bankrupt pension plans, arguing that the PBGC had failed to give due weight to other conflicting public interests involved in the bankruptcy of LTV.

12. The Supreme Court held that a company could reject a collective bargaining agreement under Section 365(a) of the Bankruptcy Code, and that rejection was not an unfair labor practice as defined by the National Labor Relations Act. According to Section 1113, a trustee or debtor in possession must make every effort to negotiate in good faith with workers' representatives any proposed change or modification to the existing collective bargaining agreements. If the relevant union has good cause to reject management proposals, management cannot arbitrarily cancel the current agreement. Any modified agreement must also have the approval of the bankruptcy court. While there is still some uncertainty about the applicability of this section to different circumstances, it is generally accepted that Section 1113 has provided organized labor with an important legal instrument for combating some types of strategic bankruptcies (witness the problem this section posed for management of Eastern Airlines in their dispute with the machinists' union). Section 1113 does not provide, though, a formula for balancing competing statutory interests.

13. See the Brief of the Respondent (Official Committee of Unsecured Creditors of LTV Corporation), Case No. 89-390, in the U.S. Supreme Court (October Term 1989), dated January 16, 1990.

14. A group of dissident retirees, organized as Solidarity U.S.A., argued in court in favor of the PBGC's decision to restore LTV's pension plans. They claimed that the company must be required to pay all promised benefits except in circumstances of severe hardship. They also suggested that the compromise worked out between the company and the union regarding pension benefits compromised their welfare and failed to respect their financial interests in receiving full benefits.

15. Many union concession agreements contain so-called snap-back conditions. These provisions were necessary because of companies' "whipsawing" tactics between plants and communities for economic concessions over the past ten years (see Clark 1989a). The USWA has used these provisions as a means of ensuring companies pay back wage and benefit concessions if concessions result in significant profit for the company and/or if circumstances change so as to radically improve corporate prosperity (a good example being the windfall profits and wage benefits that accrued from the unanticipated increase in world copper prices).

16. Bankruptcy involves regulation at two levels of government; through the federal Bankruptcy Code and through state-level collection laws. Here the focus is reserved for federal policy. While I realize the importance of state regulation of bankruptcy, it is more narrowly concerned with "providing a means for the collection of a single unpaid debt" (Warren 1987:782) than with the accommodation of diverse and competing interests justified by different statutory claims.

17. M. Shubik (1988) made a useful observation in this context about the static nature of conventional economic theory. He suggested that despite the apparent "quasi-religious meaning" attached to notions like efficiency and competition by economists, their value to judges in a "world of dynamic economies with players of different skills" is very limited. The virtues of coherence and simplicity, so important to academic theorists, may in fact translate into irrelevance and simple-mindedness in practice.

Chapter 7. Limits of Statutory Responses to Restructuring

1. Judge Robert Sweet, the federal bankruptcy judge responsible for steering LTV Corporation through Chapter 11 bankruptcy, has noted that from his perspective there is no recipe or formula for allocating the costs of restructuring between those affected (see epigraph of this book). Although he is not empowered by statute or guided by a policy or set of policies, he is required to make judgments about who is to share more or less of the burden of industrial restructuring; not surprisingly, he is involved in a complex web of argument and rhetoric that legitimates the whole (see chapter 6).

2. Wealth maximization is, according to the Chicago school of law and economics, the only legitimate reference point for evaluating the desirability of government policy (Posner 1986).

3. According to this logic, plant-closing legislation facilitates labor-market adjustment, a point borne out empirically by R. Ehrenberg and G. H. Jakubson (1988).

4. Gerald Frug (1984) describes the administrative state in terms of bureaucracy theory, its organization, scope, and powers of initiation and review. He attributes to such bureaucracies the powers and interests attributable to any organizations of such size. Cass Sunstein (1989) describes the administrative state in terms of its powers of regulation. Like Frug, Sunstein traces the evolution of such large organizations from at least the New Deal era. Frug does also suggest, however, that the bureaucratic nature of the administrative state is also attributable to a misplaced confidence in task rationality and efficient instrumental design that owes its intellectual origins to Max Weber and others (compare with Seidenfeld 1992).

5. Rubin makes an important and well-conceived argument. But it is odd that he chose to describe the opaqueness of many U.S. statutes as "intransitive." Implied is an assumption that the opaqueness of statutes is somehow illogical or invalid, referencing (presumably) an ideal, logical relationship between the intentions of statutes and their outcomes. It is as if Rubin-the-lawyer is distressed by a deliberate subversion of the logic of words and their meaning.

6. A. Mikva (1983), a federal court judge and previously a member of Congress, also believes that the legislature tends to shift responsibility for difficult questions to the courts. However, he also notes that the legislature often assumes consti-

tutional issues to be settled or, in cases where there are very pressing policy problems to be acted upon, believes that the courts ought to respect their statutory claims whatever the niceties of doctrine. Some issues are so important, and the legal context so uncertain, that Congress is willing to risk rejection in the courts: an issue of substance over form.

7. For an interesting, albeit earlier, reference on a similar topic from a public choice perspective, see W. H. Riker (1962). Using game theory and some simple assumptions about information and agents' rationality, Riker shows that as the size of "games" increase, coalitions form to ensure that individual agents have a share in winning situations.

8. See J. S. Coleman (1986:21–26) for the definitive analytical treatment of this phenomenon. Through a series of experiments involving legislators (as game players), he shows that any individual vote is contingent upon the sequence of votes played out prior to the current vote and is also contingent upon forecast future opportunities given the pattern of voting by coalition.

9. See, for example, G. L. Clark and M. Dear (1984, chap. 3), wherein we consider the various bureaucratic apparatuses of the state with reference to questions of legitimization, reproduction, and ideological coherence. It is suggested there that the state must play an active and self-interested role in organizing and deflecting dissent away from essential problems of power and privilege toward local issues of less systemic importance. Thus coherence and legitimization would demand either vague and broadly worded statutes or well-defined but local statutes of no overarching significance.

10. K. Hall (1989) has a useful discussion of the events leading up to the passage of the NIRA, and the establishment of the NRA in 1933. He notes (p. 274) that the NRA "suffered from two major defects." One was that it was difficult to justify in a constitutional sense, especially with a divided and conservative Supreme Court. The other problem was simply its dependence upon trade associations to help monitor and plan the implementation of policy. It was virtually impossible to obtain cooperative and voluntary participation in the new regulatory regime. At a broader level, W. Lasser (1988) provides a useful perspective on the conflict between the government and the court at that time, linking that conflict to a more general analysis of politics and the judiciary since the Civil War.

11. A good illustration of this argument is to be found in S. Estreicher and R. L. Revesz's (1989) assessment of the reasons why and the extent to which regulatory agencies like the NLRB and the SSA have selectively refused to respond to federal court decisions regarding the integrity of their decisionmaking processes. In some instances, like the SSA's attempts to reduce radically the numbers of disability recipients, such selective refusal amounts to a policy instituted and conducted against the interests of others (including recipients), maintained and encouraged by the executive in the context of a very hostile and critical Congress. Though an issue of immediate significance, there are many other instances less well known where agencies have refused to acquiesce to congressional review, executive orders, or judicial interventions.

12. The Japanese Ministry of International Trade and Industry (MITI) is widely credited with having directed and supported the development of the Japanese

semiconductor and computer industries. In the United States, there have been two essential responses to MITI: (1) an attempt to "neutralize the Japanese government's role" by reinforcing the power of market forces (Finan and LaMond 1985:171), or (2) establish in the United States a counterinstitutional force that could, like MITI, take a lead role in industry redevelopment. But MITI has hardly had to face the more complex problem of restructuring. Its success in growth and development is not necessarily the right formula for redevelopment. Indeed, there is very little evidence on how Japanese society would or could cope with successive waves of corporate restructuring and all that implies in terms of local job loss and poverty (Calder 1988).

13. J. Bell (1987) works through this argument, comparing Weber's principles of bureaucratic behavior with the actions and functions of judges. He finds many similarities and overlaps between these institutions, not least of which is the way actions and decisions are routinized. However, Bell also suggests that judges have a degree of political power, normative and instrumental, unmatched by the average bureaucrat. While this idea is plausible as a characterization of the difference between judges and bureaucrats, it does depend upon an unexamined presumption (implied by Weber) that bureaucrats are simply the instrumental cogs of authority. Anyone familiar with modern agencies and their responsibilities for the formation of policy would, I think, dispute this simplistic characterization.

14. R. H. Davidson (1988) goes to great length to explain to judges how the congressional process works, suggesting that judges are so ignorant of the process that their decisionmaking abilities are compromised, despite the fact that many congressional members and their staff are trained lawyers, often from the same law schools as judges.

15. Considering the issue in more detail, Judge Easterbrook (previously a law professor at the University of Chicago), rather than seeking out the intent of a statute would "look at the statutory structure and hear the words as they would sound in the mind of a skilled, objectively reasonable user of words. Words appeal to the reasonable man of tort law; private language and subjective intents should be put aside" (p. 65). Although L. Tribe (1988) says that the language of a statute ought to control its interpretation, he also observes that in any dispute over the meaning of a statute there is a choice of which words to assign priority to just as there are "background presuppositions" that guide interpreters' use of language in making arguments about meaning.

16. Forum shopping can be generally defined as a litigant's attempt "to have his action tried in a particular court or jurisdiction where he feels he will receive the most favorable judgment or verdict" (quoted from *Black's Law Dictionary* in Note 1990b:1677). I do not mean to suggest that forum shopping can be altogether avoided. There are good reasons for believing that law is not the ideal of rule-based adjudication to which many would still cling. As the Note suggests, "forum shopping exposes the tension between the ideal of the rule of law and the reality of the system created and administered by human beings" (1990b:1686). On the other hand, for equity reasons alone, we should hope that no one group of workers is so disadvantaged by reason of their judicial location (or employers advantaged by their location) that their case would receive different consideration according

to the court in which their case was heard. In this case, as in other situations, there would not be a national policy so much as a local policy, conceived and implemented by the courts (compare with Rabkin 1985).

Chapter 8. Ethics and the Strategies of Subversion

1. See also O. Williamson (1985) on corporate greed as it concerns issues of moral hazard and R. Roll (1988) on management hubris as it concerns executives' motivations for initiating corporate mergers and acquisitions.

2. A great deal of cultural-cum-social criticism is ethical in nature. Despite the denials and evasions of a generation of social theorists, social criticism is fundamentally about how we ought to live. Thus criticism of the gender orientation, racial prejudices, and class biases of social analysis are about how social analysis ought to be conducted given the relationships that condition or prescribe how analysts view the world from their particular vantage points. Implied by this kind of criticism is a notion that social analysis should be fair to those somehow maligned or excluded from social decisionmaking (see Booth 1988 for a useful discussion of these issues in the context of literacy criticism).

3. It is also possible, as suggested by H. A. Vesser (1989), that every act of criticism and argument is so related to the object of critique that there is a necessary interpenetration of the one with the other. Just as critics of economistic notions of ethics argue against the simplistic measurement of morality by costs and benefits, it is practically necessary for critics to use the language of their enemy to demonstrate the limits of that approach. The only alternative to complicity is to invoke a completely different model, a different language of ethical judgment. Yet if virtuous in intent, even that strategy is given strength by the terms of its opponent.

4. Methodologically speaking, my approach to ethical analysis is a weak version of realism. There are some theorists (like Brink 1989) who argue that there are facts of an ethical nature which transcend circumstances and thus provide a datum point for evaluating social actions, expectations, and judgments independently of agents' motivations and intentions. Inevitably, such theories have a strong thread of natural logic, suggesting an ethical theory that is at once about human nature but abstracted from human interests. My weak theory, in contrast, is more skeptical of the relevance of such ethical theories for action and evaluation. It recognizes that ethical judgments are very much contingent and contextual. This may appear as another form of simple relativism (which it is in some ways), but it does recognize something that strong realism cannot—the historical, institutional, and cultural evolution of our theories of meaning and value (see especially Taylor 1989).

5. Sissela Bok (1984:5–9), like K. L. Scheppele, emphasized that the distinguishing of secret-keeping is its "intentional concealment" of information from another party. She goes on to note that secrecy "denotes the methods used to conceal, such as codes or disguises or camouflage" (p. 6). Bok also suggested that those who would suggest that all secrets are in some sense unethical or inherently valuable makes too much about a common human trait. She prefers to treat secrets in general in a neutral manner, allowing the context of intentional concealment to help determine the significance of a secret.

6. T. Nagel (1986:176) defined the deontological perspective as that concerning the "personal demands governing one's relations with others." Nagel recognizes that deontological constraints on how people should act in relation to one another often include "restrictions against lying and betrayal" and "restrictions against imposing certain sacrifices on someone simply as means to an end." Nagel would have it that deontological constraints are in some sense obscure and puzzling. Yet other philosophers like Carol Gilligan (1982) would (presumably) protest this characterization, suggesting that deontological considerations reflect upon essential moral norms held by and promoted by women (if not men). Notwithstanding the apparent intellectual association between deontological reasoning and feminist moral thought, I would argue that deontological reasoning is in fact very common among men and women and that its persistence reflects more upon the limited nature of mainstream philosophical thought than on social reasoning.

7. It is contended by some critics of consequentialism that it would (or could be used to) condone acts of violence and barbarism all in the name of achieving the best possible outcomes for society. So-called thought experiments that demonstrate the plausibility of sacrificing the life or well-being of a person or persons for the overall good of society are taken to be indicative of possible real policies that are not so far removed from reality. By this logic it is a short step to the tyranny of the majority, even various forms of totalitarianism (see Nagel 1986).

8. Implied by this suggestion is the existence of social rules for individual behavior which are designed so as to ensure that desired outcomes are collectively achieved. This is certainly plausible as an abstract philosophical tool; it provides a mechanism for structuring otherwise unorganized actions. But it does make some ambitious assumptions about rule recognition, rule meaning, and rule-following behavior (see Pettit 1990). For instance, it requires individuals to not only identify the right rule in the right circumstances but also to understand his/her rule-oriented actions in relation to community standards. I think legitimate doubts can be raised about the integrity (or coherence) of community standards, just as doubts could be raised about the likelihood that individuals would willingly observe those standards given rather different interests. After all, this is the problem here—individuals (company executives) who subvert community standards as represented by laws and regulations.

9. As H. Putnam (1983:226) observed, there are "many versions [of the world]; the standards of rightness that determine what is right and what is wrong are corrigible, relative to the task and technique."

10. Ironically, social scientists' claims of neutrality could be seen as fundamentally an ethical claim: it promotes a mode of analysis as being correct, it invokes standards of veracity (empirical tests), and prescribes certain rules for the proper conduct of social analysis just as it denies the utility of alternative rules of social analysis. If ethics as a field of inquiry is scorned by some social scientists as being political, there are clearly grounds to suggest that ethics is about proper methodology—an issue that goes to the very heart of scientific enquiry (Brink 1989).

11. Susan Hurley (1985) makes a slightly different distinction, suggesting that *centralist* ethical theories assign notions such as "the right" and "the ought" independent status, and more specific concepts such as "just" and "unkind" a sub-

sidiary status. On the other hand, other kinds of ethical theories (described by Hurley as noncentralist coherence theories) begin with the specific ethical notions and use these to understand and inform the general concepts. The aim of this latter group of theorists (especially McDowell) is to avoid reductionism.

12. There is a real danger that membership of a union may suspect its leaders of being implicated in the relevant company's actions. This may or may not be a rational suspicion; it references a broader realization that union leaders make secret deals with companies for all kinds of reasons. Indeed, a union's membership may well expect that such dealmaking is a *necessary* reality of modern life if members' interests are to be protected. However, instances of graft and corruption among certain leaders and in certain unions tend to lend credence to suspicions that secret dealmaking is not always in the interests of the membership. An unfortunate example of this possibility is to be found in a suit brought by a small group of Steelworkers against some USWA regional directors and the president of the union, and the USX Company charging a conspiracy existed whereby certain union officials were given generous company retirement pensions in return for negotiating a limited plant-closing pension scheme for a southern plant.

13. This idea, the inadequacy of ethics as a field of systematic study, is shared by some moral philosophers as well as many social scientists (see Sayre-McCord 1988).

Chapter 9. Status of Corporations' Social Obligations

1. See S. Roach's (1990) discussion of the relationship between restructuring and labor productivity. Although he suggests that this relationship is a positive one, arguing that restructuring enables higher labor productivity, it is a difficult relationship to prove, especially in the context of changes of ownership through LBOs and the like.

2. In G. L. Clark et al. (1986, chap. 3) we showed analytically, and illustrated empirically, that internal financial liquidity is an important determinant of the levels of output and rates of capital investment. Although that analysis was for industry and regional units (assuming, for example, that a time-series equation for fabricated metals in Illinois is a fair proxy for individual firm behavior in that industry and region), it is apparent that internal liquidity has been one of the most important sources for capital investment in the United States.

3. It is not meant to be implied here that flexible manufacturing is the only new technological configuration that companies seeking higher labor productivity have tried. In fact, in many basic industries the new technology of production has been not so much flexible in the sense described by M. Piore and C. Sabel (1984) so much as highly automated and computer controlled, thereby cutting labor requirements enormously but nevertheless requiring very skilled and specialized labor. M. Gertler (1988) provides a salutary critique of the meaning and applicability of flexibility.

4. Some economic theories of the firm still assume this is the case (see Putterman 1986 for a useful compilation of the classics in this field of study).

5. The now-popular notion that a heavily indebted, specialized company run

and owned by its managers is a better performer than conglomerates suggests that, at least in some quarters of corporate strategy planning, the ultimate objective of corporate management is once again to operate individual units efficiently. Whether or not these leveraged companies will survive the real interest rates and dampened demand conditions of the 1990s remains to be seen (Asquith et al. 1991). The spectacular collapse of some of the most ballyhooed LBOs over the last few years is an indication of the fragility of many of the LBOs (compare with Stern and Chew 1986).

6. This is a common accusation leveled at American corporate executives (see Reich 1983). There is no doubt that it is correct, at least in a narrow sense—because executives receive compensation on a yearly or even a quarterly basis, there are great incentives to maximize short-run returns. *But*, this is only one part of the story because many corporations plan over quite long periods of time to achieve those goals. S. Roach (1988) provides evidence related to the most recent peak in U.S. manufacturing activity to back this claim.

7. For the sake of clarity, I assume that labor is represented by a union and thus has a formal contract with the corporation. This may not be the case, although in the sectors considered in this book it would be most likely. In any event, it may not matter that much for the analysis whether labor has an explicit contract covered by the NLRA or has prerogatives and rights of employment protected and defined in state-based contract law, the effect may be much the same—there are explicit or customary rules that define the relationship between labor and capital (see Clark 1989a, chap. 11).

8. So far, I have not considered in any detail the objectives or motives of unions in seeking higher wages and benefits. Abstractly, it is easy enough to imagine that union officials are motivated just as corporate executives are motivated, that is, by compensation levels, reputation, and power. This would suggest that there is a positive and proportionate relationship between negotiated wages and benefits and union officials' compensation. However, this kind of model is hardly adequate, given the many other issues that intrude into any analysis of union officials' objectives. We could add, for example, idealism, political commitment, and class position as relevant factors. These factors could be used, though, to "explain" unions' interests in increasing wages and benefits (see Clark 1989a, chap. 1).

9. The distinction so described may not be as obvious as I would imagine it to be. D. Gauthier (1986:167), making an analogous distinction, notes "an individual strategy is rational if and only if it maximizes one's utility given the *strategies* adopted by the other persons; a joint strategy is rational only if (but not if and only if) it maximizes one's utility given the *utilities* afforded to the other persons." In my terms, strategic alliances enable individuals the pursuit of their own interests exclusively, whereas a shared enterprise is essential to a joint strategy.

10. At issue here is the substantive strength of managers' property rights (acting as the agents of owners) in the context of other social issues. It must be realized that, in the United States at least, property rights are rarely held to have an *a priori* claim to fundamental respect or protection—claims of privilege via property rights are handled in a procedural manner, balancing those claims against other interests. See G. L. Clark (1990) for an assessment of the relative power of

property rights in the context of workers' claims for union representation wherein it is argued that the circumstances of a case, the decision rule used by the judiciary in balancing interests, and the options for achieving interests by other means all play a role in determining the power of property rights. But also see *Lucas v. South Carolina Coastal Council* (1992).

Bibliography

Cases Cited

Alexander v. Gardner-Denver Co., 415 U.S. 36 (1974).

Alman v. Danin, 801 F.2d 1 (1st Cir. 1986).

Amaro v. Continental Can Co., 724 F.2d 747 (9th Cir. 1984).

Barrowclough v. Kidder, Peabody & Co., 752 F.2d 923 (3d Cir. 1985); *cert. denied* 106 S.Ct. 863 (1986).

Chateaugay Corp. v. Farragher et al., 838 F.2d 59 (2d Cir. 1988).

In re Chateaugay Corp., 922 F.2d 86 (2d Cir. 1990).

Chateaugay Corp. v. Pension Benefit Guar. Corp., 126 B.R. 165 (Bankr. S.N.Y. 1991).

In re Consolidated Litigation Concerning Navistar's Disposition of Wisconsin Steel, No. *5-C-3251 (1987).

Cross v. NLRB, 174 F.2d 875 (1949).

Cuyamaca Meats v. San Diego & Imperial Counties Butchers' and Food Employers' Pension Trust Fund, 827 F.2d 491 (9th Cir. 1987).

Delgrasso et al. v. Spang and Co., 769 F.2d 928 (3d Cir. 1985), *denied in part*, 701 F.2d 1238 (1983).

Dorn's Transp. v. Teamsters Pension Trust Fund, 787 F.2d 897 (3d Cir. 1986).

Firestone Tire and Rubber Co. v. Pension Benefit Guar. Corp., No. 863306-OG (December 1, 1988).

Flying Tiger Line v. Teamsters Pension Trust Fund, 830 F.2d 1241 (3d Cir. 1987).

Gavalik v. Continental Can Co., Nos. 81-1519 and 82-1995 (W.D. Pa. Sept. 9, 1985), *rev'd*, 812 F.2d 834 (3d Cir. 1987), *cert. denied*, 108 S.Ct. 495 (1987).

General Motors Corp., 81 NLRB 779 (1949).

Graphic Communication Workers Local 680 v. Nabisco Brands, No. 862648 (7th Cir. 1987).

Inland Steel, 77 NLRB No. 1 (1947); Inland Steel v. NLRB, 170 F.2d 247 (1948), *cert. denied*, 336 U.S. 960 (1949).

Jones & Laughlin Hourly Pension Plan v. LTV Corp., 824 F.2d 197 (2d Cir. 1987).

Kross v. Western Electric Co., 534 F. Supp. 251 (1982), *aff'd in part, denied in part*, 701 F.2d 1238 (1983).

D. H. Lucas v. South Carolina Coastal Council, *rev'd and remanded*, 304 S.C. 376, 404 S.E. 2d 895 (1992).

Mason III et al. v. Continental Group, Inc., 569 F. Supp. 1241 (1983), *aff'd*, 763 F.2d 1219 (1985), *cert. denied*, 106 S.Ct. 863 (1986).

McClendon v. Continental Group, Inc., 602 F. Supp. 1492 (D.N.J. 1985), 7 EBC 2403 (1986).

Milwaukee Spring Division of Illinois Coil Spring Co. (Milwaukee Spring I), 265 NLRB 206 (1982), *remanded*, 718 F.2d 1102 (CA 7, 1983).

Milwaukee Spring Division of Illinois Coil Spring Co. (Milwaukee Spring II), 268 NLRB 601 (1984), *enforced*, 765 F.2d 175 (D.C. Cir. 1985).

Nachman v. PBGC, 446 U.S. 359 (1980).

Nemeth et al. v. Clark Equipment Co., 677 F. Supp. 899 (W.D. Mich. 1987).

NLRB v. Bildisco and Bildisco, 465 U.S. 513 (1983).

Otis Elevator, a Wholly Owned Subsidiary of United Technologies (Otis Elevator II), 269 NLRB 891 (1984).

Pacific Coast Association v. NLRB, 304 F.2d 760 (1962).

Parker et al. v. Connors Steel Co., No. 87-7607 (11th Cir. 1988).

Payan et al. v. Continental Can Co. No. 85-4287-LEW (1987).

Pension Benefit Guar. Corp. v. Envirodyne Industries, Inc., et al., 10 E.B.C. 1458 (1988).

Pension Benefit Guar. Corp. v. LTV Corp., 122 F.R.D. 436 (S.D.N.Y. 1988).

Pension Ben. Guar. Corp. v. LTV Corp. et al., 875 F.2d 1008 (2d Cir. 1989), *rev'd and remanded*, 110 S.Ct. 2668 (1990).

Pilot Life Insurance Co. v. Dedeaux, No. 85-1043 U.S. (1987).

Roll Coater, Inc. v. Reilly, 932 F.2d 668 (7th Gr. 1991).

Schaefer v. First National Bank of Lincolnwood, 509 F.2d 1287, 1297 (7th Cir. 1975).

Titsch v. Reliance Group, Inc., 548 F. Supp. 983 (1982).

United States v. Tabor Court Realty Corp., 803 F.2d 1288 (3d Cir. 1986).

Watkinson v. Great Atlantic & Pacific Tea Co., 585 F. Supp. 879 (1984).

West v. Butler, 621 F.2d 240 (6th Cir. 1980).

Wheeling-Pittsburgh Steel v. United Steelworkers, 791 F.2d 1074 (3d Cir. 1986).

William J. Kross v. Western Electric Co., 534 F. Supp. 251 (1982), *aff'd in part.*

Wilson v. Garcia, 471 U.S. 261 (1985).

In re Wisconsin Steel Co. v. International Harvester Co., 48 B.R. 753 (D.C. 1985).

In re Consolidated Litigation Concerning International Harvester's Disposition of Wisconsin Steel, 666 F. Supp. 1148 (1987); 681 F. Supp. 512 (N.D. Ill. 1988).

Zipf v. American Telephone and Telegraph Co., 799 F.2d 889 (3d Cir. 1986).

Secondary Sources

Aaron, H. J., B. P. Bosworth, and G. Burtless. 1989. *Can America Afford to Grow Old? Paying for Social Security*. Washington, D.C.: Brookings Institution.

Aglietta, M. 1979. *A Theory of Capitalist Regulation: The U.S. Experience*. London: New Left Books.

American Academy of Actuaries. 1992. *Preliminary Report. Results of AAA Survey of Defined Benefit Plan Terminations*. Washington, D.C.

American Law Institute. 1988. *Principles of Corporate Governance: Analysis and Recommendations*. Tentative Draft No. 8. Philadelphia.

Andrews, E. 1985. *The Changing Profile of Pensions in America*. Washington, D.C.: Employee Benefit Research Institute.

Arrington, R. L. 1989. *Rationalism, Realism, and Relativism: Perspectives in Contemporary Moral Epistemology*. Ithaca, N.Y.: Cornell University Press.

Arrow, K. 1985. The economics of agency. In *Principals and Agents: The Structure of Business*, edited by J. Pratt and R. Zeckhauser, pp. 37–51. Boston: Harvard Business School Press.

Asquith, P., R. Gertner, and D. Scharfstein. 1991. Anatomy of financial distress: An examination of junk-bond issuers. Working Paper No. 3942. Cambridge: National Bureau of Economic Research.

Atiyah, P. S. 1981. Review of *Contract as Promise*, by Charles Fried. *Harvard Law Review* 95:509–28.

———. 1983. *Law and Modern Societies*. Oxford: Oxford University Press.

Auerbach, A. J., and D. Reishus. 1988. The impact of taxation on mergers and acquisitions. In *Mergers and Acquisitions*, edited by A. J. Auerbach, pp. 69–86. Chicago: University of Chicago Press.

Baird, D. 1987. Loss distribution, forum shopping, and bankruptcy: A reply to Warren. *University of Chicago Law Review* 54:815–34.

Baker J. B. 1989. Identifying cartel policing under uncertainty: The U.S. steel industry, 1933–1939. *Journal of Law Economics* 32:547–76.

Barber, B. R. 1989. Liberal democracy and the costs of consent. In *Liberalism and the Moral Life*, edited by N. Rosenblum, pp. 54–98. Cambridge: Harvard University Press.

Barnett, R. E. 1987. Forward: Judicial conservatism v. a principled judicial activism. *Harvard Journal of Law and Public Policy* 10:273–94.

Baumol, W., J. Panzor, R. Willig, and others. 1988. *Contestable Markets and the Theory of Industry Structure*. 2d ed. New York: Harcourt Brace Jovanovich.

Beard, C. 1935. *An Economic Interpretation of the Constitution of the United States*. New York: Norton.

Bebchuk L. A. 1988. A new approach to corporate reorganizations. *Harvard Law Review* 101:775–804.

Bebchuk, L. A., ed. 1990. *Corporate Law and Economic Analysis*. New York: Cambridge University Press.

Bell, J. 1987. The judge as bureaucrat. In *Oxford Essays in Jurisprudence. Third Series*, edited by J. Eekelaar and J. Bell, pp. 33–56. Oxford: Clarendon Press.

Bensman, D., and R. Lynch. 1987. *Rusted Dreams: Hard Times in a Steel Community*. Berkeley: University of California Press.

Birch, D. 1979. *The Job Generation Process*. Cambridge: MIT Program on Neighborhood and Regional Change.

Bluestone, B., and B. Harrison. 1982. *The Deindustrialization of America: Plant Closings, Community Abandonment, and the Dismantling of Basic Industry*. New York: Basic Books.

Boden, L. I., and C. A. Jones. 1987. Occupational disease remedies: The asbestos experience. In *Public Regulation: New Perspectives on Institutions and Policies*, edited by E. Bailey, pp. 321–46. Cambridge: MIT Press.

Bodie, Z. 1990. Pensions as retirement income insurance. *Journal of Economic Literature* 28:28–49.

———. 1992. Is the PBGC the FSLIC of the nineties? *Contingencies* (March/April): 34–38.

Bodie, Z., and R. C. Merton. 1992. Pension benefit guarantees in the United States: A functional analysis. Paper presented to Symposium on the Future of Pensions in the United States. Philadelphia: Pension Research Council, Wharton School, University of Pennsylvania.

Bodie, Z., and A. H. Munnell, eds. 1992. *Pensions and the Economy: Sources, Uses, and Limitations of Data.* Philadelphia: Pension Research Council and the University of Pennsylvania Press.

Bok, S. 1984. *Secrets: On the Ethics of Concealment.* Oxford: Oxford University Press.

Booth, W. C. 1988. *The Company We Keep: An Ethics of Fiction.* Berkeley: University of California Press.

Borts, G., and J. Stein. 1964. *Economic Growth in a Free Market.* New York: Columbia University Press.

Bowles, S., D. Gordon, and T. Weisskopf. 1983. *Beyond the Wasteland: A Democratic Alternative to Economic Decline.* New York: Doubleday/Anchor Press.

Boyer, R. 1988. *La theorie de la regulation: Une analyse critique.* Paris: La Decouvert.

Braithwaite, J. 1989. *Crime, Shame, and Integration.* Cambridge: Cambridge University Press.

Braithwaite, J., and P. Pettit. 1990. *Not Just Deserts: A Republican Theory of Criminal Justice.* Cambridge: Cambridge University Press.

Brandt, R. 1983. The concept of rational action. *Social Theory and Practice* 9:143–64.

Bratman, M. 1987. *Intention, Plans, and Practical Reason.* Cambridge: Harvard University Press.

Bremner, G. 1983. *Order and Chance: The Pattern of Diderot's Thought.* Cambridge: Cambridge University Press.

Breyer, S. 1982. *Regulation and Its Reform.* Cambridge: Harvard University Press.

Brink, D. O. 1989. *Moral Realism and the Foundations of Ethics.* Cambridge: Cambridge University Press.

Brown, J. M. 1987. On applying ethics. In *Moral Philosophy and Contemporary Problems,* edited by J. D. G. Evans, pp. 81–94. Cambridge: Cambridge University Press.

Bureau of National Affairs, ed. 1974. Highlights of the new pension reform law. *Labor Relations Reporter* 87(1). Washington, D.C.

Calabresi, G. 1968. Transaction costs, resource allocation, and liability rules—a comment. *Journal of Law and Economics* 11:67–73.

———. 1970. *The Costs of Accidents. A Legal and Economic Analysis.* New Haven: Yale University Press.

———. 1982. *A Common Law for the Age of Statutes.* Cambridge: Harvard University Press.

Calder, K. 1988. *Crisis and Compensation: Public Policy and Political Stability in Japan, 1949–1986.* Princeton: Princeton University Press.

Calleo, D. P. 1992. *The Bankrupting of Ameria: How the Federal Budget Is Impoverishing the Nation.* New York: Morrow and Co.

Caplan, L. 1987. *The Tenth Justice: The Solicitor General and the Rule of Law.* New York: Knopf.

Carlton, D., and R. Gertner. 1989. Market power and mergers in durable-good industries. *Journal of Law Economics* 32:S203–26.

Chandler, A. 1990. *Scale and Scope: The Dynamics of Industrial Capitalism.* Cambridge: Harvard University Press.

Clark, G. L. 1983. *Interregional Migration, Social Justice, and National Policy.* Totowa, N.J.: Rowman and Allanheld.

———. 1985. *Judges and the Cities: Interpreting Local Autonomy.* Chicago: University of Chicago Press.

———. 1986. The crisis of the midwest auto industry. In *Production, Work, Territory*, edited by M. Storper and A. Scott, pp. 124–48.

———. 1988. Corporate restructuring in the U.S. steel industry: Adjustment strategies and local labor relations. In *America's New Market Geography*, edited by G. Sternlieb and J. Hughes, pp. 179–214. New Brunswick, N.J.: Center for Urban Policy Research, Rutgers University.

———. 1989a. *Unions and Communities under Siege: American Communities and the Crisis of Organised Labour.* Cambridge: Cambridge University Press.

———. 1989b. Commentary. Remaking the map of corporate capitalism: The arbitrage economy of the 1990s. *Environment and Planning A* 21:997–1000.

———. 1990. Virtues of location: Do property rights trump workers' rights to self-organization? *Environment and Planning D: Society and Space* 8:53–72.

———. 1993. Costs and prices, corporate competitive strategies and regions. *Environment and Planning A* 25:5–26.

Clark, G. L., and B. Fischer. 1987. An assessment of the cooperative partnership between the United States Steelworkers and National Steel, Report of Grant 85-PA/P-004 of the Federal Mediation and Conciliation Service. Pittsburgh, Center for Labor Studies, Carnegie Mellon University.

Clark, G. L., and M. Dear. 1984. *State Apparatus: Structures and Language of Legitimacy.* Winchester, Mass., and London: Unwin Hyman.

Clark, G. L., M. S. Gertler, and J. Whiteman. 1986. *Regional Dynamics: Studies in Adjustment Theory.* London and Winchester, Mass.: Unwin Hyman.

Clark, R. C. 1981. The interdisciplinary study of legal evolution. *Yale Law Journal* 90:1238–74.

Coase, R. 1960. The problem of social cost. *Journal of Law and Economics* 3:1–40.

Coffee, J. C. 1988. Shareholders versus managers: The strain in the corporate web. In *Knights, Raiders, and Targets*, edited by Coffee, Lowenstein, and Rose-Ackerman, pp. 77–134.

Coffee, J. C., L. Lowenstein, and S. Rose-Ackerman, eds. 1988. *Knights, Raiders, and Targets: The Impact of the Hostile Takeover.* New York: Oxford University Press.

Coleman, J. S. 1974. *Power and the Structure of Society.* New York: Norton.

———. 1986. *Individual Interests and Collective Action.* Cambridge: Cambridge University Press.

Collingsworth, T. 1988. ERISA Section 510—a further limitation on arbitrary discharges. *Industrial Relations Law Journal* 10:319–49.

Cowans D. R. 1978. *Bankruptcy Law and Practice*. 2d ed. St. Paul. Minn.: West.

Crandall R. W. 1989. Review of *The Decline of American Steel* by P. Tiffany. *Journal of Economic Literature* 27:1201–2.

Craypo, C. 1985. Experiences from the deindustrialization of a factory town. In *Economic Dislocation and Job Loss*, edited by B. Lall, pp. 57–66. Ithaca: New York State School of Industrial and Labor Relations, Cornell University.

Cyert, R., and D. Mowery, eds. 1988. *Technology and Employment Change in the U.S. Economy*. Washington, D.C.: National Academy of Science.

Daly, M., and M. I. Logan. 1989. *The Brittle Rim*. Sydney: Penguin.

Davidson, R. H. 1988. What judges ought to make about lawmaking in Congress. In *Judges and Legislators: Toward Institutional Comity*, edited by R. A. Katzmann, pp. 90–116. Washington, D.C.: Brookings Institution.

Delfico, J. F. 1991. *Defined Benefit Pensions: Hidden Liabilities from Underfunded Plans and Potential New Obligations Confront PBGC*. GAO/T-HRD-92-6. Washington, D.C.

Derrida, J. 1986. *Memories for Paul de Man*. New York: Columbia University Press.

Dicey, A. V. 1959. [1885] *An Introduction to the Study of the Law of the Constitution*. 10th ed. Introduction by E. C. S. Wade. London: Macmillan.

Donohue, J. J. 1989. Book review: The law and economics of tort law: The profound revolution. *Harvard Law Review* 102:1047–73.

Drache, D., and M. Gertler, eds. 1991. *The New Era of Global Competition: State Policy and Market Power*. Montreal and Kingston: McGill-Queen's University Press.

Drache, D., and H. Glasbeek. 1989. The new fordism in Canada: Capital's offensive, labor's opportunity. *Osgoode Hall Law Journal* 27:517–60.

Drucker, P. 1988. Management and the world's work. *Harvard Business Review* 88(5):65–76.

Dunlop, J. 1944. *Wage Determination under Trade Unions*. New York: Augustus Kelley.

———. 1987. The legal framework of industrial relations and the economic future of the United States. In *American Labor Policy*, edited by C. Morris, pp. 1–15. Washington, D.C.: Bureau of National Affairs.

Dworkin, R. 1978. *Taking Rights Seriously*. Cambridge: Harvard University Press.

———. 1980. Why efficiency? A response to Professors Calabresi and Posner. *Hofstra Law Review* 8:563–90.

———. 1985. *A Matter of Principle*. Cambridge: Harvard University Press.

———. 1986. *Law's Empire*. Cambridge: Harvard University Press.

Eagleton T. 1989. *The Ideology of the Aesthetic*. Oxford: Blackwell.

Easterbrook, F. 1988. The role of original intent in statutory construction. *Harvard Journal of Law and Public Policy* 11:59–66.

Ehrenberg, R., and G. H. Jakubson. 1988. *Advance Notice Provisions in Plant Closing Legislation*. Kalamazoo, Mich.: W. E. Upjohn Institute.

Eisenberg, M. A. 1988. *The Nature of the Common Law*. Cambridge: Harvard University Press.

Elster, J. 1989. *Nuts and Bolts for the Social Sciences*. Cambridge: Cambridge University Press.
———. 1990. *The Cement of Society*. Cambridge: Cambridge University Press.
Ely, J. H. 1980. *Democracy and Distrust: A Theory of Judicial Review*. Cambridge: Harvard University Press.
Estreicher, S., and R. L. Revesz. 1989. Nonacquiescence by federal administrative agencies. *Yale Law Journal* 98:679–772.
Fields, G. S., and O. Mitchell. 1984. *Retirement, Pensions, and Social Security*. Cambridge: MIT Press.
Finan, W. F., and A. LaMond. 1985. Sustaining U.S. competitiveness in micro-electronics: The challenges to U.S. policy. In *U.S. Competitiveness in the World Economy*, edited by B. Scott and G. C. Lodge, pp. 144–75. Boston: Harvard Business School Press.
Fisher, F, J. McGowan, and J. Greenwood. 1983. *Folded, Spindled, and Mutilated: Economic Analysis and U.S. v. IBM*. Cambridge: MIT Press.
Ford, W. Rep. 1985. The case for federal plant closing legislation. In *Economic Dislocation and Job Loss*, edited by B. Lall, pp. 114–21. Ithaca: New York State School of Industrial and Labor Relations, Cornell University.
Freedman, J. O. 1978. *Crisis and Legitimacy: The Administrative Process and American Government*. Cambridge: Cambridge University Press.
Freeman, R. 1985. Unions, pensions, and union pension funds. In *Pensions, Labor and Individual Choice*, edited by D. Wise, pp. 89–122. Chicago: University of Chicago Press.
Fried, C. 1981. *Contract as Promise: A Theory of Contractual Obligation*. Cambridge: Harvard University Press.
———. 1991. *Order and Law. Arguing the Reagan Revolution—A Firsthand Account*. New York: Simon and Schuster.
Friedman, B. 1988. *Day of Reckoning: The Consequences of American Economic Policy under Reagan and After*. New York: Random House.
Frug, G. 1984. The ideology of bureaucracy in American law. *Harvard Law Review* 97:1276–1388.
Gauthier, D. 1986. *Morals by Agreement*. Oxford: Clarendon Press.
General Accounting Office (GAO). 1986a. *Pension Plans. Government Data on Terminations with Excess Assets Should be Improved*. GAO/HRD-87-19. Washington, D.C.: USGPO.
———. 1986b. *Pensions. Plans with Unfunded Benefits*. GAO/HRD-87-15BR. Washington, D.C.: USGPO.
———. 1987a. *Pension Plans. Vesting Status of Participants in Selected Small Plans*. GAO/HRD-88-31. Washington, D.C.: USGPO.
———. 1987b. *Pension Plans. Government Insurance Program Threatened by its Growing Deficit*. GAO/HRD-87-42. Washington, D.C.: USGPO.
———. 1987c. *Pension Plans. Possible Effects of Requiring Employers to Make Contributions Sooner*. GAO/HRD-88-28. Washington, D.C.: USGPO.
———. 1988a. *Social Security Funds. Additional Measures Could More Fully Indicate the System's Financial Condition*. GAO/PEMD-88-11. Washington, D.C.: USGPO.

———. 1988b. *Pension Plans. Effect of the 1987 Stock Market Decline on Selected Large Plans*. GAO/HRD-88-128BR. Washington, D.C.: USGPO.

———. 1988c. *Department of Labor. Pension Plans and Corporate Takeovers*. GAO/HRD-88-58. Washington, D.C.: USGPO.

———. 1988d. *Securities Regulation. Hostile Corporate Takeovers: Synopses of Thirty-two Attempts*. GAO/GGD-88-48FS. Washington, D.C.: USGPO.

———. 1988e. *Financial Markets. Issuers, Purchasers, and purposes of High Yield, Noninvestment Grade Bonds*. GAO/GGD-88-55FS. Washington, D.C.: USGPO.

———. 1988f. *High Yield Bonds. Nature of the Market and Effect on Federally Insured Institutions*. GAO/GGD-88-75. Washington, D.C.: USGPO.

———. 1988g. *Pension Plans and Corporate Takeovers*. GAO/HRD-88-48. Washington, D.C.: USGPO.

———. 1989a. *Social Security. The Trust Fund Reserve Accumulation, the Economy and the Federal Budget*. GAO/HRD-89-44. Washington, D.C.: USGPO.

———. 1989b. *Pension Plans. Labor and IRS Enforcement of the Employee Retirement Income Security Act*. GAO/HRD-89-32. Washington, D.C.: USGPO.

———. 1989c. *Pension Plan Participation in Leveraged Buy-out Funds*. GAO/T-HRD-89-5. Washington, D.C.: USGPO.

———. 1991a. *Effect of Bankruptcy on Retiree Health Benefits*. GAO/HRD-91-115. Washington, D.C.: USGPO.

———. 1991b. *Pension Plans: IRS Needs to Strengthen its Enforcement Program*. GAO/T-HRD-91-10. Washington, D.C.: USGPO.

———. 1992a. *Pension Benefit Guaranty Corporation's 1991 and 1990 Financial Statements*. GAO/AFMD-92-35. Washington, D.C.: USGPO.

———. 1992b. *Improved Plan Reporting and CPA Audits Can Increase Protection under ERISA*. GAO/AFMD-92-14. Washington, D.C.: USGPO.

Gertler, M. 1988. The limits to flexibility: Comments on the Post-Fordist vision of production and its geography. *Transactions, Institute of British Geographers*, n.s. 13, 419–32.

Gibbard, A. 1983. A noncognitivistic analysis of rationality in action. *Social Theory and Practice* 9:199–221.

Gilligan, C. 1982. *In a Different Voice*. Cambridge: Harvard University Press.

Goldfield, M. 1987. *The Decline of Organized Labor in the United States*. Chicago: University of Chicago Press.

Goodrich, P. 1986. *Reading the Law: A Critical Introduction to Legal Method and Techniques*. Oxford: Blackwell.

Gordon, J. S. 1990. Ties that bond: Dual class common stock and the problem of shareholder choice. In *Corporate Law and Economic Analysis*, edited by Bebchuk, pp. 74–117.

Gordon, R. 1984. Critical legal histories. *Stanford Law Review* 36:57–126.

Graham, J., K. Gibson, R. Horvath, and D. Shakow. 1988. Restructuring in U.S. manufacturing: The decline of monopoly capitalism. *Annals, Association of American Geographers* 78:473–90.

Green, J. 1985. The riskiness of private pensions. In *Pensions, Labor, and Individual Choice*, edited by D. Wise, pp. 357–78. Chicago: University of Chicago Press.

Green, M. 1990. *Mergers and Acquisitions: Geographical and Sectoral Perspectives*. London: Routledge.

Grunwald, J., and K. Flamm, eds. 1985. *The Global Factory: Foreign Assembly in International Trade*. Washington, D.C.: Brookings Institution.

Gustman, A., and T. L. Steinmeier. 1988. An analysis of pension benefit formulas, pension wealth, and incentives from pensions. Working Paper 2535. Cambridge: National Bureau of Economic Research.

Hall, K. 1989. *The Magic Mirror: Law in American History*. New York: Oxford University Press.

Hall, P. 1966. *Von Thunen's Isolated State*, Oxford: Pergamon Press.

Hancher, L., and M. Moran. 1989. Organizing regulatory space. In *Capitalism, Culture, and Economic Regulation*, edited by L. Hancher and M. Moran, pp. 25–39. Oxford: Clarendon Press.

Hardin, R. 1988. *Morality within the Limits of Reason*. Chicago: University of Chicago Press.

Harrigan, K. R., and M. Porter. 1983. End-game strategies for declining industries. *Harvard Business Review* 61:111–20.

Harris, A., ed. 1987. *ERISA. The Law and the Code: 1987 Edition*. Washington, D.C.: Bureau of National Affairs.

Harrison, B. 1993. *The Ties That Bind: Producer Networks, Small Firms and Inequality in the "Age of Flexibility."* New York: Basic Books.

Harrison, B., and B. Bluestone. 1988. *The Great U-Turn*. New York: Basic Books.

Harrison, B., and J. Kluver. 1989. Re-assessing the "Massachusetts miracle": Reindustrialization and balanced growth, or convergence to "Manhattanization"? *Environment and Planning A* 21:771–801.

Harsanyi, J. 1983. Basic moral decisions and alternative concepts of rationality. *Social Theory and Practice* 9:231–44.

Hart, H. L. A. 1961. *The Concept of Law*. Oxford: Clarendon Press.

Hart, O. 1984. Comment. In *Economics and Disarray*, edited by P. Wiles and G. Routh, pp. 184–89. Oxford: Blackwell.

Harvey, D. 1988. The geographical and geopolitical consequences of the transition from Fordist to flexible accumulation. In *America's New Market Geography*, edited by G. Sternlieb and J. Hughes, pp. 101–34. New Brunswick, N.J.: Center for Urban Policy Research, Rutgers University.

Hax, A., and N. Majluf. 1984. *Strategic Management: An Integrative Perspective*. Englewood Cliffs, N.J.: Prentice Hall.

Henderson, B. 1979. *Henderson on Corporate Strategy*. Cambridge, Mass.: Abt Books.

Herz, M. 1992. Judicial textualism meets congressional micromanagement: A potential collision in Clean Air Act interpretation. *Harvard Environmental Law Review* 16:175–205.

Higgott, R., and A. Cooper. 1990. Middle power leadership and coalition building: Australia, the Cairns Group, and the Uruguay Rounds of trade negotiations. *International Organization* 44:589–632.

Hill, R. C., and C. Negrey. 1987. Deindustrialization in the Great Lakes. *Urban Affairs Quarterly* 22:580–97.

Hirsch, B., and J. T. Addison. 1986. *The Economic Analysis of Unions: New Approaches and Evidence*. London: Unwin Hyman.

Hollis, M. 1987. *The Cunning of Reason*. Cambridge: Cambridge University Press.

———. 1990. Moves and motives in the games we play. *Analysis* 50:49–62.

Hook, S. 1974. *Pragmatism and the Tragic Sense of Life*. New York: Basic Books.

Horwitz, M. J. 1992. *The Transformation of American Law, 1870–1960: The Crisis of Legal Orthodoxy*. New York: Oxford University Press.

Hovenkamp, H. 1991. Legal policy and the endowment effect. *Journal of Legal Studies* 20:225–48.

Howland, M. 1988. *Plant Closings and Worker Displacement: The Regional Issues*. Kalamazoo, Mich.: W. E. Upjohn Institute.

Hurley, S. 1985. Objectivity and disagreement. In *Morality and Objectivity: A Tribute to J. L. Mackie*, edited by T. Honderich, pp. 54–97. London: Routledge.

Jackson, T. H. 1986. *The Logic and Limits of Bankruptcy Law*. Cambridge: Harvard University Press.

Jameson, F. 1981. *The Political Unconscious: Narrative as a Socially Symbolic Act*. Ithaca: Cornell University Press.

Kagan, S. 1989. *The Limits of Morality*. Oxford: Clarendon Press.

Kahn, A. E. 1988. *The Economics of Regulation. Principles and Institutions*. Cambridge: MIT Press.

Kelley, M., and B. Harrison. 1990. Innovations in labor-management problem-solving: Do they work without unions? Working Paper 90-18. Pittsburgh: School of Urban and Public Affairs, Carnegie Mellon University .

Kelman, M. 1987. *A Guide to Critical Legal Studies*. Cambridge: Harvard University Press.

Kennedy, D. 1976. Form and substance in private law adjudication. *Harvard Law Review* 89:1685–1778.

Kotlikoff, L., and D. Smith. 1983. *Pensions in the American Economy*. Chicago: University of Chicago Press.

Kronman, A. 1981. A new champion for the will theory: Review of *Contract as Promise*. *Yale Law Journal* 91:404–23.

Kuhn, T. 1970. *The Structure of Scientific Revolutions*. 2d ed. Chicago: University of Chicago Press.

Lasser, W. 1988. *The Limits of Judicial Power: The Supreme Court in America*. Chapel Hill: University of North Carolina Press.

Lawrence, C., and R. Z. Lawrence. 1985. Manufacturing wage dispersion: An endgame interpretation. *Brookings Papers on Economic Activity* 47–106.

Lawrence, R. Z. 1984. *Can America Compete?* Washington, D.C.: Brookings Institution.

Leaver, R. 1989. Restructuring in the global economy: From Pax Americana to Pax Nipponica? *Alternatives* 14:429–62.

Levinson, S. 1991. Book review. Strolling down the path of the law (and toward critical legal studies?): The jurisprudence of Richard Posner. *Columbia Law Review* 91:1221–52.

Lewis, C. M., and R. L. Cooperstein. 1992. Estimating the current exposure of the Pension Benefit Guaranty Corporation to single-employer pension plan terminations. Paper presented to Symposium on the Future of Pensions in the

United States. Philadelphia: Pension Research Council, Wharton School, University of Pennsylvania.

Lichtenberg, F., and M. Kim. 1989. The effects of mergers on prices, costs, and capacity utilization in the U.S. air transportation industry 1970–84. Working Paper No. 3197. Cambridge, Mass.: National Bureau of Economic Research.

Lipietz, A. 1986. Behind the crisis: The exhaustion of a regime of accumulation. A regulation school perspective on some French empirical work. *Review of Radical Political Economics* 18:13–32.

———. 1987. *Mirages and Miracles: The Crisis of Global Fordism.* London: Verso.

Lockhart, J. B. 1992. Comments on pension guarantees in the U.S.: A functional analysis. Paper presented to Symposium on the Future of Pensions in the United States. Philadelphia: Pension Research Council, Wharton School, University of Pennsylvania.

MacCormick, N. 1990. Reconstruction after deconstruction: A response to CLS. *Oxford Journal of Legal Studies* 10:539–58.

McGill, D., with D. S. Grubbs. 1984. *Fundamentals of Private Pensions.* Homewood, Ill.: Richard D. Irwin, Inc.

McKenzie, R. 1981. The case for plant closures. *Policy Review* 15:119–34.

Mair, A., R. Florida, and M. Kenney. 1988. The new geography of automobile production: Japanese transplants in North America. *Economic Geography* 64:352–73.

Markusen, A., and V. Carlson. 1989. Deindustrialization in the American midwest: Causes and responses. In *Deindustrialization and Regional Economic Transformation: The Experience of the United States,* edited by L. Rodwin and H. Sazanami, pp. 29–59. Boston: Unwin Hyman.

Massey, D. 1984. *Spatial Divisions of Labor: Social Structures and the Geography of Production.* London: Macmillan.

Melman, S. 1983. *Profits without Production.* New York: Knopf.

Mikva, A. 1983. How well does Congress support and defend the Constitution? *North Carolina Law Review* 61:587–611.

Morris, C., ed. 1987. *American Labor Policy.* Washington, D.C.: Bureau of National Affairs.

Morris, D. J., P. J. N. Sinclair, M. D. E. Slater, and J. S. Vickers. 1986. Strategic behaviour and industrial competition: An introduction. In *Strategic Behaviour and Industrial Competition,* ed. Morris et al., pp. 1–8. Oxford: Clarendon Press.

Moulaert, F., and E. Swyngedouw. 1989. Survey 15. A regulation approach to the geography of flexible production systems. *Environment and Planning D: Society and Space* 7:327–45.

Mueller, D. 1989. *Public Choice II: A Revised Edition.* Cambridge: Cambridge University Press.

Nagel, T. 1986. *The View from Nowhere.* New York: Oxford University Press.

Northrup, H. R. 1984. The rise and demise of PATCO. *Industrial and Labor Relations Review* 37:167–84.

Note. 1949. Proper subjects for collective bargaining: Ad hoc v. predictive definition. *Yale Law Journal* 58:803–8.

Note. 1987. Mixing politics and justice: The office of the Solicitor General. *Journal of Law and Politics* 4:379–428.

Note. 1990. Forum shopping reconsidered. *Harvard Law Review* 103:1677–96.

Obey, D. 1986. A public economics of growth, equity, and opportunity. In *The Changing American Economy: Papers from the Fortieth Anniversary Symposium of the Joint Economic Committee of the United States Congress*, edited by D. Obey and P. Sarbanes, pp. 8–15. Cambridge, Mass.: Blackwell.

Ohlin, B. 1933. *Interregional and International Trade*. Cambridge: Harvard University Press.

Parfit, D. 1984. *Reasons and Persons*. Oxford: Clarendon Press.

Paulus, J. D., and S. Waite. 1987. Competition, junk, and the merger wave of the 1980s. Special Economic Study. Available from Morgan Stanley and Co., 1251 Avenue of the Americas, New York, N.Y. 10020.

Pension Benefit Guaranty Corporation. 1987. *13th Annual Report to Congress. Fiscal Year 1987*. Washington, D.C.: USGPO.

———. 1991. *Annual Report: Strengthening the Pension Safety Net*. Washington, D.C.: USGPO.

Pettit, P. 1989. Consequentialism and respect for persons. *Ethics* 100:116–26.

———. 1990. The reality of rule-following. *Mind* 99:1–21.

———. 1991. Consequentialism. In *A Companion to Ethics*, edited by P. Singer, pp. 230–40. Oxford: Blackwell.

Piore, M., and C. Sabel. 1984. *The Second Industrial Divide*. New York: Basic Books.

Porter, M. 1980. *Competitive Strategy: Techniques for Analyzing Industries and Competitors*. New York: Free Press.

———. 1984. *Corporate Strategy*. Boston: Harvard Business School Press.

———. 1990. *The Competitive Advantage of Nations*. New York: Free Press.

Posner, R. 1981. *The Economics of Justice*. Cambridge: Harvard University Press.

———. 1986. *The Economic Analysis of Law*. 3d ed. Boston: Little, Brown.

———. 1988. *Law and Literature: A Misunderstood Relation*. Cambridge: Harvard University Press.

Putnam, H. 1983. *Realism and Reason*. Cambridge: Cambridge University Press.

Putterman, L., ed. 1986. *The Economic Nature of the Firm: A Reader*. Cambridge: Cambridge University Press.

Quinn, D. P. 1988. *Restructuring in the Automobile Industry. A Study of Firms and States in Modern Capitalism*. New York: Columbia University Press.

Rabkin, J. 1989. *Judicial Compulsions: How Public Law Distorts Public Policy*. New York: Basic Books.

Ravenscraft, D., and F. M. Scherer. 1987. *Mergers, Sell-offs, and Economic Efficiency*. Washington, D.C.: Brookings Institution.

Rawls, J. 1971. *A Theory of Justice*. Cambridge: Harvard University Press.

Reich, R. 1983. *The Next American Frontier*. New York: New York Times Books.

Richards, D. A. J. 1989. *Foundations of American Constitutionalism*. New York: Oxford University Press.

Rifkin, J., and R. Barber. 1978. *The North Will Rise Again: Pensions, Politics, and Power in the 1980s*. Boston: Beacon Press.

Riker, W. H. 1962. *The Theory of Political Coalitions*. New Haven: Yale University Press.

Roach, S. 1988. Beyond restructuring: America's investment challenge. Special
    Economic Study. New York: Morgan Stanley and Co.
————. 1990. The restructuring of America: Lessons for Eastern Europe. Special
    Economic Study. New York: Morgan Stanley and Co.
Rodwin, L. 1989. Deindustrialization and regional economic transformation. In
    *Deindustrialization and Regional Economic Transformation: The Experience
    of the United States*, edited by L. Rodwin and H. Sazanami, pp. 3–25. Boston:
    Unwin Hyman.
Roll, R. 1988. Empirical evidence on takeover activity and shareholder wealth. In
    Knights, Raiders, and Targets, edited by Coffee, Lowenstein, and Rose-Ack-
    erman, pp. 241–52.
Rose-Ackerman, S. 1991. Risk taking and ruin: Bankruptcy and investment choice.
    Journal of Legal Studies 20:277–310.
Rosen, S. 1985. Comment. In *Pensions, Labor, and Individual Choice*, edited by
    D. Wise, pp. 248–51. Chicago: University of Chicago Press.
Roth, P. 1987. *Meaning and Method in the Social Sciences: a Case for Methodo-
    logical Pluralism*. Ithaca, N.Y.: Cornell University Press.
Rubin, E. 1989. Law and legislation in the administrative state. *Columbia Law
    Review* 89:369–426.
Salamon, L. 1981. Rethinking public management: Third-party government and
    the changing forms of government action. *Public Policy* 29:255–75.
Sanders, E. 1987. The regulatory surge of the 1970s in historical perspective. In
    Public Regulation: New Perspectives on Institutions and Policies, edited by
    E. Bailey, pp. 117–49. Cambridge: MIT Press.
Sayre-McCord, G., ed. 1988. *Essays on Moral Realism*. Ithaca, N.Y.: Cornell
    University Press.
Scheffler, S. 1982. *The Rejection of Consequentialism: A Philosophical Investi-
    gation of the Considerations Underlying Rival Moral Conceptions*. Oxford:
    Clarendon Press.
Scheppele, K. L. 1988. *Legal Secrets: Equality and Efficiency in the Common
    Law*. Chicago: University of Chicago Press.
Scott, A. 1988. *Metropolis: From the Division of Labor to Urban Form*. Berkeley:
    University of California Press.
Scott, A., and E. Kwok. 1989. Inter-firm subcontracting and locational agglom-
    eration: A case study of the printed circuits industry of southern California.
    Regional Studies 23:405–16.
Scott, A., and M. Storper, eds. 1986. *Production, Work, Territory: The Geograph-
    ical Anatomy of Industrial Capitalism*. London and Winchester, Mass.: Unwin
    Hyman.
Searle, J. 1983. *Intentionality: An Essay in the Philosophy of the Mind*. Cam-
    bridge: Cambridge University Press.
Seidenfeld, M. 1992. A civic republican justification for the bureaucratic state.
    Harvard Law Review 105:151–76.
Shleifer, A., and R. Vishny. 1988. Management buyouts as a response to market
    pressure. In *Mergers and Acquisitions*, edited by A. J. Auerbach, pp. 87–102.
    Chicago: University of Chicago Press.

Short, K., and C. Nelson. 1991. *Pensions: Worker Coverage and Retirement Benefits, 1987*. Series P-70, No. 25. Washington, D.C.: U.S. Bureau of the Census.

Shoven, J. B., and J. Waldfogel, eds. 1990. *Debt, Taxes, and Corporate Restructuring*. Washington, D.C.: Brookings Institution.

Shubik, M. 1988. Corporate control, efficient markets, and the public good. In *Knights, Raiders, and Targets*, edited by Coffee, Lowenstein, and Rose-Ackerman, pp. 31–55.

Siebers, T. 1988. *The Ethics of Criticism*. Ithaca, N.Y.: Cornell University Press.

Singer, M. 1989. Value judgments. In *Key Themes in Philosophy*, edited by A. P. Griffiths, pp. 145–72. Cambridge: Cambridge University Press.

Solow, R. M. 1985. Comment. *Brookings Papers on Economic Activity* 107–10.

Stern, J., and D. Chew, Jr., eds. 1986. *The Revolution in Corporate Finance*. Cambridge, Mass.: Blackwell.

Storper, M., and A. J. Scott, eds. 1992. *Pathways to Industrialization and Regional Development*. London: Routledge.

Storper, M., and R. Walker. 1989. *The Capitalist Imperative: Territory, Technology, and Industrial Growth*. Oxford: Blackwell.

Strauss, P. 1989. Legislative theory and the rule of law: Some comments on Rubin. *Columbia Law Review* 89:427–51.

Sunstein, C. 1987. Constitutionalism after the New Deal. *Harvard Law Review* 101:421–504.

———. 1989. Interpreting statutes in the regulatory state. *Harvard Law Review* 103:405–509.

———. 1990. *After the Rights Revolution: Reconceiving the Regulatory State*. Cambridge: Harvard University Press.

Taylor, C. 1989. *Sources of the Self: The Making of the Modern Identity*. Cambridge: Cambridge University Press.

Thompson, E. P. 1975. *Whigs and Hunters: The Origin of the Black Act*. New York: Pantheon.

Thurow, L. 1992. *Head to Head: The Coming Economic Battle among Japan, Europe, and America*. New York: Morrow and Co.

Toulmin, S. 1982. The construal of reality: Criticism in modern and postmodern science. *Critical Inquiry* 9:93–111.

Tribe, L. 1988. Statutes: Three axioms. *Harvard Journal of Law and Public Policy* 11:53–60.

———. 1989. The curvature of constitutional space: What lawyers can learn from modern physics. *Harvard Law Review* 103:1–39.

Trussell, R., ed. 1987. *U.S. Labor and Employment Laws. 1987 Edition*. Washington, D.C.: Bureau of National Affairs.

U.S. Congress. 1988. Overfunding and Underfunding of Pension Plans. Committee on Labor and Human Resources and the House Committee on Education and Labor. S. HRD. 100-431. Washington, D.C.: USGPO.

———. 1992. Are your pension rights protected? Subcommittee on Retirement Income and Employment. Comm. Pub. 102-854. Washington, D.C.: USGPO.

Unger, R. M. 1986. *The Critical Legal Studies Movement*. Cambridge: Harvard University Press.

Vesser, H. A. 1989. Introduction. In *The New Historicism*. London: Routledge, pp. ix–xvi.

Viscusi, W. K. 1985. The structure of uncertainty and the use of nontransferable pensions as a mobility-reduction device. In *Pensions, Labor, and Individual Choice*, edited by D. Wise, pp. 223–48. Chicago: University of Chicago Press.

Vogel, J. 1987. Containing medical and disability costs by cutting unhealthy employees: Does Section 510 of ERISA provide a remedy? *Notre Dame Law Review* 62:1024–62.

Wade, R. 1990. *Governing the Market: Economic Theory and the Role of Government in East Asian Industrialization*. Princeton: Princeton University Press.

Walker, R. 1989a. Regulation, flexible specialization, and the forces of production in capitalist development. Berkeley: University of California, Department of Geography.

———. 1989b. What's left to do? *Antipode* 21:133–65.

Warren E. 1987. Bankruptcy policy. *University of Chicago Law Review* 54:755–814.

Weaver, R. K. 1985. *The Politics of Industrial Change*. Washington, D.C.: Brookings Institution.

Webber, M. J., and S. Tonkin. 1990. Profitability and capital accumulation in Canadian manufacturing industries. *Environment and Planning A* 22:1051–72.

Weber, M. 1978. *Economy and Society: An Outline of Interpretive Sociology*. Berkeley: University of California Press.

Weiler, P. 1983. Promises to keep: Securing workers' rights to self-organization under the NLRA. *Harvard Law Review* 96:1769–1827.

———. 1990. *Governing the Workplace: The Future of Labor and Employment Law*. Cambridge: Harvard University Press.

White, H. 1987. *The Content of the Form: Narrative Discourse and Historical Representation*. Baltimore: Johns Hopkins University Press.

Williamson, O. 1985. *The Economic Institutions of Capitalism*. New York: Free Press.

Williamson, O. 1990. Mergers, acquisitions, and leveraged buyouts: An efficiency assessment. In *Corporate Law and Economic Analysis*, edited by Bebchuk, pp. 1–28.

Wilson, J. Q., ed. 1980. *The Politics of Regulation*. New York: Basic Books.

Wolch, J., and M. Dear, eds. 1988. *The Power of Geography: How Territory Shapes Social Life*. London: Unwin Hyman.

Index of Authors and Case Citations

Subject Index

Administrative agencies, 163–166, 168, 173–174
Administrative state, 158, 273n
Adverse selection, 111, 112, 114, 276n
AMC corporation, 265n
American Can, 77, 80–83
Antitrust Division, U.S. Department of Justice, 96–97
Antitrust violations, 130
Antiunionism, 225
Arbitration, 60–62, 64

Bankruptcy: Chapter 7, 139, 184, 203; Chapter 11, xiii, xvi, 34–35, 68, 102, 128, 133, 136, 140–141, 143–144, 146, 184, 271n–273n; strategic bankruptcy, 134, 272n
Bankruptcy Code, xvii, 137, 143; Section 365(a), 272n; Section 1113, 135, 140–141, 143, 272n
Bankruptcy policy, 142–143
Bell System, pension avoidance scheme of, 38, 42, 65, 87–89, 92–95, 97–98, 181, 185, 191
Benefit-cost analyses of respecting legal boundaries, 202, 220, 226, 230–231
Bill of Rights, 11
Bloch, Judge Alan, 63–64, 208, 265–266n
Boston Consulting Group, 95, 205–206, 244, 267n
Brademas, Rep. J. (D-Ind.), 5
Bureau of Labor Statistics *News*, 263n
Bureau of the Census, 50–51
Bush administration, 11, 43

Canning industry, 85
Carter administration, 96, 247
"Cash cows," 82, 95, 97, 178, 205
Cato Institute, 155
Chase Bank, 109–110

Chicago, 39, 92, 101, 102, 103, 269n
Chicago School of Law and Economics, 120, 125, 144–146, 171–172, 185, 197, 200, 241, 246, 273n
Clark Equipment pension avoidance scheme, 68
Clay, Rep. W. (D-Mo.), 263n
Collective bargaining, 50, 53–55, 60–61, 65, 77–78, 86, 97–98, 131, 135–136, 138–142, 144, 147–148, 191, 195–196, 210, 215–216, 218, 225–226, 264n–265n, 272n
Collective (community) welfare, 76, 222, 230
Community Adjustment and Recovery Agency (CARA), 163–164
Compensation of executives, 208, 210, 213–216, 230, 279n
Compliance and deterrence, 217–219
Concession bargaining, 59
Consequentialism, 184–186, 198–199, 201, 229, 277n
Continental Airlines, 135
Continental Can Company, xv, 10, 12–13, 18–19, 31, 37–38, 41, 48, 56–57, 75–77, 79–89, 92–99, 104, 121–122, 133, 177, 181–183, 185, 189, 191, 194–197, 204–206, 210, 225–228, 240, 244, 253, 265n, 266n, 267n, 268n; corporate history, 37; decline, 81; deunionization strategy, 93–94, 191; diversification, 81–83; ERISA cases, 60–62, 64–67, 69–72; financing of pension obligations, 87; pension avoidance scheme, 65, 68, 70–71, 84–85, 98, 191; price fixing, 97; rationalization, 62, 81–83, 86, 94–95, 191; "Red Flag" system, 88, 267n; relocation of production, 94; relocation to nonunion site, 89; restructuring strategy, 94–95. *See also* United Steelworkers of America
Continental Energy Corporation, 38
Contracts, 138, 226–230

Designed by Glen Burris; set in Century Expanded text with
Clarendon display by JDL Composition Services; and printed on 50-lb.
Glatfelter Eggshell Cream by The Maple Press Company.